The Ethnography of Tantra

The Ethnography of Tantra

Textures and Contexts of Living Tantric Traditions

Edited by

CAROLA E. LOREA AND ROHIT SINGH

SUNY
PRESS

Cover credit: Photographs by Carola E. Lorea and Rohit Singh.

Published by State University of New York Press, Albany

Printed in the United States of America

For information, contact State University of New York Press, Albany, NY
www.sunypress.edu

Library of Congress Cataloging-in-Publication Data

Names: Lorea, Carola Erika, 1987– editor. | Singh, Rohit, (Religion historian) 1981– editor.
Title: The ethnography of Tantra : textures and contexts of living Tantric traditions / Carola E. Lorea and Rohit Singh, editors.
Description: Albany : State University of New York Press, [2023]. | Includes bibliographical references and index.
Identifiers: LCCN 2022061689 | ISBN 9781438494838 (hardcover : alk. paper) | ISBN 9781438494852 (ebook) | ISBN 9781438494845 (pbk. : alk. paper)
Subjects: LCSH: Tantric Buddhism. | Tantric Buddhism—Asia—Case studies. | Tantrism. | Tantrism—Asia—Case studies.
Classification: LCC BQ8912.3 .E86 2023 | DDC 294.3/925—dc23/eng/20230509
LC record available at https://lccn.loc.gov/2022061689

10 9 8 7 6 5 4 3 2 1

Contents

Illustrations

Acknowledgments

If all knowledge is situated, the bits of knowledge one might find in this book are situated in very unusual times. The first drafts of the papers that were selected for this volume, and its final shape as a complete manuscript, are separated by a global health crisis that has changed the way we do ethnography and share research findings.

The coeditors of this volume, during the COVID pandemic, as many others, found themselves confined to unexpected locations while facing both new challenges and unexpected opportunities.

And as many others, I, Carola, was undergoing an unusual amount of stress and emotional trouble. A series of uncanny events happened—a bit too much to be mere coincidences. I first thought I was going crazy and hence sought mental health support from the university.

Unfortunately, counseling and mental health support were available only for the students, not for staff. So I decided to reach out to my *śikṣā guru* who lives in Bengal, India, via email—something I try to avoid, as he is very busy taking care of serious problems of disciples who need his help. In response to my email, he diagnosed that this was a case of black magic. He gave me a mantra to repeat aloud, with specific patterns of breath movement, to be accompanied with the visualization of a specific image that I should create and immediately destroy in my mind at each repetition. Besides the mantra practice, he prescribed a simple ritual, which I performed in an abandoned Muslim cemetery in Singapore. The instructions were followed. The problem was solved. I found myself at peace again.

In 2020, I, Rohit, transferred institutions and began the arduous process of learning how to mentor and teach online to pandemic-era students, many of them enduring trauma, anxiety, and burnout. Meanwhile, isolated from family, friends, students, and colleagues, I battled with tremendous loneliness and depression. I found two sources of solace and inspiration.

First, I would be remiss to not acknowledge the emotional support of Padma, my beloved rescue dog, who for nearly two years of quarantine was my only companion. Second, during the pandemic I observed and participated in the online Tibetan Buddhist communities. I became virtually involved in a variety of Tantric rituals, initiations, and empowerments. Many of these were broadcast globally in HD and translated in multiple languages from the Dalai Lama's residence in Dharamshala, India. During the isolating days of the quarantine, through the Tantric events on Facebook and YouTube I found a sense of connectivity with others participating in these virtual mandalas.

The stories of Carola's pandemic mantra and Rohit's participation in online Tantric ceremonies serve two purposes here. First, following a canonical Tantric custom, we employ it as a way of opening this work with an homage to our gurus. Second, these experiences contain themes that will appear throughout the book, and particularly the idea that lived Tantric worlds are not solely concerned with spiritual progression and soteriological goals, but also with pragmatic remedies, health and well-being, supernatural intervention, and the power and efficacy of sound. Echoing in many contributions to this volume is the idea that Tantric practice is not a solitary or individual enterprise; instead it weaves together broad networks of diverse people in both face-to-face and online encounters.

But Tantra is also a plethora of time-devouring deities and of resources to deal with death. And with death we had to cope indeed, in the course of this publication project. One of the contributors to this volume, Dr. Jarrod Hyam, a friend, a wonderful human, and a generous colleague, passed away just a few months before submitting this work to the publisher. Unlike many of us scholars, he was humble, genuinely modest, and deeply interested in all the various forms of embodiment and healing he was exposed to during his studies and research trips to South Asia. Tantric specialists and practices are often sought after to deal with disease and loss. So did we, when in grief and in need for powerful prayers to accompany his soul's journey. We hope this piece of his published work will allow his memory and intellectual legacy to live a long life—perhaps not up to the standards of immortality invoked by some Tantric narratives of perfected beings, the siddhas, but long enough to comfort those who miss him and to inspire present and future generations of seekers.

Besides acknowledging our debt and tribute to the gurus, the teachers, and the academic mentors, there is a long list of thanks we need to summarize here for all those who made this book possible. First, we acknowledge our heartfelt gratitude for the collaboration of local practitioners and communities whose individual members' names might not feature in this book, and yet without them there would be no such thing as the "Ethnography of Tantra" to begin with. We are also thankful to the organizers of the International Congress for Asian Studies (ICAS). This volume is largely the result of a series of panels that we have convened from ICAS 11 in Leiden in July 2019. That might have been one of the last large academic events where we participated in person before the start of the Covidian age of virtual conferences via Zoom. Carola's participation was supported by the Asia Research Institute (ARI) at National University of Singapore, her academic home for almost the entire duration of this book project. Rohit is grateful for the financial support generously given to him by ICAS. We are immensely thankful to the colleagues who agreed to read and offer generous feedback to the first, unripe drafts of this volume's introduction, particularly David G. White, Glen A. Hayes, Nicolas Sihlé, Aaron Ullrey, and Carola's colleagues at ARI's Religion and Globalisation research cluster. Lastly, we express our thankfulness to SUNY editors James Peltz and Catherine Blackwell, and to three anonymous reviewers who have shared punctual and useful comments to improve this manuscript.

Introduction

Rethinking Tantra through Ethnography

Carola E. Lorea and Rohit Singh

The word *Tantra* conjures radically different images and seemingly irreconcilable associations, ranging from spiritual enlightenment to sex and sorcery. In Indian popular culture, wealthy politicians hire "Tantriks" to secure their success through black magic. In the Netherlands, a group practicing "Tantric Dance" regularly organizes workshops and summer courses.[1] In Bengal, groups known as Bāul, Fakir, and Sahajiẏā maintain practices broadly recognized as Tantric, but they do not wish to be identified as such (Openshaw 2002). Tantric traditions gain attention in modern-day media. For example, the 2014 Kalachakra Tantric empowerment led by the Fourteenth Dalai Lama, Tenzin Gyatso, constituted a highly digitalized ceremony experienced by global audiences through Twitter, Facebook, YouTube, and other outlets. The Netflix documentary series *(Un)Well* (2020) represented Tantra in one of the episodes, focusing on expensive North American retreats to enhance sexual power in a spiritualized fashion. In 2018, the documentary *Wild Wild Country* exposed the dark side of the transnational Tantric community of Osho devotees, their morally transgressive practices, and their criminal activities. In Europe and North America, religion scholars have produced an impressive scholarship on Tantra predominantly based on disembodied texts and silent inscriptions. While their understanding of Tantric texts often emerges through the cooperation of Asian pandits and scholars, credit for such assistance remains often unacknowledged, and living voices of Tantric practitioners remain largely outside the scope of these studies. Is there a bridge for these distant milieus?

This edited volume seeks to connect distant shores of Tantric scholarship and lived Tantric practices using ethnography as the most suitable material to build this bridge. Findings unpack Tantra's relationship to the body, ritual performance, sexuality, secrecy, power hierarchies, death, magic, and healing. We approach these issues with vigilant sensitivity to the ethics of fieldwork, moving beyond the centrality of written texts, while voicing the everyday life and livelihoods of a multitude of Tantric actors: not only ritual specialists and learned elites of initiated practitioners, but also mediums, beggars, singers, healers, and craftsmen, who equally participate in the dynamic worlds of Tantra.

Attention to lived Tantric practice can decolonize and enrich Tantric studies, a field that has largely marginalized ethnographic research and has yet to give adequate attention to the experiences and discourses of living Tantric communities. Further, engaged scholarly dialogues with contemporary Tantric practitioners present new and diverse ways of imagining Tantra within the dynamic contexts of fieldwork. These dialogues potentially forge reciprocal relations between Tantric studies scholars, their respective fields of specialization, and participants of lived Tantric traditions. In an effort to critically reflect upon how to facilitate these dialogues, this introduction sets out to answer two key questions: (1) What is gained through ethnographic engagements with Tantra? (2) How do the contributions in this volume lay the groundwork for establishing a collaborative and interdisciplinary ethnography of Tantra?

Shifting Paradigms for the Study of Tantric Traditions

Tantric studies, like the academic study of religion, has developed largely with a focus on texts, while often neglecting diverse living traditions and communities involved in Tantric lifeworlds. While Tantric studies scholars have resided alongside these communities, often to conduct textual research at local archives occasionally with the aid of community members, the lived dimensions of Tantra remain absent in much of the early literature in the field. The scholarship produced through such methodology has influenced the way in which anthropologists working with Asian religious traditions relate to Tantric practices and practitioners.

Previous generations of ethnographers of Buddhism experienced, as David Gellner put it, a kind of perplexity (2017, 113): the perplexity of scholars trained exclusively in elite textual discourses, who are then confronted, in Asia, with a reality of spirit cults, magic rituals, and activities wildly differing from the monastic, rationalistic, and quasi-atheistic religion that they were exposed to in the classroom. Geoffrey Samuel shared a similar befuddlement: "I was struck by the huge gap between the way Tibetan religion was treated in Indological and Buddhological literature, and the way it was described by the smaller number of anthropologists who had worked in Tibetan societies" (2005, 4). Vasudha Narayanan articulated the same perplexity in terms of "diglossia" (2000, 761–62) between the study of Hinduism and lived religion. Soon after joining Harvard University, she realized that the everyday activities Hindus think of as "religious," from cooking the right kind of lentils to singing songs, were dismissed as "anthropological stuff" and did not make it into the textbooks. The same perplexity might arise when comparing classic academic books on Tantra with the incredible diversity of contemporary phenomena deemed as Tantric. These phenomena may include mantras and mandalas, blood sacrifice, and wrathful goddesses. They might also include online gift shops of aphrodisiacs, Dracula-like characters of Hindi movies (Iyer 2013), mainstream South Indian temple activities, massage techniques advertised in the streets of Bali and Phuket, or the choice of a life outside of conventional society, dedicated to the quest for self-realization. This cacophony of examples draws from representations of Tantra that scholars are also responsible for consuming, constructing, distorting, repeating, and disseminating through academic representations of Tantra.

This volume is born out of the necessity to bring to the forefront of Tantric studies the individuals, communities, and institutions that constitute living Tantric traditions as located in particular sociocultural environments. While Tantra has predominantly been studied through premodern scriptures of elite male priests and monks, this book underlines the multifarious life of vernacular Tantric practices and livelihoods across South Asia, Southeast Asia, and Himalayan regions. We question predominant methodological frameworks and incorporate ethnographically informed approaches to Tantra.

Ethnography is a qualitative research methodology constituted broadly by the use of fieldwork, in either face-to-face or virtual settings (e.g., "online" or "digital ethnography"). We address the need to bring more ethnographic research into the field of Tantric studies—a field that largely remains oriented to text-centric analysis. We envision the "ethnography of Tantra" as a collaborative and interdisciplinary endeavor dedicated to analyzing ethnographically drawn data on the various dimensions of Tantra in the lives of people as they manifest on the field, using theoretical frameworks from diverse domains, including history, anthropology, gender studies, and religious studies.

Dismissing lived Tantra derives from the text-centric attitude in the study of religions (King 1999; Masuzawa 2005) and, in some cases, a bias among anthropologists against local traditions they perceive as less authentic or debased because of the literature they are exposed to in their academic training (Gellner 1990). The fields of anthropology and religious studies are both entangled with colonial and Orientalist legacies. These legacies emerged through a history of imperial encounters in which, as Van der Veer (2001) has shown, notions of religious, political, and cultural identities were forged and contested in the colony and metropole through the shared experience of colonialism. Although ethnographic work can easily replicate and perpetuate problematic stereotypes and prejudiced presuppositions, the chapters in this volume demonstrate how ethnographic dialogues bring to the forefront the perspectives of lived traditions and the practices of self-reflexivity, unsettling the epistemic paradigms of modern academia.

We suggest that ethnographies of Tantra have been in part neglected because they present scholars with methodological challenges, including the problem of secrecy in Tantric esoteric practices, the limits of traditional ethnographic practices such as "participant observation" (see Hornbacher's chapter), the contested use of "Tantric" as an emic category, and stigmas associated with Tantra in both academic circles and on the ground in various fieldwork settings. Meeting such methodological challenges requires sophisticated ad hoc ethical and epistemological tools for the study of contemporary Tantric traditions.

Ethnographic studies are never situated in a vacuum of power dynamics, and in the context of British colonialism, early ethnographic accounts sustained the production of inequalities cocreating notions of deviancy and heterodoxy. The contemporary academic field of anthropology is not free from asymmetrical power relationships either, as Talal Asad (1973, 16–17) and others have saliently discussed. However, ethnographic theory and practice has grown in different directions with self-reflective criticism, particularly through the perspectives of feminist, postmodern, and post-structural lenses; critical race theory; queer theory; and postcolonial theory. Feminist ethnographers and postcolonial scholars have discussed racial and gender inequalities inherent in the history and use of ethnographic methods.

The ethnographic method began to achieve rapid legitimization by the academic research establishment only in the 1980s. According to LeCompte, ethnography was marginalized because it was subversive to positivistic, entrenched conceptions of research rigor, and it privileged alternative ways of thinking, knowing, and viewing the world (LeCompte 2002) that can challenge the epistemic ethnocentrism of the modern Western academy. Ethnographic training ideally prepares ethnographers to critically self-reflect on issues of positionality and reciprocity, while systematically addressing their own cultural bias (LeCompte 1987). With its interest in taking other lifeworlds seriously, and its narrative representations of Indigenous cultures, nonwhite communities, women, and nonbinary people, modern ethnography sustained the process of dislocating the dominance of North Atlantic objectivist and heterosexist perspectives in the social sciences and in education.

The ethnography of Tantra attempts to decolonize[2] the academic knowledge production on Tantric phenomena by questioning the importance that has been given to ancient textual traditions analyzed by European and North American scholars as normative of what constitutes "real" religion. Certainly, ethnography alone is not the solution to the legacy of colonialism and cultural imperialism, and ethnography itself needs to be decolonized in many respects (Alonso Bejarano et al. 2019). However, ethnographically informed and interdisciplinary perspectives on the voices and practices of contemporary Tantric communities can contribute to a more inclusive global history and anthropology of Tantra. This book serves as a starting point to address the lack of ethnographically informed perspectives on Tantric traditions by offering contributions by ten scholars who have engaged in long-term, linguistically competent fieldwork with living Tantric communities across diverse yet interconnected regions: South India, Southeast Asia, Bengal, Assam, the Tibetan cultural region, the sub-Himalayan region, and the digital field of online media.

***

Indologists, Buddhologists, and religion scholars have written profusely on Asian phenomena condensed into the ambiguous and problematic term *Tantra*. But why have ethnographic methods remained underutilized in exploring Tantric traditions in contrast to the preponderance of textual studies on Tantra, and what are the repercussions of the way academics generate knowledge on Tantra?

Colonial officers, missionaries, and Orientalist scholars have developed enduring paradigms for the study of Asian religions based on their own religious and sociocultural backgrounds and the Asian sources they deemed the most authoritative. In the last three decades, these paradigms have been denounced as "scriptist" (Harris 1986), "Protestant" (Schopen 1991), and "mentalistic" (Meyer in Belting et al. 2014, 207–10).[3] The assumption that the "real" religion emerges through the study of text also shaped how modern communities in Asia present their own religions to foreign audiences (Lopez 1998; Van der Veer 2001; Urban 2003). This creates biases to what scholars might observe or ignore on the field and whom they select or exclude from their studies. For example, Geoffrey Samuel observes that in the early development of Tibetan studies, "Buddhologists mostly worked with high-status refugee lamas and monastic scholars and saw little or nothing of the social and ritual context of their informants' lives within the Tibetan community as a whole" (2005, 4).

Anthropologists of religion in Asia have conducted focused studies of groups and societies that define themselves as, or are profoundly influenced by, Tantric traditions. However, they did not engage in an organized intervention toward an anthropology of Tantra. While scholars of diverse Buddhist traditions and geographic regions have strived to develop a comparative and ethnography-grounded "anthropology of Buddhism" (Gellner 2001; Sihlé and Ladwig 2017), ethnographers of Tantra have not collaborated to create a similar endeavor in the field of Tantric studies. For example, Ron Barrett's ethnography (2008) of Aghor practitioners and healers is framed as a contribution to the field of medical anthropology, but it shies away from debates and comparisons in the field of Tantric studies. Often taken as the emblem of antinomian Tantric practice, Aghoris themselves show ambivalence toward the category of Tantra: its association with sexuality and sorcery could cause misunderstandings and bring counterproductive effects in their search for social recognition. Some Aghoris eschewed the term when talking to North Indian visitors to their ashram but "reversed their position when speaking with Bengalis in Calcutta, where tantra has more positive connotations" (Barrett 2008, 11). In the lack of a systematic effort toward an ethnography of Tantra, salient works grounded in ethnographic fieldwork remain confined to the scholarship on ritual and society in a particular area and religious tradition. For example, Rich Freeman's work on Hindu Tantric traditions of Kerala and David Gellner's research on Newar Buddhism are framed as contributions to the field of South Indian Hinduism (Freeman 1997, 2003) and Mahayana Buddhism in Nepal (Gellner 1992).

In a similar manner, French ethnohistorians and social anthropologists like Raphaël Voix, Gérard Toffin, Gilles Tarabout, and Véronique Bouiller, among others, have produced exceptional scholarship on Tantric rituals, festivals, monastic traditions, and verbal arts, combining linguistic expertise and familiarity with textual sources with extensive ethnography in particular fieldwork sites.[4] However, their analysis and theoretical contribution has not addressed the field of Tantric studies at large. Hence, previous anthropological works have mostly considered their Tantric communities in specific contexts and in isolation from the rest of the inter-Asian and transregional Tantric world. What Geoffrey Samuel has noted for Tibetology thus could be easily said for previous anthropologists of Tantra: these works avoid relating the traditions under analysis to larger regional discourses and tend to remain isolated and inward-looking (Samuel 2005, 195). In the lack of an organized, inclusive, and ethnography-oriented field of Tantric studies, their bodies of knowledge have been seen in isolation rather than used to illuminate each other. Ethnography not only produces opportunities for comparison, generating empirical data on diverse sociocultural and geographical contexts (McDaniel, this volume), but comparison *is* part of the method, inherent in the analysis of the fieldworker experiencing the life of their participants. Suggesting comparative ethnographies as well as ethnography as comparison, an ethnographic future for Tantric studies would enable "the development of a sharper grasp of both emic and etic concepts" and help "us to understand distribution of traits and processes of diffusion and appropriation" (Sihlé and Ladwig 2017, 117). Ethnographies of Tantra could then offer the documentation and analytical tools needed for broader theorizations, allowing particular communities of practitioners to be seen not solely in isolation, but also in cross-regional and inter-religious connections to one another, with a global and comparative outlook.[5]

Bridging textual studies on Tantra and fieldwork-based anthropology of religion, this volume strives to do justice to the multiplicity and fluidity of Tantric traditions in practice. We propose that ethnography—including digital ethnography—and the comparative outlook inscribed in the ethnographic method, can help remap the center and periphery of Tantric traditions.[6] Furthermore, these studies help to rethink matters of authority and authenticity by accentuating the role of previously underrepresented actors of the Tantric world.

Tantras, *Tantricking,* and Tantric Culture

> Looking for God on sacred scriptures [is] like
> licking the paper where the word "sugar" is written
> The mouth doesn't learn [through it] the taste of sweetness.
>
> —Baul song of Duddu Shah

Etymologically tied to the loom as the instrument (*-tra*) for weaving and extension (its verbal root √*tan-* meaning stretching, extending, continuing, propagating, accomplishing, or performing), *tantra* is a Sanskrit term that refers to poetic composition and to textual corpora (often called *tantra*s, but also *āgama and saṁhitās*). In the colloquial compound *tantra-mantra,* used in many South Asian languages, it has a derogatory connotation (something like "hocus pocus"); it refers to incantations and magic practices for suspicious ends. Tantra can also refer to a holistic system of philosophical and ritual knowledge (Kaviraj 1966; Satpurananda 1996).

The suffix *-tra* indicates an instrument or means to an action, and *tan-* is closely related to *tanu* (the body), allowing local interpreters to address Tantra as a range of actions and things people do with their body-mind complex, "a set of techniques"—or, as Geoffrey Samuel put it (2005, 31), a matter of "procedures" (16) rather than a set of beliefs that adepts follow. Tantric texts, medieval and modern, are often practice-oriented, contain ritual instructions, and underline the importance of experiential and embodied knowledge, as illustrated in the verses of Duddu Shah—a Bengali (Muslim) composer (1841–1911) whose songs directly referenced Buddhist Tantras.[7]

Recent scholarship on religious studies has emphasized practices and performed acts rather than beliefs and texts, investigating *religioning* as a verb rather than religion as a noun for assumed crystallized entities (Nye 2000). The study of lived religion breaks away from the preoccupation with official texts, institutions, and experts and instead lays emphasis on how religiosity, spirituality, and ritual meaning are lived out in the everyday practices of ordinary people (Ammerman 2016). Earlier, Catherine Bell (1992) had argued the need to substitute static definitions of "ritual" with a more attentive approach to the ritual processes of what she calls "ritualization." Echoing these concerns, we are interested in understanding Tantra as *tantricking*, an ever-changing and complex array of things people do: actions, practices, and disciplines (*sādhana*) rather than any static or essentialized category that can be unequivocally called "Tantra" or "Tantrism." In its applied definition, "Tantra" needs to be considered as plural and dynamic.

Tantr*ism* as a single category has been questioned and ultimately abandoned as something constructed by modern, largely Western scholarship (Padoux 1986). *Tantricking* stands for doing Tantra, as a process rather than a given system, a single doctrine, or a "religion." By focusing on Tantra as *tantricking* we highlight what Tantra means in practice, in its diverse and evolving manifestations. Adding a verbal suffix, we move away from singular reifications and emphasize instead the unstable character of traditions and communities that are constantly in the making. We explore Tantric traditions in the plural form (Gray 2016), given the extensive variety of lineages, teachings, texts, and practices that bind communities across space and time, often in trans-sectarian and transregional ways. With our introduction of this term, we are not suggesting or imposing upon lived traditions a new normative category. Instead, we emphasize the need for new language we can use to discuss the dynamics encountered in the field.

The term *tāntrik* in some modern South Asian languages came to be associated with superstition, violence, and black magic. In India, negative perceptions of Tantra are generally paired with positive understandings of bhakti. These diverging popular perceptions are usually attributed to the influence of British and Christian Orientalist scholars, missionaries, and colonial administrators (Burchett 2019). As a result, some groups of practitioners, although directly connected to self-defined Tantric gurus, texts, or practices, wish to disassociate from the term. Others employ it as a source of status and prestige. In Southeast Asia and in the Tibetan region, the term *Tantra* might not be used at all. The Balinese *pedanda*s who perform "tantric rituals" (Stephen 2015), the *ngakpa* (*snags pa*) ritual specialists of northern Nepal whom Nicolas Sihlé calls "tantrists" (2013), the Newar Vajracharyas whom Gellner called "Tantric priests" (1992) do not define themselves as Tantric,[8] nor do the Fakirs and the singing beggars who populate this volume. Whether these practitioners prefer *Tantric* or other terms to define their traditions, their contribution and participation in the world of *tantricking* is unquestionable. The range of uses of the attribute *Tantric* as an etic, emic, or even post-emic term[9] is contextual and always historically and geographically contingent. Gathering the insights of diverse practitioners, from Balinese priests to Bengali Vaiṣṇava beggars, under the rubric of *tantricking* disambiguates the problem of self-definition: while it does not reflect a local noun or an emic category, it allows their voices to participate in the larger field of Tantric studies, beyond the microscale of isolated regional ethnohistories.

Tantra in the colonial encounter was insistently portrayed as the ultimate Other, the "most extreme and perverse aspect of the Indian Mind—as the 'extreme orient' and 'India's darkest heart'" (Urban 2010, 148). The Orientalist gaze of colonial ethnographers represented Tantric groups as exotic and transgressive, while implicitly assisting in the so-called civilizing mission of British imperialism (Dirks 1997). Using the case study of British responses to hook-swinging, a body-piercing tradition aimed at propitiating the goddess, Dirks examined "the institutional links between anthropological knowledge and the apparatuses of colonial state power" (1997, 186). Key to this process of policing tradition was the inclusion of elite Brahmans into colonial administration, which formed the "basis for increasing collaboration between Brahmanic precepts and Victorian morals during the nineteenth century" (1997, 200) in India.

Tantric traditions would have appeared barbaric, uncivilized, and outside the fold of Brahmanic Hinduism and "high" Buddhism in the eyes of colonial administrators and ethnographers. Colonial encounters with Tantric practitioners often came in the form of peripatetic warrior ascetics and mercenaries for hire who would go by different titles: yogis, siddhas, pirs, and *sheikhs*. Their personas challenged idealized images of Hinduism that emerged out of the Brahmin and British encounter (see Pinch 2006). The 1891 British imperial census designated many of these groups as "Miscellaneous and Disrespectable Vagrants," and colonial officials began campaigns of disarmament and criminalization against them (White 2009, 240). Influenced by European notions of how a modern religion ought to be, high-caste Hindu reformers openly condemned communities that followed Tantric cultural traits, proclaiming them deviant sects (*apasampradāyas*; see Lorea 2018b) and denouncing them as filthy, depraved, and immoral (see Bhattacharya 1896). Modern-day reform-minded Buddhists incorporate European and American understandings of "authentic" religion to critique lived ritual practices and traditions associated with Tantra (Singh 2020).

Tantric studies scholars, as well as early ethnographies, contributed eroticized and exoticized representations of Tantric traditions, with titillating academic book titles prominently featuring sexuality, secrecy, and transgression. The most direct way in which today's ethnographers of living Tantric tradition contribute to a more responsible scholarship is by de-Orientalizing representations of practitioners and their lives. For example, ethnographic portraits can demystify representations of Tantra, showing how several forms of Tantra are mainstreamed and institutionalized, where they became the official form of worship officiated by high castes or qualified monks. In Kerala, for instance, the designation *tantri* can apply only to Brahmins, and it is not tinged with any sense of heterodoxy or antinomy (Freeman 1997). In the Tiwari tribe of Assam, "mother Tantrics" (*tāntrik mā*) are female community leaders and ritual specialists who intervene when a member of the community dies in order to settle unfinished communication between the departed and the bereaved ones (Borkataky-Varma 2017). In Gujarat, a "safe, Sanskritic and Brahmanically-oriented Tantra" amenable to the taste and aspirations of upwardly mobile, urban middle classes pervades the shrines of the goddess servants (*sevak*) studied by Dinnell (2017). In Varanasi, the controversial image of the skull-bearing Aghor eating human flesh from the cremation ground has been substituted by a reformed Aghor lineage of social workers, providing sought-after cures for stigmatizing ailments like barrenness, skin diseases, and leprosy (Barrett 2008).

These portraits, rather than exceptional or eccentric, show Tantrics embedded in noncontroversial ways in their sociocultural environment; they have domains of expertise widely recognized in their social context and are not always considered unorthodox or transgressive. Ethnographies unsettle the assumption that Tantric traditions are anti-modern and anachronistic, revealing their skilful negotiation between modernizing expectations and fidelity to preexisting cosmological principles. Following Lidke (2017, 5), we could broaden the etymological root of *tan-tra* (instrument to weave) to include the ways Tantra has traditionally provided patterns and fabrics *interweaving* individuals with their social worlds.

Tantricking against the Trope of Loss

Textual studies often emphasize centers of imperial authority, elite specialists affiliated with the ruling class, and texts belonging to these groups as the starting point for understanding the origins and historical development of Tantra. Within these historical narratives, texts possessed and employed by an elite few provide the framework for writing about Tantra. For example, Ronald Davidson's groundbreaking scholarship (2002, 2005) describes the social history of esoteric Buddhism through the lens of the "Imperial Metaphor." Davidson describes how the language, rituals, and power dynamics of esoteric Buddhism came to reflect Indic feudal culture, and as esoteric Buddhism entered the Tibetan cultural sphere, "the systems of ritual, yoga, and meditation that so assisted the reemergence of Tibetan public life also embodied the Indian feudal world in its models and vocabulary" (2005, 6). While we acknowledge that the Imperial Metaphor paradigm provides insights into certain dimensions of Tantra's social history, we argue that ethnography brings in a broader range of voices and perspectives by centering the lived religious traditions of those often on the peripheries and margins of society. Through the process of fieldwork we find that Tantra does not simply come from the top down. Subaltern groups actively contribute to the ongoing practices, discourses, and experiences involved in the dynamic process of *tantricking*.

The concept of Tantra as lived processes and practices challenges the axiom that "Tantric traditions must be understood in terms of pre-modern scriptural traditions" (Flood 2006, 10) and that Indology, or "the philological study of Sanskrit[,] is the *sine qua non* for the study of Tantric traditions." This view projects authenticity into the bygone past, dislodging vernacular literature and lived practice as less authoritative than Sanskrit sources, and it inadvertently treats living lineages and contemporary practitioners as inauthentic, as spurious, or as curious remnants of an ancient past where "real" Tantric traditions (i.e., those based on scriptures) existed. We argue that participative, immersive, long-term ethnography can fill the gaps produced by such scriptist bias in the academic knowledge production on Tantra. Here, Gregory Grieve's insights on the study of Tantric rituals in Bhaktapur, Nepal, come to mind: "by privileging scriptural accounts based on the printed book, subalternative lived worlds are being lost because they are being resignified to support elite ideologies" (Grieve 2006, 5).

The focus on text contributed to a "trope of loss" that is common among Western scholars of Tantra. "Such is the broken world of Tantra at the dawn of the new millennium," asserts White (2000, 34–36)—a scenario of erosion and fragmentation after the end of royal patronage for Tantric officiants. The end of the "Tantric Age" (Burchett 2019, 60–63) is portrayed as coinciding with the spread of Turkish power across North India, from the beginning of the twelfth century, when institutional Tantra "largely collapsed, and the sphere of tantric religion underwent transformation and contraction, into less institutionalized lineages of yogis, warrior ascetics, rural tantric healers and magicians."

Studies on early Indian *tantra*s became representative of the entire Tantric world of past and present, Indian and elsewhere. Indologists' opinion that Tantra's "real nature" is not in "the world outside" but in India (Padoux 2017, 175) glossed over the textual and ritual vitality of Tantric traditions in East, Central, and Southeast Asia, as well as in Himalayan regions. Focus on premodern Indian texts also produced a lack of attention to the way Tantra adapted in the Sultanate period (thirteenth to sixteenth centuries) with the rise of influential bhakti movements, and over the colonial period to take the shape of what ethnographers find today, in Asia as well as in its global ramifications. The adaptations that took place in various specific regions and in vernacular linguistic milieus in the colonial era, mediated by occultism and the Theosophical Society, for example, often played a role in the transmission of Tantra to the West (Cantú 2021; Strube 2022).

While the so-called Tantric Age in the Indian subcontinent comes to an end with the hegemony of the Delhi Sultanate (Burchett 2019, 321; Flood 2006,71; Sanderson 2009), Tantric rituals, techniques, and imaginaries persisted, sometimes in Sufi disguise and within bhakti contexts. Tantric texts and practices traveled through inland and maritime routes and settled from India to other Asian regions. Despite the predictions of the "trope of loss," Tantric religiosity is alive and well, if in forms and contexts often quite different from the royal patronage and public spectacles of the Tantric Age in medieval India that became so paradigmatic in outlining the characteristics of "real" Tantra.

Whether erotically engaged in consort practice or meditating in haunted cremation grounds, Tantric practitioners are often represented as anachronistic survivals of a golden Tantric past, when Tantric experts were not threatened by modernization and westernization. Indologists often confess these kinds of anxieties: "The traditions that do remain will inevitably continue to undergo change and probable erosion. . . . The Tantric body is at odds with modernity. . . . The order of being in the Tantric universe remains at odds with a materialist, evolutionary understanding of the world [and with] contemporary understandings of gender" (Flood 2006, 186). Indian scholar-practitioners have also internalized this view and have proudly appropriated it to assert the superiority of Tantric "nonmodernity" vis-à-vis Western modernity (Saran 2008).

Predictions of loss and erosion remain largely unaware of the vibrant sociocultural ecologies of living Tantric communities across Asia and beyond. Tantric studies scholars faithful to textual traditions have looked with contempt at modern and contemporary incarnations of Tantra in India as well as in the "West," reducing neo-Tantra to spiritual commodification and cultural appropriation (Timalsina 2011). However, anthropological perspectives abstain from this judgment and help us to understand these phenomena as meaningful and efficacious from the perspective of participants in new ritual contexts (be it the "yoni massage" discussed in Plancke 2020, the Western Shaktas studied by Perkins 2021, or the transnational Tibetan Tantrics in Joffe 2019).

Reversing the "trope of loss," ethnographies of Tantra recover "multiple modernities" (Eisenstadt 2002) in which Tantric traditions find a significant role and shape what modernity means to a local society. Ethnographies of Tantric traditions are less occupied with the search for origin and authenticity and more interested in what people think, feel, and do within diverse social, political, and economic contexts. For Indian, urban middle classes, Tantra evolves in conversation with burgeoning bourgeois patronage. Philipp Lutgendorf (2007) exemplifies how *tantrification* has operated with the process of upward mobility, while Dinnell studies a "consumer-friendly Tantra that is sufficiently mainstream to play a part in the performance of realizing and reiterating class status" (2017). While the Imperial Metaphor emphasizes ruling institutions as the foundations of Tantric societies, ethnographic studies of Tantra in Tibetan cultural regions provide insights into the ongoing dialogues, debates, and competitions for power and authority taking place on the ground (Mills 2010; Mumford 1989; and Singh 2020). Rather than being confined to rural and uneducated milieus as remnants of a lost Tantric splendor, living Tantric agents and institutions have an active role in negotiating what modernity means in the making of contemporary religious identities, both local and transnational. Based on his ethnographic fieldwork, Jeffrey Lidke views Tantra in Nepal as "a dominant social and cultural force" that has spread across levels of Nepalese societies to the extent that "its ubiquitous presence is unquestioned" just like "all Americans are to some degree influenced by 'American values'" (2017, 17). Borrowing from Bourdieu's notion of habitus, Lidke's findings suggest that the Tantric Śrī-Vidyā tradition permeates all aspects of Nepalese society in the Kathmandu valley like a "complex cultural fiber that reveals itself in architectural codes, iconographic images, ritual practices, city layouts, regal insignia, and a host of other artifacts of material culture that stamp Nepal as a *Tantric culture*" (2017, 66, emphasis added). As suggested by Kripal (2012), Tantra in this sense, as a singular noun, can be understood as a "deep world-view" that underlies the thoughts and actions of diverse communities that may or may not define themselves as Tantric. Our use of the term *tantricking* encompasses the domains of ritual and meditation and pervades spheres of everyday action as diverse as bathing, cooking food for guests, singing, practicing martial arts, and carving conch shells. This volume demonstrates that Tantric culture as deep worldview pervades people's bodies, behaviors, and social relations in ways that can only be traced through extensive fieldwork.

Unity in Multiplicity: Key Terms and Frequent Features across Tantric Traditions

Tantric texts and practices emerged in the Indian subcontinent and formed distinct traditions in the second half of the first millennium. From India, Tantric traditions were disseminated to other parts of South, Central, East, and Southeast Asia. Modern scholarship often differentiated between Hindu and Buddhist Tantra and established that Tantric traditions significantly intersected with other religious communities, including Jainism, Sikhism, Bon traditions of Tibet, Chinese Daoism, and Shinto traditions of Japan. Mainstream academic narratives regularly omit the mutual impact of Tantric worldviews and practices on South Asian Islam, bhakti movements, and Sufi traditions (see Cashin 1995; Ernst 2005; Hatley 2007; Pechilis 2016; and Cantú 2019). These encounters and exchanges can be understood as multidirectional and mutually transformative, stemming from an early Tantric period when ritual spaces, terminologies, and technologies were shared as a common denominator (Flood 2006, 121) across diverse Asian "varieties of an over-arching tradition called Tantra" (White 2000, 8).

The Tantric way provides both a path for individual enlightenment and an empowerment for the alleviation of worldly suffering through the activities of Tantric healers (Gellner 1992, 307). Tantra according to Toffin (1984, 555) straddles various styles of religiosity being "at once an extremely popular religion . . . and an esoteric religion to the highest forms of which only a limited group has access." Scholars of living Tantric traditions have often proposed a distinction between popular and erudite Tantra, "folk" versus "classic" (McDaniel 2004), "clerical" versus "shamanic" (Samuel 1993), Brahmanic versus tribal (Borkataky-Varma 2017), and "transcendental" versus "pragmatic" (Mandelbaum 1966, in Samuel 1993). These oppositions might be meaningful for local societies, but they are also animated by constant interactions, interdependence, and productive tensions.

In short, Tantric studies scholars have cogently argued the lack of a monolithic religion called Tantra, pointing instead to a complex array of ritual, theoretical, and narrative repertoires that are shared, in different form, across various religious, cultural, sociopolitical, geographical, and historical contexts (White 2000, 5). Yet there exists a grouping of common denominators and an emic perspective for Tantra that reveals a "single" yet plural tradition. After all, as White pointed out, one of the hallmarks of Tantra itself is *unity in multiplicity* (11).

For readers unfamiliar with seminal scholarly works that discuss Tantra broadly, we summarize here some of the "refrains" that appear most frequently among the shared features of Tantric traditions, but we supplement this "polythetic definition" (Brooks 1990, 52–72) with salient characteristics that emerge from ethnographic engagements with contemporary communities.[10]

- Initiation. Ritual initiation into a lineage, typically through the transmission of a secret mantra, followed by oral instruction and transmission of knowledge from a guru (called *lama—bla ma*—in Tibetan Tantra, or *murśid* in Islamic esoteric contexts) remain vital issues in Tantric communities. Initiation not only gives access to esoteric teachings but also projects the initiate into a new social network and a spiritual kinship with the community members who share the same mantra or learn from the same guru. Access to esoteric knowledge might be restricted to members of a certain caste, clan, or patrilineal descent (as it is the case for the Vajracharyas of Nepal, Balinese *pedandas*, Nayar of Kerala, etc.) or open to anyone who commits to the guru's teachings (e.g., radically egalitarian Bauls and Fakirs of Bengal).

- *Sādhana* (in Sanskrit, and *sgrub thabs* in Tibetan). Humans are empowered with the possibility to realize the ultimate truth and / or to become themselves divine through *sādhana* by means of embodiment. The world and the body in Tantric traditions are not an illusion (in the Vedantic sense of *māyā*) nor an inconvenient burden, but rather an appropriate vehicle to gain knowledge and access liberation. This implies "a particular attitude on the part of the adept towards the cosmos" (White 2000, 8), whereby the body and the universe reflect each other in an all-embracing net of correspondences that tie microcosm and macrocosm. Progress in *sādhana* is often codified in successive stages toward self-realization.[11]

- Subtle body. With hydraulic flows, seminal essence (*bindu*), channels (*nāḍī*), and energetic centers (cakra), often represented as wheels or lotuses, the body is the central locus of Tantric practice. Yogic techniques are employed to control and manipulate these flows to enhance the practitioner's body. Several traditions emphasize the awakening and upward rising of the creative energy *kuṇḍalinī* residing at the base of the spine. Tantric traditions prioritize embodied practice (*sādhana*) of yogic and ritual disciplines; for example, controlling breath, bodily heat, and ejaculation. These practices engender transformations as a result of the manipulation of bodily substances, fluids, and winds.
- Substances that non-Tantric members of the same social context might interpret as impure, unconventional, inauspicious, or "heating." Alcohol, meat, blood, animal sacrifice, nonvegetarian offerings, and leftovers can be part of Tantric ritual offerings together with other particular means to worship or to propitiate various classes of deities. Examples might include fierce goddesses (e.g., Kali, Durga), dharma protectors (*chos skyong* or *dharmapāla*), tutelary deities (*yi dam* or *iṣṭa-deva*), and divine female entities (*ḍākinī* or *mkha' 'gro ma*). In various cultural contexts, "a Tantra is defined not by the text bearing its name but by the living tradition(s) of practice relating to the main deities involved" (Samuel 1993, 204), and, in many cases, what makes a ritual Tantric is not only the nature of the gods or demons propitiated, but the means, the

materials, and media through which people interact with them (Gellner 1992, 76). In South Asia, these means are associated with the "left-handed" path of Tantric practice (*vāmācāra* or *vāmāmārga*).

- Male and female. A bipolar Tantric cosmology portrays two opposite principles that constitute the ultimate reality: variously termed (e.g., Śiva—Śakti, *puruṣa—prakṛti*, Rādhā—Kriṣṇa, or *yab-yum* in the Tibetan context) according to the different schools and lineages, and variously neutralized into an underlying oneness (e.g., as Void, *śunya*). A sexual symbolism is always present, at least implicitly (Gellner 1992, 143).[12] Realizing the unity of these two cosmogonic principles enables the practitioner to embody the divine as a ritual technique (e.g., for worship, healing, or divination purposes), either directly or through the use of an intermediary object—sometimes the body itself, a ritual object like the *vajra*, or a mesocosmic template (White 2000, 11–12) referred to as mandala or yantra—concentrating and representing the cosmic order and its elements. Practitioners (*sādhaka*s, fem. *sādhikā*s) reproduce the process of cosmogenesis and absorption into oneness within their own psychophysiological body (see Salomon 1991; Lidke 2017, 41–42; and Lorea 2018).

- Antinomian. Certain classes of practitioners adopt the use of substances, ethical codes, and behaviors that conventional society deems as polluting or impure. Tantric practice might be viewed as conceptually opposite to mainstream religious discipline, juxtaposed to Vedic concerns for ritual purity in India or to Buddhist monastic discipline in the Tibetan region (Sihlé 2013, 21). Some stages of practice may prescribe potent and dangerous substances (e.g., wine, blood, sexual fluids, ganja, psychoactive or poisonous substances) and places (e.g., the cremation ground) for ritual, alchemical, or meditative purposes. In some interpretations, these substances are employed to achieve a transcendence of dualism (pure/impure, moral/immoral, etc.) and a state of equanimity or all-acceptance. Even in "reformed" orders like the

Kina Ram Aghoris studied by Ron Barrett (2008), cremation-ground practices remain central, while the practice of embracing polluted substances was substituted by caring for and healing leprosy patients as a form of social service.

- The ritual use of specific sonic, photic, and kinesthetic media as sensational forms (Meyer 2011), such as sacred songs and dance, the use of mantras, yantras, specific gestures (*mudrā*) and postures *āsana*s. These components, especially the use of sonically powerful formulas or syllables—mantras—for meditative and ritual purposes, and energetically empowered geometric diagrams or mesocosmic objects called yantras and mandalas, are often listed as the flagship of Tantric practice. In some contemporary traditions, Tantra is synonymous with knowledge of mantras. Mantras are crucial for mind-body transformations (Rao 2018) and for traditional modalities of healing (Hyam, this volume). The sonic rather than the semantic dimension of a mantra can perform psychophysiological transformations, evoke deities, or represent the deity itself (Gellner 1992,147). However, to complicate the picture, some traditions interiorize such elements—for example, the sound of the breath itself might be regarded as ultimate *mantra*—and disregard the use of any mantra and ritual implement except for the body.[13]

- Performing rites and practices aimed at pragmatic goals for this-worldly results. Besides offering a path to liberation, Tantra provides ritual practices using the power of the Tantric guru, Tantric deities, and/or the energies of the mandala to manipulate the conditions of the mundane world. For this reason, in certain regions Tantra and magic are often conflated dimensions. Examples of these "freelance non-liturgical" practices (Gellner 1992, 145) might include ritual healing, exorcisms, amplifying wealth, bestowing peace and blessings, divination practices, and waging magical attacks to subjugate or annihilate specific human or nonhuman targets (*ṣaṭkarman*). The Tantric practitioner's supernatural achievements (*siddhi*, often translated as "magic powers"), which enable them to control and transform the outer world, are interpreted as side effects of the spiritual attainments that result from Tantric *sādhana* (Gellner 1992, 129).

- Healing. Tantric healing (Gellner 1992, 328; Barrett 2008) is distinguished from other forms of traditional medicine (e.g., Ayurveda); its efficacy depends on the healer's knowledge of mantras, techniques for "brushing" and "blowing" (*jharphuk*), empowering water, preparing alchemical and herbal remedies, exorcising evil spirits, and "digesting" the patients' sin and impurity. Tantric healing is also a powerful source of recruitment of new adepts. For example, Aghor disciples interviewed by Ron Barrett were once nondevotee patients (2008, 83), and new disciples of Baul gurus are attracted in the lineage by their power in mastering conception and contraception (Lorea 2014b).

- Confronting death. The semantic field of death often emerges from the work of anthropological research on Tantra. Ethnographic films on *tāntrika*s emphasize and sensationalize cremation-ground practices, such as consuming human flesh from the pyre or the use of human skulls as ritual objects or drinking vessels (see Lawrence 2011). A wide range of textual and ritual traditions are preoccupied with the very art of dying (see Hornbacher, this volume). Realized practitioners are believed to acquire control over their own time of death, or even to gain immortality by becoming "dead while alive" (*jyānta marā* in Bengali). Ethnographers highlight Tantric practices that dispel the fear of death, manage loss, and professionalize communication with the spirit world (Schröder, this volume; Borkataky-Varma 2017). Confronting fears of death, sin, disease, and pollution is central to Aghor practice. Like Shiva, the Aghor guru attains the power to transform and digest these poisons in their body. Hence, laypeople can transfer on to the Aghor guru their impurities and diseases in exchange for blessings and healing (Barrett 2008).

- Divine possession. Becoming the same as a god, or temporarily mediating a deity, is the premise for Tantric ritual efficacy and healing practices. As Gellner reminds us, the line between gods and men in Tantra is far from absolute (1992, 130). Oracular possession and negative possession (by demons and *bhūtas*) are themes abundantly discussed in premodern Tantric texts and healing practices (Smith 2006; Slouber 2017). A number of ethnographies of Tantra in India highlight the role of *mātājīs*, "mothers" who undergo trance and divine possession by goddesses to answer questions, offer cures to people and cattle, and communicate with the deceased (see Erndl 2000; Dinnel 2017; and McDaniel 2004). In Kerala, the "cultural logic of formalized possession, i.e. the ability of the deity to possess and act through various media" forms a shared basis connecting both formal temple rituals by high-caste priests and the widespread Keralan folk tradition of *teyyattam* performed by untouchable dancers/oracles (Freeman 1997). Lidke's (2017, 71) ethnography suggests that the relationship between elite and non-elite Tantric traditions of Nepal is connected through music and possession (*āveśa*). The interpenetrating dimensions (Hyam 2019) of sound, healing, divination, and ritual performance are discussed in several chapters of this volume.

Although these characteristics have often been described as typical of Tantric communities of practice, we should cast this generalized taxonomic net widely (Lidke 2017, 43). This brief discussion of common traits in Tantric traditions should not be taken as normative or exhaustive. It is meant as support to readers who are new to Tantric studies, providing them with a conceptual map to navigate lived Tantric traditions through the compass of some frequent key terms and concepts that will accompany them through the course of this volume.

Tantra Research and Embodiment: Overcoming Ocularcentric and Androcentric Biases

The body is a central focus in both the ethnographic study of Tantra and the *tantricking* practitioners' journey. Here we are informed by

Hugh Urban's emphasis on embodied Tantra: "I would argue that what is needed most today is a fundamentally *embodied* approach to Tantra—a Tantra encountered 'in the flesh.' That is to say, we need to look at the peoples and traditions that we wish to identify as 'Tantric' in their most material, corporal forms, placing them firmly within their lived social, political and economic contexts" (Urban 2003, 273).

In Tantric traditions, embodied mystical experience and the oral transmission of religious knowledge are emphasized over what is written down. Like most printed literary texts in South Asia (Kersenboom 2005), rather than silent and static, Tantric texts are performed and lived through sounds, materiality, and movement. Songs constitute veritable sacred scriptures and indispensable ritual ingredients for numerous communities (Gellner 1992, 143; Lorea 2017). In the relationship between textual and embodied knowledge in the Tantras, texts are always inferior. Practitioners might be warned or explicitly ordered by the guru not to read or even touch books for several years because that knowledge, perceived as indirect and disembodied, may constitute an obstacle on their spiritual path. Such multisensory and embodied emphasis in Tantric teachings stands at odds with the scriptist and ocularcentric methodologies that are overly employed in the field of Tantric studies.

In Western theories of knowledge, seeing is considered the purer sense, epistemologically as well as morally (van Ede 2009, 62). This hegemony of the eye over other senses has been called "ocularcentrism," or the "hypertrophy of the visual" (Ong 1967). Observation has been associated in the sciences with the collection of visual data and the quality of objectivity, sustaining claims of valid knowledge. Going hand in hand, the ocularcentrism of Western knowledge and the scriptist bias of religious studies have created prejudices not only toward other senses and other ways of knowing, but also, using Hwa Yol Jung's words, toward the categories of body, woman, nature, and non-West (2002, 298). Rachel Devorah (2017) has skillfully discussed the implicit nexus between ocularcentrism and androcentrism by revealing how descriptions of the senses and sense organs are impregnated by the preconceptions of a patriarchal gender culture. She argues that ocularcentrism in modern scholarship reproduces prejudice against femininity. Traditional Western society prescribes that women must be seen and hearing, while men must be heard and seeing (Devorah 2017, 313). These kinds of critical reflections in the domain of sensory epistemology are important for the field of Tantric studies because they corroborate the fact that text-based scholarship of Tantra in particular, and of Asian religions in general, has privileged forms of knowledge preserved in written form by male elites of monks and high-caste priests as most authoritative, thus marginalizing embodied knowledge and other forms of religious authority and agency transmitted among women, queer, lower castes, and subaltern practitioners.

Feminist Buddhologist Miranda Shaw commented that concentration upon written sources at the expense of ritual and oral traditions have predisposed scholars to fail to recognize the existence of women's religious activities and leadership (Shaw 1994, 5). Previous opinions of women in Tantric rituals as servants and prostitutes at the disposal of men's liberation reflect interpretations that reproduce specific Western "protestant" and "androcentric" constructions of gender (Shaw 1994, 7).

Feminist scholars and sensory anthropologists have carefully deconstructed the ethnocentric and androcentric biases of modern academic practices based on text and vision (van Ede 2009; Classen 1998, 2005; Devorah 2017). They embraced the critique of ocularcentrism and extended it to question the validity of participant *observation* and logocentric inter*views* (Jackson 2012) as the privileged method of traditional ethnography (see van Ede 2009). Participant observation, another indication that vision-centric epistemologies are also at work in the formation of the ethnographer, stands at odds with the holistic experience of fieldwork, which is necessarily a full-body immersion involving the sensorium beyond the eye. This is particularly true when dealing with Tantric traditions and their emphasis on body, substances, and sensory experience, requiring additional heuristic tools—such as an openness to use the whole body as a research tool, or "embodied research" (Spatz 2017)—and a kind of ethnographic participation or hyperparticipation (Fakir 2005; Lorea 2016, 15) that often challenges the divide between insider and outsider.

Secrecy, Positionality, and Participation: Ethnographic Dialogues with Esoteric Traditions

Doing fieldwork with Tantric communities requires a tuned set of heuristic tools that are not necessarily part of a conventional training in ethnography. Among the authors of this volume for example, some took initiation from one or several gurus, becoming quasi-insiders; some became patients of the Tantric healers they study; some declined or accepted the proposal to become a sexual partner in esoteric rites; some learned how to sing and perform songs with their research participants; and others were required to discuss their dreams with their Tantric interlocutors and have experienced puzzling visions and divine appearances resulting from embodied research with their esoteric teachers. The ethical and epistemological facets of doing research in active Tantric contexts has profound implications for what ethnography means and how it is supposed to be conducted.

Gone are the days when ethnography was "practiced there" and "published here," produced by outsider observers taking insider practitioners as their "object" of study. The insider/outsider dichotomy in the study of religion has been dismantled (McCutcheon 2003), and anthropologists have largely abandoned it as a "pseudo-problem" that obscures more than it discloses, revealing the simple fact that knowledge is unequally distributed among subjects (Jensen 2011). The boundaries between scholarly and informant communities have largely collapsed (Barrett 2008, 19). Bridging the divide between scholar and practitioner, several researchers of esoteric traditions undertake initiation (e.g., McCarthy Brown 1991) and might become more involved as participants than they had anticipated (see Paul Christopher Johnson 2002). Modern ethnography recognizes that the exchange between researcher and informant is "rarely a clean one, without remainder" (2002, 10): the social and emotional involvement with the people we work with and write about is transformational and has deep implications for the researcher's life, well beyond the limited timeframe and goals of one's "fieldwork." Researchers might choose to locate themselves inside or outside of a particular community, deliberating and calibrating proximity and distance, participation, and detached observation, but ultimately it is the "host" community that decides if the visitor is an outsider or if, when, and to what extent her participation as an insider is welcomed (Rao 2018, 29).

The positionality and the field narratives of the ethnographers of Tantra collected in this volume cannot fall into simplistic categories of exogenous or Indigenous scholar, observing or practicing the tradition they study. Like Kirin Narayan (1993, 682), their scholarship calls for a meltdown of the divide between native and outsider anthropologist. Engaging the tension between engaged practitioner and critical observer as productive (Samuel 2005, 2), ethnographers of Tantra embody hybridity and are self-reflexive about their own genealogies of knowledge.

The secrecy that surrounds esoteric Tantric traditions has discouraged scholars to engage with living lineages and their practices. Buddhologist Edward Conze stated that in the field of esoteric knowledge, "those who know do not say and those who say do not know": either the academic author has not been initiated, then what he says is not firsthand knowledge; or he has been initiated, "then if he were to divulge the secrets [. . .] he has broken the trust placed in him and is morally so depraved that he is not worth listening to" (Conze 1967, 271–73). As Tony Stewart put it, "After the requisite time necessary to be fully knowledgeable within the tradition, the initiated scholar will have lost all pretense of academic distance [. . .] who could trust a committed scholar of an admittedly secret group that actively guards its privacy?" (2020, 155). However, ethnographic research has clearly showed that secrecy in Tantric esoteric traditions is not universal nor insurmountable. Similar to religious secrecy in Yolngu society, "interpretations lay in a relation of esoteric to exoteric along a continuum and these relations could change" (Keen 1994, 194). Secrets in Tantric traditions, like in Candomble, are unstable and transitional, rather than universal or consensual. Instead of discouraging us from any intellectual engagement, secrecy ought to be studied as a technique for the construction of social boundaries and a discursive framing of power (Johnson 2002, 24).

The esoteric character of Tantric practices led scholars to believe that "the one who knows" (one who had undergone initiation and training to access the secrets) cannot tell, and "those who speak" most likely do not know (Urban 1998). This assumption was amplified by scholarly constructions of "the myth of secrecy" (Lorea 2018c) in Tantric lineages. Textual scholars of Tantra reinforced and reified an idea of secrecy that is rarely enforced among Tantric communities. This etic emphasis on secrecy coincides with the scholarly construction of Tantric religiosity as the Other—the exotic/erotic religious group subjected to intellectual and academic scrutiny. This rigid concept of secrecy, however, is in opposition to a flexible reality of esoteric groups who continuously negotiate the balance between secrecy and disclosure, private gatherings and public audiences, subversive antinomy and widely accepted orthopraxy with overtly public dimensions. Tibetan mask dances (*'chams*), for example, are an open performance where lay spectators view monks publicly portraying Tantric deities for mass audiences (Kohn 2001).

The authors of this volume are not concerned with revealing secrets. They study the social, cultural, and religious meanings of secrecy, as well as the power dynamics entailed in the unequal distribution of, and access to, esoteric knowledge. Ethnographic work on Tantra deconstructs any monolithic notion of secrecy in Tantric contexts, instead displaying situational and variable secrets, responding to local protocols of knowledge accessibility and power, often based on an individual's stage of practice (*sādhana*) and responding to gurus' tests to understand the researcher's intentions. Keith Cantú (this volume), for example, asserts that secrets are predicated on an individual relationship and are seldom static but rather negotiated in dialogue and practice between student and teacher, and in certain cases with an additional partner and the guru's wife.

There *are* restricted truths and concealed techniques within Tantric communities, and this induces the researcher to refine conventional fieldwork methods and sharpen their ethnographic ears in a different manner. Ethnographies of Tantra are not only about what people *say* but also about what they do *not* say. Ethnographers not only base their analysis on transcriptions of interviews but also on prohibitions, silences and allusions, gestures and expressions, olfactory and tactile dimensions, coded jargons, and intuitive perceptions. As Sarbadhikary (this volume) notes, "While most ethnographers are concerned with observing and listening to semantic and articulated utterances, fieldwork in contexts that embody different kinds of concealment rather needs to be sensitive and empathically uncover the silent expressions of communities." This approach requires extensive fieldwork experience and openness to use not only participant "observation" but also participant listening, smelling, singing, and sensing, employing one's entire body as a research toolbox and engaging in ethnographic methods that are necessarily dialogical, experimental, and coproduced with research participants (see Hornbacher, this volume).

The Body, the Field, and the Work: Disputing the Borders of Ethnographic "Fieldwork" with Tantric Traditions

The challenges of doing ethnography with esoteric traditions include those inherent in all field research: finding appropriate field collaborators, gaining admittance to communities and religious events, and ensuring the trust and cooperation of a wide range of research interlocutors. Studying Yoruba society in Nigeria, anthropologist Andrew Apter realized that cult members do divulge esoteric knowledge, but they do so circuitously, in fragments, under exceptional conditions of friendship and trust. With time, and after undergoing several initiations, he was brought into restricted sacrificial groves and could ask sensitive questions without causing offense (Apter 1992, 107). Tantric contexts are not the only ones where particular protocols of knowledge, including accessibility or confidentiality, are enacted; all human societies have secrets, ways of distributing them, and relations between restricted knowledge and power. Divulging Tantric secrets to unprepared recipients, however, can have nefarious consequences that both researchers and participants need to take into account. Revealing a mantra or displaying a yantra to audiences unfit for their power might lead to insanity, wrath of deities, and even death. Tantric practice is understood as a powerful but burdensome and dangerous path, with high rewards and high risk of catastrophic failure. Any anthropological research dealing with ritual secrets must pay attention to the local concerns for knowledge restriction and disclosure and acknowledge the consequences for humans and nonhumans transgressing such protocols.

The Tantric emphasis on the human body as the site and vehicle of transformative knowledge adds ulterior challenges to ethnographic research, requiring fieldwork to become a "journey both intellectual and physical" (Shaw 1994, 15), with all the dangers and limitations such a journey implies. While traditional definitions of ethnographic research are hinged on interviews and participant observation, ethnographers of Tantra often alternate "among different degrees of insider and outsider perspective" (18) and between participation and hyperparticipation. They open themselves to blur the Western anthropologist's consecrated line between participation and "detachment," which is supposed to grant us critical distance and perspective. Clifford Geertz (1974) cautioned against yielding oneself too fully and completely to cultural integration, as it would undermine professional objectivity and the anthropologist's expertise. But in-depth research on Tantra challenges the anthropological fear of "going native." Some Tantric studies scholars are already "native" or "Indigenous" scholars in their own right, at least in one of their multiple identities; some are "halfies" or position themselves at various degrees of "hybridity" (Abu-Lughod 1991), sharing features such as nationality, caste, lineage affiliation, or bodily appearance with their research participants and their locales. Mani Rao (2018, 29) defines her positionality as a "heritage learner" who is neither experience-near nor experience-distance but rather "experience-open" in the way she engages with contemporary mantra practitioners. Conducting research in Varanasi, Ron Barrett (2008) had to juggle his roles as an ethnographer, a medical professional trained as a nurse, a white American male with all the privileges and positive discriminations it entailed, and a disciple of the Aghor guru Hari Baba.

The multiple identities of the ethnographer in relation to the group she studies aptly reflect the multiple identities of Tantric practitioners, themselves "split" between esoteric and exoteric personalities, official and "unofficial self,"[14] embodying different social roles and positions in other contexts.[15] A marked emic differentiation between secret (*guhya*) and public, inner and outer—*antaraṅga* and *bahiraṅga*—is a shared trait among many Tantric lineages (Gellner 1992, 77; Lorea 2016, 56, 60). Research with living Tantric communities require informed, tactful, and sensitive dispositions to discuss the knowledge that is meant to stay hidden, and that which is shareable.

Ethnographic research on Tantra calls for inspection and expansion of conventional understandings of fieldwork. In the global venture of anthropology, fieldwork is still carried out, largely by anthropologists from the West, in non-Western societies and cultures because "fieldwork conducted among 'exotic' natives in faraway lands has been, and still is, considered more authentic than fieldwork at home" (Kuwayama 2004, 21). Indigenous scholars have argued that the term *fieldwork* itself reflects a colonialist mentality and attitude toward colonized peoples and their lands: fieldwork ought to be conducted by physically displaced, civilized observers who will reveal what is out there in the wilderness of the "field," far away from "home." But doing ethnography within Tantric traditions often means that our field is introjected and shifts from the outside to the inside of the researcher's body-mind, requiring a degree of participation that ethnographers might be unaccustomed to and unprepared for.

The Tantric journey of *sādhana* is an inner fieldwork in its own right that explores subtle body-worlds and emotional landscapes with the tools one's own guru, lineage, or tradition puts at disposal.

As Cantú suggests (this volume), "there is an explicit link between *sādhanā* and the general process of self-exploration—that is, intensified self-reflexivity—which of course is also an important part of any ethnography." Researchers' academic practice of ethnographic fieldwork is not separate from their own bodies and their transformation, as it produces new intersubjective relationships and new relationships with one's own self. At the same time, the *sādhaka*'s practice of self-discovery generates new social relationships with, for example, guru brothers and sisters, teachers, and noninitiates, while pursuing inner knowledge through an established set of techniques of the body-mind complex. In this journey, the body-fieldwork of the *sādhaka* is specifically called a field (*khetra* or *deha-jami,* in Bengali esoteric lineages) that seeks to be cultivated through the grace of the guru. When fieldwork spatial hierarchies are taken inside out (or outside in), ethnography moves from distant lands to the inward journey of a researcher's experience. This requires a reverted gaze, which Hornbacher (this volume) calls "observing participation" as opposed to participant observation as described in classic ethnographic theory.

Tantric *sādhana* is akin to interiorized fieldwork; ethnographic fieldwork is (self-)exploratory *sādhana.* To see them as connected opens up possibilities for both semantic domains: the "field" of fieldwork, which can then revert and expand to include one's bodily and inner self, and the "work" of fieldwork, understood well beyond the mere collection of data on an "object" of study, as a kind of *sādhana* in its strive for (self-)knowledge. The work of the Tantric practitioner and the (field)work of the Tantric researcher are both conducted through an established set of research tools, whether learned in a university classroom or sitting at the guru's feet. These practices of knowledge, just like the body and the field, are usually thought of as separate, but they might inform and transform each other in ways that have been insufficiently explored.

"An Absolute Reversal": Foregrounding Living Traditions

Among recent publications dedicated to Tantric traditions, few include perspectives and sources beyond the textual.[16] Christian Wedemeyer (2013, 55–60) proposed investigating contemporary practices to understand how to interpret the notoriously transgressive rituals described in Tantric Buddhist texts. Wedemeyer relied upon the accounts of Horace Hayman Wilson, a Sanskrit scholar in early nineteenth-century Calcutta, as his ethnographic reference. From Wilson's accounts he understands that, insofar as anyone has actually witnessed them, "these wild rites turn out to be nothing but a kind of family barbecue in which the less objectionable esoteric sacraments (booze and meat) are consumed" (195). The choice of referring to the accounts of a British Orientalist as a representation of living Tantric practices is problematic at the very least.

A detailed chapter on Tantrism in the *Continuum Companion to Hindu Studies* swiftly dismisses the matter by stating that "present-day practice falls outside the scope of this survey" (Goodall and Isaacson 2011, 132). A full-length article on Tantra in *Oxford Research Encyclopaedia* (Gray 2016) counts more than 100 references but mentions only 3 authors who conducted ethnographic fieldwork. Indologists in the past have benefited from the interpretations of "local experts" elucidating unclear passages, although their perspectives on Tantra have remained unheard.[17]

These examples highlight three issues. First, the field of Tantric studies has not addressed debates on the decolonization of knowledge that call for taking into serious consideration the ways in which contemporary practitioners experience and interpret Tantra in their own terms, which is also a central concern in the study of "lived religion" (Orsi 2002, xxxiv). Second, textual scholars of tantras often lack the training to read, analyze, and effectively use ethnographic material. Third, historians of Tantra committed to philology are not interested in vernacular, oral, and contemporary sources as archival resources to understand Tantric texts and practices.

Ethnographic perspectives remain relegated to the margins of Tantric studies. David Gray informs us that "there are three primary approaches to the study of the history of Tantric traditions: textual, archaeological and ethnographic. The first two are most important [. . .] But as numerous Tantric traditions have *survived* in South, East and Central Asia, ethnographic studies in these communities are an important *additional source* of information concerning them" (2016, emphasis added). Ethnographically informed studies of Tantric traditions have been considered as only marginally important, and if useful at all, solely to represent practices that "survived" in the current era. This volume challenges this dominant view, that is, the presupposition that living Tantric traditions—regularly treated as "survivals" of a golden Tantric past—and studying Tantra through ethnography can only be an "additional" or "complementary" angle, informing "microscale" understandings and applicable to particular contemporary contexts.

This volume shows a "world of Tantra" far from eroded but not immune from change—vibrant and diverse, resonating in every aspect of people's lives, from artifacts of material culture to folk songs, from the domain of healing to the commission of black-magic rituals. We argue that practices, values, and discourses upheld by contemporary Tantric communities are not only "anthropological stuff" but should be taken into serious consideration by any scholar pursuing historical, literary, or philological engagements with Tantra.

Our contributors are not the first ones who strived to integrate living practices into the study of Tantra; rather, they follow the path of previous scholars who called for a renewed attention to non-textual sources. Gregory Schopen demonstrated the necessity for historians of Indian Buddhism to pay due attention to non-textual sources—relics, stones, bones, temple remains, and other artifacts—to gain critical insights into monastic Buddhism. Schopen established that Protestantism shaped the early paradigm of Buddhology as evinced by a conscious neglect of ample, extant material data to interpret textual archives. What Schopen (1991) calls "Protestant presuppositions" dismiss the voices and cultural artifacts of Buddhists who remain tangential to the task of finding the "real religion," situated neatly within the pages of "authentic" religious texts. The same could be said for the dominant paradigm at work within Tantric studies.

Colonialism played a pivotal role introducing these Protestant biases through the institutions, enterprises, and initiatives of studying Asian religions, both in the colonies and in the metropoles (van der Veer 2001). Textual studies were declared to be the only reliable means for the Orientalist scholar to uncover the "true" religions of Asia. For example, in tracing the history of Buddhist studies, Donald Lopez suggests that "the Buddhism that largely concerned European scholars was an historical projection derived exclusively from manuscripts and block prints, texts devoted largely to a 'philosophy' . . . . With rare exception, there was little interest in the ways in which such texts were understood by the Buddhists of Asia" (Lopez 1995, 7). This statement is still valid for Tantric studies, where literary analyses proliferate, "metaphysical and mystical elements" are privileged (Rao 2018, 38), but local perspectives on the meanings and uses of doctrinal texts and ritual manuals are absent.[18]

While trained anthropologists may need to refine their linguistic training and tackle the complex issue of incorporating the presence of text into their anthropological analysis (Gellner 2017, 113), the opposite is even more crucial. In building disciplinary bridges between Indo/Buddhological representations of Tantra and ethnographically grounded understandings, we need "an absolute reversal" (Rozemberg 2005, 42): we need to hear local voices and living practices in their own right and prioritize them over textual sources and their academic interpretations. Subverting this hierarchy, our authors take contemporary reality, with its diverse and often contradictory manifestations of *tantricking*, as the reference point for the study of Tantra.

Texts in Tantric Contexts

Tantric literature often emphasizes the priority of the gurus' oral interpretation and embodied experience of *sādhana* over texts, or the complementarity of the transmission of textual teachings, empowerment, and experiences in the oral tradition (*wang*, *lung*, and *thri*). Recent methodological efforts to access the imaginative worlds behind Tantric texts and the embodied experience of *sādhana* include the use of linguistics (metaphor theory and blending theory), cognitive science, and neuroscience (Hayes 2014; Hayes and Timalsina 2017). Goudriaan and Gupta noted that the study of Tantra without the inclusion of the testimonies of oral traditions was liable to appear incomplete and full of misinterpretations (1981, 13). Douglas Brooks observed how a text-oriented approach has been inadequate: "Tantric esotericism *requires* the translator to take seriously the insights of living adepts"; involving "more than philological ability and a vivid imagination: one must gain access to traditional interpreters and develop a critical appreciation of their input" (Brooks 1990, xvii).

On one hand, these key insights encouraged ethnographic immersion with living traditions; on the other hand, they inadvertently restricted ethnographic engagements to the learned elites of contemporary Tantric communities. Thus, several works on Tantra are based upon ethnographic fieldwork solely with ritual specialists, religious experts, lamas, monks, and hereditary priests (e.g., Saran 2008), to the detriment of the rich traditions of ritual agency and knowledge found among women and other genders, tribal communities, low classes, and castes.

Jeffrey Lidke (2017) exemplifies the advantages and values of integrating historical texts and the perspectives of living practitioners. Setting up the background to his study of the Śrī-Vidyā tradition in Nepal, Lidke stated:

> When oral tradition—the locus of ethnography—becomes institution it replicates itself as authoritative text (*śāstra*)—and thereby enters the locus of textual analysis. In a Tantric context, a text is authoritative by merit of the fact that it emblemizes the living tradition [. . .] in this symbiotic relationship between text and tradition, the living tradition (*sampradāya*) embodies its text through yogic practices which transform the written word into lived experience and makes possible liberation from the binding properties of language. (2017, 13)

Nicolas Sihlé warned us about the limitations of a logocentric approach to Tantric texts. While previous scholars often saw texts as things with meanings that await to be translated, Sihlé stressed the efficacy of texts beyond their semantic content, as instruments of mobilization of ritual power learned through repetition of the elders' bodily practices (Sihlé 2009, 39–40). Freeman (2010) looked into the liturgical details of a Tantric puja to highlight that novices rehearsed rituals directly from their teachers rather than learning from manuals. Mani Rao included in her sources modern books composed by gurus and charismatic teachers and demonstrated that these sources widely circulate among contemporary practitioners as guides, but their approach is "not that of homage but consultation" (2018, 39). Dealing with a great range of Tantric bodies, and a great range of Tantric texts such as ritual manuals, notebooks, soteriological scriptures, and popular *bazār tantra* booklets, linguistically competent ethnographers do not simply disregard textual traditions; they discuss books' usage and interpretations (Samuel 2005, 16–17), and texts as "ritualized objects" (Singh 2016). Tantric texts in this sense are "anthropologically relevant" (Sihlé 2009) and might be seen as events rather than items (Lorea 2016). Ethnography emphasizes the performative life of text in everyday practice, as Tantric "tools of the trade," subject to taboos and restrictions (see Sax and Hornbacher, this volume) or open to public worship, public singing, and transnational circulation.

Textual sources, in the chapters of this volume, are not simply dismissed. Texts are considered in their performative life, as part of a living tradition in which manuscripts and scriptures are not silent (Lambek 1990) but often actively part of rituals, recitations, and negotiations between past and present (Samuel 2005, 16–17; Sihlé 2009).

The Sex of "Tantric Sex": New Perspectives on Gender, Love, and Intimacy

The representation of copulating pairs of divine beings representing the ultimate truth through the ecstasy of a cosmic sexual union (Sanskrit *maithuna*, Tibetan *yab yum*) is perhaps the most puzzling characteristic of Tantric traditions for generations of European and North American scholars who were raised in Western contexts. This notorious entanglement of Tantric ideology and sexual imagery, reiterated in academic book covers and inflated in the market of neo-Tantric orgasmic manuals, has attracted the scorn of prudish Orientalists and the fascination of the American counterculture of the 1960s.

Primary data generated through ethnography differs from literary and iconographic analysis by engaging issues of gender, sexuality, love, intimacy, and eroticism in Tantric communities. For instance, while (white) women populate the market of neo-Tantric seminars, communes, and workshops (Saran 2008; Urban 2016; Plancke 2020; Perkins 2021), women practitioners are often absent from the studies of premodern Tantric literature in which women only appeared to be mechanistically instrumental at the service of a male *sādhaka*'s liberation (Bharati 1976, 53). Female agency and the ontological superiority of womanhood is widely attested in Vaiṣṇava Sahajiẏā and other literary archives. Not only does ethnographic evidence reveal a wide range of religious authority held by women (see Hyam's *mātājīs*, this volume) and a sophisticated spiritual discourse about other genders and nonheteronormative love (Lorea 2018), but such evidence also portrays everyday women and their participation as officiants and consumers of Tantric practices. However, this volume does not idealize a version of Tantra that is quintessentially proto-feminist, "characteristically gynocentric" (as Prem Saran argues; 2008, 131), or radically antipatriarchal, per se. While women might be exalted in Tantric ontocosmology, ritual expertise might be exclusively masculine (Sihlé 2013, 17). Women in Tantric communities might suffer seclusion and low status in society (Gellner 1992, 27) or be subjected to the same social pressures and expectations as their orthodox Hindu and Muslim neighbors (Knight 2011). Several Tantric traditions reproduce casteist and patriarchal structures, some even creating new sites to exploit women's bodies and abuse vulnerable participants (Caldwell 2001; Gray 2017).

Shifting the focus to living practices reveals specifically Tantric forms of partnership, joint renunciation, and couple practices (Openshaw 2007); the notion of spiritual companionship (Guenther 1976); and ritualized sexual intercourse that is perceived as beneficial and transformative for both male and female practitioners (Lorea 2018). These examples nuance dominant interpretations of the meaning of celibacy (*brahmacārya*) and asceticism that are otherwise only focused on the practice of lonely, single, high-caste males. Furthermore, they add layers to the otherwise simplistic binary view that Tantra in the unmarked "West" is all about full-body orgasms and cultural appropriation, while a supposedly original and authentic version of Tantra lying within Asia has grown out of, or has morally rejected any form of, erotic practice. Neo- and Western forms of Tantra contradict heteronormative values and hegemonic masculinity in contemporary societies; instead of dismissing them as "the spiritual logic of late capitalism" (Urban 2000, 270), Samuel proposed that these movements synthesize borrowings from Hindu and Buddhist sources in creative manners, while continuing themes of depth and significance within Western culture (2005, 360).

Scholars of Tantra have often uncritically perpetuated the historical notion that "older mystico-erotic forms" of Tantra, with its subversive use of sexual fluids to harness supernatural powers—as found in early Kaula traditions—are later sanitized, omitted, or reinterpreted as metaphors standing for philosophical concepts (White 2000, 17). The ethnography of Tantra can help us deconstruct the common idea of a linear history of Tantra teleologically evolving from "transgressive" to "sanitized," "sweetened," and "domesticated" (Urban 2010).

Sexual imaginaries and symbolism are still prominent across diverse Tantric traditions. A sexually active life in a consorted or conjugal relationship is what distinguishes Tantric practitioners from other religious specialists (e.g., Buddhist monks and Hindu *sannyāsīs*) in several contexts. Living traditions that transmit yogic practices performed during sexual intercourse between two initiated partners are neither remnants of a lost ancient past nor contaminated by New Age sensibilities: these contemporary practitioners are lineage heirs of continuing transmissions that, far from unchanged or unchanging, are innovative and heterogeneous, though maintaining a constant dialogue with their textual and oral history (Cantu, this volume; Lorea 2018; Salomon 1991).

Yogic and noncelibate traditions that transmit sexo-yogic teachings are often in tension with monastic and celibate ascetic institutions (Jacoby and Terrone 2009). However, both renunciation and sensuality have a place in Tantric practice. Far from the popular interpretations of Tantra as a libertine ethic of indulgence, the passions are subjected to discipline and regulations in Tantric *sādhana*. Indulgence and licentiousness are never celebrated as Tantric virtues—nondiscrimination is never an excuse for lack of discipline (Barrett 2008, 125)—but when free from attachment, and in ritual contexts, controlled infractions of taboos are part and parcel of several Tantric traditions (Gellner 1992, 144). Ethnographic work uncovers the ways pleasure, passion, and intimacy are regulated in Tantric communities, not only in accordance with ontotheological foundations but also in negotiation with changing moral values and gender roles in the societies where practitioners are embedded.

Sections and Essays

In the final part of this introduction we provide a concise, chapter-by-chapter outline of the contents in this volume. Chapters are grouped into three main parts: first, "On Materiality and Mediation: Lived Practices of Texts, Objects, and Media"; second, "Embodiment, Identity, and Experience: Conversations with Tantric Livelihoods"; and third, "Institutions and Individuals in the Making of Tantric Traditions: To Be or to Become Tantric."

On Materiality and Mediation: Lived Practices of Texts, Objects, and Media

In the past decade, scholars of lived religion have argued that while material objects and technologies of mediation (e.g., encompassing texts, digital platforms, embodied practices) are expressions of a particular religious system, materiality and media also shape the message and coproduce the ways in which religions are constituted and lived. Thus, the contemporary study of lived religion is simultaneously interested in material things, engagements of the body sensorium, and practices of mediation as inextricably connected dimensions of religion (see particularly Morgan et al. 2010; Meyer 2020). The opening section of our volume explores issues of materiality and the ways different media and mediations work in Tantric rituals, magic, and everyday practices.

William (Bo) Sax, drawing on over three decades of fieldwork, provides a critical survey of Tantric traditions in the Western Himalayas. He questions definitions of Tantra as a system serving soteriological ends and shows that Tantra in the Western Himalayas is primarily mobilized for pragmatic ends and in opposition to Vedic (*vaidik*) rituals. Tantric practices include blood sacrifices, love spells, possession by local gods and goddesses, and the use of black magic, including invocations of deities such as Bhairav, to exact revenge. The "guru" in the Western Himalayas, rather than a spiritual guide leading devotees to liberation, is a guide of the spirits: a ritual specialist who controls, bargains with, and exorcises various classes of beings to meet the desires of clients/patients. Gurus' narratives connect their histories to the kings and highlight their political power. Sax further analyzes how Sancha Vidya, an esoteric knowledge of numbers based on powerful texts written in a secret script, informs and is informed by Tantric traditions. Sancha Vidya is a complex, understudied astrological and divinatory system intended to "calculate" the right time to perform worldly actions. Sax concludes by redefining Tantra in terms of materiality: rather than abstract systems of thoughts on liberation, in the Western Himalayas tantras are defined as matter, ingredients, and material substances assembled into a yantra and empowered by mantras. Unlike Vedic rituals, they are closely connected to the material reality of the client/patient, their body, and their environment. Sax's ethnography contributes unprecedented empirical data while challenging established presuppositions in the dominant narratives around Tantra.

Connected through an ongoing collaborative research project on the life of esoteric scripts across South-Southeast Asia, William Sax's and Annette Hornbacher's chapters are in close dialogue. Hornbacher's fieldwork in Bali demonstrates that the ethnography of Tantra unsettles the scholastic boundaries of insider/outsider and complicates the distinction between emic and etic perspectives. Hornbacher employs an anthropological approach to text practices in Bali, treating texts not as systems of logocentric meaning but as vehicles for bodily transformation. Her chapter is focused on *tutur*, a genre of secret texts written in prose and dealing with esoteric cosmological and soteriological speculations, script mysticism, and magic. But instead of analyzing these texts and their oral interpretations as objects, Hornbacher embraced local epistemologies, which required her to undergo initiation and learn yogic practices. *Tutur* texts, according to their practitioners, are not to be read or commented upon but to be interiorly realized through embodied, transformative knowledge. This experimental approach subverts the conventional paradigms of participant observation. Revealing the troubled positionality of a scholar-practitioner with intellectual honesty, Hornbacher's essay not only sheds light on the understudied tradition of mystic pictographs in Bali but also contributes to the methodological and theoretical literature on the dilemmas of fieldwork with esoteric communities.

In the third chapter, Sukanya Sarbadhikary examines intersections of material, textual, and ethnographic discourses in the Tantric culture of Bengal, focusing on the material life of conch shells carved as ornaments and sound instruments. She presents the conch as a Tantric artifact due to its connections with Tantric subtle bodies, goddesses, meditative sounds, and rituals. The disparate lifeworlds of Bengali conch craftsmen (*Śāṅkhārīs*), sonic philosophy, Tantric textual conceptualizations of the cultivated human body, and Indian mathematical discourses all come together in her methodologically innovative analysis. Her study reveals that a particular number—three and a half—is a common denominator connecting the conch's interior spiral, the sonic manifestation of the mantra *aum*, and the twirls of the creative serpentine energy known as *kuṇḍalinī*. Craftsmen communities of conch-makers may not define themselves as Tantric or even know about rare ancient texts, but their lifeworlds associate them with

Tantric worldviews in unobvious yet telling ways. As Sarbadhikary navigates through twirled lives of texts, sounds, and manual labor via the lens of the conch, she shows how the ethnography of Tantra can take material objects seriously in order to critically approach the intersections of high cultural texts and everyday community practices.

Far from conservative and stagnant, the technologies of mediation engaged by Tantric traditions are constantly changing. Besides ritual objects and powerful texts, online platforms and phone apps equally constitute dynamic sites of Tantric mediation in contemporary Asian and diasporic contexts. In "WhatsApp Bagalāmukhī!" Sravana Borkataky-Varma discusses the "social" life of a Tantric goddess, her devotees, and ritual specialists; that "social" life ranges across multiple media platforms, reaching remote clients via virtual networks. Borkataky-Varma's research examines the nature of online encounters involving Tantric traditions and the ritual transactions. The author presents Tantric traditions through the lens of digital media, especially WhatsApp—arguably one of South Asia's most popular messaging services. Her work bridges the nascent field of the ethnography of Tantra with key scholarship in the field of digital religion to examine client-*tāntrika* relations, particularly those pertaining to magic rituals. The chapter highlights how digital ritual transactions are perceived as enhanced and effective religious experiences, bringing transformations into devotees' lives.

Embodiment, Identity, and Experience: Conversations with Tantric Livelihoods

The essays in this section focus on practitioners' lives and livelihoods in the complex and stratified Tantric contexts they inhabit. Essays explore participants' everyday actions, discursive strategies, and identity-making processes. Subaltern actors who perform what we call *tantricking* are embedded in webs of reciprocity and relationality with their surrounding society. Thick and vivid descriptions of their lifeworlds emerge through the authors' extensive participation in their cultural environment, repeated fieldwork visits, innumerable conversations, and immersive ethnography.

Jarrod Hyam's contribution highlights intersections of healing and Tantra, focusing on the careers of traditional healers operating outside the confines of Hindu and Buddhist institutions and within the paradigm of "folk Tantra." Hyam's case study shows how religious identities and sectarian distinctions become blurred or suspended in traditional healing. Hyam's fieldwork was conducted with healers, male (*jhākris*) and female (*mātās*), in Darjeeling and Sikkim (India). Hyam addresses the problems that emerge on the field if one relies upon traditional academic concepts of Tantra while neglecting embodied living traditions that are often highly heterogeneous. Folk Tantric healing requires knowledge and application of healing mantras; techniques of possession (i.e., by a tutelary deity, enabling the removal of harmful spiritual entities); and ritual techniques, like daily pujas and a vegetarian diet, to enhance the power of the healer. While *jhākris* perform cremation-ground practices, offer animal sacrifice, and are believed to forge alliances with evil spirits, *mātās* are apt vessels for embodying the Goddess and rely upon the sonic power of mantras drawn from sacred texts. Healing, possession, and the mobilization of sacred sounds are closely intertwined in local interpretations of Tantra in the Indo-Nepali Himalayan borderlands.

We descend from the Himalaya through North Bengal to the riverine plains of Bangladesh, where Keith Cantú interweaves vernacular religious texts and oral literature with personal engagements in *sādhanā* and long-term fieldwork with Bāul Fakirs of Bangladesh spanning over a decade. His central aim is to exemplify how participation in Bāul Fakiri *sādhanā* can present new methodological approaches to the ethnography of Tantra "as inspired by Bengali practitioners' perspectives." Bāul Fakirs (men) and Fakiranis (women) participate in the social network of the *sādhu* phenomenon in South Asia, but they do so as consort couples in a Muslim society. Cantú's empirical data counterbalances the overwhelming focus given to *sādhus* as celibate Hindu male ascetics. His approach enriches both anthropological and philological studies of South Asian religious traditions. Moving beyond scholarly constructions of Tantric authenticity, predominantly anchored in Hindu and Buddhist pasts, Cantú endeavors to conceptualize Tantra as defined by his informants: receiving a mantra and implementing practical instructions from a guru, which when enacted toward accomplishment (*siddhi*) becomes *sādhanā*. Arguing for a crosspollination of philology and ethnography, Cantú employs a full disclosure of his positionality in the field to advocate for "a responsible ethnography on *sādhana*," engaging in genuine dialogues, building lasting friendships, and creating multidirectional learning with fieldwork participants.

Set on the other side of the border, in the Indian state of West Bengal, the next chapter explores a contiguous cultural and historical region with closely affiliated lineages of musicians as well as spiritual practitioners. Kristin Hanssen worked with communities of Bengali Tantric Vaiṣṇavism, documenting their lives as beggars. She observes that scholars have understudied begging, which is a key practice for Bāuls and Vaiṣṇava mendicants. Begging provides insights into the social and economic networks in which they are situated; it is also embedded in their religious ethos and employs a religious vocabulary. Hanssen examines how begging is understood relationally, as mutually nourishing social obligations and reciprocity, integrating marginalized Bāuls within the larger society. Begging also constitutes a key aspect of their spiritual path: by framing their mendicancy in terms of the ceremonial language associated with sharing a meal and performing songs, these acts are included under the spiritual rubric of *sevā* (selfless service out of love for other humans). Hanssen demonstrates three important dimensions of the ethnography of Tantra. First, seemingly mundane economic realities, such as begging, serve as windows to understand how groups like the Bāuls involve themselves in social and religious networks. Second, while Tantric practitioners are often exoticized as isolated esoteric subjects, Hanssen shows that they are integrated in fundamental social relationships and exchanges in the public realm of rural societies. Third, practices with contents that emphasize social equality and inner divinity, including the songs of the Bāuls, also reinforce social distinctions, foster religious transactions, and facilitate the assembling and disassembling of social ties.

Institutions and Individuals in the Making of Tantric Traditions: To Be or to Become Tantric

The final section explores the different social layering of Tantric traditions—individual, clan, caste, lineage—and their dynamic and interactive role in transmission and institutionalization. Individual life stories and tensions between social expectations and personal aspirations are presented side by side with lasting Tantric formations supporting spiritual and political authority. This section explores Tantric practices and deities not only as apotropaic and salvific, but also, perhaps most importantly, as status markers, defining and reinforcing one's identity and belonging to lineage, group, or clan (see Gellner 1992, 313).

While historical and textual scholarship in Tantric studies often lacks individual voices, Nike-Ann Schröder worked closely with the life events and religious choices of a specific Tibetan practitioner to understand "what makes the fabric of an individual Tantric encounter." Schröder's ethnographic research was conducted over eight years in the Himalayan region of Ladakh. Working with the Tibetan refugee community in the region, she analyzes the rituals of *chöd* (*gcod*, or cutting), a cremation-ground practice that confronts death and brings pacification of suffering. Drawing on her experience with a local *chöd* practitioner, her analysis weaves together ritual descriptions, ritual texts, philosophical doctrines, anthropological fieldwork, and biographical research. Schröder cogently argues that to understand the complexity of the enacted dimension of Tantric practice we have to consider the motivations and the experiences individuals bring into the practice. The chapter centers on the personal experience of Pema Wangchuk, a Tibetan *chöd* practitioner whose Tantric engagements find meaning in relation to various life events such as the loss of his homeland and family roots, the tragic death of relatives, and the involvement in the armed resistance, which brought him to spend nine years in labor camps where a multitude of people died of starvation. Pema Wangchuk sought initiation and expertise in *chöd* practice to deal with painful memories and karmic residues, harnessing spiritual power to pacify restless spirits. Schröder's case study persuasively argues that Tantric lives and ritual agency may emerge as a choice that is not only soteriological but profoundly personal, political, and affective.

Maciej Karasinski's essay explores creative transformations of Tantric traditions in Kerala as revealed by an individual guru of the contemporary Meppaṭ *sampradāya* who combines ritual innovations with clan heritage. Karasinski examines collective identity formation among the members of the Nāyar caste belonging to the Meppaṭ tradition of Kerala through their daily ritual worship. The Meppaṭ order integrates various elements of Śākta and Kaula traditions within its rituals. Karasinski's ethnographic observations challenge conventional sectarian divisions. Combining both historical and ethnographic perspectives, he shows the heterogeneity of an elusive Tantric identity that is rooted in Pan-Indian philosophical Tantric traditions as much as it is entangled with the local religious relevance of sacred groves and martial arts gymnasia. Karasinski argues that the Meppaṭ tradition shapes its identity by referring to the authority of the clan (Nāyar), the esoteric knowledge of sophisticated philosophical traditions of Kashmir, and the Śrī-Vidyā tradition as practiced at the South Indian site where the Meppaṭ guru was initiated and trained. Far from unchanged, this case study of the dynamic Meppaṭ tradition exemplifies how Tantric communities engage in "opening, reviving, or in some cases reinventing traditions." Karasinski concludes by suggesting that research on Tantric identities prompts scholars to redefine notions of tradition and orthodoxy within Keralan Hinduism. Ethnography thus equips scholars of Tantra with tools to unpack how community bonds and individual experiences both create and are created by Tantric traditions.

The final chapter by June McDaniel employs a comparative perspective to bring together ethnographic data gathered across several decades of fieldwork research, tackling the difficult question of what prompts an individual to become a *tāntrika* and what are the social repercussions of that decision. She compares interview data gathered in West Bengal and Bali, Indonesia. Both locations maintain living traditions of Tantric practice dating back several centuries. McDaniel argues that different expectations of *sannyās*—renunciation—constitute "a major contributing factor to the different styles of Tantric experience" in the two societies. Her essay incorporates interviews with *tāntrika*s and lay audiences to compare the social identity, careers, and status of Tantric renunciants. In West Bengal, McDaniel observed that locals often ostracize *tāntrikas*, and practitioners struggle to preserve their livelihood and their dignity as ritual specialists in the context of modern India. In Bali, however, *tāntrikas* remain well integrated in society, staying with family, counseling people about their problems, and ensuring blessings for those surrounding them. McDaniel's contribution toward a comparative ethnography of Tantra demonstrates how Tantric lifestyles and the motivation for joining a Tantric tradition differ across diverse sociocultural contexts.

Conclusion

Through diverse ethnographies of Tantra, our contributors employ their case studies to challenge normative definitions of Tantra, to map the diversity of Tantric traditions, to bring individual experiences and life stories to the forefront, and to provide comparative perspectives on Tantric societies across regions and religious backgrounds. These studies conceive Tantra as lived religion and compel scholars to reflect upon what it means to be an ethnographer working in a Tantric field site.

The esoteric character of many Tantric traditions has discouraged fieldwork engagements, and secrecy has been repeatedly invoked as a pretext for neglecting living traditions. Further, many generations of scholars of religion have been trained only in historical and literary analyses, lacking the ethnographic tools to work within contemporary societies. Personal and collaborative engagement in fieldwork, conducted in ethical, empathetic, and responsible ways, can fruitfully discuss Tantra as plural and dynamic, as *tantricking*—an open-ended process coproduced by heterogeneous agencies—rather than reified as a set of texts, syllables, and images. From this perspective, Tantra reveals important social functions "of which, unlike magic and healing, one gets little hint in the scriptures" (Gellner 1992, 307).

Collectively, these chapters hope to contribute to the development of Tantric studies as a field undergoing a process of emancipation from exclusively scriptist interpretations. This emerging scholarly project is the shared endeavor by a community of scholars ethnographically grounded but also historically informed, linguistically competent in colloquial and literary idioms, and engaged in the study of varied Tantric traditions in context. *The Ethnography of Tantra* aspires toward a thorough definition of Tantric traditions that is not indicative of the textual production of a minority of learned theologians and other elites, but rather is closer to the lived practices and embodied experiences of a wide variety of actors. Far from aspiring to exhaustively represent all living Tantric traditions, this volume is but a first move to create a long-lasting intellectual framework that will support ethnographically rooted future research on Tantric traditions.

We coined the phrase *tantricking* to indicate a shift from the study of Tantra as a timeless and unalterable essence, to a focus on the active ways in which Tantric traditions are performed, mediated, and articulated within dynamic cultural contexts. However, this is a vast and complex world spanning across centuries and continents, and this publication project does not have the pretense of exhaustiveness. We had to limit the scope of our volume to particular regions, ritual communities, and traditions. Various geographical and cultural contexts had to be excluded, such as East Asia and Western forms of "neo-Tantra." What we offer is an initial step toward a new trajectory for Tantric studies, which includes a discussion on the decolonization of knowledge and a sincere interest in prioritizing community members and their living traditions.[19]

What emerges from this book is a rich and multilayered reality of Tantric traditions, vibrant and heterogeneous, freed—but not separate from—the silent folios of Tantric manuscripts, and deeply interwoven with the mind and body sensorium of the practitioner as well as that of the researcher, bringing up a new range of questions and possibilities for the future of Tantric studies.

Notes

1. See "Art of Loving," www.artofloving.nl.

2. The debate about decolonizing academia gained momentum since 2015. The legacy of the colonial era continues to influence many aspects of academic work through systematic biases in the hiring process, the syllabus, teaching perspectives, and the authors cited in scholarly papers. The movement to decolonize universities, academic conventions, and classrooms is about challenging longstanding biases and omissions that limit how we understand the world. Advocates of decolonization interrogate the canons of academia and the assumptions of its power structure, with the aim of broadening our intellectual vision by including a wider range of perspectives, authors, teachers, theories, and epistemologies (e.g., from the global South). Strong voices arguing for the decolonization of academic knowledge include Achille Mbembe, Walter Mignolo, Clelia Rodriguez, and many others. On decolonizing the field of religious studies, see Nye (2017).

3. The "scriptist" bias refers to the tendency in Western educational systems to assume that reliable information is naturally found in writing and print. "Protestant" presuppositions refers to the assumption that real or genuine religion lies not in daily religious praxis but rather within texts. Scholarship on religion has been defined as heavily "mentalistic," operating under the

assumption that religion is constituted by beliefs, metaphysical concerns, and abstract speculation rather than embodied practices and sensory engagements.

4. Voix has studied Tantric practices, political violence, and utopia in West Bengal. Toffin studied masked dances and goddess worship in Newar religion, where the dance troupe is a secret society structured through Tantric initiation and masks are consecrated by Tantric Hindu priests. Bouiller worked with historical sources (e.g., land endowments, monastic foundation acts, judicial records) and conducted extensive fieldwork to study Kanphata and Nath yogis. The work of Tarabout contributed to our understanding of body, possession, temple ritual, and Keralan countermagic rites where passions are operative tools for the Tantric *mantravādī* specialist.

5. Geoffrey Samuel has pioneered cross-cultural and transregional studies of Tantric traditions. Rather than studying Tibetan societies in isolation from other communities, he interrogates the possibility to study Tibet as part of upland Southeast Asia (2005) and connects it to Sub-Saharian Africa, while drawing informed comparison with South and Southeast Asia (2005, 31, 218).

6. Kripal and Saran portray South Asian Tantrism as lying at the core of Indic civilization, even as it flourishes as a counter-system on the geographical and doctrinal fringes (Saran 2008, preface).

7. See song n. 141 in Jha (2012) discussed in Lorea (2022).

8. Gellner used the term *Tantric* as a synonym of Vajrayana Buddhism because its usage "is well established in Western sources" (1992, 252), but only a few learned Vajracharyas named Tantra as "the knowledge which saves from the cycle of rebirths" and Tantrayana as "the ability to cure someone at a distance." Most Newars instead understood *tantra* as magical spells (*tantra-mantra*).

9. For example, Bāul-Fakir practitioners of Bengal do not desire to be associated with anything explicitly "Tantric." However, many receive initiation and Tantric training (e.g., in cremation-ground practices) from a *śākta tāntrik* preceptor. Their songs may refer explicitly to Tantric texts, as in the case of the composers Lalan Fakir (d. 1890) and Duddu Shah (1841–1911). However, explicit reference to this Tantric legacy seems to wind down toward the end of the nineteenth century. This is what is meant by Tantric as a post-emic category (see Lorea 2022).

10. Previous scholars have outlined some basic characteristics of Tantric traditions, often built upon the extensive lists of Sanjukta Gupta, Teun Goudriaan, and Dirk Jan Hoens (1979, 8–9), and Douglas Brooks (1990, 53). Brooks calls for a polythetic definition by describing a number of characteristics that do not have to be invariably present at the same time for a certain tradition to be considered Tantric, while recognizing that certain traits tend to converge.

11. Tibetan Tantric traditions often divide these practices into two stages. First, one engages an initial generation stage (*bskyed rim*) when practitioners

visualize themselves as the tutelary deity (*yi dam*) residing within a mandala (*dkyil 'khor*) surrounded by a retinue of dharma protectors (*chos skyong*) and other beings. The completion stage (*rdzogs rim*) is the second stage of practice involving yogic practices for manipulating subtle winds and channels in the subtle body.

12. Prem Saran goes as far as to define Tantra as "the centuries-old South Asian cults of erotic yoga which use ritualized sexual intercourse, either physically performed or only visualized, as a means to attain the mystical experience" (2008, 14).

13. The internalization of all ritual components particularly applies to the followers of the *sahaja* ideal, also called *Sahajiẏā* in the Bengali Vaiṣṇava context and *Sahajayāna* in the study of Buddhist Tantra.

14. Most Tantric communities are not interested in displaying antinomian behaviours to attract social contempt and public scorn. Dimock distinguished between an outer and inner dimension of Vaiṣṇava Sahajiẏā practitioners: "The Vaiṣṇava self is the 'official self' of a Vaiṣṇava Sahajiẏā. This self is a social being. The unofficial self is the Sahajiẏā self, his elect nature goes against all normal standards. The personality of the Vaiṣṇava Sahajiẏā, it would seem, was somewhat schizophrenic" (Dimock 1966: 105–9).

15. As the Tibetan saying goes "outwardly Hinayana, inwardly Mahayana, secretly Vajrayana" (Samuel 2005, 58). A similar saying is found in the Hindu Tantras: "Secretly Kaula, outwardly Śaiva, and Vaishnava among [common] men" (Avalon and Vidyarnava 1917, 11, 83).

16. The volumes edited by White (2000) and Keul (2012) feature one or two essays based on firsthand ethnography.

17. For example, Hélène Brunner-Lachaux's critical edition of *Somaśambhupaddhati*, an eleventh-century Śaiva text, is equipped with photos of a contemporary practitioner whose "patient explanations have clarified several obscure terms" (1963, xlvi, our translation). Czech linguist and Tamil expert Kamil Zvelebil (1927–2009) and his in-depth engagement with Tamil siddhas is also worth mentioning. In his words: "We must avoid the 'tunnel vision' (D.D. Kosambi) of armchair Indologists who avoid any disagreeable contact with fieldwork—with anthropology, sociology, folklore, or reality at large. The long and exclusive concentration of such scholars on written, particularly Sanskrit, Brahmin-produced documents seems to have impaired their ability to distinguish between myth and reality" (1991).

18. With the notable exception of Nicolas Sihlé and his attention toward an anthropology of written media among "tantrist" householder specialists (2013).

19. Our commitment to decolonizing knowledge production is constrained by systemic inequalities and exclusionary politics within academia (e.g., the need to publish in English and with an American university press

in order to gain recognition for our work). Operating within these constrains, it is difficult to provide the kind of diversity of voices we would have hoped for. Nevertheless, this volume is inclusive of authors from very diverse backgrounds, including authors of Indigenous, Latino, Indian, Bengali, Native American, and southern and eastern European origins. Several of them/us are trained in Asia and/or based in Asia and/or originally from Asia (even though our surname might not reveal such heritage). In addition to this, we do not believe that adding nonwhite scholars would per se make a volume more germane to the project of knowledge decolonization. Epistemic decolonization is a slow process of encompassing transformation. Our contribution to epistemic decolonization is but a little step to de-exoticize Tantric traditions, recognizing and valuing other ways of knowing and epistemologies from the global South (see Walter Mignolo and Boaventura de Sousa Santos) by subverting conventional hierarchies of authoritative sources and methods. We hope this volume will establish the ethnography of Tantra as a relevant area of research, so that more scholars from the global South and from regions with active Tantric traditions will feel encouraged to engage in these topics.

Bibliography

Abu-Lughod, Lila. 1991. "Writing Against Culture." In *Recapturing Anthropology: Working in the Present*, edited by Richard Fox, 137–54. Santa Fe: School of American Research Press.

Alonso Bejarano, Carolina, Lucia López Juárez, Mirian A. Mijangos García, and Daniel M. Goldstein. 2019. *Decolonizing Ethnography: Undocumented Immigrants and New Directions in Social Science*. Durham, NC: Duke University Press.

Ammerman, Nancy T. 2016. "Lived Religion as an Emerging Field: An Assessment of its Contours and Frontiers." *Nordic Journal of Religion and Society* 29, no. 2: 83–99. https://doi.org/10.3167/arrs.2014.050114.

Apter, Andrew. 1992. *Black Critics and Kings: The Hermeneutics of Power in Yoruba Society*. Chicago: University of Chicago Press.

Asad, Talal, ed. 1973. *Anthropology and the Colonial Encounter*. Ithaca: Ithaca Press.

Avalon, Arthur, and T. Vidyarnava, eds. 1917. *Kulārṇava Tantra*. Vol. 5. London: Tantrik Texts.

Bell, Catherine. 1992. *Ritual Theory, Ritual Practice*. New York: Oxford University Press.

Belting, Hans, Pamela Klassen, Birgit Meyer, Christopher Pinney, and Monique Scheer. 2014. "An Author Meets Her Critics: Around Birgit Meyer's 'Mediation and the Genesis of Presence: Toward a Material Approach to Religion.'" *Religion and Society* 5, no. 1: 205–54.

Bharati, Agehananda. 1976. "Making Sense Out of Tantrism and Tantrics." *Loka 2: A Journal from Naropa*: 52–55.

Borkataky-Varma, Sravana. 2017. "The Dead Speak: A Case Study from the Tiwa Tribe Highlighting the Hybrid World of Śākta Tantra in Assam." *Religions* 8, no. 221. https://doi.org/10.3390/rel8100221.

Brooks, Douglas. 1990. *The Secret of the Three Cities: An Introduction to Hindu Shakta Tantrism*. Chicago: University of Chicago Press.

Brunner-Lachaux, Hélène. 1963. *Somaśambhupaddhati*. First Part. Pondichéry: Institut Français d'Indologie.

Burchett, Patton E. 2019. *A Genealogy of Devotion: Bhakti, Tantra, Yoga, and Sufism in North India*. New York: Columbia University Press.

Caldwell, Sarah Lee. 2001. "The Heart of the Secret: A Personal and Scholarly Encounter with Shakta Tantrism in Siddha Yoga." *Nova Religio* 5, no. 1: 9–51.

Cantú, Keith. 2019. "Islamic Esotericism in the Bengali Bāul Songs of Lālan Fakir." *Correspondences* 7, no. 1: 109–65.

———. 2021. Sri Sabhapati Swami and the "Translocalization" of Śivarājayoga. PhD diss., University of California Santa Barbara.

Cashin, David. 1995. *The Ocean of Love: Middle Bengali Sufi Literature and the Fakirs of Bengal*. Stockholm: Stockholm University Association of Oriental Studies.

Classen, Constance. 1998. *The Color of Angels: Cosmology, Gender and the Aesthetic Imagination*. London: Routledge.

———. 2005. "The Witch's Senses: Sensory Ideologies and Transgressive Feminities from the Renaissance to Modernity." In *Empire of the Senses*, edited by David Howes, 70–84. Oxford: Berg Publishers.

Conze, Edward. 1967. *Buddhist Thought in India: Three Phases of Buddhist Philosophy*. Ann Arbor: University of Michigan.

Davidson, Ronald M. 2002. *Indian Esoteric Buddhism: A Social History of the Tantric Movement*. New York: Columbia University Press.

Davidson, Ronald M. 2005. *Tibetan Renaissance: Tantric Buddhism in the Rebirth of Tibetan Culture*. New York: Columbia University Press.

Devorah, Rachel. 2017. "Ocularcentrism, Androcentrism." *Parallax* 23, no. 3: 305–15.

Dinnell, Darry. 2017. "Can Tantra Make a Mātā Middle-Class? Jogaṇī Mātā, a Uniquely Gujarati Chinnamastā." *Religions* 8, no. 8: 142.

Dirks, Nicholas B. 1997. "The Policing of Tradition: Colonialism and Anthropology in Southern India." *Comparative Studies in Society and History* 39, no. 1: 182–212.

Eisenstadt, Shmuel N. 2002. "Some Observations on Multiple Modernities." In *Reflections on Multiple Modernities: European, Chinese and other inter-*

pretations, edited by Dominic Sachsenmaier, Jens Riedel and Shmuel N. Eisenstadt, 27–41. Leiden: Brill.

Erndl, Kathleen M. 2000. "A Trance Healing Session with Mataji." In *Tantra in Practice*, edited by David G. White, 97–116. Princeton: Princeton University Press.

Ernst, Carl W. 2005. "Situating Sufism and Yoga." *Journal of the Royal Asiatic Society* 15, no. 1: 15–43.

Fakir, Rudrani. 2005. *The Goddess and the Slave: The Fakir, the Mother and Maldevelopment*. New Delhi: Indica Books.

Flood, Gavin D. 2006. *The Tantric Body: The Secret Tradition of Hindu Religion*. London: I.B. Tauris.

Freeman, J. Rich. 1997. "Possession Rites in the Tantric Temples: A Case Study from Northern Kerala." *DISKUS Internet Journal of Religion* 2, no. 2. Accessed November 4, 2021. http://jbasr.com/basr/diskus/diskus1-6/index.html.

———. 2003. "The Teyyam Tradition of Kerala." In *The Blackwell Companion to Hinduism*, edited by Gavin Flood, 307–26. Oxford: Wiley Blackwell.

———. 2010. "Pedagogy and Practice. The Meta-Pragmatics of Tantric Rites in Kerala." In *Ritual Dynamics and the Science of Ritual*, vol. 1, edited by Axel Michaels and Anand Mishra, 275–305. Wiesbaden: Harrassowitz.

Geertz, Clifford. 1974. "'From the Native's Point of View': On the Nature of Anthropological Understanding." *Bulletin of the American Academy of Arts and Sciences* 28, no. 1: 26–45.

Gellner, David N. 1990. "Introduction: What Is the Anthropology of Buddhism About?" *Journal of the Anthropological Society of Oxford* 21, no. 2: 95–112.

———. 1992. *Monk, Householder, and Tantric Priest: Newar Buddhist and Its Hierarchy of Ritual*. Cambridge: Cambridge University Press.

———. 2001. *The Anthropology of Buddhism and Hinduism: Weberian Themes*. Delhi: Oxford University Press.

———. 2017. "Afterword: So What Is the Anthropology of Buddhism About?" *Religion and Society* 8, no. 1: 203–9.

Goodall, Dominic and Harunaga Isaacson. 2011. "Tantric Traditions." In *The Continuum Companion to Hindu Studies*, edited by Jessica Frazier, 122–37. London: Continuum Books.

Goudriaan, Teun, and Sanjukta Gupta. 1981. *Hindu Tantric and Śākta Literature*. Wiesbaden: Otto Harrasowitz.

Goudriaan, Teun, Sanjukta Gupta, and Dirk Jan Hoens. 1979. *Hindu Tantrism*. Vol. 2. Leiden: Brill.

Gray, David B. 2016. "Tantra and the Tantric Traditions of Hinduism and Buddhism." *Oxford Research Encyclopedia of Religion*. April 5, 2016; accessed August 18, 2020. https://oxfordre.com/religion/view/10.1093/acrefore/9780199340378.001.0001/acrefore-9780199340378-e-59.

———. 2017. "Contemporary Tantric Buddhist Traditions." In *The Oxford Handbook of Contemporary Buddhism*, edited by Michael Jerryson, 606–18. New York: Oxford University Press. https://doi.org/10.1093/oxfordhb/9780199362387.013.40.

Grieve, Gregory. 2006. *Retheorizing Religion in Nepal*. New York: Palgrave MacMillan.

Guenther, Herbert. 1976 [1969]. *The Tantric View of Life*. Boulder, CO: Shambhala.

Hayes, Glen A. 2014. "Possible Selves, Body Schemas, and Sādhana: Using Cognitive Science and Neuroscience in the Study of Medieval Vaiṣṇava Sahajiyā Hindu Tantric Texts." *Religions* 5, no. 3: 684–99.

Hayes, Glen A., and Sthaneshwar Timalsina. 2017. "Introduction to Cognitive Science and the Study of Yoga and Tantra." *Religions* 8, no. 9: 181.

Hatley, Shaman. 2007. "Mapping the Esoteric Body in the Islamic Yoga of Bengal." *History of Religions* 46, no. 4: 351–68.

Hyam, Jarrod. 2019. "The Transformational Body: Bāul and Jhākri Approaches to Embodied Healing." PhD diss., University of Sydney.

Iyer, Usha. 2013. "Nevla as Dracula: Figurations of the Tantric as Monster in the Hindi Horror Film." In *Figurations in Indian Film*, edited by Meheli Sen and Anustup Basu, 101–15. London: Palgrave Macmillan.

Jackson, Cecile. 2012. "Speech, Gender and Power: Beyond Testimony." *Development and Change* 43, no. 5: 999–1023. https://doi.org/10.1111/j.1467-7660.2012.01791.x.

Jacoby, Susan, and Antonio Terrone, eds. 2009. *Buddhism Beyond the Monastery: Tantric Practices and their Performers in Tibet and the Himalayas*. Leiden: Brill, 2009.

Jensen, Jeppe Sinding. 2011. "Revisiting the Insider-Outsider Debate: Dismantling a Pseudo-problem in the Study of Religion." *Method and Theory in the Study of Religion* 23, no. 1: 29–47. http://dx.doi.org/10.1163/157006811X549689.

Joffe, Ben Philip. 2019. "White Robes, Matted Hair: Tibetan Tantric Householders, Moral Sexuality, and the Ambiguities of Esoteric Buddhist Expertise in Exile." PhD diss., University of Colorado.

Jha, Shakti Nath. 2012. *Duddu Śā'r Padābalī*. Kolkata: Sahajapath.

Johnson, Paul Christopher. 2002. *Secrets, Gossip and Gods: The Transformations of Brazilian Candomble*. New York: Oxford University Press.

Jung, Hwa Yol. 2002. "Enlightenment and the Question of the Other: A Postmodern Audition." *Human Studies* 25, no. 3: 297–306.

Kaviraj, Gopinath. 1966. *Aspects of Indian Thought*. Burdwan: University of Burdwan Press.

Keen, Ian. 1994. *Knowledge and Secrecy in an Aboriginal Religion*. New York: Oxford University Press.

Kersenboom, Saskia. 1995. *Word, Sound, Image: The Life of a Tamil Text*. Oxford: Berg Publishers.

King, Richard. 1999. *Orientalism and Religion: Postcolonial Theory, India and 'The Mystic East'*. Delhi: Oxford University Press.
Knight, Lisa I. 2011. *Contradictory Lives: Baul Women in India and Bangladesh*. New York: Oxford University Press.
Kohn, Richard J. 2001. *Lord of the Dance: The Mani Rimdu Festival in Tibet and Nepal*. Albany: SUNY Press.
Kripal, Jeffrey. 2012. "Remembering Ourselves: On Some Countercultural Echoes of Contemporary Tantric Studies." In *Transformations and Transfer of Tantra in Asia and Beyond*, edited by Istevan Keul, 435–56. New York: De Gruyter.
Kuwayama, Takami. 2004. *Native Anthropology: The Japanese Challenge to Western Academic Hegemony*. Melbourne: Trans Pacific Press.
Lambek, Michael. 1990. "Certain Knowledge, Contestable Authority: Power and Practice on the Islamic Periphery." *Asian Ethnologist* 17, no. 1: 23–40.
Lawrence, Andrew, dir. 2011. *The Lover and the Beloved; A Journey into Tantra*.
LeCompte, Margaret D. 1987. "Bias in the Biography: Bias and Subjectivity in Ethnographic Research." *Anthropology and Education Quarterly* 18, no. 2: 43–52.
———. 2002. "The Transformation of Ethnographic Practice: Past and Current Challenges." *Qualitative Research* 2, no. 3: 283–99. https://doi.org/10.1177/146879410200200301.
Lidke, Jeffrey. 2017. *The Goddess Within and Beyond the Three Cities: Shakta Tantra and the Paradox of Power in Nepala-Mandala*. New Delhi: DK Printworld.
Lopez, Donald S. 1995. Introduction to *Curators of the Buddha: The Study of Buddhism Under Colonialism*, edited by Donald S. Lopez, 1–30. Chicago: University of Chicago Press.
Lorea, Carola E. 2014. "Searching for the Divine, Handling Mobile Phones: Baul Lyrics and Their Osmotic Response to Globalization." *Journal of History and Sociology of South Asia* 8, no. 1: 59–88.
———. 2014b. "Why Do You Go Swimming in the River Full of Algae? Conception and Contraception in Baul Songs and Oral Teachings." *Journal of Folklore and Folkloristics* 7, no. 1: 9–45.
———. 2016. *Folklore, Religion and the Songs of a Bengali Madman: A Journey Between Performance and the Politics of Cultural Representation*. Leiden: Brill.
———. 2017. "The Difference Between a Paṇḍit and a Wise Man: A Study of Bengali Songs as Literature Against Literature." *Sanskrti Charcha / Cultural Studies* 1, no. 1: 8–22. http://www.culturalstudies.in/.
———. 2018. "Pregnant Males, Barren Mothers and Religious Transvestism: Transcending Gender in the Songs and Practices of 'Heterodox' Bengali Lineages." *Asian Ethnology* 77, nos. 1/2: 169–213.
———. 2018b. "Sectarian Scissions, Vaishnava Deviancy, and Trajectories of Oral Literature: A Virtual Dialogue between the Bengali Songs of

Bhaktivinod Thakur (1838–1914) and Duddu Shah (1841–1911)." *Zeitschrift für Indologie und Südasienstudien. Band* 35: 83–114.

———. 2018c. "I Am Afraid of Telling You This, Lest You'd Be Scared Shitless!": The Myth of Secrecy and the Study of the Esoteric Traditions of Bengal." *Religions* 9, no. 6. https://doi.org/10.3390/rel9060172.

———. 2022. "Singing Tantra: Aural Media and Sonic Soteriology in Bengali Esoteric Lineages." In *The Oxford Handbook of Tantric Studies* (online edition, Oxford Academic, 18 Aug. 2022), edited by Richard K. Payne, and Glen A. Hayes. https://doi.org/10.1093/oxfordhb/9780197549889.013.37, accessed 12 June 2023.

Lutgendorf, Philip. 2007. *Hanuman's Tale: The Messages of a Divine Monkey.* New York: Oxford University Press.

Masuzawa, Tomoko. 2005. *The Invention of World Religions.* Chicago: University of Chicago Press.

McCarthy Brown, Karen. 1991. *Mama Lola: A Vodou Priestess in Brooklyn.* Berkeley: University of California Press.

McCutcheon, Russell T. 2003. "The Ideology of Closure and the Problem with the Insider/Outsider Problem in the Study of Religion." *Studies in Religion* 32, no. 3: 337–52.

McDaniel, June. 2004. *Offering Flowers, Feeding Skulls: Popular Goddess Worship in West Bengal.* New York: Oxford University Press.

Meyer, Birgit. 2011. "Mediation and Immediacy: Sensational Forms, Semiotic Ideologies and the Question of the Medium." *Social Anthropology* 19, no. 1: 23–39.

———. 2020. "Religion as Mediation." *Entangled Religions* 11, no. 3. https://doi.org/10.13154/er.11.2020.8444.

Mills, Martin A. 1993. *Identity, Ritual, and State in Tibetan Buddhism: The Foundations of Authority in Gelukpa Monasticism.* London: Routledge-Curzon.

Morgan, David, Birgit Meyer, Brent Plate, and Crispin Paine. 2010. "The Origin and Mission of Material Religion." *Religion* 40, no. 3: 207–11. https://doi.org/10.1016/j.religion.2010.01.010.

Mumford, Stan. 1989. *Himalayan Dialogue: Tibetan Lamas and Gurung Shamans in Nepal.* Madison: University of Wisconsin Press.

Narayan, Kirin. 1993. "How Native is a Native Anthropologist?" *American Anthropologist* 95, no. 3: 671–86.

Narayanan, Vasudha, 2000. "Diglossic Hinduism: Liberation and Lentils." *Journal of the American Academy of Religion* 68, no. 4: 761–79.

Nye, Malory. 2000. "Religion, Post-Religionism, and Religioning: Religious Studies and Contemporary Cultural Debates." *Method & Theory in the Study of Religion* 12, nos. 1–4: 447–76. https://doi.org/10.1163/157006800X00300.

———. 2017. "Some Thoughts on the Decolonization of Religious Studies: Postcolonialism, Decoloniality, and the Cultural Study of Religion." *Medium,*

Religion Bites, October 15, 2017. https://medium.com/religion-bites/decolonisation-of-religious-studies-993727c6d1bc.

Ong, Walter J. 1967. *The Presence of the Word: Some Prolegomena for Cultural and Religious History*. New Haven, CT: Yale University Press.

Openshaw, Jeanne. 2002. *Seeking Bauls of Bengal*. New York: Cambridge University Press.

———. 2007. "Renunciation Feminised? Joint Renunciation of Female–Male Pairs in Bengali Vaishnavism." *Religion* 37, no. 4: 319–32, https://doi.org/10.1016/j.religion.2007.06.007.

Orsi, Robert. 2002. *The Madonna of 115th Street: Faith and Community in Italian Harlem, 1880–1950*. New Haven: Yale University Press.

Padoux, André. 1986. "Tantrism: An Overview." In *Encyclopedia of Religion*, vol. 14, edited by Mircea Eliade, 271–72. New York: Macmillan.

———. 2017. *The Hindu Tantric World: An Overview*. Chicago: University of Chicago Press.

Pechilis, Karen. 2016. "Bhakti and Tantra Intertwined: The Explorations of the Tamil Poetess Kāraikkāl Ammaiyār." *International Journal of Dharma Studies* 4, no. 2: 1–10.

Perkins, Sophie-Anne. 2021. "Conserving the 'Container' of Tantric Secrecy: A Discussion with Western Śākta Practitioners." *Religions* 12, no. 9: 729.

Pinch, William R. 2006. *Warrior Ascetics and Indian Empires*. New York: Cambridge University Press.

Plancke, Carine. 2020. "Bodily Intimacy and Ritual Healing in Women's Tantric Retreats." *Anthropology and Medicine* 27, no. 3: 285–99.

Rao, Mani. 2018. *Living Mantra: Mantra, Deity, and Visionary Experience Today*. London: Palgrave Macmillan.

Rozemberg, Guillaume. 2005. "Anthropology and the Buddhological Imagination: Reconstructing the Invisible Life of Texts." *Aséanie, Sciences Humaines en Asie du Sud-Est* 16: 41–59.

Salomon, Carol. 1991. "Cosmogonic Riddles of Lalon Fakir." In *Gender, Genre, and Power in South Asian Expressive Traditions*, edited by Frank J. Korom, Arjun Appadurai, and Margaret A. Mills, 267–304. Philadelphia: University of Pennsylvania Press.

Samuel, Geoffrey. 1993. *Civilized Shamans: Buddhism in Tibetan Societies*. Washington, DC: Smithsonian Institution Press.

———. 2017 [2005]. *Tantric Revisionings: New Understandings of Tibetan Buddhism and Indian Religion*. New York: Routledge.

Sanderson, Alexis. 2009. "The Śaiva Age: The Rise and Dominance of Śaivism during the Early Medieval Period." In *Genesis and Development of Tantrism*, Institute of Oriental Culture Special Series 23, edited by Shingo Einoo, 41–350. Tokyo: Institute of Oriental Culture, University of Tokyo.

Saran, Prem. 2008. *Yoga, Bhoga and Ardhanariswara: Individuality, Wellbeing and Gender in Tantra.* New Delhi: Routledge.

Satpurananda, Kulavadhuta. 1996. "Tantra in its Essential Nature." *Bibliotheca Sikkim Himalayca Series 1. Symposium Volume, Guru Duechen* (July issue).

Schopen, Gregory. 1991. "Archaeology and Protestant Presuppositions in the Study of Indian Buddhism." *History of Religions* 31, no. 1: 1–23.

Shaw, Miranda. 1995. *Passionate Enlightenment: Women in Tantric Buddhism.* Princeton: Princeton University Press.

Sihlé, Nicolas 2009. "Written Texts at the Juncture of the Local and the Global: Some Anthropological Considerations on a Local Corpus of Tantric Ritual Manuals (Lower Mustang, Nepal)." In *Tibetan Ritual,* edited by José Cabezón, 35–52. New York: Oxford University Press.

———. 2013. *Rituels Bouddhiques de Pouvoir et de Violence: la Figure du Tantriste Tibétain.* Turnhout, Belgium: Brepols.

Sihlé, Nicolas, and Patrice Ladwig. 2017. "Introduction: Legacies, Trajectories and Comparison in the Anthropology of Buddhism." *Religion and Society* 8, no. 1: 109–28. https://doi.org/10.3167/arrs.2017.080107.

Singh, Rohit. 2016. "Buddhists and Muslims in Ladakh: Negotiating Tradition and Modernity." PhD diss., University of California, Santa Barbara.

———. 2020. "Authenticating Buddhism in the Public Sphere: Moral Dialogues in Ladakh." *Journal of Global Buddhism* 86, no. 1: 171–86.

Slouber, Michael. 2017. *Early Tantric Medicine: Snakebite, Mantras, and Healing in the Garuda Tantras.* New York: Oxford University Press.

Smith, Frederick. 2006. *The Self Possessed: Deity and Spirit Possession in South Asian Literature.* New York: Columbia University Press.

Spatz, Ben. 2017. "Embodied Research: A Methodology." *Liminalities: A Journal of Performance Studies* 13, no. 2: 1–31. http://liminalities.net/13-2/embodied.pdf.

Stephen, Michele. 2015. "*Sūrya-Sevana*: A Balinese Tantric Practice." *Archipel* 89: 95–124. https://doi.org/10.4000/archipel.492.

Stewart, Tony K. 2020. "The Power of the Secret: The Tantalizing Discourse of Vaiṣṇava Sahajiyā Scholarship." In *The Legacy of Vaiṣṇavism in Colonial Bengal,* edited by Ferdinando Sardella and Lucian Wong, 125–66. London: Routledge.

Strube, Julian. 2022. *Global Tantra: Religion, Science, and Nationalism in Colonial Modernity.* New York: Oxford University Press.

Timalsina, Sthaneswar. 2011. "Encountering the Other: Tantra in the Cross-cultural Context." *The Journal of Hindu Studies* 4: 274–89.

(Un)well. 2020. Episode 2: *Tantric Sex.* 48 min. USA: Netflix.

Urban, Hugh B. 1998. "The Torment of Secrecy: Ethical and Epistemological Problems in the Study of Esoteric Traditions." *History of Religions* 37, no. 3: 209–48. https://doi.org/10.1086/463503.

———. 2000. "The Cult of Ecstasy: Tantrism, the New Age, and the Spiritual Logic of Late Capitalism." *History of Religions* 39, no. 3: 268–304.
———. 2003. *Tantra: Sex, Secrecy, Politics, and Power in the Study of Religion*. Oakland: University of California Press.
———. 2010. *The Power of Tantra: Religion, Sexuality, and the Politics of South Asian Studies*. New York: I.B. Tauris.
———. 2016. *Zorba the Buddha: Sex, Spirituality, and Capitalism in the Global Osho Movement*. Oakland: University of California Press.
Van der Veer, Peter. 2001. *Imperial Encounters: Religion and Modernity in India and Britain*. Princeton: Princeton University Press.
van Ede, Yolanda. 2009. "Sensuous Anthropology: Sense and Sensibility and the Rehabilitation of Skill." *Anthropological Notebooks* 15, no. 2: 61–75.
Wedemeyer, Christian K. 2013. *Making Sense of Tantric Buddhism: History, Semiology, and Transgression in the Indian Traditions*. New York: Columbia University Press.
White, David Gordon. 2000. "Introduction: Tantra in Practice: Mapping a Tradition." In *Tantra in Practice*, edited by David G. White, 3–38. Princeton: Princeton University Press.
———. 2003. *Kiss of the Yogini: "Tantric Sex" in its South Asian Contexts*. Chicago: University of Chicago Press.
———. 2009. *Sinister Yogis*. Chicago: University of Chicago Press.
Zvelebil, Kamil. 1991. *Tamil Traditions on Subrahmanya-Murugan*. Madras: Institute of Asian Studies.

Part I

On Materiality and Mediation: Lived Practices of Texts, Objects, and Media

1

An Ethnography of Tantra in the Western Himalayas

The Material Substance of Practical Rituals

William S. Sax

Indology, Anthropology, and Tantra

Most scholarly works on Tantra over the past century have focused on the texts known as *tantras*. These texts have been translated, analyzed, interpreted, and ordered so as to establish their provenance and genealogy, to distinguish between particular traditions or schools, and to characterize the development of Tantric (*tāntrik)* thought; or, they have been used as the basis for generalizations about Tantra as a particular kind of religious practice. But despite nearly a century of effort, text-focused scholarship has failed to produce a widely accepted definition of Tantra. On the contrary, definitions of Tantra vary dramatically, and over time they have shifted from negative to positive. When the late nineteenth-century Hindu reformer Dayananda Saraswati was given *tāntrik* texts by a local Brahman near Rishikesh, he noted in his diary: "No sooner had I opened them, that my eye fell upon such an amount of incredible obscenities, mistranslations, misinterpretations of text and absurdity, that I felt perfectly horrified" (1879–1880, 66, cited in Salmond 2006, 111). In his book on Hinduism published in

1894, the Oxford Indologist Monier-Williams rejected Tantra as backward and depraved, and in 1932 Benoytosh Bhattacharya opined that "Mahayana philosophy . . . led . . . to evil and culminated in Tantrism" (1964 [1932], 22). In the course of time, this thesis generated several related counter-theses. Sir John Woodroffe, a stalwart apologist for Tantra, defined it in 1914 as "the repository of a high philosophical doctrine, and of the means whereby its truth may through bodily psychic and spiritual development be realized" (Avalon 1978, 3). More recently, Teun Gourdriaan called Tantra "a systematic quest for salvation or for spiritual excellence by realizing and fostering the bipolar, bisexual divinity within one's own body" (Gourdriaan 1981, 1), and Herbert Guenther wrote that "Buddhist Tantrism aims at developing man's cognitive capacities so that he may be, here and now, and may enact the harmony of sensuousness and spirituality" (Guenther 1972, 2). Müller-Ortega asserts that the *jīvanmukta* searches "not just for freedom that releases a person from suffering and transmigration, but for a powerful, even magical perfection (siddhi) and autonomy (svātantrya)" (Müller-Ortega 1989, 50). Both David Gordon White and Müller-Ortega cite André Padoux, who in turn cites Madeleine Biardeau, for a definition that found favor among many academics in the last quarter of the twentieth century, perhaps because it captures a certain longing for a form of spirituality in which eroticism finds a place: Tantra is "an attempt to place *kāma,* desire, in every sense of the word, in the service of liberation . . . not to sacrifice this world for liberation's sake, but to reinstate it, in varying ways, within the perspective of salvation" (Padoux 1986, 273).

Perhaps we must, when all is said and done, agree with Padoux and admit that Tantra is "a hazy and ill-defined sort of notion; it can cover, in fact, so vast a field as to include almost all of Hinduism" (2002, 18–19). But perhaps not. The material I have collected over decades of research in the Western Himalaya supports yet another definition, one proposed by Narendranath Bhattacharyya, according to whom Tantra denotes

> a way of life that sought the significance of knowledge, not in the realization of an illusory absolute, but in the day-to-day activities of men, in the simple facts of life as agriculture, cattle-breeding, distillation, iron-smelting, etc., and in the experimental sciences like alchemy, medicine,

> embryology, physiology and so forth, with a deliberate theoretical orientation that the structures of the microcosm and the macrocosm are identical and that the key to the knowledge of nature is to be found in the body. (Bhattacharyya 1987, 1)

This characterization has not found much favor among Indologists, perhaps because it is more pragmatic than "spiritual." It is however confirmed by the rather surprising and (to the best of my knowledge) unprecedented definition of Tantra that was given to us by all the *tāntriks* in the Western Himalaya with whom we spoke—a definition with which this chapter concludes.

In order to obtain a clearer grasp of what Tantra is, we must focus more on its historical and ethnographic context than has normally been the case. With notable exceptions (in particular, Davidson 2002 and the seminal writings of Alexis Sanderson), scholarly works on Tantra pay scant attention to the social historical background of *tāntrik* texts, and even less to the question of what relation, if any, these written words may have had to actual practice. This is in part due to the notorious difficulty of establishing the provenance of ancient Indian texts. But although Indological research on *tāntrik* texts has made great strides in recent years, it is not and perhaps cannot be known with any certainty which (if any) practices were historically linked to particular texts. There is only a handful of ethnographic studies of what *tāntriks* actually do, as opposed to what they claim to do in their teachings and writings, but in my view, the meaning of a text is *only* to be found in its use. A published book, or a manuscript written on birchbark or palm leaf, has no meaning whatsoever until it is used by someone in some fashion. Such manuscripts are, of course, designed to be read, and the practice of reading is the primary way in which they become meaningful. But even reading has many variations: aloud or silently, in a known or an unknown language, as instructions to be followed for ritual or meditation or as illustrations of forbidden or censured practices. A book or manuscript may be displayed to gain authority, kept as an inherently powerful object of manifestation of divinity, burned or destroyed as an act of iconoclastic piety, and so forth. However, until the text is used in some way, it is nothing more than ink on paper, and it has no inherent meaning (cf. Sax 2005).[1] Research on Tantra has focused on texts and will most probably continue to do so:

Nevertheless, the inclusion of ethnographic descriptions (where this is possible) of precisely how such texts are used is a desideratum for further research in this area.[2] In our research project *Tantrik Text Practices*, Annette Hornbacher and I respond to this desideratum by comparing how the uses of *tāntrik* texts, and the practices associated with them, have changed (or not) over the centuries in Indonesia and India. We rely on Indological research, which has demonstrated "the deep and pervasive influence which *tāntrik* traditions . . . have had throughout Asia."[3] Philologists and historians have clearly shown that a number of texts widely regarded as "*tāntrik*" circulated for centuries in a large swathe of Asia that included these two regions, and this has inspired Hornbacher and I to search not only for texts or text fragments that may have common origins, but more importantly (given our ethnographic methodology) for related text practices. Utilizing the method of "text anthropology" developed by Hornbacher's SFB 933 research project on the materiality and use of Balinese *tutur* and script (Hornbacher 2016a, 2016b) and by Fox's (2018) research on the use of letters in Balinese ritual, we seek to enhance the classical historical-critical interpretation of texts with a self-consciously ethnographic approach based on the assumption that the significance of esoteric texts, scripts, and characters emerges from their actual use by living practitioners. Such an approach does not oppose historical-critical interpretation nor seek to replace it, but rather complements it by analyzing the different ways in which a complex text tradition is reinterpreted and changed in the course of its use by successive generations of practitioners. It allows us to look at the practical and ritual frameworks, not necessarily mentioned in the texts themselves, in which texts are used or performed (Cf. Hornbacher 2007), and it builds on the general ethnographic method of participant observation including forms of text embodiment such as meditation, ritual, and magic.

Tantra in the Western Himalayas

My part of our joint research focuses on Tantra in the Western Himalayas. In this region, as elsewhere in North India, the terms *tantra* and *tāntrik* almost never refer to the soteriological traditions that are the focus of so much Indological and Buddhological research, but rather to a set of practices one might call "black magic" or "sorcery":

love magic, rituals of possession by local gods and goddesses, and techniques to cause harm to others via supernatural means. According to a common stereotype, such practices are especially common in the Himalayas, so that the term *pahārī paṇḍit* (Himalayan Brahman priest) is virtually synonymous with *tāntrik*. And indeed, my forty years of research in the North Indian state of Uttarakhand have confirmed not only that such practices are rather common, but that they are directly related to classical *tāntrik* texts in several ways. First, there are remarkably detailed correspondences between the vernacular demonology of Uttarakhand (Sax 2009, 2010) and that of the ninth-century *Netratantra,* as commented on by Abhinavagupta's pupil Ksemaraja (White 2012). Sanderson (2004) cites the same source in connection with a *tāntrik* tradition associated with Jayavarman II, who allegedly resided in Java under Shailendra rule when he imported the cult of divine kingship into Cambodia and employed it to unify the Khmer Empire. A second factor directly linking contemporary Tantra in Uttarakhand to classical *tāntrik* texts is the salience of the cremation ground as the site of the all-important ritual of initiation, the location for various rituals of cursing and healing, a source of human bones for *tāntrik* rituals, and an inspiration for images invoked in mantras and forms of ritual music (Sax 2009). A third factor linking popular Tantra in Uttarakhand to classical texts is the prominence of the god Bhairav, the eponymous "God of Justice" in my 2009 monograph and one of the most important *tāntrik* deities in both North Indian Hindu and Tibetan Buddhist Tantra. A fourth characteristic shared by classical texts and the popular practices of Uttarakhand is the widespread existence of rituals involving possession by numerous local deities, something that is a "hallmark" of Śaiva Kaula Tantra (Sanderson 2009, 133 ff).[4]

In Garhwal, Tantra is focused on the ritual specialists known as "gurus" (*gurū*). The novice requires a guru (often his own father) to teach him the relevant mantras, songs, rituals, and other techniques. The process that can take years (although a good friend of mine, who was cajoled into becoming a *tāntrik* by his dying father, received a "crash course," with many beatings to aid his memory, over a period of months). Eventually there comes a day when the novice feels he is ready to perform the *smaśān kī pūjā*, the "ritual of the cremation ground." All the gurus I know claim to have done this by going to the cremation ground along with one or several helpers (who watched from a safe distance), stripping naked, and then summoning Masan, "king of the burning ground," in the middle of the night. Masan plays many tricks to frighten the aspirant: ghosts and wild animals appear, gale winds blow, there are noises, there is pleading from loved ones, but one must stay firmly seated inside the magic circle. Shortly before dawn, Masan appears with his two queens, who offer three bowls to the aspirant from which he must choose. One of the bowls contains boiled rice, which indicates success. Another contains water, which is neutral. The third bowl contains meat, and if the aspirant chooses it, he will die. When one of my closest colleagues, himself a guru, was attempting to persuade me to undergo this initiation, arguing that the novelty of a white American guru would guarantee a handsome income, I asked him, "But what if I choose the meat?" With a soft smile, he replied, "No one ever chooses the meat."

The word "guru" in this context does not mean "spiritual master" but rather "master of the spirits." The guru's main task is to summon local gods and demons on behalf of his client and, by means of praise, negotiation, bribery, and threats, to make them do his bidding. The most important deity is Bhairav, who has multiple local manifestations. Other important deities include Narsingh (Skt. Narasiṃha) and the spirits mentioned by Ksemaraja (e.g., *chal*—Pahari *chaḷ—chāyā, cidra, ḍākinī, śākinī, yoginī*). Often, these beings are pacified by inviting them to "possess" the client or a member of his family. Once they are "dancing" in someone's body, one can offer them gifts (bribes, actually) in return for leaving the client alone. If they are reluctant or unwilling to do so, the guru might shift registers and begin threatening them. I have, for example, heard a guru threatening a ghost (who was at that moment possessing the client's wife) that he would cover his bones with pig shit and bury them at a crossroads, where people will continually tread on them.

Whether playing a drum, chanting a mantra, exorcizing a ghost, or sacrificing an animal, the guru must always be calm and self-assured; what the Germans (using a French word) would call *souverän* (see figure 1.1). He may cause possession in others, but he himself is never possessed—this simple fact is fundamental for what it means to be a guru. The guru is a counterpoint to another prominent ritual specialist, the oracle (called *bākī*, "the one who speaks"; or *pūchwāṛī*, "the one who answers questions"), who diagnoses the client's problems while possessed by local gods and goddesses. The oracle is the patient of agentive local gods and goddesses, while the guru is a

Figure 1.1. The Guru-Musician Satyeshwar Himalaya playing the *huṛakī* drum and accompanied by Dinesh Mistari on the thālī. Chamoli District, Uttarakhand, 2010. *Source*: Photograph by the author.

paradigmatic agent whose patients are local deities and people; this distinction exemplifies much about power, relationality, life, and death in Tantra as practiced in the West Himalayas.

The most frequently performed healing ritual in Chamoli District is the *chaḷ kī pūjā*, or "worship of the *chaḷ*" (one of Ksemaraja's supernatural beings), that is usually performed for women during their first few years of marriage. Should an oracle inform a woman that she is afflicted by *chaḷ* from her natal village, she returns there to supplicate it and return it to the soil from which it sprang. The ritual has many variations, but it always involves transferring the *chaḷ* by means of mantras, offerings, and *jhār-phūk* ("sweeping" the body of the victim with feathers or plants while reciting mantras, a very widespread practice in northern South Asia) to a small doll made of barley flour. Later, the *chaḷ* is transferred once again, this time from the barley flour doll to a chicken or goat, which is sacrificed to the *chaḷ*, who in turn agrees to stop afflicting the victim. The client's "village brothers" (young men from her natal home) eat the sacrifice in a males-only feast and later defecate in local fields, thus returning the *chaḷ* to its place of origin.

Another common ritual is the *thān kī pūjā,* a ritual for establishing or renewing the shrine (*thān*) of a deity. These can be performed for many reasons: to give thanks, because the family is moving to a new house, or perhaps because the deity demands that a new shrine be built in return for its ceasing to afflict someone. The *thān* is constructed according to measurements based on the body of the patron. A complicated ritual follows involving mantras, a fire sacrifice, and many different kinds of offerings, the central purpose of which is to invite the deity to come and take up residence in the shrine. The ritual has a number of steps. First, negative energies are driven out and the area where the shrine is to be constructed is purified. After that, the guru leads the family in the *kas pūjā* proper, which resembles the fire sacrifice that is part of a conventional *saṁkalpa* ritual in this region. This is normally followed by the "dancing" of the *devtās*. "Dancing" is the term used for what one would call "possession" in English. The guru summons local gods by singing their songs, after which (if all goes well) they possess their human vehicles, or "beasts," and dance (see figure 1.2).

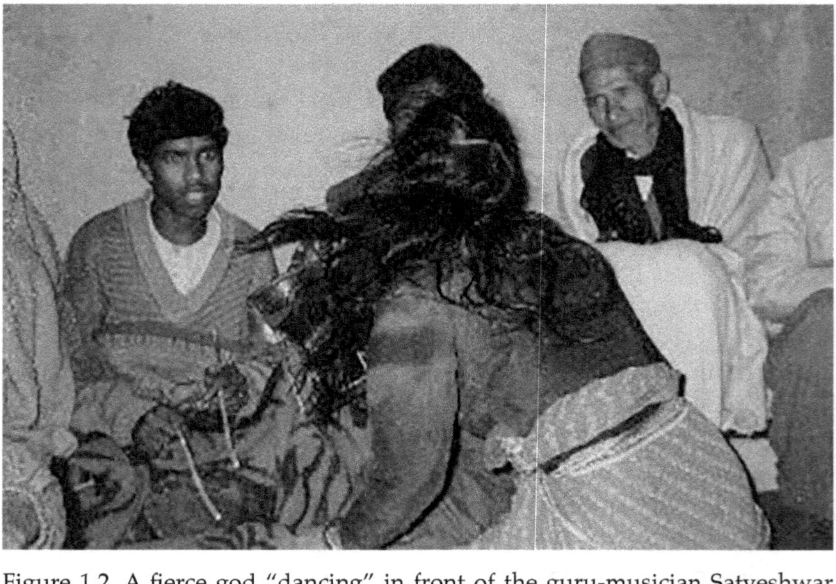

Figure 1.2. A fierce god "dancing" in front of the guru-musician Satyeshwar Himalaya. Chamoli District, Uttarakhand, 2002. *Source*: Photograph by the author.

This music and dancing can be very dramatic and exciting: More than any other factor, it is these sessions that draw crowds (not only for the *kas pūjā*, but for all such public rituals). Not only do the *devtās* dance, but they also speak, and people negotiate with them. The shrines of peaceful *devtās* are usually inside the house, while shrines of the more dangerous *devtās* are outdoors. The *thān kī pūjā* for the latter type of shrine culminates with the sacrifice of further animals, normally decapitating them and spraying the blood into a pit in front of the shrine, which is the dwelling place of the deity's fierce and violent followers. The *thān kī pūjā* thus constitutes the sacrificial pit as a place of concentrated violence. Goats, chickens, and sometimes sheep or even pigs are sacrificed and their blood poured into the pit. Fish, crabs, spiders, worms, and other creatures are also sacrificed, especially to the fierce, dangerous beings accompanying Bhairav. The idea is to attract these beings with blood, to localize them in the pit, and to bind them there with mantras so that their fierce and dangerous energy can later be used for the benefit of the client and his family. They can also be used for bloody revenge: people (especially women) who feel they have been the victim of injustice go there, remove the rock cover, and shed tears into the pit, calling upon the god to bring them justice and punish their oppressors.

At the beginning of my research, I doubted that local *tāntriks* really performed black magic to harm and even kill their clients' enemies. Such practices are so thoroughly condemned, and have such frightening karmic consequences, that I thought no one would really perform them. But I was wrong, as I discovered when I was invited to witness such a ritual (see Sax 2009, chapter 7). As I have noted elsewhere, *tāntriks* normally justify these "rituals of aggression" by claiming that they are, in fact, acts of defense. Such a redefinition of aggression as defense is typical of witches and sorcerers around the world; for example, those in rural France who were the subjects of Favret-Saada's brilliant ethnography *Deadly Words* (Favret-Saada 1980). When Hornbacher and I asked local *tāntriks* whether their activities were morally problematic or even sinful, they responded in different ways. Several said that in fact their work was justified because it removed the suffering of patients by curing their illnesses. When I asked one *tāntrik* if he would harm someone at the request of his client, he replied, "Yes. Shouldn't I save him if he asks me? And how can I save him if I can't save myself? If my magic doesn't work, then it may rebound on me. Therefore, I need to know how to protect myself." I asked him several times about the ethics of sorcery; for example, if he did not perhaps agree that it was wrong to harm someone in this way. But he answered only in terms of danger and (his own) survival. In elaborating on this point, he said such actions could indeed damage his karma, and that is why he needed to know how to defend himself—otherwise he might have problems or even die. He said that if he does immoral things ("bad work"), then the bad karma is shared with his client. But if he is powerful enough, then it won't harm him.

These are some of the principal ways in which the rituals performed by *tāntrik* gurus in the West Himalayas are linked to classical texts. More examples could be added. Another factor that links contemporary West Himalayan *tāntriks* to the earlier *tāntrik* tradition is the significance of the king. In his influential essays on the social history of Shaivism, Alexis Sanderson has clearly shown how the growth and increasing prestige of *mantramārga* Shaivism was partly a result of the close links to Hindu kings that it was able to forge in the early medieval period (2004; see also Sanderson 2009, 252), and the close relations of *tāntriks*, or *tāntrik*-like figures, to kings throughout South and Southeast Asia is well documented. Two West Himalayan Brahman *tāntriks* of the Uniyal caste were also keen to establish the importance of their ancestors' relation to local kings. One of them told us:

> According to the older people, we were the royal priests of the goddess Rajarajeshwari. The king's elder daughter died: She was eaten by a demon (*daint*). A ghost (*pretātmā*). Kali of the cremation ground. The demon took one victim every day. But after she was eaten, the daughter herself became a ghost and said to the king, "Find someone among your subjects who can subdue this demon!" So, the king sent a message to my ancestor, who had *tāntrik* knowledge (*vidyā*). The message said, "Come to the capital right away, otherwise I might have you hanged. Stop this demon, and I will recognize your *tāntrik vidyā* as true (*saccī*).
>
> And so, my ancestor went with his fourteen-year-old son, and reached the court on the very day that the king was due to sacrifice his second daughter to the demon. He

> told the king that if the demon came, he would offer his own son instead of the king's daughter. Then the goddess Rajarajeshwari possessed someone and said, "This is a good *tāntrik*; he won't allow the demon to take anyone. He will stop him." After that there were no more human sacrifices, Rajarejeshvari was established, and the eightfold animal sacrifice (*aṣṭhabali*) was also established.

Another Uniyal Brahman *tāntrik* told us a different story, which also linked his *tāntrik* ancestors to the king.

> The king invited a number of Brahmins for his fire sacrifice, including my ancestor. At that time the Uniyals were not very knowledgeable about Vedic worship, but still he took part, and performed the puja in his own way. Our local deity (*kṣetrapāl*) is Bhairav, who was born from Shiva. We had his *siddha mantras*. Anyway, this was during the time of Kirti Shah (late 19th c.) My ancestor, the Uniyal pandit, complained to the king, saying that the other Brahmins were insulting him, calling him a "*tantra-mantra*" priest who did not understand Vedic ritual. So, the king challenged him to show his power. He called upon Bhairav, and threw a loincloth (*varaṇī*) that the king had given him into the fire. The king felt insulted, and got angry: "Why did you do that?"
>
> The Uniyial asked the king to give him some time to show his power. The king agreed, and the Uniyal meditated on Bhairav and prayed to Rajarajeshwari, who appeared in the form of a girl. She asked what he wished, and he said, "You give the king whatever he wants." The king asked her to restore the loincloth, and she did. The king was amazed, and said, "How did you do that? What is this miracle?" My ancestor told him that it was due to the power of his *mantra* and the blessings of Rajarajeshvari. And so, the king told the other Brahmans that he didn't accept them but rather my ancestor. They replied that his knowledge was of a lower kind, but the king wanted to acquire the knowledge of the Uniyal. He thought that in this way he could extend his power without having to bother with an army, soldiers, and so forth. But the Uniyal refused to share

> his books and his knowledge. He said, "This has been given to us. Why should we give it to you?"
>
> Then the king got angry. He said, "With your knowledge I could run the kingdom by myself. I wouldn't need soldiers, an army, and all that." But when the Uniyal refused to share his books or teach him, the king became angry. He said that if the Uniyal would not share his literature, he would destroy it all! He sent his soldiers to find such books and burn them, so the pandits hid their manuscripts. Some hid them in water, others in the ground. Only those which had been kept in dry places survived, and they are the ones we use to worship Bhairav.

That is one version of a story one frequently hears in the region, according to which a medieval king of Garhwal, worried about the growth of rival centers of power, ordered all the *tāntrik* manuscripts in his kingdom to be destroyed. But fortunately, not all were destroyed, and all the *tāntriks* with whom we spoke had their own, handwritten manuscripts (see figure 1.3).

Such stories are partly corroborated by our colleague, Professor Dinesh Saklani, who remembers that his great-uncle used to regale him and the other village children with stories of how, in his function as police inspector for a minor local landlord, he would periodically

Figure 1.3. A typical *tāntrik* manuscript from the Western Himalaya. District Chamoli, Uttarakhand, 2020. *Source*: Photograph by the author.

destroy the books and smash the equipment of local *tāntriks*. He even showed village children the special metal-tipped boots that he used to smash the *tāntriks'* devices, and the military greatcoat that he wore when he was on such search-and-destroy missions. Saklani says that according to his great uncle, such assignments were received after the landlord's investigators had concluded that some *tāntrik* was causing discord and factionalism amongst the villagers.

Sāñcā Vidyā

In over ten years of regular fieldwork on Tantra in Garhwal, I met many practitioners, documented numerous rituals, and photographed and transcribed several manuscripts, most of which consisted of mantras addressed to the main gods of the *tāntrik* pantheon: Narsingh, Bhairav, and the *chaḷ, cidra, chāyā,* and other beings mentioned by Ksemaraja in his *Nīlatantra*. But while some of these traditions involved elaborate oral narratives and mantras, none of them included anything that might be described as a sophisticated textual tradition. The most suitable candidate for this is *sāñcā vidyā* ("the knowledge of numbers"), an esoteric tradition found on the border of Uttarakhand and the neighboring Indian Himalayan state of Himachal Pradesh. The tradition is esoteric, not only because the texts with which it is associated are handwritten in "secret" scripts that cannot be read by those unfamiliar with them, but also because in order to practice it, one requires initiation from a guru (often one's father). *Sāñcā vidyā* is regarded by local people as *tāntrik* because it is associated with human and animal sacrifice, with oracular and divinatory techniques, with rituals involving possession, and because of the centrality of mantra and yantra within it.

The tradition is found in an area broadly comprising the parts of Uttarakhand known as "Rawain" and "Jaunsar-Bawar," along with parts of Shimla and Sirmaur districts in neighboring Himachal Pradesh. This region is culturally distinctive, and in precolonial times it consisted of several tiny kingdoms ruled by gods from their temples (see Sax 1998, 1999, 2000, 2003, 2006, 2023). Other unusual cultural features included the widespread practice of fraternal polyandry where brothers shared a single wife; and a highly developed system of pastoral feuding involving the taking of enemies' heads, which were offered to aniconic forms of the goddess at clan temples. Two categories of Kshatriyas are found there: the high-status Rawats or Khas Rajputs, and the pugnacious Khund of the lower, warrior caste, whose name is derived by folk etymology from *khūn* or blood; the Khund are those who are eager to shed the blood of their enemies. *Sāñcā vidyā* was employed by particular Brahmin lineages to serve the Rajputs, and the texts themselves were (and remain) a monopoly of the Brahmins. Manuscripts are written in secret scripts, which is another reason why some consider them to be *tāntrik*. One of the primary traditional tasks of these Brahmans was to determine the optimal times for attacking enemies, burning villages, and beheading opponents. There is some evidence that they also practiced human sacrifice.

Historically speaking, the heartland of *sāñcā vidyā*, in the area around the town of Shillai, was part of Sirmaur, which was one of the smallest "hill states" at the time of Indian independence but which had previously been one of the largest and most influential kingdoms during the tenth and eleventh centuries. According to legend, in the eleventh century a low-caste woman was deceived by the king of Sirmaur and died[5], but before her death she cursed him, that his lineage would come to an end. Local historians write that in 1095 he sent his two advisors Raigopal and Raimohan to the court of the king of Kashmir to ask him to send his son to rule Sirmaur. Instead, the king sent his pregnant second queen, Sumitra, back with them, and she reached Sirmaur in the company of the Brahman, Rai Bhat. According to the historian Raman, a second set of learned Brahmans from Kashmir had accompanied another Kashmiri princess to Rajasthan for her wedding, after which they traveled on to Sirmaur, and because they were regarded as particularly pure—ostensibly because of the pure food in Rajasthan—they were called "Pavuch" (Raman 2013, 2). They settled in Sirmaur with their books and manuscripts and *tāntrik* knowledge, where they remain today.

Of particular interest are the manuscripts at the center of the tradition (see figure 1.4), which are often beautifully produced with drawings of various animals, gods, plants, and so forth (see figure 1.5), sometimes using differently colored inks; large numbers of yantras (abstract "geometrical" diagrams used for divination, magic, and healing; see figure 1.6); and of course the "secret scripts" mentioned above (see figure 1.7). The manuscripts are regarded as inherently powerful objects. Some practitioners are reluctant to handle them or

Figure 1.4. Page from a *Sāñcā vidyā* manuscript. *Source*: Photograph by the author.

Figure 1.5. A "calculator" in the form of a cow, used in conjunction with the building of a house. *Source*: Photograph by the author.

to show them to inquisitive anthropologists, and I once saw a local Brahman fall into trance merely from touching one. Others say that they may only be unwrapped after one has sacrificed a goat.

The core of *sāñcā vidyā* consists of its numerous methods for astro-numerological prognostication. In fact, the whole system has

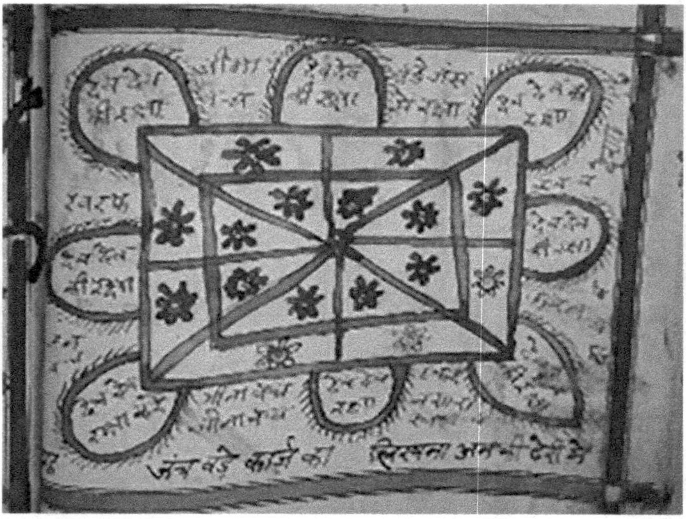

Figure 1.6. A *yantra* for generating wealth. Dehra Dun, Uttarakhand, 2019. *Source*: Photograph by the author.

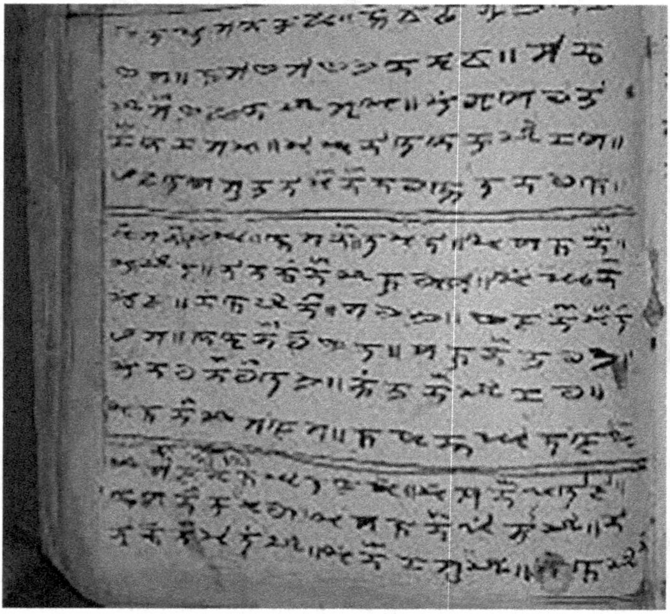

Figure 1.7. An example of one of the four "secret scripts" of Sāñcā Vidyā. Dehra Dun, Uttarakhand, 2019. *Source*: Photograph by the author.

primarily to do with finding the most auspicious times (and avoiding the least auspicious ones) for a variety of activities. A client visits the *sāñcā* Pandit with a question ("When should I break ground to build my house? or celebrate my son's wedding? or begin a long journey? or plant a particular crop?") or a difficulty (e.g., recurring health problems, affliction by ghosts or demons, strife within the extended family, financial problems), and the Pandit uses a variety of techniques to calculate the answer. I use the word "calculate" advisedly, since the multiple techniques generate numerical equivalents of astrological forces (stellar asterisms, lunar phases, planetary influences, etc.), which in turn become elements in complex mathematical formulae that point toward an answer to the client's question, or a solution to his problem. Other techniques involve auguries associated with the client (i.e., the time and direction of his arrival, the clothes he is wearing, the first words he says), casting a four-sided die called the "Mother of Wisdom" (*vidyāmātā*) fashioned from the bones of a vulture or a hyena, the sprinkling of rice grains over a special yantra made by the *sāñcā* priest from soil brought by the client from his home, astro-numerological calculations made directly on the basis of name of the client or his family member(s) or his village, and many other techniques as well. In effect, these techniques replace the oracular possession so characteristic of Tantra in Garhwal; in other words, books replace *bākīs*. The system is exceedingly complex, and in my experience the only specialists who retain some mastery over it are the Brahmans of Kharkaham Village near Shillai in Himachal Pradesh, especially our colleague, the renowned scholar Pandit Deviram Paboch.

As a complex system of astro-numerology, *sāñcā vidyā* with its diagnostic techniques is unique, but not particularly *tāntrik*. However, the rituals performed by the *sāñcā* Pandits are of a piece with those performed by the "gurus" of Garhwal—namely, controlling and pacifying local spirits by means of flattery, gifts, bribes, and threats; capturing ghosts and demons and taking them to holy places where they may be "liberated"; fashioning and "establishing" powerful yantras to strengthen and protect clients and their families; sending black magic back to the enemy who loosed it upon the client; "purifying" clients from supernatural pollution and thus healing them of their diseases and infertility; and several other techniques and procedures. Many of these involve the construction of magical yantras that are "empowered" by the force of mantra. Performing such rituals and making such yantras is, in Garhwal, not limited to Brahmans. Men from other castes can and do such things as well. However, I do not know if these rituals can also be performed by men from lower castes in Himachal Pradesh.

Tantra, Yantra, Mantra

All the experts we spoke with said that Tantra, yantra, and mantra are three aspects of a unified ritual practice in which all are essential, and none can be left out. What is rather surprising in this regard is that the term *tantra* is not used to indicate any particular "system" per se. It seems that only modern scholars use the term in this way. The experts with whom we spoke used the word *tāntrik* as a noun to indicate themselves as practitioners, and as an adjective to distinguish their rituals from *vaidik* rituals, performed as prescribed in the Vedic manner; but the word *tantra* was never used as a substantive to indicate a particular system as such. Rather, the word *tantra* simply means "material"; that is, the physical materials—plants, soil, water, stones, paper, colored powders, and so forth—that are used to construct a yantra. The yantra is normally a two-dimensional diagram or cakra, but it can also be a puppet or some other ritual device, which is subsequently empowered or enlivened by means of mantra, which is the proximate source of energy for the ritual. In certain parts of District Rudraprayag in Uttarakhand, for example, rival *tāntriks* are said to weave "rams" out of the branches of a particular tree and cause them to fight with each other so as to establish who is most powerful. One *tāntrik* showed us a kind of sieve with dozens of holes in it, which he called the *sahasradhārā* or "thousand streams," which was used to bathe patients with purifying water before performing certain rituals (see figure 1.8).

Both of these constructions might well be regarded as "yantras," in addition to the more familiar two-dimensional drawings. As Pandit Paboch, the very learned exponent of *sāñcā vidyā*, put it, "First you have to do the *tantra* and then, on the basis of your practical knowledge, the *yantra*, and then the *mantra*. . . . *Tantra* is all the material you bring; rice, flour, etc.—with which you make the *yantra*. The *yantra* is made from the *tantra*." During this interview, I explained to him that according to many researchers, Tantra means "becoming one with the

Figure 1.8. A Himalayan Tantric exhibiting the *sahasradhārā yantra*, along with a bird's claw. District Rudraprayag, Uttarakhand, February 2020. *Source*: Photograph by the author.

deity," and I asked what he thought of that, but he didn't respond to my question. Instead, he continued in the same vein: using English terms (underlined), he said,

> First and foremost, *tantra* is the matter. It's the material. Whatever material you use to cure the patient, that is *tantra*. And the yantra is what you make from this material: it could be a lamp or a *piṇḍ* [a ball made of dough] or an image of some kind. And it is on the basis of the mantra of this yantra that everything becomes effective: When this combination is there, it's set. . . . If someone is struck by a *bāṇ* (supernatural arrow), then you first have to "do *tantra*" by collecting milk, cow's urine, etc.

Professor Saklani described the *pañcamakāra* ritual to Pandit-ji, who was horrified and could only mutter, "That's nothing for me." Later, while speaking about a different ritual, he said, "First you have to buy the *tantra*, and then use it to make the *yantra*." He spoke of gathering the *tantra* for the ritual: water from the left and right banks of a river, the roots from twenty trees, and so forth: "You make a *yantra* with this, and then you have to order more *tantra*: flour, a chili, etc."

Radhakrishna Uniyal, another learned Brahman whom we interviewed in a region quite far from Pandit Paboch's home, said something very similar:

> There is Tantra and there is mantra. Tantra is that thing which I prepare with my own hand. Tantra is the thing that we make.
>
> Saklani: What about the yantra?
>
> RU: Yes there is a yantra, but first comes the Tantra. For example, I make something for someone to wear [an amulet]. And it will keep the ghosts away. [He indicates a six-pointed yantra:] Like this one: it's a Bhagavati yantra, a Durga yantra. I can use it for many purposes, for mental problems or if someone's stars are bad or if medicine is not working, etc. But it will only work when I empower it with a mantra.
>
> WS: What is *tantra*?
>
> RU: The *tantra* is prepared by making it. It is prepared in a certain form/design/shape. First comes the *tantra*, which I enliven with my mantra. Only then is it a yantra, which is efficacious.

For these West Himalayan practitioners, the distinction between Tantra and Veda is crucial. These days, learned *tāntriks* like Uniyal and Paboch are proficient in Vedic as well as *tāntrik* worship, but perhaps this was not always the case. Recall Radhakrishna Uniyal's story, reproduced above, of the learned Vedic priests who criticized his ancestor for being an ignorant "*tantra-mantra* priest." And indeed, prominent scholars have argued that Tantra should be understood as a kind of anti-Veda (Sanderson 2004; Gokhale n.d.). This is confirmed by the fact that the *tāntrik* guru's work (making and empowering yantras, dealing with ghosts and demons, etc.) can be done just as well by low-caste gurus as by high-caste ones: in nearly twenty years of research on the topic, I have never once heard anyone say that a low-caste man would be disqualified from such work.[6] By the same token, however, it is quite unthinkable that anyone other than a Brahman male priest could perform *vaidik* puja. For the *tāntriks* we interviewed, the distinction between *tāntrik* and *vaidik* puja has not only to do with caste qualifications, but also with the materials that are used. The *tantra*—that is, the material that is used to make the *yantra*—has one very important overarching characteristic: it is taken from the immediate environment of the patient. It is soil from *his* (or her or their) land, wood from *his* house, hair from *his* body, milk from *his* cow, and so on that are used for the ritual. This reminds us of the *tāntrik* rituals of Garhwal discussed earlier, where the *chaḷ* demon is returned to the soil from which it sprang. It also reminds us that when a *thān* (shrine) is built, its dimensions are based on the body measurements of the patron. Practitioners say it is precisely the fact that this *tantra* or material is personalized and "tailor-made" that makes it much more powerful and effective than *vaidik* puja, and they distinguish such materials from those used in mainstream Vedic worship, which are identical for every client. Pandit Paboch insisted over and over that *tantra* is more *saṭhīk* (precise), but it also takes less time, and therefore his fees are less than those for more prestigious *vaidik* rituals. Vedic ritual, he said, is "like a showroom" where one purchases a car resembling the display models one sees, whereas *tantra* is like a shop where you buy the car and drive it off.

Such notions are remarkably consistent with the widespread South Asian idea, discussed in a number of ethnographies (e.g., Daniel 1984; Mines 2005; Moore 1985; Sax 1991), that people and the places they live are mutually determining. The air one breathes, the water one drinks, the soil in which one grows one's food—all of these affect one's body and mind, and the village environment is in turn affected by the people who work its soil, care for it, perform rituals on it, and return their waste products to it. This is not an abstract or sentimental connection, but rather a matter of shared mutual substance. You are not only "what you eat" but also "where you live," so that in a very real sense the substantial and moral natures of West Himalayan villagers are partly determined by their constant transactions with the houses, villages, fields, and forests that make up their environment.

Tantra in the Western Himalayas thus resembles Narendranath Bhattacharyya's characterization more than the characterizations of other scholars mentioned in the first paragraphs of this chapter. In other words, it looks more like a system of practical rituals for dealing with life's problems than a system for spiritual advancement. The human being is seen as being intimately and substantially related to their environment: soil, water, air, family members, domestic animals, and astrological conditions. The rituals labeled "*tāntrik*" make use of these mundane physical and temporal elements to solve people's problems with respect to love, enmity, health, success, and other fundamental aspects of life. Unlike *vaidik* rituals, such *tāntrik* rituals may be performed by men of any caste. But the *tantra* itself—by which local practitioners mean the physical elements employed in the ritual—is not effective without being assembled into a yantra and empowered by mantra. Such a view shares certain elements with classical Indological and Buddhological descriptions, but at the same time it differs profoundly from them and could only be discovered by conducting ethnographic research.

Notes

1. I have been particularly inspired in this regard by Connerton's brilliant book *How Societies Remember* (1989), which advocates a "hermeneutics of the body" in addition to the well-known "hermeneutics of the text."

2. Introducing her research project *Sacred and Holy Scripture. On the Materiality and Function of Competing Systems of Writing during the Formation of the Religious Field in Bali, which is part of the Collaborative Research Centre 933 Material Text Cultures: Materiality and Presence of Writing in Non-Typographic Societies,* funded by the German Research Foundation, Hornbacher usefully distinguishes between the linguistic meaning of a text, which she regards as the proper object of hermeneutics, and the various uses (and corresponding meanings) of texts regarded as material objects. https://en.mtk-online.urz.uni-heidelberg.de/subproject.php?tp=C07&up=, accessed July 26, 2020.

3. Internet introduction to the University of Hamburg's "Tantrik Studies Volume," No. 2: https://www.tantrik-studies.uni-hamburg.de/en/series/tantrik-studies-2.html, accessed August 31, 2017. Cf. Goodall 2015. Acri 2016.

4. Cf. Smith (2006, 368) where he claims that "along with the Vedas and the two Sanskrit epics, the Tantras provide the richest sources for the phenomenology of religious possession in premodern India."

5. According to Pandit Deviram Paboch, her death was connected with the infamous *bheḍā jāt*, the Himalayan "rope-sliding ritual" banned by the British, which was a kind of human sacrifice. See Alter (2009), Berreman (1961), and Fiol (2010).

6. Low-caste gurus are in fact the focus of my 2009 monograph *God of Justice.*

Bibliography

Alter, Andrew. 2009. "The Significance of Tantric Sects for Drum Practice in the Central Himalayas." *Yearbook for Traditional Music* 41: 187–98. https://doi.org/10.1017/S0740155800004197.

Avalon, Arthur. 1978 [1960]. *Principles of Tantra: The Tantrasattva of Sriyukta Siva Candra Vidyarnava Bhattacarya Mahodaya.* Part 1. Madras: Ganesh & Company.

Berreman, Gerald D. 1961. "Himalayan Rope Sliding and Village Hinduism: An Analysis." *Southwestern Journal of Anthropology* 17, no. 4: 326–42.

Bhattacharya, Benoytosh. 1964 [1932]. *An Introduction to Buddhist Esoterism.* Varanasi: Vidya Vilas Press.

Bhattacharyya, Narendranath. 1987 [1982]. *History of the Tantrik Religion: A Historical, Ritualistic, and Philosophical Study.* New Delhi: Manohar.

Connerton, Paul. 1989. *How Societies Remember.* Cambridge: Cambridge University Press.

Daniel, E. Valentine. 1984. *Fluid Signs: Being a Person the Tamil Way.* Berkeley: University of California Press.

Davidson, Ronald M. 2002. *Indian Esoteric Buddhism: A Social History of the Tantric Movement.* New York: Columbia University Press.

Favret-Saada, Jeanne. 1980. *Deadly Words: Witchcraft in the Bocage.* New York: Cambridge University Press.

Fiol, Stefan. 2010. "Sacred, Polluted and Anachronous: Deconstructing Liminality among the Baddī of the Central Himalayas." *Ethnomusicology Forum* 19, no. 2: 137–63.

Gokhale, Pradeep P. n.d. "The Philosophical Geography of Kashmir Śaivism." *Asiatic Society Journal,* Mumbai, Volume 88. Accessed January 4, 2023. https://www.academia.edu/42736954/The_Philosophical_Geography_of_Kashmir_%C5%9Aaivism.

Gourdriaan, Teun, and Sanjukta Gupta. 1981. *Hindu Tantrik and Śākta Literature.* Wiesbaden: Otto Harrassowitz.

Guenther, Herbert. 1972. *The Tantrik View of Life.* Berkeley: Shambala.

Hornbacher, Annette. 2007. "Sounding the Word: Prosody and Poetics in Wayang Kulit Reflected by Western and Balinese Concepts of Language." In *The Power of Discourse in Ritual Performance*, edited by Ulrich Demmer and Martin Gaenszle, 121–47. Bielefeld: Lit Verlag.

———. 2014. "Machtvolle Zeichen: Schrift als Medium esoterischer Spekulation, ritueller Wirkung und religiöser Kanonisierung in Bali." In *Erscheinungsformen und Handhabungen Heiliger Schriften*, edited by Joachim F. Quack and Daniela Luft, 311–36. De Gruyter.

———. 2016a. "Introduction—Balinese Practices of Script and Western Paradigms of Text: An Anthropological Approach to a Philological Topic." In *The Materiality and Efficacy of Script: Situating Scriptural Practices*, edited by Richard Fox and Annette Hornbacher, 1–22. Leiden: Brill.

———. 2016b. "The Body of Letters: Balinese Aksara as an Intersection Between Script, Power and Knowledge." In *Balinese Aksara: On Materiality and Efficacy of Script*, edited by Richard Fox and Hornbacher Annette, 70–99. Leiden: Brill.

Mines, Diane P. 2005. *Fierce Gods: Inequality, Ritual, and the Politics of Dignity in a South Indian Village*. Bloomington: Indiana University Press.

Moore, Melinda A. 1985. "A New Look at the Nayar Taravad." *Man* 2, no. 3: 523–41.

Müller-Ortega, Paul E. 1989. *The Triadic Heart of Siva: Kaula Tantricism of Abhinavagupta in the Non-dual Shaivism of Kashmir*. Albany: SUNY Press.

Padoux, André. 2002. "What Do We Mean by Tantrism?" In *The Roots of Tantra*, edited by K. A. Harper and R. L. Brown, 17–25. Albany: SUNY Press.

Raman, Tulasi. 2013. *Himachal Pradesh: Abhilekh aur Pandulipiyam (Shodhgranth)*. Shimla: Himachal Akademi.

Salmond, Noel. 2006. *Hindu Iconoclasts: Rammohun Roy, Dayananda Sarasvati, and Nineteenth-Century Polemics against Idolatry*. Vol. 28. Waterloo, Ontario: Wilfrid Laurier University Press, Canadian Corporation for Studies in Religion.

Sanderson, Alexis. 2004. "Religion and the State: Śaiva Officiants in the Territory of the King's Brahmanical Chaplain." *Indo-Iranian Journal* 47, nos. 3–4: 229–300.

———. 2009. "The Śaiva Age—The Rise and Dominance of Śaivism during the Early Medieval Period." In *Genesis and Development of Tantrism*, edited by Shingo Einoo, 41–350. Tokyo: Institute of Oriental Culture.

Sax, William S. 1991. *Mountain Goddess: Gender and Politics in a Himalayan Pilgrimage*. New York: Oxford University Press.

———. 1998. "The Hall of Mirrors: Orientalism, Anthropology, and the Other." *American Anthropologist* 100, no. 2: 22–31.

———. 1999. "Worshiping Epic Villains: A Kaurava Cult in the Central Himalayas." In *Epic Traditions in the Contemporary World: The Poetics of Community*, edited by Margaret Beissinger, Jane Tylus, and Susanne Wofford, 169–86. Berkeley: University of California Press.

———. 2000. "In Karna's Realm: An Ontology of Action." *Journal of Indian Philosophy* 28, no. 3: 295–324.

———. 2003. "Divine Kingdoms in the Central Himalayas." In *Sacred Landscapes of the Himalaya*, edited by Niels Gutschow et al. Vienna: Verlag der Österreichischan Akademie der Wissenschaften.

———. 2005. "Response to Reviews of 'Dancing the Self.'" *Journal of Ritual Studies* 19, no. 1: 141–45

———. 2006. "Divine Kingship in the Western Himalayas." *European Bulletin of Himalayan Research* 29–30: 7–13.

———. 2009. *God of Justice: Ritual Healing in the Central Himalaya*. New York: Oxford University Press.

———. 2023. *In the Valley of the Kauravas: Divine Kingship in the Western Himalaya*. London: OUP.

White, David Gordon, 2012. "Netra Tantra at the Crossroads of the Demonological Cosmopolis." *The Journal of Hindu Studies* 5, no. 2: 145–71.

2

Observing Participation, Transgressing Hermeneutics

Bali's Tantric Script Practices and the Limits of Participant Observation

Annette Hornbacher

Tantra between Philology and Anthropology

Tantra has fascinated Western scholars for over a century and for very different reasons. Early nineteenth-century protestant missionaries in India referred to Tantric practices and teachings as scandalous, transgressive, and obscene. Evidently, similar ideas were shared by many Indians of that time. Chakravarthi defended Tantra as a philosophical and ritual tradition of scholarly value, writing that "the very name of Tantra shocks our nerves" but adding that "two thirds of our religious rites are tantrik, and almost half of our medicine is tantrik" (Woodroffe 1991, 20).

The "we" here is obviously an Indian one, which means that by the end of the nineteenth century Tantra was commonly dismissed not only among Western protestants but also among modern Indians. They, too, associated Tantra with "shocking" practices like blood sacrifices, ritual sex, black magic, meditation on the cremation ground, and the consumption of impure substances, among which alcohol might have been the least problematic.

Nevertheless Chakravarthi (and for that matter Woodroffe, who quotes him) wished to advance a new paradigm for Tantra, insisting that such dubious practices were based on a misconception of Tantra, which should be understood as a *śāstrik* tradition related to metaphysical or religious teachings (the *āgamas* and the *tantras*) about soteriological issues.

This distinction between a popular view of Tantra as black magic and a deeper understanding of Tantra as revealed religious literature with soteriological goals marks the beginning of the scholarly—and until today almost exclusively philological and historical—research on Tantra, which is based on textual sources (Woodroffe 1991; Goudriaan and Gupta 1981; Müller-Ortega 1989; Sanderson 1988, 2009; Padoux 2002; Flood 2006; Hatley 2010; Bäumer 2011; Goodall 2015). But critical-historical interpretations of Tantric texts must involve knowledge of their social and cultural contexts, as Sanderson (2009) has brilliantly shown in his work on Tantra and early Shaivism. In the case of an esoteric textual tradition, such an interpretation must also include the private and secret practices that transform a human body into a divine one, which is a distinctive aspect of the realization of Tantric texts, as Flood (2006) and Padoux (2011) have suggested. In this chapter, I will show how such lived Tantric practices realize the meaning of texts.

In recent years, critical-historical research has provided important insights into the development of early Tantric texts and motifs and their distribution beyond the Indian subcontinent (Nihom 1994; Sanderson 2003; Sundberg 2004; Acri 2006, 2016b). But while this important corpus of work has focused on written sources of the past, I suggest a new, complementary, and strictly anthropological approach to Tantric text practices on the island of Bali, where I did most of my fieldwork over the last two decades. Rather than reconstructing the historical origins of Indic Tantras, I will examine the relation between esoteric texts, practices, and body techniques in which Tantric traditions persist in modern Bali.

This requires some clarification regarding the respective approaches to Tantra of anthropology and philology. Both disciplines interpret what people from different linguistic, cultural, or historical backgrounds think and reflect about individual texts or statements in relation to specific contexts. In other words, both disciplines share a hermeneutical approach. But while philology focuses primarily on written texts, anthropology observes contemporary lifeworlds consisting not only of language but also of embodied practices, techniques, technologies, and all the many ambiguities of social interaction. In other words, by means of fieldwork, anthropologists investigate not only the said but also the unsaid of social life, and this distinctive form of research is not only interpretive but also holistic and interactive.

Malinowski calls this specifically anthropological approach "participant observation" because it involves both participation *and* observation, and indeed embodiment *and* reflexivity. Ingold (2014) has more recently reemphasized the fundamental priority of the embodied—not just discursive or objectifying—form of participant learning of unfamiliar practices and perceptions of the world as opposed to a theoretical reconstruction of "cultures" that uses participant observation merely as a method for the generation of allegedly "objective" data. Both Ingold (2014) and Shah (2017) emphasize that participant observation is actually a genuinely human and open-ended engagement with a specific lifeworld, a process of "learning from the inside" that puts the ethnographer's own theoretical and ontological convictions at risk and thus has to be understood as a "potentially revolutionary praxis" (Shah 2017, 45) rather than merely an attempt to produce ethnographic texts about or representations of others (Ingold 2014).

In what follows, I try to do exactly this: to reflect on my attempt to find out what Tantra in Bali means from "the inside," based upon my participation in a secret and esoteric script tradition that cannot be studied from "the outside," according to Balinese practitioners. This raised a series of ethical, methodological, and epistemological questions: Who is allowed to participate? Where does participation begin and where does it end? And what is the role of observation and reflexive distancing when the very goal of the practice is self-transformation of the observing (or rather, self-observing) participant? Such questions became crucial for me when I started my fieldwork on *tutur*, a specifically Balinese genre of esoteric palm-leaf manuscripts that have been associated with early Tantric influences from India by philologists, although the term Tantra was not used in Bali until very recently (Goudriaan and Gupta 1981; Acri 2006).

Tutur are part of an elaborate palm-leaf literature consisting of hundreds of manuscripts (lontar) and different genres written in Old Javanese (Kawi) that appeared in Hindu-Javanese kingdoms around the eighth-century CE but came to be mainly associated with Bali from the fourteenth century. In this historical period, the Javanese courts were in decline due to the growing influence of Islam while the island of Bali maintained and developed the formerly shared Shaiva-Buddhist tradition. Philologists and historians regard *tutur* as the Balinese equivalent of and response to the South Asian *tantras* (Goudriaan 1981; Nihom 1987; Acri 2006, 2016a).

The Kawi literary heritage is thus preserved and developed to this day in Bali as a living (and therefore changing) tradition, and it is likely that most *tutur* were composed, copied, and compiled in Bali where they are kept and venerated in family shrines. Each of these manuscripts is regarded as a sacred and inherently powerful object able to influence its environment and those who engage with it, even if they do not study or open the text (Hornbacher 2014; Fox 2018). At the same time, *tutur* address a wide range of cosmological and soteriological topics, which are ultimately connected in a monistic cosmology where everything emerges from one absolute principle that appears under different Old Javanese or Sanskrit names in different Shaiva and Buddhist texts, such as Paramasiva, Sunyata or Sanghyang Nora (the Venerated Nothingness).

Some *tutur* deal with healing, death, and the art of dying, or the relation of life and death. Others focus on complex and sometimes obscure speculations about the relations among mind (*idep*), speech (*sabda*), and the letters (*aksara*) of the Balinese syllabary, or about esoteric pictorial arrangements of these letters (*aksara modré*) for magical purposes (Rubinstein 2000; Hunter 2007; Hornbacher 2016a). Finally, there are *tutur* dealing with esoteric or meditative body techniques and a specific form of yoga related to these teachings (Acri 2013).

Since *tutur* are secret texts, I was hoping to find a practitioner who could help me understand what this textual tradition means in contemporary Bali. But this was more difficult than I thought: On one hand, *tutur* are difficult to study, inherently dangerous, and associated with black magic. Most Balinese assured me that they had no intention whatsoever to expose themselves to such a risk and had little if any knowledge about this esoteric tradition. On the other hand, and for the same reasons, *tutur* and the practices associated with them are regarded as secret knowledge that should only be shared with initiated practitioners, which explains the almost complete lack of comprehensive research on this topic in the anthropology of Bali.[1]

Thus, I felt fortunate when I finally met a practitioner willing to share his knowledge under the condition that I was willing to undergo a ritual initiation in order to protect me. I did not realize though that the hermeneutical problems of "understanding the other" and his esoteric practices would not be solved by being initiated; on the contrary, they would only begin. In some respects, my initiation made it more difficult than I had expected to understand Tantric ideas and practices in Bali because it confronted me with an unresolvable hermeneutical dilemma. Although I thought at first that participant observation of the script practices would help me translate Tantric knowledge into my own terms, I came to realize that embodied participation required the transgression of these very terms, including my paradigms for reality and self. Indeed, it turned out to be a "revolutionary" practice regarding my epistemic as well as ontological assumptions.

To investigate Tantra in Bali implies a whole series of fundamental hermeneutical challenges, the first of which emerges from the anachronistic character of "Tantra" as an analytical modern term that is retrospectively applied to a range of different practices and texts that belong to different regions, historical periods, and societies. Although there is a corpus of texts called *tantras* written between the sixth and twelfth centuries, there is no consistent "tantrism" in the sense of an accepted, institutionalized, or singular system that includes all the texts, practices, and features, which are today subsumed under the term. "Tantra" can thus best be understood as a dynamic discourse that involves texts as well as practices and is often confusing because it refers not to one empirical object, but to very disparate and sometimes incommensurable texts and practices.[2] And if "Tantra" is difficult to determine in South Asia, it is even more problematic in Bali, where Western archaeologists and historians were quick to define Indo-Balinese mandala structures, sculptures, mantras, and esoteric texts as "Tantric" even though the term is absent from the old Javano-Balinese vocabulary and emerges only as a new label in contemporary discourse (Bosch 1947; Kempers 1991; Kandahjaya 2016).[3] For anthropologists, this raises the first fundamental hermeneutical problem: How can one investigate "Tantra" in Bali if the term does not even exist? This question is of crucial importance for an anthropological research ethos that tries to take other epistemic traditions and terms seriously rather than projecting the assumptions and categories of the researcher. A second and perhaps even more serious challenge emerges from a structural contradiction between, on one hand, an understanding of ethnography as a method for the description of other people's knowledge and, on the other hand, as embodied learning "from the inside." Ingold (2018) reminds us that participant observation is indeed more than an objectifying method for the representation of others. If it involves the embodied participation of the researcher, it is a form of transformative learning.

This is usually not a problem as long as anthropologists share the public practices of the people they study, such as farming, cooking, and conversing—even healing rituals, which are at the same time object of public reflection. But Tantric practices related to *tutur* are of a somewhat different status, as they do not constitute public social practice in Bali: they are secret practices reserved for trained specialists, involve initiation by a guru, and require an existential engagement because their aim is transformation of the consciousness and body of the initiate.

Tantra in Bali?

None of the Balinese *tutur* is a direct translation of an Indian Tantra; even so, they are the most promising starting point for an anthropological investigation of Tantra in Bali because they are historically associated with Buddhist and Shaiva Tantras from the Indian subcontinent, and they are crucial for contemporary esoteric practices that transform a human practitioner into a being imbued with divine power (*sakti*) by means of mantras, mystical letters, and specific yoga techniques.

As such, only a few scholars were concerned with *tutur* texts (e.g., Weck 1937; Hooykaas 1980; Rubinstein 2000; Acri 2016b). Stephen (2014), who conducted research on *tutur* and mystical drawings as an anthropologist, based her interpretation of Balinese Tantra on Indian texts or on interviews with Brahmin informants rather than on an engagement with Balinese script mystical practitioners. All these scholars provide helpful insights, but none of them engages with contemporary esoteric practices. One reason is probably the secrecy and ambiguity surrounding them. Even though hundreds of *tuturs* have been copied, collected, and even scanned since the first lontar archive was founded by the Dutch in 1928, most Balinese I met regarded *tutur* not just as books representing a doctrine but as inherently powerful and ambiguous objects, and they would not dream of reading them without proper initiation and the guidance of a guru. I was told many stories of spiritually unprepared disciples who suffered mental confusion, physical harm, and even early death (see Fox 2018). But the opposite is also true: experts famed as powerful balian (healer or sorcerer) told me proudly that they were fascinated with this kind of "science" (*ilmu*) and had engaged with *tutur* since their youth, one of them without a guru. Nevertheless, many *tutur* start with an apotropaic opening line (*ajawerea*) warning the student not to reveal this knowledge to the uninitiated, and this advice seems to be taken quite seriously. My interlocutors did not regard this as an unjustified restriction of individual freedom but rather as a form of protection on the part of those who had taken the risk of engaging with such knowledge, which may involve meditating all night long in highly inauspicious and spiritually dangerous places such as burial grounds so as to transform into the wrathful deity Bhairav (Lovric 1987, 127).

This restrictive access to *tutur* is associated with restricted knowledge about them. A priest from an old temple associated with Tantric traditions told me that hardly anyone dared to study these things anymore because they were too difficult and demanding, although they were crucial for the specifically Balinese "art of dying" that was mastered one or two generations ago by certain people; for example, his grandfather. Such masters were experts in a particular form of meditation or *yoga semedi*, had knowledge of mystical script practices, and were able not only to foresee the moment of their death, but also to perform it as a free act in the company of their family members rather than suffering it passively.

But because he had not studied this tradition, he could not tell me what those teachings were. Much later, when I found my guru in east Bali, he told me of a crucial practice in script mysticism associated with the union and separation, the mutual entering (*pasuk*) and exiting (*wetu*) of father and mother as described in the *tutur rwa bhineda tanpa sastra*.[4] Elsewhere, a temple priestess informed me that much of Bali's ritual aesthetics manifests this mystical union and separation of complementary macro- and microcosmic powers and agents associated with opposite pairs such as Siva and Sakti, *dewa* and *dewi*, father and mother, male and female, heaven and earth, water and fire, and so forth. This cosmological model also informs Balinese ideas about health, where it appears as the dynamic union of water and fire (Weck 1937, 51) in the living body, which is the microcosmic counterpart (*bhuwana alit*) to the macrocosmic order of the world (*bhuwana agung*). It represents the metaphysical model of Balinese speculation about a monist cosmogony that teaches the dynamic union and mutual transition of creation and dissolution, life and death. In Balinese philosophical terms it is called *rwa bhineda,* usually translated as the 'union of differences. In Balinese script mysticism, *rwa bhineda* is manifest in the mystical letters ***a*** and ***ang*** representing male and female, father and mother, *amerta* (the water of immortality) and the internal fire, all of which are ultimately one, just like the speculative *aksara* for *ang* that is drawn as a combination of the usual letter for the vowel ***a*** with the mystical diacritic *hulucandra,* a sign without independent phonetic value that causes the nasalization of vowels and is the upper part of the cosmic syllable Om (*ongkara*), which manifests Paramasiva as the absolute and primordial unity before creation. In Balinese script, the *hulucandra* consists of three elements: *ardhacandra* (half-moon), *windu* (dot), and *nada* (stroke) that are, according to some speculations, associated with the *trisakti,* the three creative powers of energy, voice, and mind (*bayu, sabda,* and *idep*; Weck 1937, 40). The Balinese *aksaras* ***a*** and ***ang*** are thus visually related to the *ongkara* and can be regarded as a speculative explication of what the primordial unity of Om implies: emanation and creation as well as the annihilation of distinctions (Hornbacher 2014, 2016a). The more I learned about *tutur* and script speculations, the more I realized that these philosophical teachings were not just theories about life and death but were also concerned with the dynamic transfiguration of a practitioner and ultimately with the creation of the world, as the *tutur mareka bhwuana* indicates when it describes cosmogony as a process of creative yoga on the part of Siva in his absolute existence, from which first the god of script Sanghyang Reka and subsequently the entire world with its gods, humans, and elements emerged.

Learning Balinese Tantra—Learning One's Self?

To learn more about this relation between script mysticism, cosmogony, magic, and esoteric body techniques, I decided to study with esoteric script practitioners. This proved to be difficult because these teachings are associated with black magic or witchcraft. Balinese friends told me to contact learned Brahmin priests (*pedanda*) who are regarded as script specialists, but soon I learned that these days few of them focus on esoteric teachings. Some told me they were not interested in literature but rather in rituals, and others showed me printed books about magical letters, which they could no longer understand.

Eventually I met a man in his seventies, Jero Gede[5] from a village in Karangasem, who had been recommended as an expert on esoteric script practices. Although he was a Sudra, or commoner, he had studied esoteric teachings since his youth together with several Brahmin gurus and is now a healer, diagnosing the hidden causes of his clients' afflictions and offering them ritual protection against black magic or attacks from spirits of the invisible dimension (*niskala*) of the material world (*sekala*). Jero told me that although he had never attended a formal school, he had studied Balinese script and Old Javanese because he was interested in the *tutur* literature, which he reads fluently. His family was poor, but his father had collected esoteric *tutur* dealing with soteriological and spiritual topics. He was also familiar with the *tutur rwa bhineda tanpa sastra,* which he associated with the highest form of knowledge: the knowledge of one's own death. Beyond that, he had copied some *tutur* related to healing from his Brahmin guru in the town of Sanur. Although Jero emphasized that knowing one's "self" and thus one's death was indeed the ultimate goal of esoteric learning, he admitted that he himself had not yet reached the ultimate state because he was still bound to his family and not ready to die. Moreover, his focus was more practical, especially in his youth. In those days he was "still ambitious" (*masih ambisi*), as he put it, by which he meant something like "eager to develop supernatural powers" (including black magic). He wanted to learn powerful techniques so as to influence the world. In fact, his desire to develop magical skills for transformation and change (*perubahan*) was the central topic of his spiritual path, and a recurring theme in his teaching, as he kept on reminding me: "There will be a change, certainly!"

To achieve this goal, he had studied his family's *tutur,* but he found them too theoretical. He said reading alone didn't change anything, and hence he began to search for specialists famous for their powerful knowledge. His first guru was the high priest of his village, who taught him how to install the ten magical syllables (*dasaksara*) in different parts of his body, which is a common script-mystical practice in many rituals (Rubinstein 2000; Stephen 2010) and a topic of many *tutur* (Acri 2016a). The *dasaksara* represent Siva's names and manifest his power as a mantra. They are installed in the body parts or organs of a practitioner in a way that can thus be regarded as a transformative divinization of the physical body. The imposition of mantras is a common Tantric technique in the Indian subcontinent, known as *nyāsa,* and is crucial for the transformation of the human body into a divine one (Padoux 2011; Flood 2006).

Similar ideas informed the Balinese practices that Jero had studied, and a variation is used on effigies in public cremation rituals (Stephen 2010; Hornbacher 2016b). Jero had learned this technique, but he dismissed it because it had no lasting effect and did not increase his power. Finally, his family collected all the money they could afford so that Jero could contact a new guru who had been recommended to him and who lived in Sanur, a famous center of black magic.

But at that point of his narrative, he became reluctant to talk about what he had learned from his guru unless I would undergo an initiation. He feared that contact with these teachings would harm me, especially since he had diagnosed that I was a target of black-magic attacks from someone in Germany. Before considering my initiation, however, he examined my motivation. Did I plan to harm others? Did I want to get rich by selling his powerful knowledge in Europe? Despite his own initial interest in black magic, he had radically changed his focus after studying with a Brahmin guru, who taught him that it was not only unnecessary but also potentially harmful for him to continue with black magic (*pengiwa*) and who persuaded him to ritually remove it from his body because otherwise he might have died at a young age, as had many other practitioners of black magic.

During our conversations I was wondering if his reluctance to reveal more of his knowledge was perhaps not only ethically motivated. He seemed also uncertain about me taking his knowledge seriously; he asked me repeatedly what a university professor from Germany could possibly learn from someone who had not even attended a school. I got the impression that his reluctance to teach me also reflected some of his own ambiguities about a knowledge tradition for which he and his family had invested so much money and time, and for which he was highly respected by his clients, but which seemed also to have lost much of its former prestige during the few decades of mass tourism business that began back in 1972 with the opening of an international airport. New economic options and pressures brought about by tourism combined with the modernization both of society and the education system had imposed an entirely different value system regarding the relation of knowledge and power, which was now defined by money and modern formal education rather than mystical transformation or supernatural achievements. Jero was obviously struggling with the incommensurability of this clash: he had expected that his older son would pursue the family tradition and was slightly disappointed to learn that he preferred to make money with a small business in the capital Denpasar. While he thought it would be good to protect at least parts of this specific Balinese knowledge tradition from being forgotten by sharing it with an anthropologist who appreciated it, I found it very difficult to explain that I was motivated by philosophical questions regarding life and death rather than by an interest in gaining supernatural powers. He, on his part, found my intellectual passion strange if not pointless, and he insisted time and again that his knowledge would allow me to heal—or to curse—people in Germany, and to make lots of money, implying that I should reward him accordingly.

Whatever his motives might have been, after examining my ethical stance with regard to harming, healing, and secrecy, he agreed to share his teachings gradually with me if I would promise not to reveal the secrets without his permission, nor perform black magic except in self-defense. The ultimate decision to initiate me was made after his personal Brahmin priest agreed that a person from Europe could also study the esoteric teachings. For his Buddhist *pedanda,* a European woman over fifty years of age was an ideal initiate since she would be able to grasp the esoteric truth related to script and *tutur,* which is, after all, about dying.

It was then I realized that Jero Gede's ideas about knowledge, and his role as a teacher, might differ significantly from mine. I hoped to receive detailed interpretations of and discursive comments on esoteric texts from a Balinese practitioner, but in his view I could only understand what I was able to realize in my own existence and body. Understanding was change. Of course, I had known that Tantra is never a matter of sheer intellectual curiosity but may involve forms of existential engagement, and that it requires surrender to a guru. But I had known this only theoretically.

I had to realize that my fieldwork could no longer be based on my own paradigms about knowledge, but rather on his, which implied that I could only begin to learn after a ritual purification of my whole body (*sarira*), understood by Jero to be my "self" (*sendiri*). The initiation culminated in the enthronement of Saraswati, the goddess of learning, who manifests in the letters (*aksara*) of the Balinese syllabary and who is particularly associated with both the esoteric script speculations of *tutur* and human reason and insight. She had to be literally written on my body, and particularly on my tongue. Jero arranged baskets full of complex and costly offerings by a specialist and performed an elaborate ritual that began with prayers in front of his meditation chamber and ended with me being showered with different sorts of holy water, including the sweet water of young coconuts, until I was dripping wet and sticky from head to toe. Only then was Saraswati enshrined in my body to ensure my ability to learn without being confused.[6] Sticky and with wet hair, I waited for Jero to reveal what he considered the most important piece of knowledge, but my expectations were disappointed: I assumed that after my initiation he would finally share his knowledge by explaining to me one of the *tutur* about which we had spoken. But even though Jero has a thorough understanding of some of the most mysterious *tutur*, as I discovered later, he dismissed altogether the idea of reading esoteric texts because in his opinion this was merely theory (*teori*) or empty (*suong*) knowledge as long as I had not yet realized the mystical and transformative power of mystical letters and mantras—the *sakti* that was the ultimate goal of his teaching—in my own life and body. What he envisaged was a much more existential form of learning for which I was not really prepared, and for which he accepted only one criterion: a radical change (*perubahan*) in my life, perceptions, and abilities, which was his precondition for further metaphysical readings, not vice versa. I was puzzled, but also curious to see where this experiment would lead us.

Without losing any time, Jero Gede began to explain what his guru had taught him in the 1960s and I now needed to learn: a particular form of yoga to awaken and to raise *kundalini* in my body, which he identified with *sakti*, a magical power associated with supernatural agency and skills. It was this technique, along with a mantra he received from his guru, that enabled his change or transformation, and which he has practiced to this day. He was about to pass it on to me with the understanding that I would never reveal it, nor the mystical script that was part of his form of yoga, to the noninitiated. Whatever I am going to describe in the following is thus an exoteric and general description of this transformative script-practice, the esoteric truth of which is derived from the specific pictographic form of the letters and the mantra involved.

It is worth noting that Jero used the terms *kundalini* and *yoga*, which are popular terms in the modern global imaginary but hardly common in Bali except for the emerging market of modern and Western yoga as found in tourism centers with which he was certainly not linked. In fact, he did not even know that yoga was an Indic technique involving bodily postures, nor did he think that *kundalini* could be imagined as a snake. His understanding was obviously based on a more abstract and perhaps older version of yoga as a form of meditation (*semedi*) and internal movement of specifically shaped *aksara* that he associated with *rwa bhineda*, the internal union of complementary agents and forces.[7] *Kundalini* to him was just the energy sitting in the belly of the practitioner that had to be raised up by means of a specific body technique he called *yoganidra*, the yoga of wakeful sleep, which he described as a state of trancelike consciousness resulting from a concentration on specific *aksara* that were drawn into the body. He associated this technique with several supernatural abilities I would develop if I were to practice daily: I would be able to hear the voice of God inside my head as if it was my own; to perceive the hidden causes or agents of misfortune and affliction; to see the future; to travel afar while lying on my bed; and, finally, to change my shape, becoming huge like a giant or threatening like a tiger, as he did several times according to clients who claimed they had witnessed it. In short, *yoganidra* would radically change my perceptions and bodily abilities. I would develop the supernatural skills and knowledge called *siddhis* in South Asian *tantras*. But such supernatural skills were only one indicator of a much deeper process. Jero consistently stressed that the ultimate goal of this learning and transformation was not power over others but "to know myself" (*tahu diri sendiri*), which he expressed in Indonesian with the abstract notion of "self" but in Balinese with the word for "body" (*sarira*).[8] This meant I would realize that my embodied self was the same as God, that his thoughts would be mine, and that mortality and immortality were one and the same. This, he said while apologizing to God (*tuhan*) for his boldness, was what he learned: "I am God." This was not arrogance, but rather the reason why he could help other people with his knowledge. At the same time, it was the final, esoteric truth of the *tutur*, the embodiment of mystical script. There was nothing more I could learn. Puzzled by this truly Delphic program of knowing myself, I asked him why he had studied not only the right-handed knowledge (*pengenang*) leading to the union with God but also black magic (*pengiwa*), which was, after all, the Balinese paradigm for destruction and evil. He smiled and answered calmly, "Because we have a right and a left hand, and we can only pray with both together."

Jero began to teach me his technique of *yoganidra*, a term already known in the Upanishads and the Mahabharata. Whereas current forms of *yoganidra* in India emphasize breath control, Jero highlighted the visualization and internalization of mystical-script pictograms, which seem absent from Indian versions. What is important for both, though, is the position of the body lying on the back with closed eyes on a bed "as if" sleeping but awake, as Jero said. Alternatively, he added, I could assume a lotus seat position and close my eyes or focus my gaze on the tip of my nose. In fact, he mostly sat in this position for his daily meditation.

In any case, what mattered was not the position of the body nor the control of breath, but rather the visualization and strictly controlled internal movement of mystical letters (*aksara*). *Nyasa*, the imposition of sacred letters or mantras in different parts of the human body or in organs, is a well-known Indic tradition that can be understood as a transformative union of the physical human body with deities manifesting their powers in the sonic form of mantras. This concept is related to the *matrikas*, the "mothers," but also the letters of the alphabet as the matrix of mantras (Törzsök 2009). A similar idea of letters as the creative matrix of gods and the entire world is present in the *tutur bhwana mareka*, where Siva manifests himself as the world via yoga as *aksara*. Jero's version of *yoganidra* represents the complementary process where a human practitioner transforms themself into God via *aksara* yoga. But unlike Indic traditions, Balinese *aksara* speculations do not focus on sound. The magical power of letters does not emerge from their sonic quality but rather from the speculative pictographic combination of a basically phonetic letter of the Balinese syllabary with diacritic signs that have no phonetic but rather cosmological significance (Hornbacher 2014; Hunter 2016). This fundamentally pictographic Balinese script mysticism has been described in previous works as a form of *nyasa* (Rubinstein 2000; Stephen 2014; Acri 2016a).

During my initiation, however, I learned that in Bali it is more than a static imposition of letters, because *aksara* are dynamic agents in the process of yogic meditation connecting macro- and microcosm, the human body with the cosmic environment. Jero revealed to me that I should not imagine or impose but rather inhale the mystical letters of *rwa bhineda*, ***a*** and ***ang***, from their cosmic places in the world. He called them mother earth (*ibu pertiwi*) and father ether (*bapak akasa*), and I had to bring them through breath from their cosmic locations in the world below and above me into my body so that they could interact.

He advised me to begin by inhaling mother earth out of the ground in the form of a secret mystical drawing for the syllable ***ang*** and install her temporarily in my lower belly. After that, I had to do the same with *bapak akasa* from above. But both *aksara* were not installed in different places of my body; instead, they constantly moved and finally united according to a prescribed choreography. After a complex circulation and union of both letters in my body, I was supposed to imaginatively write a secret mantra across my chest, starting from the heart and moving toward the right side. With the same *aksara* dramaturgy, I could visualize this energy into a glass of water to be used as a medicine.

Thus, the yogic process enacted the union of the macrocosmic spheres of ether and earth, father and mother visually as a dynamic interaction of secret *aksara* pictograms (*modré*), in the body and culminated, so to speak, in the birth of a mantra that was able to heal others (Hornbacher 2016b, 93). Jero warned me that this mantra and the *aksara* must never be spoken aloud, since pronouncing them would release their power, whereas they should instead transform my self. I should not even imagine the *aksara* as an internal sound but only and specifically as mystically written letters. The initiation was therefore only complete when he drew in my notebook what I had to remember visually and, in fact, what I had to visualize every day during *yoganidra*.

For Jero, it was solely this yogic script practice that contained the truth about *tutur* and brought the real transformation. But what did this mean to me? How would I know that the transformation he was talking about had taken place? I felt I needed more information, but Jero finished his teaching with an order that raised the more serious hermeneutical problem of fieldwork on esoteric and Tantric practices. He said, "From now on I will no longer tell you what this knowledge is all about: You will tell me! You are initiated and have to practice. If you are capable of realizing this knowledge it will have an impact on you that you can report. All the rest is just theory. And if there is no change, I cannot help you. It no longer depends on me."

With this, I reached the limit of "participant observation" as it has been traditionally understood since the times of Malinowski. Jero had brought me into an aporetic position: were I to follow his instructions, and "participatorily" observe what he said, then I could no longer observe "the other" but only myself. But this was clearly at odds with the most fundamental requirement of fieldwork that tries to overcome the conceptual limitations and subjective presumptions of the anthropologist in her relation with others. Although the autoethnographic method offers a solution by suggesting a retreat to subjective feelings or personal experiences, it was at odds with the basic principle of hermeneutics as a mode of translation and thus with my research goal, which was to understand Jero's radically different epistemic paradigm rather than talking about my personal experiences.[9] And yet, Jero Gede's epistemic regime required participant observation not of his actions, thoughts, or stories, but of myself. But upon what, exactly, should I focus? What should I observe while observing myself? In any case, his order was clear inasmuch as it required a radical willingness to expose myself to his regime of knowledge and to accept it as a possible way to truth, rather than insisting on my idea of understanding, observing, and participating.

I began my experiment by practicing *yoganidra* for thirty to forty minutes every evening. At first nothing much happened except for some thoughts, feelings, and personal memories, which I shared with Jero. But my "autoethnographic" reports about subjective experiences did not interest him at all. He interrupted me to ask if I had already "seen" or "heard" something, thus guiding my attention away from my inner psychological states. I began to focus on the *aksara* outside and inside of me, which indeed made a difference as I realized when I began to sense that someone was moving behind me, that the ground in front of me was opening when I inhaled *ibu pertiwi*, and that there was fire in an abyss in front of me. It started to become interesting for both of us because we agreed that these perceptions were an effect of his technique. He assured me that I was on the right path, and one day I would see in front of me what I now felt behind me. But I should not follow the fire into the abyss: I might not come back.

Clearly what was important for his technique were not changes in my subjective feelings or thoughts, but only what I could perceive in the world while practicing *yoganidra*. To him this was an external (though usually invisible) reality, not a psychological state, whereas my personal doubts, feelings, or beliefs were as unimportant as the fact that I was not Hindu and that I had to return to my academic routine in Germany after a month. Our respective religions were never a topic of our discussion, and he accepted my limiting circumstances just as I accepted his preconditions. Thus, for several years, until our cooperation was interrupted by the COVID-19 pandemic, I would meet him during the few months of my semester break, which were reserved for my research. And I would practice *yoganidra* only during this time and always alone to continue an experiment that we had started and are still developing together.

However, in the second year after my initiation, something happened that I had never expected, and about which I hesitate to write since it transgresses not only the limits of intercultural hermeneutics but also my paradigm of reality and thought. In other words: I have no satisfying scholarly explanation because explaining in the terms of modern epistemology would require me to deny its reality.

While practicing *yoganidra* under a banyan tree, without any particular expectation, I saw all of a sudden the terrifying goddess of the graveyard and witchcraft, Rangda, as clearly as the rest of the world sitting in front of me. She was meditating, mirroring my position, peaceful in spite of her frightening face with wild hair framing it, her bulging eyes staring at me, the fangs, and the long protruding tongue. I was shocked, not because I was afraid of the goddess of divine destruction and death, who is indeed feared as much as venerated in Bali, but rather because I had been sure that something like this could never happen to me. When I saw Rangda, it was equally clear to me: this was not just my subjective imagination, nor was it the result of Jero's suggestion. He had never remotely mentioned the possibility that Rangda or any other god could appear as a result of *yoganidra*. But indeed, she appeared to me as a reality of the world around me—a world to which Jero had drawn my attention with his *aksara*-yoga technique, nothing I or he would have fantasized about.

At the same time, I was absolutely aware of the fact that this could not have happened in my modern Western mode of perception, or, if so, then only as subjective hallucination. Modern Western ontology is based on the dichotomy of material reality versus subjective imagination, which leaves no place for the agency or intentionality of beings who manifest as visible realities only to disappear in the very moment when one begins to reflect upon their impossibility. My experiment had led me to the shocking awareness that it was possible to live an irreconcilable contradiction between two modes of being in and perceiving the world. My perception of the world had clearly changed due to my participation in Jero's technique, and yet there was no way to translate this properly into modern categories. My successful participant observation left me in a hermeneutical dilemma of intranslatability.

When I reported my encounter to Jero, he was delighted and not at all surprised. He told me that what I had encountered was the blissful presence of both the goddess Bhairavi and myself, or rather that the goddess was myself, recommending that I should absorb her into my body, whenever I met her again, and continue to practice yoga. In his opinion, I had reached the next level of transformative knowing of myself. Unfortunately, our cooperation has stopped since the beginning of the COVID-19 pandemic, but we both hope I can return.

Concluding Remarks

I have claimed that philological and historical research on Tantra as a textual tradition requires the complementary hermeneutical approach offered by anthropological fieldwork and participant observation, which engages not only with texts but also with their contexts, particularly with practices in which texts are embedded, and even with esoteric body techniques through which texts have to be "realized" according to the practitioners.

My ethnographic engagement revealed a new dimension of text practice: I found it most interesting to learn that Jero Gede regards *tutur* per se as "empty" and insists that the realization of this written knowledge requires a transformative yogic technique, rather than merely theoretical forms of reading and contemplation. Moreover, I learned that in his understanding, magic, cosmology, and soteriology, which seem to belong to entirely different strata of knowledge—at least from the perspective of *tāntrika*s in North India[10]—are mutually connected aspects or degrees of one and the same esoteric teachings. These interconnected dimensions can be regarded as moments of a dynamic biography of knowledge aiming at an ultimate self-realization via transfiguration. This explains why *tutur* address topics as different as magic and soteriology, and it resonates with what Goodall (2015) describes as a common feature of early Tantra in the Indian subcontinent with regard to the *Niśvāsatattvasaṃhitā*.

All of these findings are solely matters of situational exchange and oral advice between a guru and their disciple, but not topics discussed in *tutur*. This practical framework of learning is open to permanent innovation and reinterpretation, even if texts do not change. The cooperation with Jero paradigmatically shows how *tutur* are not representations of timeless, written doctrines but rather elements of individual engagement and situational interpretations, which are both secret and fluid because they are transformative, innovative, and, thus indeed as Jero warned me, not just *teori*.

But, by the same token, ethnographic participant observation and intercultural hermeneutics reach a limit in the case of esoteric knowledge practices that require bodily engagement, and transfiguration to the extent that it forces the observer to transcend her own interpretative framework and mode of perception. Because I followed Jero's invitation to participate and engaged in initiation rituals and yoga techniques, the consequences of this learning "from the inside" made a classical ethnography of Tantra—one that stuck to representations of others' ideas, practices, and experiences—impossible. Anthropology can be understood as an ongoing discussion about the question of how to engage with "the other" or how to combine "participation" and "observation" in adequate representations, especially when it comes to paranormal phenomena or witchcraft (Bowie 2019). The postmodern crisis of representation reminds us of the power-knowledge relation inherent in our ethnographies. In my case, however, the hermeneutical problem arises not from a colonizing representation of another knowledge tradition, but, on the contrary, from the crumbling of scholarly categories under the transformative impact of an embodied form of learning that was not only esoteric but also highly individual. My vision of Rangda/Bhairavi was not a foreseeable step in a standard learning program, but rather my way to realize through participant observation a body technique that changed my own perceptions but was not exactly what Jero himself had experienced.

What Jero Gede offered was something more radical than the embodied knowledge of another society. He insisted that in order to participate in his epistemic world, I had to put my own ideas about self, world, and knowledge at risk and see what happened. What is at stake in this unfinished process is not an alternative interpretation of an external or internal reality, but rather the question of what to do when participant observation opens another world by using the body as a means of revelation. Whatever I saw was neither suggested by Jero nor a projection of my expectations. It was an individual result of my learning to direct my attention differently, not quite, or not any more toward the "worldview," "ontology," or metaphysics of "the Balinese," but rather toward observing my own participation.

Notes

1. The only exception I am aware of is the PhD of Barbara Lovric (1987), who passed away before she was able to publish her extensive fieldwork on black magic, a fact that my Balinese interlocutors (and some colleagues) regard as clear evidence for the existential threat associated with this kind of research. This is different in the case of the emerging anthropology of Tantra in India, where Tantra is a well-established and self-defining set of practices including healing rituals and magical techniques that are public rather than esoteric and that can be studied ethnographically via participant observation and even without initiation (see William Sax, this volume; Bradbury 2020; Hyam, this volume).

2. See also David White (2000, 4–7) and Shaman Hatley (2020).

3. This situation is currently changing: To achieve political recognition as Hindus, Balinese were eager to claim that their religious rituals were a blend of local traditions and a Vedic world religion. Since the fall of the Suharto regime, and under the influence of academic training including global research on Tantra, young Balinese tend to reinterpret and qualify local ritual practices as "Tantric."

4. This esoteric doctrine was first mentioned by Weck (1937, 40). I refer to a translation of this manuscript provided by Dr. IBP Suamba, who translated around thirty-six *tutur* during his collaboration in the SFB 933 project.

5. The name Jero Gede is actually a combination of an honorific title, Jero—referring to "insider," which can be related to the inner circle of a high-caste person or, as Jero explained, to those who have gained deep insight about their self—and Gede, which means "big." He is usually addressed as Jero.

6. This is related to a Balinese story according to which humans were unable to understand Siva until he installed Saraswati via the *aksara* on their

tongues. From this perspective, knowing and insight are not natural abilities of the human mind, as in Western thought, but rather the result of the embodiment of a goddess in the shape of mystical letters (Rubinstein 2000; Hornbacher 2014).

7. With respect to *tutur*, Acri mentions an ancient form of Saiddhantika yoga without reference to bodily postures but associated with some mystical centers in the body. It would be interesting to know if this yoga is still practiced somewhere in Bali. However, it is not related to what I learned, except for the lack of postures (Acri 2006, 128).

8. Our conversations were basically in Bahasa Indonesia, but we discussed such key terms in the high-Balinese register of *tutur*, which in this case provides the Sanskrit word *sarira* for something that Jero would always refer to with the abstract term "self," or *sendiri* in Indonesian.

9. In his phenomenological research on Nepalese Shamans, Desjarlais (1992) describes with admirable honesty, how he—in his intimate engagement with shamans—suddenly fell in trance during a Shamanic session emphasizing that his experience and his performance differed from those of local shamans. What makes his account relevant is that it is presented as a personal side effect of his fieldwork, but not as its actual focus, which seemed to be Jero's suggestion.

10. See William Sax's chapter in this volume.

Bibliography

Acri, Andrea. 2006. "The Sanskrit-Old Javanese Tutur Literature from Bali: The Textual Basis of Śaivism in Ancient Indonesia." *Rivista di Studi Sudasiatici* 1, no. 1: 7–37.

———. 2008. "The Vaimala Sect of the Pāśupatas. New Data from Old Javanese Sources." *Tantric Studies* 1: 193–208.

———. 2011. "Glimpses of Early Shaiva Siddhanta. Echoes of Doctrines Ascribed to Brhaspati in the Sanskrit-Old Javanese Vrhaspatitattva." *Indo-Iranian Journal* 54: 209–29.

———, ed. 2016a. *Esoteric Buddhism in Medieval Maritime Asia: Networks of Masters, Texts, Icons*. Singapore: ISEAS Yusof Ishak Institute.

———. 2016b. "Imposition of the Syllabary (svaravyañjana-nyāsa) in the Old Javano-Balinese Tradition in the Light of South Asian Tantric Sources." In *The Materiality and Efficacy of Balinese Letters*, edited by Richard Fox and Annette Hornbacher. 123–65. Leiden: Brill.

Bäumer, Bettina. 2011. *Abhinavagupta's Hermeneutics of the Absolute Anuttaraprakriya*. New Delhi: D.K. Printworld.

Bowie, Fiona. 2019. "Negotiating Blurred Boundaries: Ethnographic and methodological considerations." In *The Insider/Outsider Debate: New Perspectives in the Study of Religion*, edited by George D. Chryssides and Stephen E. Gregg, 110–29. Bristol: Equinox Sheffield.

Bradbury, James S. 2020. "Where is the Tantric Mainstream? Discussions with a Bengali Brahmin Godmaker in Kolkata." *The Journal of Hindu Studies* 13, no. 2: 172–200.

Calo, Ambra. 2020. "Durgā Mahiṣāsuramardinī in Likely Tantric Buddhist Context from the Northern Indian Subcontinent to 11th-Century Bali." *Pratu: Journal of Buddhist and Hindu Art, Architecture and Archaeology of Ancient to Premodern Southeast Asia* 1, no. 3: 1–20.

De Castro, Eduardo Viveiros. 1998. "Cosmological Deixis and Amerindian Perspectivism." *Journal of the Royal Anthropological Institute* 4, no. 3: 469–88.

Decleer, Hubert. 2007. "Atiśa's Journey to Tibet." In *Religions of Tibet in Practice: Abridged Edition*, edited by Donald S. Lopez, 107–27. Princeton: Princeton University Press.

Descola, Philippe. 2013. *Beyond Nature and Culture*. Chicago: University of Chicago Press.

Desjarlais, Robert. 1992. *Emotion and Healing. The Aesthetics of Illness and Healing in the Nepal Himalayas*. Philadelphia: University of Pennsylvania Press.

Flood, Gavin. 2006. *The Tantric Body: The Secret Tradition of Hindu Religion*. London: Tauris.

Fox, Richard. 2018. *More than Words: Transforming Script, Agency, and Collective Life in Bali*. Ithaca: Cornell University Press.

Geertz, Clifford. 1973. "Thick Description: Toward an Interpretive Theory of Culture." In *Turning Points in Qualitative Research: Tying Knots in a Handkerchief*, edited by Yvonna S. Lincoln and Norman K. Denzin, 143–68. Walnut Creek, CA: AltaMira Press.

Gonda, Jan. 1975. *The Indian Religions in Pre-Islamic Indonesia and Their Survival in Bali*. Indonesia: Brill.

Goudriaan, Teun. 1981. "Two Stanzas of Balinese Sanskrit Located in an Indian Tantra." *Bijdragen tot de taal-, land- en volkenkunde / Journal of the Humanities and Social Sciences of Southeast Asia* 137, no. 4: 477–79.

Gourdriaan, Teun, and Sanjukta Gupta. 1981. *Hindu Tantrik and Śākta Literature*. Wiesbaden: Otto Harrassowitz.

Hatley, Shaman. 2010. "Tantric Śaivism in Early Medieval India: Recent Research and Future Directions." *Religion Compass* 4, no. 10: 615–28.

———. 2020. "Tantra (Overview)." In *Hinduism and Tribal Religions*, edited by Jeffery D. Long, Rita D. Sherma, Pankaj Jain, and Madhu Khanna, 1602–12. Dodrecht: Springer.

Hazra, Kanai Lal. 1983. *Buddhism in India as Described by the Chinese Pilgrims, AD 399—689*. New Delhi: Munshiram Manoharlal.

Hornbacher, Annette. 2005. *Zuschreibung und Befremden: Postmoderne Repräsentationskrise und verkörpertes Wissen im balinesischen Tanz*. Berlin: Reimer.

———. 2014. "Machtvolle Zeichen: Schrift als Medium esoterischer Spekulation, ritueller Wirkung und religiöser Kanonisierung in Bali." In *Erscheinungsformen und Handhabungen heiliger Schriften*, edited by Joachim Friedrich Quack und Daniela C. Luft. Berlin, 311–36. München: De Gruyter.

———. 2016a. "Introduction—Balinese Practices of Script and Western Paradigms of Text: An Anthropological Approach to a Philological Topic." In *The Materiality and Efficacy of Script: Situating Scriptural Practices*, edited by Richard Fox and Annette Hornbacher, 1–22. Leiden: Brill.

———. 2016b. "The Body of Letters: Balinese Aksara as an Intersection Between Script, Power and Knowledge." In *Balinese Aksara: On Materiality and Efficacy of Script*, edited by Richard Fox and Hornbacher Annette, 70–99. Leiden: Brill.

Hooykaas, Christiaan. 1962. "Saiva-Siddhanta in Java and Bali." *Bijdragen tot de taal-, land- en volkenkunde* 118, no. 3: 309–27.

———, ed. 1980. *Drawings of Balinese Sorcery*. Leiden: Brill.

Hunter, Thomas M. 2007. "The Poetics of Grammar in the Javano-Balinese Tradition." *The Poetics of Grammar and the Metaphysics of Sound and Sign*, edited by Sergio la Porta, 271–303. Leiden: Brill.

Ingold, Tim. 2014. "That's Enough about Ethnography." *HAU Journal of Ethnographic Theory* 4, no. 1: 383–95.

Bernet Kempers, August Johan. 2013. *Monumental Bali: Introduction to Balinese Archaeology & Guide to the Monuments*. Berkeley: Tuttle Publishing.

Lovric, Barbara Joyce A. 1987. *Rhetoric and Reality: The Hidden Nightmare: Myth and Magic as Representations and Reverberations of Morbid Realities*. PhD diss., The University of Sydney.

Muller-Ortega, Paul E. 1989. *The Triadic Heart of Śiva: Kaula Tantricism of Abhinavagupta in the Non-dual Shaivism of Kashmir*. Albany: SUNY Press.

Nihom, Max. 1994. *Studies in Indian and Indo-Indonesian Tantrism: The Kuñjarakarṇadharmakathana and the YogaTantra*. Vienna: Institute für Indologie der University Wien.

Nihom, Max. 1998. "The Mandala of Candi Gumpung (Sumatra) and the Indo-Tibetan VajrasekharaTantra." *Indo-Iranian Journal* 41, no. 3: 245–54.

O'Connor, Stanley J. 1985. "Metallurgy and Immortality at Caṇḍi Sukuh, Central Java." *Indonesia* 39: 52–70.

Padoux, André. 2002. "What Do We Mean by Tantrism?" In *The Roots of Tantra*, edited by Katherine Anne Harper and Robert L. Brown, 17–25. Albany: SUNY Press.

Padoux, André. 2011. *Tantric Mantras: Studies on Mantrasastra*. London: Routledge.

Rubinstein, Raechelle. 2000. *Beyond the Realm of the Senses: The Balinese Ritual of Kakawin Composition*. Leiden: KITLV Press.

Sanderson, Alexis. 1988. "Śaivism and the Tantric Traditions." In *The World's Religions,* edited by S. Sutherland et al., 660–704. London: Routledge and Kegan Paul.

———. 2003. "The Śaiva Religion among the Khmers Part I." *Bulletin De L'École Française D'Extrême-Orient* 90/91: 349–462.

———. 2009. "The Śaiva Age: The Rise and Dominance of Śaivism during the Early Medieval Period." In *Genesis and Development of Tantrism,* edited by Shingo Einoo, 41–350. Tokyo: University of Tokyo, Institute of Oriental Culture.

———. 2015. "How Public was Shaivism?" Keynote lecture presented at the Symposium for Tantric Communities in Context: Sacred Secrets and Public Rituals, Vienna.

Schoterman, Jan A., and Andrea Acri. 2016. "Traces of Indonesian Influences in Tibet." In *Esoteric Buddhism in Medieval Maritime Asia: Networks of Masters, Texts, Icons,* edited by Andrea Acri, 113–22. Singapore: ISEAS Publishing.

Shah, Alep. 2017. "Ethnography? Participant Observation, a Potentially Revolutionary Praxis." *HAU: Journal of Ethnographic Theory* 7, no. 1: 45–59. https://doi.org/10.14318/hau7.1.008.

Stephen, Michele. 2010. "The Yogic art of Dying, Kundalinī Yoga, and the Balinese Pitra Yadnya." *Bijdragen tot de taal-, land- en volkenkunde / Journal of the Humanities and Social Sciences of Southeast Asia* 166, no. 4: 426–74.

Stephen, Michele. 2014. "The Dasaksara and Yoga in Bali." *Journal of Hindu Studies* 7, no. 2: 179–216.

Sundberg, Jeffrey Roger. 2003. "A Buddhist Mantra Recovered from the Ratu Baka Plateau; A Preliminary Study of its Implications for Sailendra-era Java." *Bijdragen tot de taal-, land-en volkenkunde/Journal of the Humanities and Social Sciences of Southeast Asia* 159, no. 1: 163–88.

Törzsök, Judit. 2009. "The Alphabet Goddess Mātṛkā in Some Early Śaiva Tantras." Second International Workshop on Early Tantras, Pondicherry, India.

Weck, Wolfgang. 1986. *Heilkunde und Volkstum auf Bali.* Jakarta: Bap Bali.

White, David G. 2012. "Netra Tantra at the Crossroads of the Demonological Cosmopolis." *Journal of Hindu Studies* 5, no. 2: 145–71.

Woodroffe, John. 1991. *Principles of Tantra.* Part 1. Madras: Ganesh & Company.

Woodward, Hiram. 2004. "Esoteric Buddhism in Southeast Asia in the Light of Recent Scholarship." *Journal of Southeast Asian Studies* 35, no. 2: 329–54.

3

The Conch as a Tantric Artefact

Metaphysics of a Number and the Twirled Lives of Text and Practice

Sukanya Sarbadhikary

Introduction: Serendipities of Practice and Text

The vital breath (*prāṇa*) of all life is awake in your existence
Don't be indifferent, rise, rise to it.
Listen, the eternal conch resonates in the consciousness-mansion of your heart
Don't be indifferent, rise, rise to it.

—Rabindranath Tagore (1993, 117)[1]

One is not sure, but there are roughly a little more than three folds in the conch navel, and there resides its *prāṇa* (life-force). The saying goes, "*śāṅkher sāṛe tin*" (the conch's 3½).

—Conch craftsman in Barrackpore, West Bengal

The AUM̐ buzz is the first cosmic resonance. But it does not end with the three sounds: A, U, M. There is an extra nasal echo (after M) we symbolize as *candrabindu*.[2]

—Musician in Navadvip, West Bengal

Nādācchaiva Samutpannā Ardhabindurmaheśvari,
Sārdhatritayabindubhyo bhujaṅgī kulakuṇḍalī.[3]

—*Kubjikā Tantra* 1.53 (in Das 2018, 11)

If we consider *Tantra* as etymologically meaning the interweaving of threads, then the fabric of the words, people, symbols, and numbers represented in these citations have been vibrating together, through history, in a "*Tantra*" of metaphysical connections. What may be binding the lives and intuitions of one of the most significant Tantra texts, *Kubjikā Tantra* (eleventh century), a religious sound practitioner, a contemporary craftsman with no explicit knowledge of difficult religious texts, and a modern poet? Are the worlds of high concept, manual practice, and intuitive experience independent domains, or are there pulsating echoes among these apparently disparate lifeworlds, originating in some deep-seated cultural habitus? It is approximations of the number 3½ that shall be the focus of the paper's analysis and discursive connections. The number will be demonstrated as especially significant in imaginations of the sacred conch, perfected yogic body, and cosmic sonic vibration.

The material object of the paper's concerns is the conch shell, known in Bengali as *śāṅkh* or *śaṅkha*. It is collected from the sea, cleaned, crafted, and made appropriate for critical ritual roles in homes and temples. While it is widely sounded for religious and musical purposes in South Asia, it is also of everyday domestic sacred use in Hindu Bengal. Women sound it during dusk for homely well-being, and conch bangles are worn by married women as symbols of fertile nourishment.

I encountered the number 3½ for the first time while conducting ethnographic work with Śāṅkhārīs, a Bengali lower-caste group of primarily men who work as conch collectors and craftsmen. After my exposure to this mysteriously recurrent number among Śāṅkhārīs, I was also alerted to its traces in ideas of sound meditation, and thus I was led to texts of Tantra, especially sound yoga.[4] Rather than finding a "fit" of the world of practice with cultural texts, the journey was interestingly the other way around: texts resounded the words and hands of ordinary people. I was thus fortunate to experience serendipity of the best kind: drawn rather spontaneously, from people's voices, to sounds, *ślokas*, and texts.

As the above excerpts indicate, the body's empty spaces, like the consciousness-filled heart, life-breath (*prāṇa*), the conch's twirls, the lunar image of the metaphysical first sound, and the conch-like serpentine corporeal manifestation (*kuṇḍalinī*), are entwined in a coherent worldview. I suggest that this lifeworld also echoes in mathematical intuitions of a transcendental, infinite number. However, ethnographic discussions shall demonstrate that these abstract connections are grounded and expressed in mundane practices concerning the conch, its insides, its curves, and its acoustic generation. Reminding me of the image of god as earthmaker, a potter in West Bengal's Bishnupur town, adept in making clay conches, told me (referring to a Puranic story), "The conch was born from the first churning of the sea by gods, so its sound is eternal. . . . The sound cannot originate without the conch's life (*prāṇa*) in its navel's folds. This is all natural. But through years of practice, I have learnt how to make earthen conches, which will sound! So, I need to know how to *make* those twirls with my fingers." The potter's fingers—materially entangled with and almost indistinguishable from the most immanent matter, clay—resonate the primordial sound of sacred abstraction.

Thus, while Tantra has mostly been approached as a scriptural heritage describing initiate esoteric practices of sophisticated religious traditions, I argue that these worldviews may also be sedimented in people's bodies, objects, and everyday narrations. My ethnography expands the dominant textual methods of studying Tantra by demonstrating ways in which complex understandings of sacred embodiment and sonic theology echo in the material practices of conch-people. Further, these materialities play agentive roles in perpetuating the embodied traditions through both texts and practices. The spiritual is thus equally tangible, inner lives of meditative contemplation having potent resonances in the world of outer matter (see Houtman and Meyer 2012, 1–26). In my study of everyday religiosities of the conch-world, I try to understand processes of the conch's production, the mythmaking and textual imaginations centering the conch, and the conch's material-aural effects that reflect and surpass the human intentions of the craftsmen working with them (see Flueckiger 2020, 4–5). Therefore, modern Western epistemologies differentiating text and matter, inner contemplation and external reality, transcendence and immanence, or Sanskrit texts and vernacular practices do not hold in this case. I concur with Richard D. Mann when he says—critiquing dominant Western tropes of religious studies that have privileged script over matter, as well as recent understandings of materiality that divorce themselves from textual studies—that "the multidisciplinary effort of the materiality of religion needs to include all aspects of the study of religion from ancient texts to everyday moments of lived religion" (2014, 271). Further, while earlier studies of Tantra often understood the human body as a microcosm of textually defined universal principles (see Hayes 2000; White 1996), I extend the analytic to include the enriched domain of sacred objects.

If Tantra literally means a system of nuanced texture, then this ethnography spins a weave encompassing the conch's body, the human body, and sound. While Tantra implies secrecy, the spectrum between revelation and obscurity may work in interesting ways in ethnographic contexts: not as confidentiality literally, but as a kind of concealment. Although the ethnographer may be able to trace similar genealogies of thought and practice between high texts and everyday lives, these discourses may be implicit in people's lifeworlds. They may allude to esoteric dimensions underlying their practices, but another layer of concealment is what Victor Turner terms a "block in native exegesis" (1967, 38, cited in Obeyesekere 2008, 360). Explaining and articulating their practices in words is something practitioners might not be used to. Their relationship with Tantric cosmology is rather intensely ingrained in their habitus, their hands, and their intuitions.

Even though people may not be consciously aware of the discourses of which they are part, their vocabulary, craftsmanship, myths, and stories have intuitive links that echo textual conceptualizations. Intuition, as Merleau-Ponty reminds us, works at the interface of mind and body, concept and percept, text and practice (see Carman 2008, 18). It establishes a spontaneous relation between one's unconscious habitus background and embodied foreground of activities and objects. People's "block" in exegesis thus often exists because so profoundly are the discursive connections embedded in their body-minds that they may not surface to conversational levels. While most ethnographers are concerned with observing and listening to semantic and articulated utterances, fieldwork in esoteric contexts rather needs to empathetically uncover the silent expressions of communities. Such empathy may involve a sinking oceanic "immersion" in peoples' lifeworlds (Helmreich 2008), an appropriate metaphor in my context concerning a sea artefact, the conch.

Being a Bengali Hindu and a Bengali-speaking person enabled me particularly during fieldwork—at cognitive, bodily, and ethical levels—to productively associate with peoples' embodied allusions of conch-sound relationality. I could resonate spontaneously with people's myths, metaphors, and other everyday cosmological tropes because I have grown up in the same discursive lifeworld, even hearing the daily dusk conch-sounding at home, through childhood, adulthood, and to this day. My participatory sonic immersion thus allowed me to appreciate the intuitive habitus binding sounds, bodies, texts, and metaphysics. My methodology is primarily what McCutcheon identifies as phenomenological-hermeneutic (1999, 1–10), but it also involves a psychological dimension as I try to understand relatively concealed affective and material links between high theory, popular practice, sounding, listening, and understanding of the conch. While my higher-class, higher-caste, educated and urban background set me apart from the craftsmen's world, and my being a woman interviewer remained stark in the male-dominated skilled worksphere, the conch-acoustic universe always acted as an equalizer, binding our conversations, understandings, and memories about the *śaṅkha*. The object's materiality had a strong force in if not dissolving then at least marginalizing our social differences through shared sonic appraisals of a most commonly used, everyday sacred matter.

The critical theoretical issue this paper engages with is the continuities of text, practice, and experience. An ethnography of Tantra here involves the analysis of an artefact's (conch's) life as a Tantric one: constituted through textual representations as well as practiced traditions of tactile craftsmanship. I argue that people's habitus and intuition form phenomenological continuities with texts that have significant discursive impact. I describe ethnographic ways in which narratives of caste communities working with conches connect their labor, lives, and imaginations with literary traditions. My chapter thus reconciles two spheres that both mainstream Indological and popular narratives imagine as necessarily separate: texts and everyday experience.

Several ethnographic analyses have influenced my perspectives. Openshaw (2002) clearly demonstrated the embodied dimensions of Bengal's popular religiosity, while Fruzzetti and Ostor (1984, 109) have shown that abstract (Tantric) ideas, such as that of essential maleness and femaleness (*puruṣa* and *prakṛti*), may be analogous with everyday

Bengali life, as in linguistic kinship structuration; for instance, in conceptions of "seed" and "earth." While McDaniel classifies Bengal's Tantric practitioners as either folk or scholastic, distinguishing domains of practice from theory (2004, 9–10), I find some other ethnographic cues more apposite than such categorizations. This might be due to the fact that my work is not about practitioners explicitly, but rather more implicit connections between a sonic artefact, Tantric cosmology, and the meditative body.

Richard Wolf states that South Asian musical instruments have intimate relations with community lives and bodies, and they carry traditions of textual messages, even when listeners may not immediately understand semantic details (2014, 7). These acoustics thus constitute ingrained visceral ethics of responsive listening through what Charles Hirschkind calls "infrastructural affects and sensibilities" (2006, 2–9). I find Jeffrey Lidke's understanding about Tantric-embodied spirituality—which he defines as tying performance, psychology, philosophy of language, sonic metaphysics, and even "divinely inspired mathematic vision"—as particularly useful (2015, 7). Lidke proposes a hermeneutic approach to engage with deep Tantric symbolic meanings, which have become ritually encoded and veiled in centuries of popular cultural practice. In my work, too, I find throbbing resonances of a number as weaving text and practice, deities, materialities, yogic bodies, and the buzzing universe.

Based both on Tantric texts and ethnographic insights developed in two important Śāṅkhārī settlements of West Bengal—Barrackpore and Bishnupur—this paper reflects on ontological substructures that constitute a productive habitus space between philosophy and the everyday, metaphysics and embodiment, textual imaginaries and manual labor. The specific focus shall be on discourses and practices centering the number of the conch's coils, the powerful 3½.

The Twists of a Tantric Artefact

I conducted ethnographic work among Śāṅkhārīs over several small intervals in the period between 2017 and 2018 in Barrackpore (North 24 Parganas district). Here, Śāṅkhārīs live and work in a cluster of a 6-kilometer radius. Almost all families of this congregation—the largest of Śāṅkhārīs—migrated from Bangladesh. I also worked among a settlement of 105 Śāṅkhārī families in Bishnupur, Bankura district.

Śāṅkhārīs follow a hereditary line of caste profession and specialize in different activities involving the conch. Conches are first collected from the sea by Muslim fishermen, and then they bring those extremely smelly raw products to warehouses and clean them. All subsequent work is conducted by Śāṅkhārīs. They clean the objects further, segregate them according to health and type, and craft decorative conches, ritual ones for sounding (*bādya-śaṅkha*), others for storing sacred Ganga water (*jal-śaṅkha*), and still others for making *śāṅkhās* (the white conch bangles worn by married women). They make elaborate machine designs on these products, grind ayurvedic medicines from different conch parts and dust, and, finally, sell all products in shops they own hereditarily. Each of these processes requires tremendous expertise Śāṅkhārīs inherit and cultivate.[5]

The conch is centrally associated with the deity Vishnu/Narayana's persona, as evident especially in the Pan-Hindu consecration of Krishna's conch, Pancajanya. In the *Bhagavad Gita* it is narrated that the god robustly sounded the conch to announce the war of Mahabharata. Ubiquitous in the ritual sphere, Bengali Hindus have a special relation with the conch: it is blown during dusk in every home and venerated as the direct embodiment of Lakshmi's and Narayana's restorative qualities (*maṅgal*, or auspiciousness). It is an indispensable material object bringing domestic and *sāṃsārik* (both this-worldly and cosmic) well-being, peace, health, and wealth. The discourse of *maṅgal* binds Bengali imagination of sacred domesticity (see Chakrabarty 1993). Simply, the conch is generally understood to be a Vishnuite or Vaiṣṇava symbol signifying peace-bearing qualities and cooling properties. It has a specific association with femininity in Bengal, not only because women blow it during the evening puja, but also since they wear conch bangles, which are believed to keep their body-minds calm and bring domestic harmony. However, while I was also aware of Buddhists' figuration of somber conch sounds as depicting Buddha-like meditative stillness, my fieldwork among Śāṅkhārīs exposed me to a dimension of conch sacrality unknown before: the object's essential connectedness to the Tantric deity-consort, Shiva-Parvati/Durga; that is, a Śaivite (Shiva worship–oriented) and Śākta (mother-goddess worshipping) religiosity. Elsewhere, I have analyzed unexplored associations of conches with snakes, serpentine motifs, and the snake goddess Manasa based primarily on their coiled similarity (Sarbadhikary 2019). Ethnography revealed further esoteric connections, which I argue establish the conch as a Tantric artefact.[6]

While one would expect conch shops to be named after Lakshmi/Narayana, these are in fact rare. Most shops are named after Shiva and goddess forms, such as Kali, Parvati, Manasa, Sitala, Karunamayi, and Bhavatarini. Śāṅkhārīs' narrations of conch stories and their caste genealogies amply demonstrate that the artefact is related by them to Shiva and his consort, *puruṣa* and *prakṛti*, and, further, to the Shiva devotee, sage Agastya. References to Vishnu are formulaic and Puranic, but to Shiva they are more immediate and embodied. I shall discuss these stories, the conch's astrological uses, and evocative narratives of crafting the ritual object—especially concepts of its inside, its coils, and related issues of breath, life, body-space, and cosmogonic primordialism—to emphasize popular insinuations of the artefact's *tantricity*. The conch's 3½ twirls become crucial in these castings.

Śāṅkhārīs say that the conch, although sacred, is never directly ready for ritual use when collected from the waters; their labor transforms the object. Most natural conches are twirled to the left side (*bām-ābarta*) and closed; they are perforated at the mouth for sounding purposes. Then the stinky, fleshy portions are scraped from the conch's spiraled inside, followed by cleaning with sand and acid water. Śāṅkhārīs refer to this coiled portion as the conch's navel (*nābhi*), vital breath (*prāṇa*), life (*jān*), twists, folds, or knots (*pyañc, guli, gyañṛā,* or *giñt*). Most Śāṅkhārīs said that the conch-navel spiral has roughly 3½ folds, and they showed three faint lines on the conch's exterior as indication of its thrice-twisted inside. Some said that after the mouth is perforated and the inside cleaned, they can actually see through the spirals of three and a little extra (see figures 3.1 and 3.2).

Śāṅkhārīs have intuitive senses about which conches will sound well, depending on their inner space and breathing capacities. Those that have more expansive interiors are chosen to be crafted as wind instruments (*bādya-śaṅkha*). In these, the knotted portion is retained inside, since, as Śāṅkhārīs carefully observed, it is the internal balance of emptiness and obstruction that causes the conch to resonate. Blown air twirls through the 3+ coils and pushes against the walls to produce the desired echo.

If bangles (*śāṅkhās*) are made, the internal twirled portion (*guli*) is drilled out. Since the conch navel is a spiral and gets scooped out,

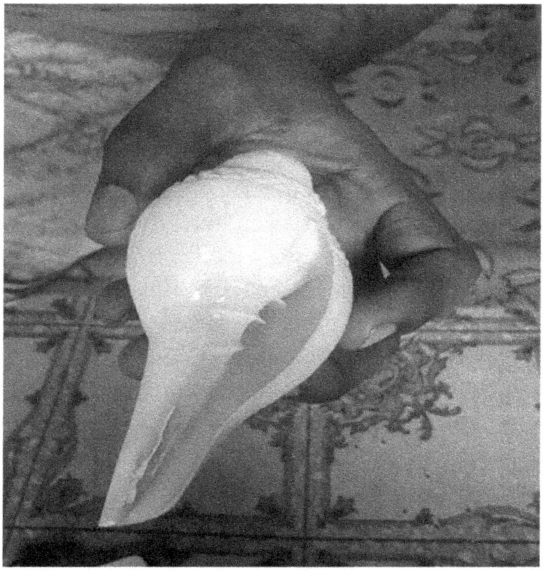

Figure 3.1. The three fold-lines on the conch's exterior surface. *Source*: Photograph by the author.

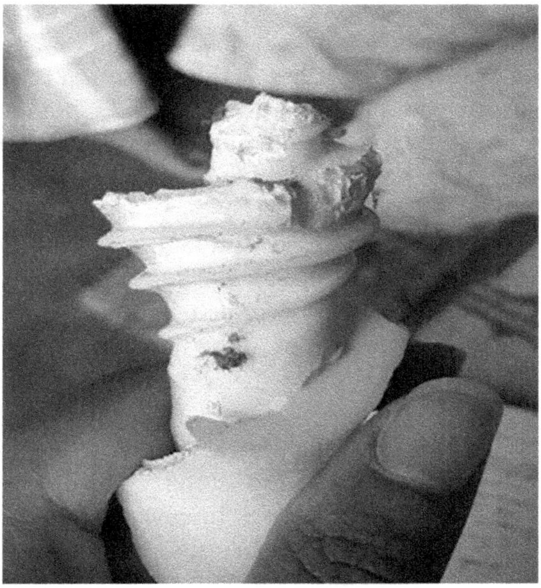

Figure 3.2. The three and a half spirals of the conch-navel. *Source*: Photograph by the author.

śāṅkhās are never perfectly round. Each pair of the married woman's *śāṅkhās* is unique. The conch's originality depends on its breath, life, and 3½ coiled navel. This removed part is then used for lunar astrological functions, since the moon, sea, and conch are all seen as connected and as offering cooling, fertility, and prosperity to the body and to the home. So, the internal portion is variously deployed in treating stomach and skin diseases, fertility problems, warding off evil, ensuring children's and cows' health, and controlling temperamental issues. Some people also wear amulets made of conch navels and the seed of the *rudrākṣa* plant sacred to Shiva.

As will be evident when Tantric texts are discussed, all the above narratives—which evoke notions of the conch's twirled body-space, 3½ folds, airing/sounding capacity, healing properties, and moonlike cooling impact—have connections with esoteric constructions of the body. As many sonic meditators explained, the human body, indeed, is a perforated vessel, which with practiced, perfected breathing attains perception of an originary sound that resonates in its empty cavities.[7] This buzz, known as *anāhatanāda* (the primordial, unstruck, uncaused, cosmic vibration), is the AUM̐ sound. Śāṅkhārīs told me that the conch, the AUM̐ sound, and Lakshmi emanated simultaneously from the sea's churning. This sound can be heard, they say, simply by placing the conch mouth on the ear cavity. Thus, ideas of gushing air-water primordial sound are immanent in the first forms of life: sea, conch, and divinized body. When breath/life is activated for the first time, it sounds the original vibration. These discourses come together in Tantric texts and are foreshadowed in everyday narratives of conch-people.

In addition to Tantric sonic cosmologies draping the conch, its more popular associations with Shiva, his consort, and Agastya are palpable in Śāṅkhārīs' myths and practices. Śāṅkhārīs claim descent from Agastya, who not only represents ideal Shaivite devotion but also strict "Shiva-like" asceticism. Thus, there are mythical overlaps in Shiva-Agastya narratives.

Śāṅkhārīs recount how Shiva once wanted to gift Parvati conch bangles. Even Vishwakarma, the god of craftsmanship, failed to make them through the complex processes involved. However, Agastya—Shiva's ideal devotee—crafted the bangles, and Shiva, dressed as a Śāṅkhārī, offered them to Durga on Ashtami puja day (see Fruzzetti 1990, 69–70). Ever since, married Bengali women have worn conch bangles and, customarily, a Śāṅkhārī puts the first pair on the bride's hands on her marriage day. The bangles' sales also increase during Durga puja, following the same narrative tradition. In another story narrated by Śāṅkhārīs, there is a devout Kali worshipper who desperately seeks her presence in his life. One morning, a young girl visits a Śāṅkhārī in the same village and asks to buy a pair of conch bangles. When requested to pay, she points to the man's house and says she is his daughter. When the Śāṅkhārī visits him to collect his due and narrates the story, the man tells him that he has no daughter. The two men immediately realize that Kali herself had descended in disguise. They run toward her and come upon a pond, and the tale ends on an evocative note: from inside the blue waters, shining black hands with red vermillion and sparkling-white conch bangles surface with the goddess' eternal blessing gesture.

Śāṅkhārīs' narrative connections with Agastya are equally suggestive. In a famous Puranic chronicle, Agastya drank up the entire sea to kill demons hiding there. Agastya is renowned as a pious embodiment of celibate devotion, and his powers are ascribed to his yogic accomplishments. Later, however, Agastya returned the sea and all aquatic life with it, including the source of Śāṅkhārīs' caste occupation: the conch. Thus, Śāṅkhārīs are respectful of Agastya, who they venerate as their first ancestor and lineage guru.

During the monsoon month of *Bhādra*, Śāṅkhārīs worship Agastya for four consecutive days, ending on Vishwakarma puja. In another story, Śāṅkhārīs, too busy with their difficult work, could not attend to their passerby guest, Agastya, who, known for his Shiva-like anger, refused to return. This would imply the loss of all fortune, so Śāṅkhārīs decided to appease him through annual worship. In their ritual observances during this period, however, Śāṅkhārīs, who are almost exclusively men, themselves embody Agastya's/Shiva's asceticism: observing strict celibacy, fasting, and abstaining from market activities. Some emphasized that they do not touch conches during this period. They construct the sage's idol anew every year, who sits as an embodiment of Shiva's *tapas* (yogic discipline) in a meditative posture, draped in tiger skin, with *rudrākṣa* in his hands. Two striking features accompany him: a pot, and two reptilian creatures (or crocodiles) at his feet to symbolize Agastya's control over aquatic life. These coiled, conch-like reptilian motifs are also replicated in bangle designs that Śāṅkhārīs craft (for a typical Agastya idol, see figure 3.3).

Figure 3.3. An Agastya idol worshipped by Bishnupur Śāṅkhārīs. *Source*: Photograph by the author.

Agastya's physical and spiritual representation thus brings together Tantric dimensions of Shivaite asceticism and goddess power (*śakti*), celibacy and creation, masculine principle and *kuṇḍalinī* (Tantric body's coiled feminine serpent energy). The next section discusses Tantric discursive understandings of primordial male-female union in the body and its sounding capacities through the body-conch's 3½ folded spiral. Śāṅkhārīs' tracing their genealogy to Agastya indeed evokes implicit Tantric connections.

Why would a community dependent on waters derive lineage imaginations from a sage who drank up the sea? This is not simply explicable as fearful reverence. I argue that, in a Tantric vein, celibacy and life, *tapas* and fertility, retention and breath, power and overflowing creativity, *puruṣa* and *prakṛti*, are necessarily entangled, as demonstrated in the story of Agastya and the conch he returns life to. While popular lore and texts identify sage Jaratkaru as snake goddess Manasa's husband (see Haq 2015), many Śāṅkhārīs, in an interesting oral-mythical version, told me that Manasa is married to Agastya. Manasa, like Agastya, is worshipped on the last day of *Bhādra*. During Manasa's worship, the goddess is also represented by a pot, and the reptiles at Agastya's feet represent Manasa's power over snakes and aquatic creatures.[8] While the left-sided twirled conches are sounded, the rare right-sided ones (*dakṣiṇa-ābarta*), considered to be Narayana's direct embodiment under the sea, are held in greatest reverence. Their mouths are not slit; thus, they cannot be sounded, and women are disallowed from touching them. Similarly, in the ascetic guise, during their temporary celibate period of four-day Agastya puja, Śāṅkhārīs don't touch feminine conches. This conch world of resonance and silence, creation and abstinence, represents what Tantric texts describe as the cosmic continuum of *nāda* (sound) and *nādānta* (stillness) and their feminine-masculine expressions. Their union in the body is represented as the first unstruck vibrating moment, the 3+ conch-coiled *kuṇḍalinī* buzzing continuously with the original hum, AUṀ.

I had a fascinating encounter with people who approximate these originary features of the natural conch with their hands. These potters of terracotta conches develop intuitive manual relations with conch navel and breath, just as the Tantric body realizes cosmic sounds within itself by reflecting the conch's luminosity. If a spiritual progression can be imagined—from the closed mouth *śaṅkha* to the one with breathing holes; from the cosmic male principle to feminine life force; from meditative stillness to the practicing, sounding Tantric body—then a further level of manifestation proceeds from the natural to the human world, from conches collected from underwater to those crafted by human hands. Abhinavagupta's Tantric theory of reflection (*prativimba-vāda*) is appropriate to understand this phenomenon of successively manifested forms of creation as reflecting original vibration and, further back, primordial stillness (Ratie 2017, 207–40).

I conducted fieldwork among Kumbhakār or Kumor (potters) communities of Panchmura village, about 36 kilometers from Bishnupur. Panchmura is renowned for terracotta work and has a significant number of National Award for Master Craftsmen winners. Almost every household among its eighty-four families specializes in earthenware work and develops expertise in perfecting clay consistency, finger dexterity, and balancing traditional methods and new designs through generations of embodied learning from family and neighbors. Kumbhakāras agreed that among the many earthen products they craft, conch-making is toughest.

While currently many potters have learned conch art, late Ganapati Kumbhokar (a National Award winner) was the first to create an earthen conch. I had the privilege of interacting with him and observing intense methods of conch creation. He said, "Conch is a natural object. But as a child, I developed the imagination of making one with the play of earth and hands. . . . A clay conch is man-made, so its sound can never be the same as that made by god, but that my conch can sound, is itself so much pleasure!" So, in the image of god-as-earthmaker, a child's fantasy of the natural connection between playful fingers and malleable clay gives us the first human handmade conch. It evokes the idea of divine approximation through artistic methods, expressed specifically, in the mirror of sound production. Indeed, the conch's aural life is what makes it challenging to craft an earthen one. Ganapati explained, "If it were only a decorative conch, it would be easy. But we make conches which one can blow in. The clay, making, are planned accordingly. But the most critical aspect is the conch's coils, which without a lot of training and concentration, is impossible to create."[9] Kumbhakāras work on the conch with meditative attention, and it can take up to three days if the conch is fully handmade. These days, potters have casts with which they make conch exteriors, and they engrave them with elaborate religious motifs. They choose clay thickened with water (*en̐tel māṭi*) and fired well (*poṛā māṭi*) to make the consistency resistant and solid. Air/breath can then twirl through coils and rebound in the conch's walls even during hard blowing, rather than scatter through porous clay texture (figure 3.4 illustrates a Bishnupur potter with his cast). In other contexts of my work with musician-meditators, the practitioners of the sacred drum (*khol*) used the *poṛā māṭi* metaphor to assert that human body—heated through Tantric-yogic *tapas* and with the right breathing balance—mirrors processed clay in its divinity and ability to hear transcendental sounds.

For Kumbhakāras, what remains critical is the shaping of the sound hole—the inner cave's coils—since as Śān̐khārīs also explained, breath-air twists around the conch-navel folds, then strikes against the conch walls, to finally produce the conch's booming buzz. These

Figure 3.4. Potter casting a conch. *Source*: Photograph by the author.

twirls, the conch's navel life, are the most originary form, almost impossible to replicate. But adept Kumbhakāras, through the finest intuitive poise of skin touch, eyes, and an inimitable cognitive awareness about the amount and kind of space to be crafted between the twists in a way that air can twirl through, rub and coil the clay "like snails on fingertips," as a craftsman evocatively put it, to "make" the conch's primordial inside. The cast is then used, and different parts assembled, to graft the conch body around it. Ganapati said, "Machines can make the body. But only human touch can imagine the coils, because they are most natural. That is why not everyone can make an earthen conch, and not all sound the same." Kumbhakāras also have ways to test how the conch sounds. They look through the entangled passage and strike on the perforated mouth to assess twirled perfection in reverberating sound. This obviously involves great sensory nimbleness. Finally, they drill three artificial lines near the external body's stomach to indicate the presence of loops inside.

These traces of the interior are human-made to replicate the appearance of the original conch's twirls in terracotta *śaṅkhas*.

Despite this most complex method of gifting embodied breath-life to the earthen conch through human hands, of approximating natural aurality, there remains a distinct lack. Ganapati's cousin, who has mastered conch-making, explained, "The conch's *prāṇa* is in 3½ loops inside. But our hands can produce 2½ twists at most, due to lack of maneuverable space inside. That automatically affects sound quality." Earthen conches, he said, have a sweet sound, but they cannot produce the somber reverberation (and tactile vibrating impact) like the sea ones. "Its sound can enter our ears, but not hearts."

This primitive expression—of vibrating resonance of the conch's navel sound, emanating in the 3½ life center—also enables Śāṅkhārīs and Kumbhakāras to make ontological claims to originality. These caste groups have an interesting association through the conch/pot imaginary. Kumbhakāra literally means "one who makes a *kumbha*" (a clay pot), and the clay pot is used in worshipping Agastya, Śāṅkhārīs' guru-ancestor, as well as his coiled serpentine consort, Manasa.

The 3½ breathing tangles of the conch interior propel discourses of sound and stillness, craftsmanship and untouched eternity, knowledge and unknowability, *prakṛti* and *puruṣa*. A clear, unspiraled space passage could not have produced sound—neither in the conch nor the human body—and this animates connections evident in Tantric texts of sonic metaphysics.

The Turns of Tantric Texts

The ethnographic threads of 3½ coils, breath/air passages, and transcendental acoustics are finely entwined with classical textual traditions, which tie the conch with the body's "esoteric physiology of sound" (Beck 1993, 97). The conch as a Tantric artefact is thus established also through its associations with a cosmic anatomy.

Gavin Flood, following Andre Padoux, says some Upaniṣads have clear Tantric concerns (2006, 8). Thus, *Kauṣītaki Upaniṣad* posits vital breath (*prāṇa*) and sound/speech (*vāc*) as each other's intimately united shadows (see Anirban 1992, 23–41, 96–127). Such entanglements of breath and sound vibrations—both principles of body/conch functioning—are essentially dependent on the empty space of sound holes. Thus, *Chāndogya Upaniṣad* considers sound to be the main function of *ākāśa*, or empty space. Accordingly, the text also describes the heart space's inner cavity as *cidākāśa*, the vibrating/reflective capacity (*ākāśa*) of consciousness (*cit*), which manifests as cosmic sound.[10] The *Mahābhārata* also mentions *ākāśa*'s primordial unstruckness and presence in the body's orifices (Sinha 1987, 793). Unstruck sound (*anāhata nāda*) is thus conceptually derived as incessantly flowing with life-breath through corporeal openings. Upaniṣads' and *Mahābhārata*'s deliberations about *ākāśa* and sound relate to the Tantric idea of the first cosmic tremor of life, coeval with the primal sexual union of eternal male-female energies, being felt as an unstruck, uncaused AUM̐ buzz throughout the body. The same AUM̐ buzz is described by Śāṅkhārīs as booming in conch insides.

The following discussion, while based on texts, closely dialogues with my ethnography. Both are concerned with constructions of perfected bodies. The Tantric-yogic body as divided into six circular energy centers (cakras) was first mentioned in the eleventh century, in *Kubjikā Tantra*, where the crooked goddess, Kubjika, is identified as goddess Kuṇḍalinī (Flood 2006, 158). These cakras are associated with hidden sounds/phonemes. *Sārdhatriśaktikālottara Tantra* (Tantra of the eternally powerful 3½) mentions 72,000 nervous channels springing from the navel center and carrying blood and ten kinds of breaths through ten main spinal currents, the central one being *suṣumnā* (2006, 159). Of these sounding/buzzing currents mentioned by Abhinavagupta and Gorakhnath, the tenth one is named *śaṅkhinī* (the female conch) (Silburn 1988, 28, 124). Like *Netra Tantra*, *Kubjikā Tantra* also describes the upward-rising serpentine energy associated with the sonic life of mantras and speech as the coiled one, *kuṇḍalinī* (Flood 2006, 160), also called *śaṅkhinī*/conch because she is looped 3½ times (Silburn 1988, 129).[11] The 3½ twirls around the Shiva *liṅga*—which approximate the form of a conch interior—have roots in *Ṛg Vedā*'s serpent queen image, according to S. C. Banerji (1992, 60).

Lilian Silburn discusses the Nāth-Śaiva text *Amaraughaśāsana*, where Gorakhnath identifies *śaṅkhinī*/conch nerve as *kuṇḍalinī*. The text describes how the inner spontaneous sound, *anāhata nāda*, gets aroused through yogic methods and stimulates *kuṇḍalinī*. *Kuṇḍalinī*, goddess energy, the first sense of life's vibration emanating from

Shiva's stillness, is thus acknowledged as the primordial conch. In different ways, Śāṅkhārīs also alluded to the conch's sound as life's originary expression.

Silburn translates:

> Between the anus and the sexual organ sits the *trikoṇa* [triangle] with three circles around it. . . . In the middle of the three knots sits a lotus with four downward-turned petals. There, in the center of the pericarp, is found a conch of extreme subtlety . . . wherein rests the Kuṇḍalinī energy, the coiled one . . .
>
> Along the central channel, this path [of Kuṇḍalinī] extends up to the braincase; there, in the moon circle, resides the supreme *liṅga* of the skull. . . . In the inner space, the *garbha* situated in the middle of the forehead, . . . *śaṅkhinī* releases its flow. (Silburn 1988, 125–26)

Thus, we find constant references to upward-rising breath (*prāṇa*), the moon (in the forehead middle, also the seat of AUM̐'s after-buzz), *kuṇḍalinī* (*prakṛti*) rising up to entwine with Shiva (*puruṣa*), and the number 3½. This discourse resonates in ethnographic narratives about the conch's twirls, breath, sound, astrological lunar significance, and relation between masculine celibacy and feminine creative excess as embodied, for instance, in Agastya's stories. Also, like the earthen conch approximates the natural one, yogic bodies, perfected, apprehend conched/sonic divinity.

From the rising conch arise all primary sounds (*śabda*) and phonemes (*mātṛkā*), together constituting both language and cosmos (Silburn 1988, 130–31). Shiva's moon nectar is carried by the aroused, conched *kuṇḍalinī* from the cranium throughout the body, throbbing as AUM̐ or *anāhata nāda* (Omkarnathdev 2012, 60). The Tantric body is thus dependent on the 3½ coiled conch-serpent energy. From here, other Tantric sonic theorizations proceed.[12]

Sound/speech (*śabda*) arises through four bodily levels corresponding to cosmic sonic emanation. This movement is directed toward creation of external sonic life; it manifests as progressive vibrational differentiation and ultimately retreats back into silence (see Baumer 2019, 46). The first stage, *parā* (corresponding to the anus center), is the still state of Shiva's formless wisdom, bound with his yet-unmanifested feminine *śakti*, the sleeping conch/snake *kuṇḍalinī*. This is followed by *paśyanti* (navel), *madhyamā* (heart), and *vaikharī* (tongue/speech). In the first stage, vibration is undifferentiated and is merged with the 21,600 daily breaths, resounding *anāhata nāda* in the body. This *nāda*, AUM̐, is the cosmic/corporeal murmur representing the sexually united form of Shiva/Parvati, *bindu*/*bīja*, stasis/dynamicity, *prakāśa/vimarśa*. Their union then gives rise to different levels of vibration, sound, and time felt throughout the body.[13]

The conch is thus the ideal counterpart of the human body: when not yet blown, it embodies *parā*'s stillness, and its inner buzz then hums like the primordial sound (the sea and AUM̐). Its 3½ twists are like the coils of the bodily serpent energy, *kuṇḍalinī*. When breathed into, the insistent somber sound progressively finds outlet. It also enters into empty interstices of the listener's body, through the ear and heart cavities (*madhyamā*), and, further, in reverse direction, is internalized through the navel (*paśyanti*) toward the anus (*parā*) to resonate as *anāhata nāda*. The 3½ twirls, both of the conch and of the body, then sound—in the most subtle, unuttered form—the 3½ acoustic components of AUM̐: A, U, M, followed by *candrabindu*, the full moon's power, which, reaching the forehead is transformed into *ardha-candra* (̐).[14] The nasal buzz and the after-sound (½) beyond 3 both condenses and transcends A-U-M's power. The everyday activity of blowing the domestic conch—three times exactly, then followed by a distinct humming resonance after the third—internalized by listeners in the home, is thus intensely intertwined with century-old Tantric textual traditions.

The dot beyond AUM̐ is known as *bindu*, Shiva's subtlest manifestation and creative energy, located in the middle of the eyebrows, and the first of a yogi's nine corporeal acoustic stations. These sonic meditative levels are progressively subtle lands in the cranium, moving from manifest sound back toward silence, creativity toward stillness, *prakṛti* toward *puruṣa* (Omkarnathdev 1990, 22, 26). The 3½ twists thus connect the sonic transcendence of the yogic Tantric body and the conch's aurality, as well as the craftsmen's narratives, manual intuitions, and imaginaries of cosmogonic creativity.

In positing the conch as a Tantric artefact, my methodological contribution to the ethnography of Tantra thus lies in establishing insistent associations between living traditions, embodied practices, oral exegeses, and esoteric texts. These connections, while often hidden from ordinary parlance, find outlets in people's intertwined voices when the ethnographer identifies often-obvious metaphorical overlaps in people's mythical recountings, textual conceptual deployments, and understandings about how to sanctify an object—the conch, in this instance. Material objects are thus equal participants in a Tantric lifeworld, discursively emplotted by texts, people, and everyday experiences, although they have not been adequately analyzed in studies of South Asian Tantra.

The potent symbol of 3½ that connects the conch, *kuṇḍalinī*, and AUM̐ also has significant resonances in some mantric and mathematical theorizations. I shall briefly indicate those directions. The 3½ snake breathes AUM̐, and since phonemes manifest in time, she also births temporality. However, in the cranium, completely united with Shiva, she embodies the moon's fullest potential (*kāmakalārūpiṇī*), silent and timeless, when all sounds/time fuse in the primordial buzz vibrating throughout the body. The conch's resolute and pregnant hum, sounding 3 times and then fading in a powerful echo (the ½ after 3), is the ideal parallel. In this form, as Shiva's *parā* (transcendental) *śakti*, she is known as goddess Tripurāsundarī. *Mātṛkābhed Tantra* conceptualizes her as including and surpassing the 3½ powers of AUM̐. She holds the key to knowledge (*jñāna*), science (*vijñāna*), and transcendence (Tarkatirtha 2013, 36–38, 70). Her seed *mantra* (*aing*) is thus common to the knowledge goddess Saraswati, to the guru who is the knowledge imparter, and to the serpentine energy Kuṇḍalini who is knowledge herself (Tarkatirtha 2013, 36; Das 2018, 8).

Tripurāsundarī's Saraswati powers, in the Tantric discourse, congeal as intuitive concentration in the third eye space, and her 3½ AUM̐ energy gives birth to language (sound/phonemes) and mathematics (through units of time and rhythm) (see Beck 1993, 136–44; McDaniel 2004, 258). These sensibilities, at the interface of metaphysics and mathematics, echo in one of the most important theorizations in the history of science—phenomenal in its abstraction and ubiquitous in application—the number pi, by the famous Indian mathematician Srinivasa Ramanujan, renowned for his purely "intuitive" approximations. Ramanujan (1887–1920) ascribed his conceptual intelligence entirely to the knowledge goddess, Namagiri. Among others, it was his theorization of pi as 3.1415 . . . , and the relationship he brilliantly imagined between pi and the formation of natural spirals like the conch (phi), that became hallmarks of his instinctual mathematics.

Thus, Ramanujan submitted his mathematical visions of 3+ . . . to the goddess. The 3½ twirls of *kuṇḍalinī*, conch, and AUM̐ propel Tantric imaginaries of language and mathematics. So, I end this chapter by extending the discursive web of a Tantric imagination from the world of ethnographic material objects to the apprehensions of conceptual mathematics: woven together as the fabric of the 3½ spiraled cosmos.

Ramanujan had a deeply religious upbringing, and his family was devoted to goddess Namagiri. His maternal grandmother would be possessed by the goddess, and Ramanujan also claimed to "receive" his formulae of infinity, pi, zero, and so forth, from the goddess herself in his dreams (Kanigel 1991, 13–36). Of interest here is pi (3+ . . .) and its relation to the conched golden ratio (phi). Spirals have often been connected with cosmology, and the golden ratio, especially, analyzes the conceptual aesthetics of twirled creation—from the universe to petals, conches, and shells.

Pi is the ratio of a circle's circumference to diameter. It is considered an enthralling enigma of science, the exact value of its infinite series still unreached. It is an irrational and transcendental number. Absolutely any set of numbers and Ascii values, as the present status of mathematics suggests, is contained in it.

In 1913–1914 Ramanujan offered a complex formula for the pi-phi relation. Phi (length: width), or golden ratio—an irrational, nonrecurring number like pi—is of the value 1.618 . . . It is embodied in natural spirals, like seashells and conches, and represents the aesthetics of asymmetrical compositions.

The number 3+ . . . and its relation to phi are thus significantly related to the conch's lifeworld, primarily through its aspects of spiral whirl and potentiality. Like the infinite portion of the number, the sonic eternal buzz gives life to all sound, and as Tantra posits, the 3½ coiled *śaṅkhinī*/*kuṇḍalinī*/AUM̐ springs language, numbers, and creation. These aspects are beautifully spiraled in the conch's inside: the navel of conception, the embodiment of *puruṣa-prakṛti* union, the first form of phenomenal vibrating existence.

The mystical number 3½ thus embroils apparently diverse worlds of the conch's folds, the yogic human body, the original sonic buzz, and mathematical theory. Such entwinement, however, is not only explicit in abstract texts but also equally intuited in everyday practices and oral narratives of popular worldviews. My ethnography thus shows that material culture and lived practices of conch craftsmen and sonic meditators are not separate from Tantric textual cosmologies. They throb together the pulsations of a cultural habitus. People receive traditions of manual labor, ritual worship, and symbolisms, co-constituted through discursive and embodied traditions of which they are critical participants. So, when a reader of "high" Tantra comes across understandings of *kuṇḍalinī*, when a potter discusses measures of the conch's navel turns, when a conch craftsman imagines creation through mythical symbolisms concerning Tantric deities, or when a mathematician's work connects measures of time, aesthetics, spirals, and sound, the boundaries between these otherwise distinct realms collapse. I have tried to propose a methodological sensitivity in studies of Tantra wherein texts come to life, literally, with human hands, breath, and imagination, throbbing with the shared understandings of an originary sonic vibrational universe. Further, practices do not only validate texts; the two are synchronous rhythms and proceed together through time.

Conclusion

This case study demonstrates that an ethnography of Tantra needs to work at the nodal interfaces of whatever constitutes its particular Tantric lifeworld; in this case, acoustic networks of high cultural texts, everyday community practices and lore, and particular artefacts. It foregrounds the material object, the conch (*śaṅkha*), and shows that the worlds of Tantric text and practice around it are intensely embroiled through knots of the number 3½. The natural conch, human body, and yogic sonic cosmos are represented in textual discourses and narrativized through everyday embodiments as bearing numerous correspondences. Creation, which is the goddess's impulse, finds life in Śāṅkhārīs' (conch craftsmen's), Kumbhakāras' (potters'), and Tantra authors' hands. They approximate, through their nuanced practices of embodiment and thought, the first moments of existence and give form to the life of sound. Śāṅkhārīs do this through complex understandings of conch matter; Kumbhakāras, by creating the coiled conch with clay; and authors, by conceptualizing the constitution of the human body and its energies within its twirled *śaṅkhinī/kuṇḍalinī*.

This chapter has thus established the conch as a Tantric artefact and has methodologically foregrounded the critical importance of understanding the material resonances of Tantric philosophical speculations. It concurs in its arguments with Gavin Flood (2006) that "entextualised bodies" are inscribed by texts, as also that cosmic formations, language, and tradition are understood in corporeal terms. Indeed, "entextualisation is a topos operative from the king to the village washerwoman" (30). Texts, techniques, and practices are thus warped and woofed into a Tantric whole; texts are congealed practices, while practices have internalized textual, metaphorical whispers over centuries. However, I extend the argument from human bodies to sacred material objects, such that, to worship the gods, "entextualized bodies" become necessarily intertwined with the often-underexamined materiality of lived Tantric traditions, as demonstrated by my ethnographic analysis of the conch (11). Divinization is thus a process enmeshing people, artefacts, and texts through the habitus of intuitive sacrality. Such intuitions also affect mathematical imaginations. The conch, with its 3½ coils, which Śāṅkhārīs say itself reaches maturity at 3+ years, is the connecting node in this entangled world of numbers, language, artistry, and mantric sound.

Notes

1. All translations of vernacular texts are by the author.

2. The Sanskrit diacritic sign shaped like a lower half circle with a dot above (ँ); phonetically, it is a half-alphabet, or *ardhamātrā*.

3. "The half-moon emanated with the primordial sound, *nāda*. The sound coils 3½ times as the serpentine *kuṇḍalinī*, at the body's spinal base, and is the embodiment of the first, subtlest manifestation of [Shiva's] creative consciousness, *bindu*." *Kuṇḍalinī* refers to the Tantric idea of a coiled feminine serpent energy dormant in every person, which awaits awakening through yogic methods.

4. There are strong yogic traditions and practices centering the cultivation and realization of cosmic sacred sound (*nāda*) in the body, constituting the significant paradigm of Nāda Yoga.

5. Dr. Sujay Kumar Mandal (Kalyani University, Department of Folklore) has published in Bengali language on the conch and conch craftsmen of Bengal. Due to the COVID-19 pandemic, I was unable to access these publications.

6. While I focus on the object's tantricity in a Hindu context, it is also used in other Tantric liturgical contexts, including among Newar Buddhists, while even being ubiquitous in non-Tantric orthodox Hindu worship rituals.

7. During my larger work on devotional (musical) sound in Bengal, which I have been conducting since 2010 with intensive focus during 2017–2019, and which included fieldwork in different rural districts, I encountered several people learned in concepts of *nāda yoga*, mostly lower-caste instrumentalists of sacred drums, flutes, and so forth, whom I call sonic meditators. Some of them are well versed with texts and cultivate realizations of sacred sound within bodies and material instruments.

8. These thematics also surface in King Chandradhvaj's story, as described in the nineteenth-century text *Bṛhat Kṛṣṇalīlā Sārāvali*. The king had refrained from drinking water blessed by Agastya to relieve his ailment, since it had worms in it. He smelled the water instead. So powerful was the blessed water that the king was cured, but since he refused to drink it, he was cursed and born as a snake, albeit the strongest one with a hundred heads, the famous serpent Kāliya. This story suggests Agastya's powers over the serpent world (Ghosh 2018, 168–69).

9. However, earthen conches are not used in ritual contexts, where only natural conches are sanctified.

10. See Olivelle (1998, 181, 207, 209–11, 229–31, 273–74).

11. For further significance of 3½, see Tarkatirtha 2013, 69, 76.

12. The following discussion is primarily based upon Banerji (1992, 81, 327); Baumer (2019, 17, 111–68); Lakshmanjoo (2011, 7–9, 31–32, 67–69, 77); Matilal (2017, 105); Omkarnathdev (1990, 7–28, 32–33, 110–11, 129); Padoux (1992, 14–21, 51, 83–222, 272); and Silburn (1988, 48–49).

13. This is especially elaborated in *Vijñāna Bhairava Tantra* (Lakshmanjoo 2011, 32).

14. This extra after 3 is also associated with the number 4 and its cosmic correspondences: the fourth Veda, *Puruṣa*, four states of consciousness, and so forth (Baumer 2019, 168; Padoux 1992, 19–21).

Bibliography

Anirban, Srimad. 1992. *Upaniṣad Prasaṅga, Part 5: Kauṣītaki Upaniṣhad*. Bardhaman: University of Bardhhaman.

Banerji, S. C. 1992 (1978). *Tantra in Bengal: A Study in its Origin, Development and Influence*. New Delhi: Manohar Publications.

Baumer, Bettina Sharada. 2019. *The Yoga of Netra Tantra: Third Eye and Overcoming Death*. Shimla: Indian Institute of Advanced Study.

Beck, Guy L. 1993. *Sonic Theology*. Columbia: University of South Carolina Press.

Carman, Taylor. 2008. *Merleau-Ponty*. London: Routledge.

Chakrabarty, Dipesh. 1993. "Deferral of (A) Colonial Modernity: Public Debates on Domesticity in British Bengal." *History Workshop* 36, no. 1: 1–34.

Das, Jyotirlal, ed. 2018. *Kubjikātantram*. Kolkata: Nababharat Publishers.
Flood, Gavin. 2006. *The Tantric Body: The Secret Tradition of Hindu Religion*. London: I.B. Tauris.
Flueckiger, Joyce Burkhalter. 2020. *Material Acts in Everyday Hindu Worlds*. Albany: SUNY Press.
Fruzzetti, Lina M. 1990. *The Gift of a Virgin: Women, Marriage, and Ritual in a Bengali Society*. Delhi: Oxford University Press.
Fruzzetti, Lina M., and Akos Ostor. 1984. *Kinship and Ritual in Bengal: Anthropological Essays*. New Delhi: South Asian Publishers.
Ghosh, Radhamadhav. 2018. *Bṛhat Kṛṣṇalīlā Sārāvali*. Kolkata: Akshay Library.
Guillén, Beatriz. 2016. "Ramanujan, the Man who saw the Number Pi in Dreams." *Open Mind*. Accessed December 13, 2019. https://www.bbvaopenmind.com/en/science/leading-figures/ramanujan-the-man-who-saw-the-number-pi-in-dreams/.
Gupta, Mahendranath. 2008. *Sri Sri Rāmakṛṣṇa Kathāmṛta*. Kolkata: Shubham.
Haq, Kaiser. 2015. *The Triumph of the Snake Goddess*. Cambridge, MA: Harvard University Press.
Hayes, Glen A. 2000. "The Necklace of Immortality: A Seventeenth-Century Vaiṣṇava Sahajiyā Text." In *Tantra in Practice*, edited by David Gordon White, 308–25. Princeton: Princeton University Press.
Helmreich. Stefan. 2008. "An Anthropologist Underwater: Immersive Soundscapes, Submarine Cyborgs, and Transductive Ethnography." *American Ethnologist* 34, no. 4: 621–41.
Hirschkind, Charles. 2006. *The Ethical Soundscape: Cassette Sermons and Islamic Counterpublics*. New York: Columbia University Press.
Houtman, Dick, and Birgit Meyer, eds. 2012. *Things: Religion and the Question of Materiality (The Future of the Religious Past)*. New York: Fordham University Press.
Kanigel, Robert. 1991. *The Man Who Knew Infinity: A Life of the Genius Ramanujan*. New York: Washington Square Press.
Lakshmanjoo, Swami. 2011. *Vijñāna Bhairava: The Manual for Self-Realization*. New Delhi: Munshiram Manoharlal.
Lidke, Jeffrey. 2015. "Dancing Forth the Divine Beloved: A *Tāntric* Semiotics of the Body as Rasa in Classical Indian Dance." *Sutra Journal* 1, no. 2: 1–11.
Mann, Richard D. 2014. "Material Culture and the Study of Hinduism and Buddhism." *Religion Compass* 8, no. 8: 264–73.
Matilal, Bimal Krishna. 2017 (2001). *The Word and the World: India's Contribution to the Study of Language*. New Delhi: Oxford University Press.
McCutcheon, Russell T., ed. 1999. *The Insider/Outsider Problem in the Study of Religion: A Reader*. London and New York: Continuum.
McDaniel, June. 2004. *Offering Flowers, Feeding Skulls: Popular Goddess Worship in West Bengal*. Oxford: University Press.

Obeyesekere, Gananath. 2008. "Medusa's Hair: An Essay on Personal Symbols and Religious Experience." In *A Reader in the Anthropology of Religion*, edited by Michael Lambek, 356–67. Oxford: Blackwell Publishing.

Olivelle, Patrick. 1998. *The Early Upanisads: Annotated Text and Translation*. New Delhi: Munshiram Manoharlal.

Omkarnathdev, Sitaramdas. 1990. *Sri Omkārnāth-Racanāvalī, Volume 10*. Kolkata: Akhil Bharata Joyguru Sampraday.

———. 2012. *Sri Sri Guru Gitā*. Kolkata: Sriguru Prakashan.

Openshaw, Jeanne. 2002. *Seeking Bauls of Bengal*. Cambridge: Cambridge University Press.

Padoux, Andre. 1992. *Vāc: The Concept of the Word in Selected Hindu Tantras*. Delhi: Sri Satguru Publications.

Ratie, Isabelle. 2017. "An Indian Debate on Optical Reflections and its Metaphysical Implications." In *Indian Epistemology and Metaphysics*, edited by Joerg Tuske, 207–40. Maryland: Bloomsbury.

Sarbadhikary, Sukanya. 2019. "Shankh-er Shongshar, Afterlife Everyday: Religious Experience of the Evening Conch and Goddesses in Bengali Hindu Homes." *Religions* 10, no. 53: 1–19.

Silburn, Lilian. 1988. *Kuṇḍalinī: The Energy of the Depths*. Albany: SUNY Press.

Sinha, Kaliprasanna. 1987. *Mahābhārata, Volume 2*. Tulikalam: Kolkata.

Tagore, Rabindranath. 1993 [1910]. *Gītabitān*. Kolkata: Visvabharati Granthanavibhaga.

Tarkatirtha, Hemantakumar, ed. 2013. *Mātṛkābhedtantram*. Kolkata: Nababharat Publishers.

Thakur, Rajesh Kumar. 2016. *Mathematics in Religion*. Rupa: New Delhi.

Wolf, Richard K. 2014. *The Voice in the Drum: Music, Language, and Emotion in Islamicate South Asia*. Urbana: University of Illinois Press.

White, David Gordon. 1996. *The Alchemical Body: Siddha Traditions in Medieval India*. Chicago: University of Chicago Press.

4

WhatsApp Bagalāmukhī!

Social Life and Experiences of a Tantric Goddess

SRAVANA BORKATAKY-VARMA

Bagalāmukhī is one of the ten great-goddesses (*daśa mahāvidyās*) in Śākta Tantra. She is also worshipped in pragmatic transactions that ultimately foster meaningful experiences and enhance personal devotion. And all this may happen online! WhatsApp, a social media platform, is transforming religious experiences by providing unprecedented access to Bagalāmukhī's puja space and ritual specialists; in this way, social media are a pathway to and a space for ritual engagement with the larger world of Śākta Tantra. In this chapter, Bagalāmukhī rituals and devotion are represented in varied media: oral (structured interviews and casual conversations), textual (devotional and ritual texts in vernacular languages), and digital (websites and WhatsApp). While this study analyzes all these media, special focus is placed on digital media to represent continuity and innovation as devotees interact with the goddess and her experts. While Tantric studies generally work with premodern textual data as their conventional canon, the study of devotees' relationships with the goddess Bagalāmukhī and her ritual experts using WhatsApp suggests a new avenue to explore contemporary, lived Tantric religion using non-textual, oral-aural, and digital-textual sources.

While some scholars and insiders question the legitimacy of digital experiences as religious, the informants who participated in this study do not, and a *selective* application of Ann Taves' ascriptive model for religious experience[1], in which "experiences deemed religious" are affirmed (Taves 2011, 14), legitimates devotees' statements as significant. Taves' ascription model assumes experiences are not inherently religious or nonreligious; rather, they are designated as religious or not by the experiencer. In this way, diverse experiences may be deemed religious—mystical, spiritual, transcendental, and so forth. Using the lens of the ascription model, comparisons are made to show that certain similar features are shared outside of a "pure" or normative religious experience framework. Taves importantly critiques *sui generis* models of religion that argue only experiences deemed religious by authorities are genuinely religious and worthy of studies. Tantra studies scholars might be tempted to dismiss Taves' model, citing cognitive reductionism and claiming her data from American Pentecostalism invalidates interpretative use for non-Western sources. I will demonstrate, however, that Taves' embrace and valuation of experience opens new avenues for analysis and data collection. This will be accomplished by analyzing experiences among Bagalāmukhī devotees.

While I conducted field research on Bagalāmukhī, I came upon her complex relationship with devotees when they engage her and her ritual officiants on the digital platform of WhatsApp. On-the-ground research was conducted over two years (2017–2019) in Kāmākhyā, Assam, India, but I continue to gather digital data using WhatsApp and by staying in touch with my informants remotely. My use of digital research methods is informed by the scholarship of Heinz Scheifinger (2013, 2020), Christopher Helland (2013), Heidi Campbell (2013, 2017), and Knut Lundby (2013).

To situate my positionality in short, I am a scholar-practitioner of Śākta Tantra from Assam. I adopted an "insider with an outsider lens" perspective, which enabled easier acceptance into these tight-knit communities than possibly an "outsider" anthropologist might receive. My ethnographic methods included conversations with devotees and ritual specialists, participant observation and recorded face-to-face interactions both in person and remotely (i.e., using WhatsApp), and a standard questionnaire. The boundary between the participants and the observer (i.e., this author) was not rigidly dichotomous. Great care was taken to sift through and separate the disclosed religious world of the devotees and the way the author experienced the religious world of the devotees.

Most of the interviews cited below were conducted during the annual Ambubachi Mela in 2019. Attended by approximately two million visitors (*The Diplomat*, 2019), Ambubachi Mela is a three-day, monsoon-season festival celebrating the yearly menstruation of the goddess Kāmākhyā.[2] This large devotee population is gathered not only in one physical place, but devotees also use smart phones widely, making WhatsApp a powerful tool for data collection. The questionnaire that was circulated to informants during the festival consisted of the following questions: Have you heard of the goddess Bagalāmukhī? If yes, have you either performed Bagalāmukhī puja based on requests received on WhatsApp, or requested Bagalāmukhī puja, or know people who have requested Bagalāmukhī puja via WhatsApp? If yes, what was the purpose behind the puja? Where was the puja performed (temple or house or a community center or cremation ground)? Have you sent pictures and/or recordings of the puja via WhatsApp? Have you ever used WhatsApp live video to share the puja with the devotees? Were you happy with the results of the puja?

As I worked through the above inquires, the boundaries between the insider and the outsider often blurred. Through my ethnographic interactions, I navigated between the world of the scholar and the religious devotees I engaged with. These intersubjective experiences compelled deep self-reflections on how I experienced the religious world of the devotees.

In this chapter, I will first explore the nature of religious experience in the history of the study of religion, making an argument that Taves' theories fruitfully interpret South Asian devotees' interaction with Bagalāmukhī in a digital realm. I will also survey the important disciplinary shifts in digital religious studies that enable this very project. Next, the section titled "Bagalā from Myths to Screens" discusses the growing popularity of online Bagalāmukhī pujas and other ritual services that expand on traditional depictions and appeals to this goddess. The subsequent section, "WhatsApp, Bagalā!," focuses on devotees' use of the social media platform WhatsApp and what they declare to be advantages to online religious services. In other words, I am using the emic category of religion, taking into account what devotees and ritual experts consider to be religious to study the religious space of Bagalāmukhī *while* I adopt the etic lens of experience, to analyze the experiences of the devotees. Finally, I conclude by examining the devotees' "experiences deemed religious"; that is, innovative, discrete interactions with the goddess. Further, these interactions over time may transition into more conventional understandings of "religious experiences." In short, experiences of the sacred through digital platforms for some can be as effective and transformative as the experience of the divine in offline, physical spaces such as temples, altars, and pilgrimage sites.

Mapping the Encounters

Religions consistently enable humans to "make contact" with something superhuman, something extraordinaire, transcending time and space, and this is reflected in scholarship on religions. Martin Riesebrodt, somewhat echoing Milford Spiro's (1966) religion as "an institution consisting of culturally patterned interaction with culturally postulated superhuman beings," defines religion as a "complex of practices that are based on the premise of the existence of superhuman powers, whether personal or impersonal, that are generally invisible" (Riesebrodt 2009, 74–75). Jeffery Kripal argues that religion enables contact with the "Other"; it is "any set of established stories, ritual performances, mind disciplines, bodily practices, and social institutions that have been built up over time around extreme encounters with some anomalous presence, energy, hidden order, or power that is experienced as radically Other or More" (Kripal 2014, 94). Religions enable humans to glimpse and recognize that Other-than-human via religious experience.

But what is "religious experience"? And what makes such experiences authentic? Wayne Proudfoot (1985) made a pivotal methodological intervention, arguing that scholars must aim for "explanatory reductionism" as opposed to "descriptive reductionism" in which scholars of religions painstakingly describe any religious experience precisely as the experiencer reports it and only interpret it after such careful description. Scholars must document devotees' experiences without passing judgment. From this perspective, digital Bagalāmukhī and her followers are revealed as a vibrant development in Tantra and goddess worship.

But what is digital religion, and how can scholars study this innovative religious context? The topics for the study of religion and media are often divided into three categories: producers of content, media itself, and the effects. Horace Newcomb proposes that media culture be considered as a "cultural forum" where important ideas are presented, discussed, and evaluated (Newcomb and Hirsch 1976); I will extend this category to include social media engagements with the goddess Bagalāmukhī and her media artifacts. Religion and media analysis initially documented and analyzed the effects of religious broadcasting and televangelism in the 1950s, as pioneered by Barry Parker (1955) and continued in 1985 by Gary Gaddy and David Pritchard. By 1993, as explained by Hoover and Kim (2016, 122), the focus of these studies shifted away from televised sermons toward "practices and experiences of individuals in making religious and spiritual meanings," though this was rooted in "American religious culture, including its disestablishment, its pluralism, its adaptability, and its aspirations to individual empowerment" (122).

The field of religion and media today interacts and overlaps in a wide range of religions—well beyond American Christianity—and on multiple platforms (websites, social networking platforms like Facebook and Instagram, and encrypted platforms like WhatsApp). These democratic and diffuse shifts lead to newfound individual religious autonomy—"Individuals today increasingly think of their religiosity as an ongoing project of constructing an ideal faith or spirituality suited to their biography and their own needs" (Hoover and Kim 2016, 122). Autonomy as a value is on the rise, and people are seeking new platforms for religious experience and expression. In this digital realm, religion rapidly becomes a marketplace, leading to structural and economic changes; for example, when folks interact with a goddess via technological platforms, or when Bagalā goes on-screen online.

Traditional structuralist and functionalist approaches fail in these new contexts. The rapidly growing academic field of digital religion explores how living religious practices are impacted by digital media and documents the significant changes occurring due to that interaction. The digital is more than a medium of technology, for it affects the ways people seek religions and do religions. As such, the religious and the arena of spirituality are changing. New phenomena generated by digital culture must embody culture, authenticity, authority, and experience(s)—all issues for which the term "religion" can stand (Hoover 2012). The digital encourages generative encounters in which novel forms of religious experiences arise—for example, through video games like "The Durga Puja Mystery," or by connecting faith through the use of virtual reality (VR)—which brings us back to Taves' claim that there can hardly be a single and universal paradigm to define *a* religious experience.

Bagalā from Myths to Screens

The so-called dot-com movement started in the mid- to late 1990s, initiating a shift in the ways cultural technologies, including religion, are transmitted, stored, cataloged, and disseminated. Helland (2007) proposes a distinction between "religion online" and "online religion." Online religion essentially represents how the fluid and flexible nature of the Internet allows for new forms of religiosity and lived religious practice online. Within this larger space, issues about tradition, authority, authenticity, and efficacy are fiercely debated. What is the actual influence of the digital on religions and religiosity? This investigative lens is called digital religion.

Studies on the Internet and religious traditions have flourished in recent decades. During the 1990s and 2000s, scholarship on religion and the Internet focused on basic questions How is religion represented in new media environments? How do religious groups use new media to serve their causes and needs? What challenges do new media technologies pose to traditional religious communities and institutions? (Lövheim and Campbell 2017, 6). The next phase of research was followed by more nuanced questions about identity and community-making via online interactions and networks.

Scholarship on Hinduism and the Internet addresses a wide range of relevant topics to this chapter. Emilia Bachrach (2014) focuses on the growing presence of gurus and their impact online. Vinay Lal (2014), Sriram Mohan (2015), and Sahana Udupa (2015) discuss cyberspace and Hindus, diasporic and Indian residents. Maya Warrier (2014) concentrates on the online presence of bhakti. Xenia Zeiler (2018) describes online Durgā puja, and I recently explored how the Internet perpetuates normative understandings of Tantra (Borkataky-Varma 2019). Nicole Karapanagiotis (2010) explores the virtual sacred space in the context of Vaishnava Hindus and asks some pertinent questions around rules and protocols of ritual purity. Let us turn to some specific media artifacts. Websites like onlinepuja.com, shubhpuja.com, onlineprashad.com, and epuja.co.in, as well as temple webpages like emeenakshi.org and kamakhya-temple.com, all bring the Hindu divine to the screens. Furthermore, pujas are facilitated online daily through social media platforms like Facebook live stream. Prominent examples include the Kali Mandir Ramakrishna Ashram and Puja with Mangaldeep. Facebook Messenger and WhatsApp, in particular, are growing in popularity for securing ritual and worship services. The popularity of such digital pujas is not just marketed to Hindus, for they appeal to non-Hindus as well. In 2017, the widely publicized teen-music icon Miley Cyrus performed Lakṣmī puja during the Super Bowl (NDTV 2017). Other celebrities like Priyanka Chopra Jonas and Nick Jonas are tagged under ritual testimonials found on shubhpuja.com.

To appreciate the scope of pujas on the Internet, examining one particular website can be informative. Shubhpuja.com was founded by Saumyaa Vardhan, a graduate from Imperial College of London, and according to her website profile under "Our Craftsmen": "She has previously worked in London for over 7 years as a Mergers & Acquisition executive with KPMG London, EY London, and Rolls-Royce UK. Vardhan picked up not just a valuable education and top corporate experience along her journey; but also collected a maze of life experiences whilst retaining her belief in ancient Hindu philosophy. Honing her focus toward this philosophy, Vardhan founded Shubhpuja.com in 2013" (Shubhpuja n.d.). Vardhan's degrees are listed on the website, and they include "Advanced degree in Vedic Astrology, Numerology (Western & Vedic) & Vaastu Shastra / Feng Shui" (Shubhpuja n.d.). In 2018, five years after the site's inception, shubhpuja.com became the top Vedic-spirituality-based online venture, and 500 professionals, including Vedic Brahmins, make up their team. Tapping into a USD 30 billion USD Indian spiritual market, the site appears extensively in leading media channels and newspapers. The *New York Times* named subhpuja.com the "Uber for God" (Shubhpuja n.d.).

The role of smartphones and the expansion of the digital spiritual market in India today is being studied by scholars like Kathinka Frøystad (2019) and Varuni Bhatia (2020). Bhatia follows the circulation of visual imagery of god Śani on the Internet, where Hindu devotees can not only find ritual experts, but also follow rituals and listen to mantras and stories all at the click of the button. Bhatia succinctly concludes her essay with these words: "In doing so, virality fundamentally contributes to the vitality and lifeness of the sacred object within digital Hinduism" (2020, 16). Now let us turn to the goddess Bagalāmukhī, whom we find readily dwelling on the Internet, and explore the larger question of religious experiences.

Goddess Bagalāmukhī is also known as Pītāmbarā-devī, "The Goddess Dressed in Yellow Robes." Like all *mahāvidyās* (a group of ten wisdom goddesses), Bagalāmukhī has several mythological story sequences. According to one of these, in the *Kṛta Yuga* (the first cosmic age), an incredible storm threatened to destroy the universe. Viṣṇu was disturbed. He went to a sacred pond, prayed to the goddess Tripurasundarī, and undertook austerities. Tripurasundarī brought forth Bagalāmukhī, who calmed the storm (Kinsley 1997, 199). Another myth, however, is the most popular among Ambubachi festival participants: The demon Madan undertook austerities that won him the boon of exceptional speech (*vāk siddhi*). He started abusing his powers and killing people. The gods invoked Bagalāmukhī, and she removed Madan's boon by taking hold of his tongue and paralyzing (*stambhana*) his speech. More generally, Bagalāmukhī is associated with "supernatural or magical powers, the ability to immobilize and attract others" (Kinsley 1997, 197). Paralyzing is one result of the magic rituals I describe in the next section.

Materials on magic, especially those circulating in the twentieth century, are published widely in Indian vernacular languages. Some publications contain extensive Sanskrit root texts, and others are entirely vernacular except for mantras. The main concern of these texts is magic rituals, rites that cause specific, usually aggressive, changes in the world, though texts may also contain devotional hymns, mystic mathematical diagrams, medical remedies, and even sleight-of-hand tricks. These sources should be considered secondary interpretations of prior Sanskrit texts; namely, what Aaron Ullrey calls "Magic Tantras" (Ullrey 2016). Almost all these publications have caveats at their beginning (and sometimes in text boxes throughout) that absolve printers, publishers, and authors from liability if successful rituals cause negative results or if rites fail and thereby cause harm to practitioners.

According to Ullrey, magic *tantras* are texts whose primary concern is pragmatic rituals. Three categories constitute magic rituals in South Asia: (1) the six results (*ṣaṭkarman*), (2) fantastic feats and enchanted items (*kautukakarman, indrajāla*), and (3) conjuring of (mostly female) entities who grant wealth, spiritual expedients, and worldly power (*yakṣinīsādhana*). The six results include pacification, murder, bewildering, eradication, dissent, attraction, and so forth. Fantastic feats include alchemy, erotic augmentation, revivifying the dead, and more. Enchanted items locate hidden treasure, enable the sorcerer to walk upon the water, and may divine the future. Conjuring calls forth and manifests deities or spirits, mostly female, who grant the petitioner wealth and powers (Ullrey 2016, 18–19).

The *Yakṣinī Bhūtinī Sādhanā aur Devi Siddhiyāṃ* is a modern book of magic in Hindi with select Sanskrit quotes and mantras. A long section within the book is about perfecting goddesses (*Devī siddhiyāṃ*), and Bagalāmukhī is the fourth goddess among Tārā, Dhumāvatī, Bhuvaneśvarī, Bagalāmukhī, Mātaṃgī, Chinnamastā, Ṣoḍaśī, Ucchiśṭa Cāṇḍālinī, Ucchiṣṭa Gaṇeśa, Dhandā, Nityā, Karṇa Piśacinī, Haridrā Gaṇeśa, Annupūrṇā, and Durgā.[3] Repetition of the mantra "*Oṃ hrīṃ bagalāmukhī sarvaduṣṭānāṃ vācaṃ mukhaṃ padaṃ stambhaya jihvāṃ kīlaya buddhiṃ vināśaya hlīṃ oṃ svāḥā*" invokes Bagalāmukhī directly (Śobhanā 2004, 44). The mantra stresses her power to immobilize (*stambhaya*), an enemy's body and speech, to bind his tongue and destroy his mind.

Bagalāmukhī destroys an enemy by halting his speech, but also, it appears, by slandering his or her very name, presumably casting vile speech back upon the slanderer. Recall the goddess grabbing demon Madan's tongue to stop his mighty speech powers. One thousand repetitions on a rosary made of turmeric or some generally yellow rosary is prescribed to please the goddess. In this text, as in most depictions, Bagalāmukhī is portrayed as a furious goddess, and she is accompanied by a yantra (a magic diagram) with intersecting triangles and a dot at its center, surrounded by two rings of lotus flowers, numbering eight and sixteen petals, respectively. Opposite the yantra is a line drawing of the goddess restraining a human-headed figure by the tongue as she prepares to strike him with a club while water rushes about above him, connecting the story of Madan and the tale of calming a cosmic flood. She displays a flag inscribed with a swan (see figure 4.1).

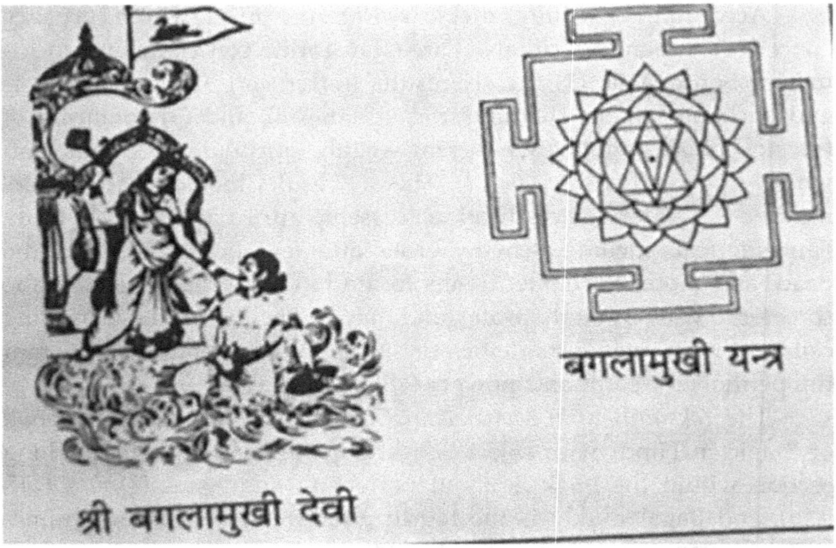

Figure 4.1. On the left, the anthropomorphic representation of the Goddess; on the right, her cosmic-geometric diagram or yantra. *Source*: Śobhanā (2004: 45).

Specific oblations to affect the six results (*ṣaṭkarman*) are also prescribed as the domain of Bagalāmukhī. Below are a few examples (see Śobhanā 2004):

> Honey (*madhu*)[4], ghee (*ghṛya*), and sugar (*śakkar*) mixed with sesame should be oblated to subjugate (*vaś*) humans.
>
> Creating discord (*kalaha*) [i.e., *vidveṣaṇa*]—Mix neem leaves into oil [mustard oil][5]. Oblating this causes mutual conflict [between and among the victims].
>
> Immobilizing Enemies (*śatru stambhana*)—Palm leaf, salt, and turmeric root [emend *halkī* to *haldī*] are oblated to cause the immobilization of an enemy. Aloe (*agar*), mustard seed (*rāi*), buffalo ghee, bdellium (*guggula*) are oblated at night to bring about the swift destruction of enemies.
>
> Eradication (*uccāṭana*)—Vulture and crow feathers are mixed with mustard oil which are oblated into a funeral pyre (*citā par havan*), causing eradication of enemies.

A large majority of the devotees and almost all priests either contacted or interviewed mention the *Ṣaṭkarman* rituals to be central to Bagalāmukhī ritual space. Informants describe the goddess Bagalāmukhī as wearing yellow and having the power to paralyze (*stambhana*) speech, movement, and activities of the enemy. At the same time, she may grant the devotee the power of exceptional speech (*vāk siddhi*) by which the opponent may be defeated. Lived religion and printed magic sources are thereby consistent and connected. Paralyzing the enemy's speech while at the same time sharpening the devotees' tongue is an interesting interpretive move. Nevertheless, it was consistent among interviewees and magic sources. When asked why they offer puja to Bagalāmukhī, a wide range of reasons were provided, but all sought to address a dispute: divorce, property quarrel, financial problems, court cases, obstacles in the profession, troublesome in-laws, business deals not materialized due to lack of approval, and so forth. The complexity of the specified problem determined the length of the puja. For example, if the devotee seeks a promotion or to win a business deal, one to two days of puja is recommended and deemed enough. However, if the believer is caught in a web of disputes—property, marital, contractual, and so forth—extensive pujas are performed over three to fourteen days.

A quick Internet search for "Bagalamukhi puja" yields a few website results. Zeenews.com, a popular Indian news channel, under their program *Manthan*, aired an entire segment titled "Bagalāmukhī: History and Benefits of Praying to Her" containing the following description: "Bagalamukhi is one of the ten mahavidyas (great wisdom goddesses) in Hinduism. Bagalamukhi Devi smashes the devotee's misconceptions and delusions (or the devotee's enemies) with her cudgel. She is also known as Pitambara Maa in North India" (YouTube 2014). In another leading newspaper, *The Times of India*, an author describes the results Bagalāmukhī may confer:

> Removes the debts and enhances prosperity at home. • Fear of enemies is removed and the devotee experiences a great degree of comfort in mind. The enemies will no more be able to confront you. They will grow powerless when trying to act against you and their vicious plots will turn futile and ineffective. [. . .] • The devotee triumphs over lawsuits and succeeds in quarrels and competitions. • If there are fluctuations in your life, this mantra can help balance the positive and negative aspects and establish harmony in home and life. (Sathya Narayanan 2018)

Her worship remedies physical and magical attacks but also grants prosperity. According to Shivology.com, her puja "will remove the effects of black magic. Maa Baglamukhi is known to resolve ongoing court cases and all legal matters. It protects you from your enemies. You will get the divine grace and blessings of Devi Baglamukhi. This puja will help you to get good health and prosperity. It will also help you to remove all the obstacles from your success path" (Shivology.com 2018).

Devotees can place an order online from various websites for Bagalāmukhī puja. The prices are steep. Shubhpuja.com charges $196.98 for one day, and for seven days the cost is $459.63. Almost all websites post long testimonials and screenshots of message exchanges from Facebook, Instagram, and WhatsApp. From Goa, India, one devotee writes:

> I can't thank Shubhpuja enough for the issues they have solved for me. I consulted shubhpuja.com for a complete diagnostic solution. I came to consult them after spending lacs of rupees (approx. 2.36 lacs) on a personal problem for which I could not find a solution for the last two years. [. . .]. First, they scientifically checked my horoscope and I was very surprised at the precision of their analysis upto each date. [. . .]. I did not believe in these things earlier. But decided to give it a try as I was finding no solutions for my problem. They organized the puja which was customized for my requirements. It was very professionally organized with top ingredients and pandits. For the first time in my life I could feel the vibrations within my body through mantra chanting when I sat for the puja. [. . .]. All of a sudden there were situations that developed on their own, which nobody including professionals had not thought about in my case. It happened on its own and was a solution created by the higher force for me. [. . .]. The problem could have costed me minimum 5–7 lacs more and would have persisted for another 7–10 years. I have saved unbelievable amount of money just through a consultation, small vedic pujas and colour therapy solution suggested by Shubhpuja. [. . .] Thank you for truly changing my life for good. (Shubhpuja.com)

Analysis of customer testimonials and reviews on other popular websites (including onlinepuja.org, onlinetemple.com, and divine-rudraksha.com) reveals sophisticated target marketing that appeals to a wide, global audience. The next example addresses the Indian diaspora.

> NRI people [Non-Resident Indians] performing a Puja in a proper way either becomes impossible or otherwise exorbitantly expensive. It is due to these situations that a concept of Online Pujas has been invented wherein a client residing abroad can book a Puja through our Online Puja service providers. Once the puja is booked, the client can get the Puja performed on their behalf that too in a perfect way and at affordable cost. Any Puja that is ordered Online is performed by a team of Brahmins (usually at least 3–5 Brahmins). Out of them, one of the Brahmins takes a "Sankalp" [intention] in client's name who has booked the Puja and then he performs all the recitals and rituals that were supposed to have been done by the person if he was himself physically present in the Puja. This means that the Brahmin who has taken the sankalp virtually represents the client who has booked the puja during the entire puja procedure. (divine-rudraksha.com 2016)

Such websites meet NRIs' needs in innovative ways (Borkataky-Varma 2019). Aggressive rituals such as *vaśikaraṇ* (subjugation, especially "love magic") and *sammohan* (hypnosis) are widely popular online, though in prior times they could be ordered through mail correspondence. Lee Siegel (2014) provides detailed testimonials and experiences about sorcerers and hypnotists operating online and over the phone. While discussing a sorcerer named Swamiji Mohan Kamacharan, Siegel lists Kamacharan's self-description: "Specialist in love and other problems, gold medalist of Tantra winner, and fulfill all your Love desire today. Get your true Love now and keep him or her faithful and devoted to you as long as your like" (Siegel 2014, 37).

Describing the effectiveness of online pujas, divine-rudraksha.com states the following: "We are pleased to declare that the online Pujas have already benefited a large number of people which is confirmed by the very fact that the same people have given repeated bookings for other Pujas after their initial order [. . .] beneficial and effective is further ascertained by large number of feedbacks and testimonials sent by our grateful and esteemed clients" (divine-rudraksha.com 2016). Social media platforms, especially WhatsApp, as we shall see, enable even greater engagement among devotees and between ritualists and clients compared to the websites above. This greater engagement using social media and messaging applications increases the notion of greater access to the goddess, which further enhances "experiences deemed religious."

WhatsApp, Bagalā!

Messaging applications like WhatsApp, Viber, and WeChat are extremely popular among smartphone users worldwide. WhatsApp blends a short messaging service (SMS) and social networking. Users send instant messages but also create and share user groups, called WhatsApp groups, that spread widely. These groups are used for varied non-text purposes such as sharing images, audio, and video messages and media. Duncan Omanga (2019), in the context of Kenya, writes: "WhatsApp and WhatsApp groups have lately become important loci of sociality and political 'talk,' from mundane, routine messaging to more organized, structured groups with a more or less formal agenda. [. . .] As [a] social media platform, it is capable of convening groups, for both spirited debates and routine conversations with a typical WhatsApp group ranging from 3 to a maximum of 256 participants" (Omanga 2019, 176). In 2019, WhatsApp reached 400 million users in India (Singh 2019). Sharing pictures and videos of festivals, temple visits, pilgrimages, and pujas is common. What about the goddess Bagalāmukhī on WhatsApp? My ethnography reveals that pujas are ordered over WhatsApp. All names are changed to protect the identity of the respondent, except if the name was published by a website. According to one priest respondent:

> When you are stuck in a court case or a serious dispute, you cannot come to the temple. You may not be in Guwahati or India for that matter. What do you do? You can WhatsApp your personal details like name, *gotra*, date of birth, court date, the case details, and desired outcome. Depending of the desired outcome I will tell you what puja is needed, for how long, and substances required. For example, if

> you want *vaśikaraṇ* or *māraṇ* I will need hair, nail clippings or some fabric from the person's personal attire. You can courier that to me. I will tell you the cost of the puja and you transfer the money to my bank. My account can take money from anywhere in the world. After the puja I will send you a video of the puja and if needed I will courier you a *tabiz* (amulet) and/or ash or dried fruits. After receiving the package, you WhatsApp me and I will tell you what to do with the stuff I have sent you.[6]

All interviewees in Kāmākhyā preferred to directly order pujas using WhatsApp rather than indirectly ordering rituals requested through online portals. Ordering via a website, as opposed to direct WhatsApp communication with a ritualist, creates an additional layer of separation from the priest beyond physical distance. WhatsApp is perceived to be more intimate and personalized than webpages. Contact details are saved in WhatsApp's phone book, and profile pictures appear next to contacts' names, though some users prefer not to display these. There are options to video call and/or voice call. At the time when the interviews were conducted and even now, it is true for most people (in this context) that the riding assumption while using WhatsApp is that the messages are encrypted. Recent findings, however, have proven to be otherwise. But that is outside the scope of this chapter. Users feel more privacy and, thereby, comfort than other communication services. Informants report their "secret" is safe on WhatsApp, which is especially important when addressing or requesting aggressive magic rites. Pronita Sarkar, a twenty-seven-year-old devotee, said:

> I use only WhatsApp to speak to *deo* [priest]. Black magic was performed on me by my husband's family and because of that my husband wanted a divorce, but I have not left the house. I also cannot come every day to the temple because my husband and his family will know that I am getting puja [Bagalāmukhī] done. *Deo* sends me puja videos. After I receive the blessings via the video, I delete them. *Deo* has given me *tābīj* [amulet] which again I wear hidden from my family. My relationship with my husband has improved a lot, but I think the best solution is for us to live separately from my in-laws. *Deo* has said that *devī* [Bagalāmukhī] will grant my wish, soon. I must have faith and patience.[7]

Stories like Pronita's use of WhatsApp come up repeatedly in the field. It is of no surprise, therefore, that most popular online puja websites now have a dedicated WhatsApp tab, showing that WhatsApp is influencing older, stand-alone, web-based ritual commerce sites. These websites also publish screenshots of WhatsApp text exchanges between the customer (devotee) and the provider (priest) to demonstrate the close connections between priests and clients. An entire section of "testimonials" on shubhpuja.com indicates personal conversations like checking weather, health, birthday wishes, festival wishes, and so forth. In addressing the specialists, both men and women (e.g., priest, astrologer, palmist, *vāstu* consultant) as "Uncle" or "Aunty," sharing events as they unfold, there is an important sense of urgency and a feeling of immediacy. Here are some sample threads.

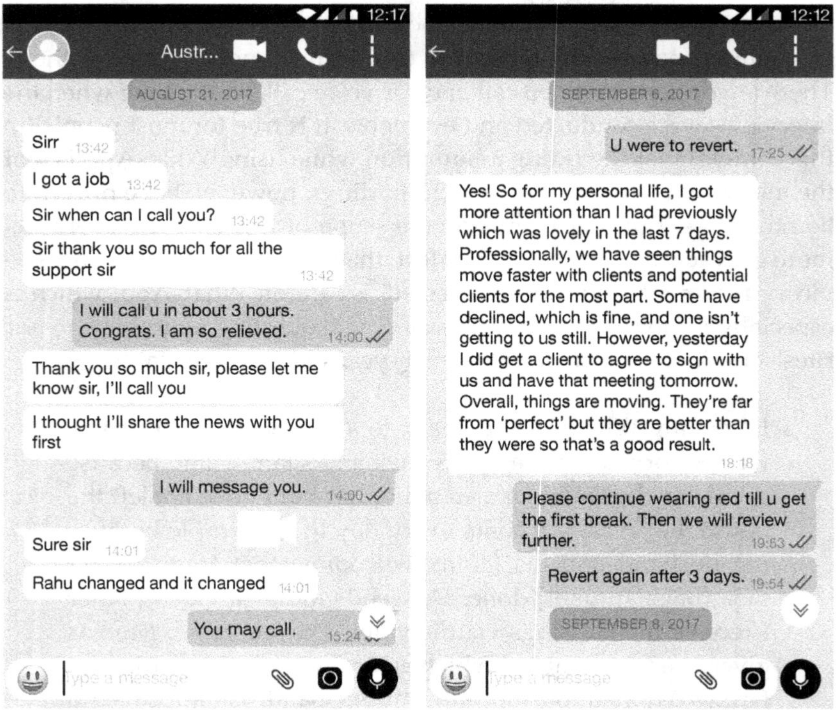

Figure 4.2a and b. Recreation of anonymized WhatsApp conversations between client and ritual specialist. Credit: shubhpuja.com, accessed on June 21, 2020.

Experiencing Bagalā on Screens

We opened this chapter with the question of religious "experience." How does "experience" operate in WhatsApp? In the context of Hinduism, experiences of the divine have been extensively written in the larger concept of *darśan* (in Hindi; *darśana* in Sanskrit). *Darśan* means "sacred vision" or "auspicious sight," sometimes achieved as the end product of pilgrimage, sometimes through seeing a famous or holy person or persons. Pilgrims are sometimes called *darśaniyas*—those who come to see (Vidyarthi 1961, 84–85). Diana Eck (1985) explains *darśan* whereby a Hindu does not say, "I am going to worship," but instead says, "I am going for a *darśan*," or, "I am going to take *darśan*." In this section, I am asking the reader to shift from considering *darśan* as *only* a physical-visual centric experience to also considering plural forms of seeking *darśan*.[8] That is the vision of the "divine" on screens is equally powerful, at least for certain devotees.

In the context of ISKCON (International Society for Krishna Consciousness) and online *darśan*, Nicole Karapanagiotis (2019) concludes that there is no qualitative difference between being physically present in front of the deity in the temple and experiencing Krishna online. By extension, online rituals are just as effective and authentic as those solicited and performed in public. This is not completely settled, however. Questions of authenticity for online puja appear consistently in conversations with informants, and while the digital medium is rapidly growing, there are occasional doubts.

Heinz Scheifinger succinctly investigates *darśan* in online puja, and though he is not referring to WhatsApp in particular, his observations are instructive.

> The practice of *darshan*—the key feature of puja—can be successfully mediated via the Internet. While the other senses may not be stimulated in the way that they are when conducting puja in the offline setting, the importance of the sense of sight remains in an online puja. In both cases, a devotee is able to see and be seen by the deity. Therefore, in this crucial respect, the puja is not altered radically in its online-form [. . .] Hindu puja rituals that are performed online are not fundamentally different from traditional forms of the ritual and hence possess efficacy. (Scheifinger 2013, 126)

Darśan experiences online are perceived to be heightened, rather than lessened as one might initially expect. WhatsApp, likewise, heightens experiences by mediating increased intimacy between priest and client, let alone goddess and devotee, on the social media platform.

Experiencing a ritual through synchronous or asynchronous WhatsApp videos may lead to an enhanced ritual experience since it can foster greater intimacy, but also, paradoxically, because it creates additional levels of separation. The lack of physical presence keeps devotees and clients insulated from the actual ritual performance, which is especially desired when extreme methods or aggressive results, such as the "six results" (*ṣaṭkarman*), are sought. One couple, Ravi and Lakshita, sought the death of their rival (*māran*) as an outcome, and they sent the so-called enemy's hair to a ritual specialist.[9] They did not ask what and how the hair would be used. They did not request any videos. They did not ask any questions. All that mattered was the result.[10]

The sorcerer and client are intimate enough that the rite may be solicited and ingredients conferred, but the separation between the client and the physical performance of the ritual is crucial. For several months after I heard it in the field, I thought about that couples' statement describing a murder ritual. I repeatedly drew parallels to goats and goat meat, which were instructive in several hypothetical scenarios. In scenario one, a customer goes to a livestock farm, selects a goat, butchers the goat, and consumes the goat meat. In scenario two, a customer selects the goat, the farmer butchers it, and the customer pays for the goat and consumes the goat meat. Scenario three is a religious setting in which a devotee offers a goat sacrifice (*balī*)—in Kāmākhyā, for instance, as is common. He pays for the ritual, but he may choose to be part of the beheading or not. He may also take the meat home or simply ask for it to be distributed among temple priests and priest families or for it to feed the less fortunate. In Ravi and Lakshita's case, they did not want to know "how the sausage was made"; they just cared that the goat was transformed into a "sausage." WhatsApp enables clients to solicit, sponsor, and secure the results of ambivalent rituals, but the service insulates them from the "dirty business" of aggressive rituals, like witnessing how the sausage is made.

Devotees process the experience of interacting with priests and the goddess via social media. Mediated digitally, these are not traditional "religious experiences," but they are "experiences deemed religious" according to Taves' ascription model. Different experiences demonstrated by interviewees show that experiences may shift from (1) a potent, discrete ritual instance, to (2) an understanding of the importance and effectiveness of ritual, and to (3) an abstracted religious experience of the goddess inspiring devotion to her.

For the first category, a specific experience is out of the ordinary, thereby "special." Devotee informants shared and continue to report embodied experiences—such as feeling vibrations or hearing or sensing the presence of the deity, smells, and so forth—during the puja or soon after. These embodied experiences are considered exceptional and intimate, often enhanced by the relationship with the priest and the rites' direct fit to devotees' needs.

Second, as cumulative abstraction, devotees' personalized experience is linked directly to ritual results. Witnessing results' fruition, the devotee makes a cumulative abstraction that the rites are effective. The devotee seeks the puja because she seeks an outcome, and when that outcome is achieved, her faith in the puja intensifies. When outcomes are not achieved, the devotees do not necessarily question the goddess or the puja; instead, they usually pin the blame on themselves. Priyanka Sarma, interviewed during Ambubachi Mela in 2019, had visited Bagalāmukhī every Tuesday at 7:00 a.m. for more than a year. She stated that she had not missed a single Tuesday, no matter what. She had been offering pujas, as suggested by the temple priest, and she wore yellow beads and yellow garments (inner or outer) every day. But her wish had not been fulfilled. When asked how she felt about the lack of benevolence on the part of the goddess, she said, "The fault is mine. I may have done some bad karma and have not accrued enough good deeds for *Mā* [honorific term for the goddess, here Bagalāmukhī] to grant me my wish. This only means I must try harder. Prove myself worthy of her love and blessings."[11]

In 2020, I asked Mohit Sarma, a priest serving in a Kāmākhyā temple to Bagalāmukhī, about failed outcomes, and he swiftly absolved himself: "The devotee did not receive the desired outcome not because of an error in my part of doing the puja or chanting the mantra. The puja failed because either devotee was unclear of his or her intention or lack of faith."[12] Mohit Sarma also alluded to fears about counter-puja offerings: an opposing party might have also performed pujas or performed counter-spells; consequently, pujas must be repeated.

Another devotee describes receiving positive results, and those results increased his belief in the rituals' effectiveness and affirmed his faith in the power of devotion to Bagalāmukhī. Rishi Das is a forty-four-year-old civil contractor who declares he is very happy with the outcomes of worshipping Bagalāmukhī. Das left his government job a few years earlier because he wanted to establish his consulting firm, work for himself, and not be salaried. For the first five years, he did not secure any contracts. His savings were depleted, and there were growing tensions at home. Das consulted several religious experts—including astrologers, palm readers, and sorcerers—and then decided to turn to Bagalāmukhī. Within a year of puja offerings, he landed his first contract. Das was reluctant to give details about what kinds of puja he had been offering and whether he had sent any bodily traces to an officiant, hallmarks of aggressive magic such as nail clippings, hair, or dust from feet or shoes. Since that success, he has been an ardent devotee of Bagalāmukhī. In March of 2020, when I interviewed Das, it was his twenty-third weekly visit to the temple without a single skipped week. He plans to visit the goddess until his last breath.

The combination of abstract experiences and concrete experiences is the third category. The experiences are considered generally "religious" and overlap with traditional conceptions of "the religious." Encountering Bagalāmukhī leads to a devotee performing regular rituals and fosters the belief that the goddess now loves and protects her followers. An American devotee whom I will name June was introduced to Bagalāmukhī through a public, online course taught by a scholar-practitioner. June is not South Asian, nor was she interviewed in Assam, but her experiences of goddess Bagalāmukhī map perfectly onto Taves' concept of abstract experiences. Before the course, June had heard of the *mahāvidyās* and was part of a Kālī *sādhanā* group led by a USA-based guru whose followers were largely westerners. During the course she felt "the call," and, in time, she became a devotee of Bagalāmukhī. As of May 2020, June had not visited any Bagalāmukhī temples or shrines yet, though she expressed her desire to visit India and Kāmākhyā in 2021.

Learning about Bagalāmukhī online was so transformative that June now maintains a Bagalāmukhī shrine in her home, with an image of Bagalāmukhī and a printout of her mantra. June chants the mantra, wears yellow beads, puts a small dot of turmeric (yellow) in her heart center, and is convinced Bagalāmukhī is her *iṣṭa devī* (cherished goddess). June's discrete experiences, which so far have been purely digital, inspired deep devotion leading to abstract religious experience. "Experiences deemed religious" evolve into "religious experiences." In June's case, there is no difference between seeking the goddess, experiencing the goddess, believing in the divine through online platforms, and practicing in the physical temple. The virtual is authentic, as is the physical space of a temple—in our case, Kāmākhyā.

To conclude, while various media have been consulted for this study, special focus was placed on digital media to show instances of continuity and innovation as devotees interact with the goddess and her ritual experts. While Tantric studies is generally focused on the historical and philological analysis of premodern textual data, the study of devotees' relationships with the goddess Bagalāmukhī and their experiences, traveling all the way from the pilgrimage site to the screen of a smartphone, suggest a fruitful avenue to explore contemporary, lived Tantric religious experiences and ritual efficacy, especially in the ever-expanding context of digital media. Ethnographic research on the experience of Tantra in digital worlds provides critical insights into how the scholar and the communities we study negotiate what constitutes the sacred in cross-cultural and transnational virtual spaces.

Notes

1. Debates around religious experiences are not new. Historical to present times, scholars have either considered experience a legitimate category that calls for further research and contemplation or simply a figment of the imagination and, hence, dismissed. Robert Sharf (1998), for example, suggests that the category of "experience" is a modern Western invention and was nowhere to be found in Asian religions (Rao 2018).

2. This chapter exclusively focuses on the experiences of the Bagalāmukhī devotees through the use of websites and WhatsApp at Kāmākhyā. Historic and present-day scholarship on the rituals, Tantric traditions, and politics of power surrounding the temple and this goddess' tradition is not included. The work of scholars like Irene Majo Garigliano (2015), Sundari Johansen Hurwitt (2019), Paolo E. Rosati (2019), Jae Yun Shin (2016), and Hugh Urban (2010) should be consulted to arrive at a better understanding of the place and its relevance in the larger space of Śākta Tantra.

3. Sections of the text was generously shared by Aaron Michael Ullrey.

4. The term *madhu,* including *madhura* and *madhuka,* is to be understood as honey, but there is some ambiguity, as elsewhere these terms may refer to alcoholic liquids.

5. This technique is supported by my interview of Mahakal Tilkdhari in 2020.

6. Kushal Sarma, Priest, Bagalāmukhī temple, Kāmākhyā, interview with the author, June 22, 2019

7. Pronita Sarkar, Devotee, Bagalāmukhī temple, Kāmākhyā, interview with the author, June 20, 2019.

8. On visions as more than optical experiences, see Rao (2019, 191–92).

9. Ravi and Lakshita, Devotees, Bagalāmukhī temple, Kāmākhyā, interview with the author, June 23, 2019.

10. Ullrey confirms that body traces, especially footprint dust and hair, are common ingredients in murder rituals throughout the magic *tantras* (Ullrey 2016, 321–42).

11. Sarma, Devotee, Bagalāmukhī temple, Kāmākhyā, interview with the author, June 20, 2019.

12. Mohit Sarma, in conversation with the author, March 2020.

Bibliography

Bachrach, Emilia. 2014. "Is Guruji Online? Internet Advice Forums and Transnational Encounters in a Vaishnav Sectarian Community." In *Indian Transnationalism Online: New Perspectives on the Diaspora,* edited by Ajaya Kumar Sahoo and Johannes G. de Kruijf, 163–76. New York: Routledge.

Bhatia, Varuni. 2020. "Shani on the Web: Virality and Vitality in Digital Popular Hinduism." *Religions* 11, no. 9: 456. https://doi.org/10.3390/rel11090456.

Borkataky-Varma, Sravana. 2019. "Taming Hindu *Śākta* on the Internet: Online pūjās for the goddess Tripurasundarī." In *Digital Hinduism,* edited by Xenia Zeiler, 186–206. Oxon: Routledge.

Campbell, Heidi, and Mia Lövheim. 2013. "Introduction: The Rise of the Study of Digital Religion." In *Digital Religion: Understanding Religious Practice in New Media Worlds,* edited by Heidi A. Campbell, 1–22. Oxon: Routledge.

———. 2017. "Considering Critical Methods and Theoretical Lenses in Digital Religion Studies." *New Media & Society* 19, no. 1: 5–14. https://doi.org/10.1177/1461444816649911.

Divine-rudraksha.com. 2016. "Tripura-Sundari Yantra." Accessed September 1, 2020. https://www.divine-rudraksha.com/products/tripura-sundari-yantra#desc-bookmark.

Eck, Diana. 1981. *Darśan: Seeing the Divine Image in India.* New York: Columbia University Press.

Frøystad, Kathinka. 2019. "Affective Digital Images: Shiva in the Kaaba and the Smartphone Revolution." In *Outrage: The Rise of Religious Offence in Contemporary South Asia,* edited by Paul Rollier, Kathinka Froystad, and Arild Engelsen Ruud, 123–48. London: UCL Press.

Gaddy, Gary, and David Pritchard. 1985. "When Watching Religious TV Is Like Attending Church." *Journal of Communication* 35, no. 1: 123–31.

Garigliano, Irene M. 2015. "Les Brahmanes du Complexe du Temples de Kāmākhyā (Assam). Droits héréditaires, relation avec les pèlerins et pouvoir administratif." PhD diss., Sapienza University of Rome and Paris Ouest Nanterre La Défense University.

Helland, Christopher. 2007. "Diaspora on the Electronic Frontier: Developing Virtual Connections with Sacred Homelands." *Journal of Computer-Mediated Communication* 12, no. 3: 956–76. https://doi.org/10.1111/j.1083-6101.2007.00358.x.

———. 2013. "Ritual." In *Digital Religion: Understanding Religious Practice in New Media Worlds,* edited by Heidi A. Campbell, 25–40. Oxon: Routledge.

Hoover, Stewart, M. 2012. "Foreword: Practice, Autonomy, and Authority in the Digitally Religious and Digitally Spiritual." In *Digital Religion, Social Media, and Culture: Perspectives, Practices, Futures,* edited by Pauline Hope Cheong, Peter Fischer-Nielsen, Stefan Gelfgren, and Charles Ess, vii–xii. New York: Peter Lang.

Hoover, Stewart M., and Seung Soo Kim. 2016. "Media." In *Handbook of Religion and Society, Handbooks of Sociology and Social Research,* edited by David Yamane, 117–32. Switzerland: Springer International Publishing. https://doi.org/10.1007/978-3-319-31395-5_7.

Hurwitt, Sundari J. 2019. "The Voracious Virgin: The Concept and Worship of the Kumārī in Kaula Tantrism." PhD diss., California Institute of Integral Studies.

Karapanagiotis, Nicole. 2010. "Vaishnava Cyber-Pūjā Problems of Purity & Novel Ritual Solution." *Heidelberg Journal of Religions on the Internet* 4, no. 1. http://dx.doi.org/10.11588/rel.2010.1.9391.

———. 2019. "Automatic Rituals and inadvertent audiences: ISKCON, Krishna and the Ritual Mechanics of Facebook." In *Digital Hinduism,* edited by Xenia Zeiler, 51–77. New York: Routledge.

Kinsley, David. 1997. *Tantric Visions of the Divine Feminine.* Berkeley: University of California Press.

Kripal, Jeffrey J., ed. 2014. *Comparing Religions: Coming to Terms.*New York: John Wiley & Sons.

Lal, Vinay. 2014. "Cyberspace, the Globalisation of Hinduism, and the protocols of Citizenship in the Digital Age." In *Indian Transnationalism Online: New Perspectives on the Diaspora,* edited by Ajaya Kumar Sahoo and Johannes G. de Kruijf, 121–46. New York: Routledge.

Lundby, Knut. 2013. "Theoretical Frameworks for Approaching Religion and New Media." In *Digital Religion: Understanding Religious Practice in New Media Worlds*, edited by Heidi A. Campbell, 225–37. Oxon: Routledge.

Mohan, Sriram. 2015. "Locating the "Internet Hindu": Political Speech and Performance in Indian Cyberspace." *Television and New Media* 16, no. 4: 339–45. https://doi.org/10.1177/1527476415575491.

NDTV. 2017. "Miley Cyrus Chooses Lakshmi Puja Over Super *Bowl*." Accessed April 29, 2019. https://www.ndtv.com/offbeat/miley-cyrus-chooses-lakshmi-puja-over-super-bowl-1656521.

Newcomb, Horace, and Paul Hirsch. 1976. "Television as a Cultural Forum." In *Television: The Critical View*, edited by Horace Newcomb, 561–73. New York: Oxford University Press.

Omanga, Duncan, 2019. "WhatsApp as 'Digital Publics': The *Nakuru Analysts* and the Evolution of Participation in County Governance in Kenya." *Journal of Eastern African Studies* 13, no. 1: 175–91.

Parker, Everett C., David W. Barry, and Dallas W. Smythe. 1955. *The Television-Radio Audience and Religion*. New York: Harper.

Pink, Sarah. 2011. "Multimodality, Multisensoriality and Ethnographic Knowing: Social Semiotics and Phenomenology of Perception." *Qualitative Research* 11, no. 1: 261–76.

Proudfoot, Wayne.1985. *Religious Experience*. Berkeley: University of California Press.

Rao, Mani. 2018. *Living Mantra: Mantra, Deity, and Visionary Experience Today*. Cham, Switzerland: Palgrave Macmilan.

Riesebrodt, Martin. 2009. *The Promise of Salvation: A Theory of religion*. Chicago: University of Chicago Press.

Rosati, Paolo E. 2019. "The Yoni of Kāmākhyā: The Intersection of Power and Gender in its Mythology." *Religion of South Asia* 13, no. 3: 317–47. https://doi.org/10.1558/rosa.19013.

Sathya Narayanan, A. 2018. "Baglamukhi Mantra Meaning and Benefits." *Times of India*. January 16, 2018. Accessed August 18, 2020. http://timesofindia.indiatimes.com/articleshow/68205254.cms.

Scheifinger, Heinz. 2010. "Internet Threats to Hindu Authority: Puja Ordering Websites and the Kalighat Temple." *Asian Journal of Social Science* 38, no. 4: 636–56.

———. 2013. "Hindu Worship Online and Offline." In *Digital Religion: Understanding Religious Practice in New Media Worlds*, edited by Heidi A. Campbell, 121–28. Oxon: Routledge.

Sharf, Robert. 1998. "Experience." In *Critical Terms for Religious Studies*, edited by Mark Taylor, 94–116. Chicago: University of Chicago Press.

Shin, Jae Yun. 2016. "Searching for Kāmarūpa: Historiography of the Early Brahmaputra Valley in the Colonial and Post-Colonial Period." *Puravritta:*

Journal of the Directorate of Archaeology & Museums 23, no. 1: 115–32. https://doi.org/10.1080/14631369.2020.1750945.

Shivology.com. 2018. "Baglamukhi Puja Significance, Importance & Benefits." October 10, 2018. Accessed August 10, 2020. https://shivology.com/puja/vedic-puja-rituals/goddess-baglamukhi-puja/469.

Shubhpuja.com. n.d. "Our Team." Accessed May 16, 2020. http://shubhpuja.com/our-team/.

Siegel, Lee. 2014. *Trance Migrations: Stories of India, Tales of Hypnosis*. Chicago: The University of Chicago Press.

Singh, Manish, 2019. "WhatsApp Reaches 400 Million Users in India, Its Biggest Market." *TechCrunch*, July 26, 2019. https://techcrunch.com/2019/07/26/whatsapp-india-users-400-million/.

Śobhanā, Kanakavati. 2004. *Yakṣinī Bhūtinī Sādhanā aur Devī Siddhiyāṃ*. Haridvar: Randhir Prakashan.

Taves, Ann. 2011. *Religious Experience Reconsidered: A Building-Block Approach to the Study of Religion and Other Special Things*. Princeton: Princeton University Press.

Udupa, Sahana. 2015. "Internet Hindus: New India's Ideological Warriors." In *Handbook of Religion and the Asian City: Aspiration and Urbanization in the Twenty-First Century*, edited by Peter van der Veer, 432–50. Berkley: University of California Press.

Ullrey, Aaron. 2016. "Grim Grimoires: Pragmatic Ritual in the Magic Tantras." PhD diss., University of California–Santa Barbara.

Urban, Hugh B. 2010. *The Power of Tantra Religion, Sexuality, and the Politics of South Asian Studies*. New York: I.B. Tauris.

Warrier, Maya. 2014. "Online Bhakti in a Modern Guru Organisation." In *Gurus of Modern Yoga*, edited by Mark Singleton and Ellen Goldberg, 308–23. New York: Oxford University Press.

YouTube. 2014. "How to Perform Maa Bagalamukhi Sadhna?" Zeenews.com. May 2, 2014. Accessed January 5, 2020. https://www.youtube.com/watch?v=1lKIVnjQ1gg.

Zeiler, Xenia. 2018. "Durgā Pūjā Committees. Community Origin and Transformed Mediatized Practices Employing Social Media." In *Nine Nights of the Goddess: The Navaratri Festival in South Asia*, edited by Caleb Simmons, Moumita Sen, and Hillary Rodrigues, 121–38. Albany: SUNY Press.

Part II

Embodiment, Identity, and Experience: Conversations with Tantric Livelihoods

5

Folk Tantra and Healing

An Ethnography of Traditional Healers in the Darjeeling Hills and Sikkim

Jarrod Hyam

The Indo-Himalayan region of the Darjeeling Hills exemplifies a unique set of geographical and sociocultural confluences. Situated at the border of India and Nepal in the upper reaches of northeastern West Bengal, this area exhibits a complex array of borderland influences from the cultures of Bengal, Nepal, and Tibet. Both Hindus and Buddhists attend the Mahākāla Temple in the city center of Darjeeling. Originally housing a Buddhist monastery, the main attractions at the temple complex include a sacred cave and a Śiva lingam attended by Hindu Brahmins. It is widely held that Mahākāla as a *dharmapāla* or wrathful Vajrayāna protective deity manifests in this location as Śiva.

The name Darjeeling itself illustrates a Tibetan Buddhist influence: the word is purportedly of Tibetan origin, *rDo rje gling,* "region of the *Dorje*" (in Sanskrit, *vajra*). Originally included in the Kingdom of Sikkim with a large population of Lepcha inhabitants, it was invaded in the nineteenth century by the Gorkhas of western Nepal. Later, the British Empire subsumed the area into India, and it became a district of West Bengal after independence. Following the People's Liberation Army's annexation of Tibet in the early 1950s, many Tibetan refugees fled to the Darjeeling area. These many mergers and invasions resulted in a particularly vibrant sociocultural diversity and a wide array of religious practices, both institutionalized and "folk" traditions. My sense of "folk" religious practitioners applied within this chapter refers to small networks of traditional healers who operate at a grassroots-level organization, outside the purview of organized Hindu and Buddhist religious institutions. I return to this concept in my discussion of folk Tantra and healing. The Darjeeling Hills area reveals a striking confluence of ethnic, cultural, and religious communities due to its geographical positioning as a borderland. Though located in West Bengal and called the "crown of West Bengal," its majority Nepali inhabitants distinguish themselves ethnoculturally and call for the establishment of a new Indian state—Gorkhaland. There is a multitude of Nepali ethnic groups, including the Tamang, Gurung, Limbu, Newar, and Rāi, as well as Sikkimese Tibetan groups such as the Bhutia.

The cultural confluence flows from several directions, both from the Gangetic plain regions of northern India and from Nepal and Tibet. The immediate effect of the physical geographical conditions of subsistence in the Himalayan region of Darjeeling and adjacent areas is striking; the climate limits the growth of vegetable crops, and the rugged mountainous terrain provides geographical seclusion while limiting the influx of goods from other regions of India. Winters can be profoundly cold, and village residents often live in poorly insulated cottages while relying on the burning of coal as a heating source. The nearest urban center relative to the Darjeeling district is Siliguri, West Bengal, which is located in a valley just below the mountainous terrain of the district. A large region straddling the Indo-Nepali border along northern Bengal and Sikkim depends on Siliguri for the supply of general goods and petroleum; many local residents referred to the rest of India generically as the "plains," illustrating a geographical rift between the Himalayan and Gangetic plain areas, both topographically and socioculturally. It is this uniquely porous borderland geography that appealed to me as a research site. As the Darjeeling area is inhabited by significant communities of Nepali and Tibetan ethnic groups, I grew curious regarding what, if any, Hindu-Buddhist syntheses formed in the religious praxis adopted by traditional healers in this region (see figure 5.1). I also wondered what forms of Tantric practice were integrated into this regional traditional healing modality and if there was a unique application and understanding of Tantra

Figure 5.1. It is common in the Darjeeling region to see simultaneous depictions of Śakyamuni Buddha, Ganeśa, and Śiva. This artistic depiction illustrates the pluralistic syntheses of traditions applied in the eclectic approaches of traditional healers and Tantric practitioners in the region. *Source*: Photograph by the author.

within this context. I began initial ethnographic fieldwork in the Darjeeling Hills with these inquiries in mind.

Notes on Methodology and Positionality

I conducted fieldwork on four consecutive trips between 2016 and 2020. Among Nepali traditional healers in the Darjeeling Hills district and Sikkim, I observed healing pujas for various kinds of afflictions; I also received healing pujas myself. Along with *jhākris*[1] and *mātās*, I interviewed a Lepcha *bongthing* in rural Sikkim. I used a digital audio recorder to record interviews and informal conversations. I conducted interviews and participant observations with eleven Nepali traditional healers, including three *mātās* and eight *jhākris*. This chapter includes interview excerpts with four of these research participants. Much of the fieldwork centered on quotidian activities relating to subsistence. While staying at a friend's cottage adjacent to the Takdah Tea Estate, he introduced me to *jhākris* and *mātājīs* at their familial homes. I stayed at their homes and observed while they busied themselves with gardening, cooking, manual labor, and domestic duties. I also observed healing pujas performed by practitioners for various kinds of ailments, including the treatment of chronic stomach (in Nepali, *gastrik*) problems and persistent physical and mental symptoms diagnosed as relating to malignant witchcraft.

My interest in Indigenous healing practices is inspired by my own indigenous American heritage and personal experience with traditional healing methods to treat debilitating psychosomatic illnesses that developed during childhood. My mother's family lived in the borderland area of what is now the Southwest United States and northern Mexico, eventually settling in the San Antonio valley area in southern Texas. Our ethnic and cultural identity is a hybridized mixture of indigenous Coahuiltecan and Hispanic ancestry. Akin to the traditional healers in this ethnography, this borderland heritage was porous to cultural influences from numerous geographical directions. Without delving into overt autoethnography, I am training in traditional healing methods drawn from my indigenous heritage. Reclamation of traditional healing and religious practices connects to the larger decolonial projects of indigenous cultural revitalization.

My research methodology rests on the importance of relationships rather than an attempt to extract information; thus, my engagement in fieldwork depends on a nuanced set of relationships with participants, with ecologies—with places. This methodology is inspired by the decolonial and indigenous methodologies of Gloria Anzaldúa (1987), Margaret Kovach (2021), and Patrisia Gonzales (2012). I occasionally describe analyses from a first-person perspective to acknowledge my lack of detached objectivity in my position as a researcher. Before beginning interviews in the field, I describe my training in an indigenous American healing tradition, which inspires my research interests and worldviews related to this work. I explain that my interest is in *sharing* knowledge and gaining a mutual understanding, rather than simply taking information as an object of study and accumulation of data.

Though I began my research as a PhD student with minimal income, being a Western researcher who is affluent relative to rural Himalayan villagers impacted my positionality within fieldwork; not only was I perceived as an outsider, but I was also perceived as someone with Western cultural status who is presumably wealthy. I spoke about this tension with my advisor Geoffrey Samuel. Having extensive ethnographic experience, he reflected on the inevitability of these kinds of cultural tensions and how ignoring the issue of positionality as a foreign researcher is naïve and lacks self-reflexivity (see Samuel 2007, 2017). We both have discovered that it is an ongoing struggle to navigate *how* one can effectively approach fieldwork with wealth and power differentials. He advised that one simple strategy would be to bring a gift or donation to anyone who participates in the research. I thus attempted to apply my relationally focused methodology as effectively as I could. Even so, I question to what degree I can effectively mitigate this struggle. I often set up field interviews by explaining that my goal was not to document the healers' work impersonally or to extract knowledge, but rather to engage with them as a fellow storyteller, to share stories and experiences with participants. This sometimes involved sharing private details of my dreams, as dream content may reveal the knowledge and skill sets required by traditional healers in this ethnography. The primary research participants included *jhākris*, *mātās*, Tibetan Buddhist lamas, and villagers in this field site. The fieldwork research area was in a radius of about 40 kilometers, stretching from Darjeeling and nearby rural villages, to the Takdah, Teesta and Lopchu Tea Estate areas and the adjacent village of Lamahatta, also including the villages adjacent to Pakyong in southeast Sikkim and the hilly region slightly beyond Gangtok city limits. As I spent extended time in rural areas throughout the Darjeeling Hills and southeast Sikkim, much of my assistance came from villagers I met during fieldwork, who were extremely welcoming and who often warmly volunteered to assist me with directions to adjacent villages and other confusions. I gradually grew a network of acquaintances directly embedded in the local village-based health-care system, which has minimal access to physicians and hospitals due to the remote locations in the Himalayan borderlands. Because of this, relying on traditional healers during health emergencies is crucial. Some villagers were hesitant to admit that certain *jhākris* are legitimate healers, and this was often countered with skepticism; a common argument given was that these healers apply old-fashioned methods that modern biomedicine will eventually replace. Thus, the ongoing discourse surrounding the legitimacy and trustworthiness of *jhākris* and *mātās* along the Indo-Nepali borderland regions is an important aspect of the social exchanges and negotiations within the local health-care system. While traveling in the Darjeeling Hills, I rented a small cottage near the village of Lamahatta from Tashi Bhutia, who gradually became a close friend. After we cultivated a relationship of mutual trust, Tashi agreed to help as a research assistant as the ethnography developed. He initially introduced me to Lakṣmī Mātājī, a guru who initiates *mātās* in the vicinity surrounding the Takdah Tea Estate, because of her advanced experience and knowledge. Lakṣmī offered edifying, nuanced descriptions of the differing approaches and methods applied by traditional healers in the area. I therefore primarily visited *mātās* within her lineage. Research-participant *jhākris* came from differing local lineages, and some explicitly defined themselves as *not* being a part of a specific lineage or *paramparā*; everything they learned, including medicinal compounds and healing mantras, appeared directly through dreams or visions. Knowledge is also transmitted from incorporeal beings and gurus who are no longer human beings.

Himalayan Traditional Healers

The ritual practitioners I engaged with during fieldwork in Sikkim and the Darjeeling Hills often self-designated as the general Nepali appellation *jhākri*, while others self-designated using a term specific to their ethnocultural group, such as *bijuwa* among the Rāi. *Jhākris* are traditional healers, ritual specialists who work part-time as psychophysiological healers, intermediaries between human beings and local spirits, and assistants in funerary rites. *Jhākris* in my field site also worked as agrarian laborers, tending to livestock, or tilling the land for local vegetable crops, with minimal monetary income other than what is given from patients during healing pujas. *Jhākris* can be of any gender; female practitioners who apply parallel healing repertoires are known as *mātājīs*, or Mother Goddesses.

The practitioners I interviewed saw themselves as fitting within the larger Indo-Nepali Hindu community, yet they tended to avoid a specific religious identity, having no issue with integrating Buddhist deities (in Sanskrit, *devas*) and ritual praxis (in Sanskrit, *sādhana*), as well as incorporating a complex local cosmology and ecology of spirits and incorporeal entities. *Mātās* are defined both by themselves and by local villagers as women possessed by Goddess Devī in her many manifestations. Those who are receptacles for the goddess gain healing powers from her presence. While men can be possessed by Devī, I was told by *mātās* that this calling is for women alone, who become instruments of Devī. However, this was contradicted by other *mātās* who claimed that men can also be Devī—gender is not relevant. Every *mātā* I encountered during fieldwork was vegetarian and eschewed the sacrifice of chickens that is typically performed by *jhākris* to appease harmful spirits, specifically offering their blood to hungry ghosts; in fact, *mātās* defined themselves in contrast to *jhākris* by refusing to partake in this ritual. Visitors to *mātās* are not allowed to eat meat on the day they visit the *mātājī*.

Regarding the phenomenon of spirit possession, Rex L. Jones (1976) develops four potential categories within the context of Nepali traditional healers, including "tutelary possession" (5–6). He posits that reincarnate Tibetan Buddhist lamas or *tulkus* are "reincarnate possessions" whose careers parallel shamanic practitioners insofar as they master "controlled possession" as a source of ritual praxis throughout their life (5). Jones suggests that lower-caste people, particularly women of lower caste or social status, are more susceptible to pathological spirit possession. This often applies to unmarried women or women who work as servants. Unmarried women in Nepali societies are often relegated to inferior social status with little chance of advancing their social positions. Men of lower castes without wealth or social status are also more commonly subject to spirit possession, as "an approved means for 'social protest' " (9).

Gurung et al. (2014) relatedly comment on the social implications of their psychiatric study of a collective possession experience in a rural Nepali village: "Possession states allowed women to speak in ways that were socially proscribed, including expressing frank criticism and using disrespectful, or obscene language, which they would usually not utter in a conscious state. For example, when possessed, some women accused their neighbors, mother-in-laws, or daughter-in-laws of being *boksiharu* [witches] and inflicting harm on them" (657). The implication is that possession is deeply tied to sociopolitical positioning and contexts and may serve as a subversive attempt to aggressively respond to social oppression. In a sense, these possessed women, including the *mātās* in this chapter, embody a new kind of self, no longer subject to the constraints related to their social positions as women. During volatile possession experiences, those who are socially marginalized and neglected can no longer be ignored, and the intensity of the ritual experience draws attention to needs that must be attended to. These experiences also ease the ability of possessed women to speak frankly without social censure, as well as to express socially inappropriate and emotionally charged content.

Folk Tantra and Healing

Tantric practitioners (in Sanskrit, *tāntrikas*) have long been associated with itinerant sorcerers and healers throughout South Asia. In the context of rural low-caste communities, David Gordon White (2003) situates possession, exorcism, divination, and healing as "the most pervasive forms of Tantric practice," and it was in their role as healers "and ground-level problem solvers that popular Tantric specialists first established and have continued to maintain their closest ties with every level of South Asian society" (260). Because healers were often perceived as "polluted" due to their physical contact with those from numerous castes, Kenneth Zysk (1991) notes the affinity between heterodox yogis and healers, since itinerant healers found shelter among heterodox renunciate communities. He argues that these wandering healers gradually became "indistinguishable from the ascetics with whom they were in close contact" (5). A sharing of techniques occurred among these communities, including the use of plant and herbal preparations, charged amulets, and magical mantras. This relates to the existence of a unique "folk Tantra" social niche in which *jhākris* and *mātās* are similarly situated in low-caste rural communities, having close contact with all castes and genders, and applying "Tantra-mantra" and herbal and *āyurvedic* medicines; they are sometimes viewed suspiciously by local villagers as untrustworthy *tāntrikas*, particularly *jhākris*, who are rumored to revivify the dead and make pacts with spirits.

White (2000) continues regarding the current perceptions of Tantric practitioners in South Asia who lack a cohesive social position after the dissolution of monarchic patronage. Modern Tantric practice is often viewed as "little more than black magic": "On the one hand, the powerful Tantric rites of subjugation, immobilization, annihilation, and so on—the 'Six Practices' or 'Six Rites of Magic'—have become the sole province of individuals practicing for their own prestige and profit. . . It is in this context that many Hindus in India today deny the relevance of Tantra to their tradition, past or present, and identify what they call 'Tantra-mantra' as so much mumbo jumbo" (35).

I observed similar prejudgments during fieldwork in India. Among the *bhadralok* or middle-class Bengalis I spoke to regarding *tāntrikas*, such practitioners are typically viewed as untrustworthy individuals whose motives are unknown and therefore questionable (see McDaniel, chapter 10, this volume). Mirroring White's discussion of "mumbo jumbo," during my fieldwork in the Indo-Nepali borderland areas, nonpractitioners often associated the term "Tantra-mantra" with superstitious scam artistry and practitioners of black magic. Part of this suspicion relates to financial opportunism, as many so-called *tāntrikas* are perceived as greedy charlatans who capitalize on individuals' vulnerabilities by preying on the gullible. This social denouncement continued in discourse related to Nepali traditional healers: *jhākris* are often referred to as *tāntrikas,* greedy scam artists who use questionable methods and are not to be trusted.

Kathleen Erndl (2000) conducted fieldwork with *mātās* in Himachal Pradesh near Dharamsala, another Himalayan borderland area that exemplifies a wide range of cultural confluences. Regarding the healing practices of *mātās,* Erndl makes an important observation about "practical" Tantric paradigms, which aims to fulfill mundane, pragmatic desires as much as it seeks soteriological goals: "The powers gained through Tantric practice can be used for both worldly (*bhukti*) and spiritual (*mukti*) purposes. In the non-dualist ontology of Tantra, these two are part of the same reality. Mātājī and her devotees are part of a broadly based grassroots religious expression, a kind of 'folk Tantra' that connects the more formal textual and esoteric Tantric traditions with exoteric village religion" (98).

Folk Tantra forms the intersection for the practices applied by *jhākris* and *mātās*. The healing repertoires expressed by these traditional healers are certainly grassroots, connected to the larger framework of South Asian religious traditions, yet function independently in terms of how Hindu texts (*śāstra*) are applied and interpreted. Brahmanical hegemony and hierarchy also tend to be ideologically and geographically distanced from rural village religious traditions, allowing for a flexibility and novelty that is more focused on praxis than caste-bound formal orthodoxy. Among *mātās,* texts such as the Bhagavad-Gītā may be interpreted as a guide toward ultimate liberation while simultaneously being a source of powerful, healing mantras to deflect afflictions caused by malignant sorcery and capricious spirits.

Frederick Smith (2006) notes Vedic literary descriptions of *āveśa,* a process analogous to possession he describes as "pervasion" (17). This term is applied in various contexts of South Asian embodied spirit-possession rituals. *Āveśa* correlates with South Asian shamanic-type possession states, often occurring in village-based, rural contexts. The phenomenon of spirit possession will be further discussed below, and it forms a foundational aspect of my understanding of folk Tantra. The central āyurvedic medicinal text *Caraka saṃhitā* identifies *bhūtāveśa,* possession by ghosts, as a major source of disease in section 6.3.123, which may manifest as trembling, sobbing, and related outbursts of emotion.

June McDaniel (2004) developed an important argument regarding the existence of folk Tantra in Bengal. She notes the initiatory connection shared between "tribal shaman-healers (*ojhas*)" and Śākta Tantric practitioners at cremation grounds (9). She continues to describe folk Tantra as primarily an oral tradition, focusing on praxis (in Sanskrit, *sādhanā*) and related magical powers (in Sanskrit, *siddhi*) rather than textual and philosophical exegesis (10). These aspects strongly align with my ethnographic observations and my understanding of the unique positioning of folk Tantra along the Indo-Nepali borderland regions.

Regarding the healing practices of *ojhās*, Patricia Cook's (1997) ethnographic work addresses sacred music therapy in northern Indian villages near Varanasi practiced by *ojhās*. Akin to the Nepali word *jhākri*, there is a certain semantic looseness and imprecision with European-language translations, and this term is often translated as the English "exorcist" or "healer." Cook discusses the Vedic literary influence on these musical healing practices. The Sāma Veda, for example, prescribes the recitation of mantras for healing diseases; specific, sung words affect ailing bodily areas (1997, 63). Rural-village musical healing practice in this region of India "has evolved from Vedic, Tantric and Hindu folk traditions over many centuries" (63). This synthesis parallels the healing repertoires of Nepali traditional healers, who employ mantras from the Vedas and the Gītā as incantations with powerful healing abilities, rather than interpreting these passages soteriologically.

One female *ojhā* she interviewed is often possessed by Śītalā, a goddess capable of healing pox and other diseases. The Devī demands offerings such as flowers to prevent the provocation of her wrath. This goddess, in addition to Hārītī, an ambivalent deity who is also associated with smallpox, is significant to Nepali *mātājīs* and is often embodied by them. Darry Dinnell (2017) describes an intriguing parallel in the praxis of *mātās* in contemporary Gujarat, who primarily embody Jogaṇī Mātā, a wrathful goddess associated with cholera and closely tied to the fierce Tantric goddess Chinnamastā. Dinnell notes an important feature found in this modern context: the growing popularity of a "safe" Sanskritic Tantric tradition applied by the Gujarati *mātās*, which appeals to middle and upper-class devotees (2017, 1). While my research participants operate primarily within oral traditions, I observed influences from and dialectical exchanges with Sanskritic literary cultures that manifest within the contemporary practices applied by Nepali traditional healers. Margaret Trawick (1990) similarly discusses how these tensions arise within South Asian village-based religious practices as "the multiplicity of contexts in which the rules of the texts might or might not be more or less enacted" (23). How these textual "rules" are and are not enacted will be described more specifically in the next sections.

The general structure of folk Tantra applied in this chapter contains these key elements adopted by practitioners:

1. Integration of healing methods, which includes mantra recitation, herbal and āyurvedic medicinal compounds, song, dance, and related palliative aesthetic modalities.
2. Working with scriptural and/or philosophical texts (*śāstra*) for pragmatic and healing purposes rather than soteriological ones.
3. Emphasis on the removal of harmful spiritual entities, such as malignant spirits or *bhūt*. This occurs through the direct embodiment of and possession by tutelary deities (*deutā*) leading to the subsequent exorcism of harmful spirit influences.

While not exhaustive, these elements are recurring themes applied by traditional healers in my ethnography. These aspects represent an inherently eclectic and pragmatic approach to religious practice and healing, a model influenced by the need to respond to immediate, quotidian necessities and health crises more so than the pursuit of abstractly philosophical exegeses.

Folk Tantra Healers

I met Pumpha Regmi Mātājī (see fig. 5.2) in a rural area of southeast Sikkim near Pakyong in 2016. She is a well-known healer in her local district. Adjacent to her home is her personal *mandir* or temple,

Figure 5.2. Traditional healer Pumpha Regmi near Pakyong, Sikkim. *Source*: Photograph by the author.

where she practices *dhyān* or meditation and *jap* (mantra recitation). Her mandir is also where the afflicted are taken during healing pujas. Pumpha explicitly defined how *mātās* differ from *jhākris*, though their methods are similar and they attend to a related cosmological framework and related healing methods. She emphasized the difference by claiming that *jhākris* work with Tantric methods while *mātās* do not, an intriguingly nuanced position.

Jhākris and *mātās* occupy the same ritual space and participate in a kind of division of labor related to healing work. Female Hindu and Buddhist villagers I interviewed generally chose to consult whichever practitioner was closest or known to be practically effective with healing; Hindu female villagers sometimes preferred seeking *mātās* for healing due to their specific spiritual hygienic practices, including the eschewing of animal sacrifice.

Mātās I interviewed repeated consistent key themes that appear to differentiate the work of *mātās* from *jhākris*, including the framework with which entities are called upon during ritual praxis:

1. *Jhākris* typically perform healing work publicly, while *mātās* perform healing sessions privately, usually in their home temple (mandir).

2. *Jhākris* summon an entire array of deities and spirits and can embody such entities, while *mātās* are possessed by a manifestation of Devī alone.

3. While both kinds of healers often suffer an early life initiatory crisis/sickness, *mātās* are known for being spontaneously possessed by Devī, a necessary requirement to establish their vocation as *mātās*.

Pumpha expanded on her analysis of the Tantric methods applied by *jhākris* that she does not share. She associates "Tantra" generally with graveyard praxis and questionable pacts made with ghosts and other entities: "The *jhākris* work through Tantra and Tantric ways, whereas we [*mātās*] work through Devīs like Mahā-Kālī and Śakti. Tantric practices pertain to magic [black magic] and *masāns* [restless ghosts]. *Jhākris* derive their power from these sources. We instead derive our powers from the divine goddesses like Durga, Kālī. We get knowledge and wisdom from the books that have been written on the Devī Śakti."

Pumpha referred to the infamous practice of *śmaśān sādhanā* (charnel ground practice), a Tantric rite shared among Śaiva, Buddhist, and Tibetan Chöd practitioners. This practice is engaged among different Tantric ritual contexts for different purposes. Systems of mutual exchange among disparate localized, Indigenous traditions and Tantric systems is pronounced throughout the Himalayan regions. The thighbone trumpet commonly used by *jhākris* is often gathered from recently deceased persons. They employ Śiva's hand drum (*ḍamaru*) as a main instrument for puja, and they often refer to Mahādeu or Śiva as their patron deity; thus, their charnel or cremation-ground practice is situated within the ritual framework of wrathful Śaiva praxis. Śiva is the preeminent deva for many *jhākris*—he dances in the cremation grounds and is the supreme healer, god of medicine, and master of Tantric yoga, both sensually indulgent and restrained. Romano Mastromattei (1989) refers to the Nepali shamanic complex as "proto-Śivaismo," which was possibly "adopted as an ideological and ritual corset for ancient autochthonous and purely shamanistic practices and beliefs" (229).

Charnel-ground practice is not practiced by all *jhākris*; according to research participants, since interaction with potentially harmful entities and ghosts such as *bhūt* and *pret* are inevitable for their work, some practitioners actively forge relationships with spirits in charnel grounds and potentially "enhance their powers," as Pumpha claims. Pumpha described *jhākris* who are known for meditating, contacting spirits, and engaging in other practices in secluded caves at night, which adds to suspicion about their intentions and abilities to perform black magic.

Pumpha's initial comments show a noteworthy ambivalence. While noninitiates and villagers often included *mātās* within the generic term of *tāntriks*, Pumpha finds it necessary to distance herself from this term and its associated methods completely. Interestingly, other *mātās* had no issue referring to their practices as connected to Śākta-Tantra! This is part of a larger cultural discourse prevalent in modern South Asia that equates "Tantra" with all things scandalous, erotic, depraved, and dangerous, which explains some of Pumpha's skepticism.

I revisited Sikkim during the particularly frigid and cloud-strewn winter month of January 2020. I prefer to stay a few kilometers from the city center when visiting Gangtok, so I based myself at a higher altitude on a hilltop near the famous mandir of Gaṇeś Tok. The bone-piercing Himalayan cold was especially striking during this time, and I often slept with a coat and scarf on! I was fortunate enough to be introduced to the well-known healer Yam Bahadur Thapa—who identifies as a Himalayan healer—while staying at a hotel in this area (see figure 5.3). He is generally referred to with the honorific title of

Figure 5.3. Yam Bahadur Thapa, Himalayan traditional healer. Gangtok, Sikkim, January 2020. *Source*: Photograph by the author.

gurujī. Yam explained his unique initiatory background in the early evening hours at the hotel's outdoor courtyard:

> This was my birth gift . . . when I was still in my mother's womb, the *deutā* (deities) came to me.
>
> When I was only three years old, I was taken by the *ban jhākri*.[2] I was taken away to the jungle and stayed there for a long time. I was lost taken deep within the jungle. All food came from nature—it all tasted sweet and pure (like desserts: *sandesh*). I am a healer by birth, through my heritage.

After the age of 11, I came back to my home from the jungle. I roamed around my home village practicing healing arts. This was written in a biography in a book about Sikkimese healers [*Faith Healers of Sikkim* by Yishey Doma].

Everything was taught to me by the *ban jhākri*. This includes divination [in Nepali, *jokhānā*] with rice grains, how to see what is ailing a sick person. . . . This could be health-related "natural" diseases or those related to ghosts: *bhūt, pret*. I can only cure these second cases; this is my specialty. Recently deceased souls [*ātma*] wander around everywhere after death—some people are simply more vulnerable to these spirits.

My primary method is through mantra. I cure through this way. If one is not cured this way—I also apply Tantra.

Jarrod: What kind of Tantric methods do you work with?

By "Tantra" I mean that I will call on a dead person, a restless spirit who is harming someone. I command the harmful spirit to leave this person alone, to stop haunting them or making them sick. This is Tantra-mantra.

This relates to my primary *deutā*. They enter my body—this is the only way I can heal [others].

The *ban jhākri* has seven brothers . . . among these seven brothers, one is Buddhist. The eldest one comes to my body during Tantra-mantra. They [the brothers] are both Hindu and Buddhist. I forget everything; I do not remember what happens when the *deutā* enters my body.

I begin giving healing pujas as soon as I wake up in the morning, 6 a.m. I also give pujas to people in different countries on the phone. Many seek me who are *pāgala* [mentally imbalanced]—they are suffering from infection by *bhūt*. If they take a [psychedelic] drug and act *pāgala*, though, I cannot help [laughing].

I can cure those affected by *boksī*,[3] by *bhūt* and *pret*. I help women suffering from menstrual-related diseases—this can also come from *bhūt-pret*. All I need is the right mantra—this draws the harmful presence away from sick peoples' bodies. I help many kinds of people all over Sikkim—simple people and even top politicians!

> The *ban jhākri* keeps guardian spirits in the forest. Some of these are hunter spirits [in Nepali, *śikārī*]. Human beings cross their paths when they should not—they will become completely crazed [*pāgala*], depressed, or have other kinds of mental imbalance. They will need help from me or another healer.
>
> I feel much power [*śakti*] when I do my daily pujas. This is how I remain strong and healthy, avoiding sicknesses. This power grows with the more practice and pujas I perform.

Yam referred to Tantric methods with the general compound term "Tantra-mantra." His understanding of this term refers to the recitation of mantras and a set of practices related to harmful spirits and tutelary deities (in Nepali, *deutā*), which are exorcized or invoked for various purposes. This conception is comparable to the definition given by other nearby traditional healers I interviewed. In Yam's case, he embodies his main tutelary deity—the *ban jhākri*—in addition to other guardian spirits, which enables him to perform Tantric healing practices after they fully suffuse his body. The *deutā* empower him with this ability, as they can see directly into the incorporeal domains, the realm of spirits and invisible entities. This was also discussed as generating the sufficient power (*śakti*) necessary to heal others with Tantric methods. Paralleling Pumpha Mātājī, his primary healing method is sonic: centered on the inherent vibratory power of the recitation of healing mantras. As I further discuss in the next sections, chronic illnesses that are not "natural" (in Nepali, *prākṛtika*), such as microbial infections and broken limbs, are often diagnosed as resulting from restless spirits, *bhūt-pret*, or harmful witchcraft directed from *boksī*. Such malignant sorcery, often generalized as the English term "black magic," is to be countered by the magical Tantric powers of a competent traditional healer.

Embodiment, Affliction, and Spirit Possession

Among the Nepali traditional healers I interviewed, the role of embodiment is approached in several ways. One integral aspect is how practitioners relate to their bodies. *Mātās* often referred to their bodies as "vessels" (in Nepali, *pōta*) with which they are to serve Devī simply and humbly. Certain lifestyle constraints are needed to keep the body pure, such as maintaining a vegetarian diet, ingesting and working with herbal medicines, adhering to disciplined hygiene and daily pujas (often one in the morning and one at night), and avoiding polluted places like graveyards and areas where people committed suicide. Kumar Sarki, a female *jhākri*, told me that a vegetarian diet is indeed ideal for her work, but chicken is acceptable as it is a "neutral" meat and women need to replace iron lost in menstruation. Other *jhākris* have uniquely individual approaches to bodily discipline and purification, and some spend considerable time in graveyards communicating with and even embodying restless spirits—practices eschewed by *mātās*, according to interviewed research participants. This connects to my earlier discussion of the association with itinerant healers and wandering Tantric practitioners, both of whom purposely break caste-bound distinctions of purity and social propriety.

The embodiment of powerful deities unique to specific Tantric traditions illustrates that the self is subject to transformative processes; that is, individual subjectivity dissolves into ultimate union with the sacred powers and entities invoked. As Tantric revelation is esoterically encrypted textually—often within mantras or in poetic and song form—so too can revelations be "written" onto the body as it is reconfigured in physical praxis, to continue with the metaphor of culturally embodied structures. Dominik Wujastyk (2009) refers to the "Tantric body" as an analytical referent for understanding perceptions of the human body in premodern India: "The Tantric body is yet another example of a non-anatomical body. Just as the Vedic body was profoundly implicated in ritual meaning, the Tantric body is an instantiation of the universe in miniature and a conduit for mystical energies that awaken consciousness" (200). I agree with Wujastyk's conclusion about the development of numerous bodies in premodern India, including nonanatomical bodies; in addition to the "Tantric body," Wujastyk describes the medical body, the Buddhist body, the yogic body, and so on. India's premodern period "produced a rich and diverse world of bodily discourse all of her own . . . various intellectual disciplines and religious faiths . . . developed distinct and different imagined bodies" (190). My analysis of embodiment rests on the assumption that such differently imagined bodies are crucial to the development of Tantric bodily praxis in which the materially existent body is presented as coexistent with not-quite-material subtle bodies.

Thomas J. Csordas (1990) contributed an important phenomenological argument to anthropological theories of embodiment. He distinguishes his position from Mark Johnson's cognitivist-oriented model of embodiment: "this approach to embodiment begins from the methodological postulate that the body is not an *object* to be studied in relation to culture, but is to be considered as the *subject* of culture, or in other words as the existential ground of culture" (5). This approach aligns closely with the paradigm underlying my research methodologies. I argue that *healing is an embodied shift in the totality of one's being*. In its strongest potentiality, this can result in a complete, even disorienting ontological transformation.

Csordas continues by discussing the phenomenological project of "pre-reflective," first-order accounts as the initiating catalyst of research: "The collapse of the subject-object distinction requires us to recognize that if 'hard science' deals with hard facts, they are the result of a hardening process, a process of objectification" (1990, 38). Objectification implies that the body is a mechanical *object* to be studied—an entity to detach from and to analyze, as per the medicalization of the human body in Western biomedical theory and praxis. It is in second-order reflective self-awareness that one conceptually detaches from directly embodied experience, viewing the body from afar—objectively—which in turn enables one to easily view others and physical environments as objects, as mere things. My research framework instead rests on a nondual model of embodiment. From this position, all forms of mentation, as well as cultural narratives, illnesses, psychophysiological imbalances, and the possibilities for healing and transformation, are *embedded in the enfleshed physicality of human bodies*.

Embodying spirits and tutelary *deutā* requires a certain yielding of the body in which individual bodily agency gives way to the receptivity requisite to invite beings to cohabitate their body. Frederick Smith (2011) presents an argument regarding mind-body dualism in psychological interpretations of spirit possession:

> If mind and body are considered separately, as has usually been the case in studies of possession states, the consensus

> has been that the individual experiences dissociation, which is invariably described as a mental state. . . . It is true that in possession the status or quality of consciousness, of mind, becomes transformed; it becomes unpredictable, reflecting unusual, dangerous, or socially inappropriate speech and bodily actions. However, within relatively small and closed circles in which possession is negotiated, such behavior is sanctioned, even commended. . . . It is regarded as therapeutic, indeed as successful therapy. (11)

This discussion again turns to the central role of embodiment in relation to healing as well as the analytical conflicts that result from presuming a mind-body duality. Psychological concepts about discrete "mental states" differing from physical embodiment, resulting from a foundationally dualistic premise, convolute the embodied nature of possession and can reduce the phenomenon itself to psychopathology. If the "mind-body complex [exists] as an indivisible unit" (Smith 2011, 11), then possession may be understood in a different perspective—an analytical framework that does not imply dissociative pathology. As Smith notes, whatever volatile behavior results from the negotiation or healing of possession can potentially be successful therapy.

J. R. Freeman (1997) developed a theory of "formalized possession" that resulted from his ethnographic work in South India, specifically in the state of Kerala. Paralleling the social contexts within the folk Tantra healing systems described in this chapter, Freeman worked with practitioners of the folk tradition of *teyyattam*, wherein spirit possession rituals are common occurrences. Given his observations of these contexts, Freeman defines "formalized possession" as being: "1) culturally constructed and codified at the conceptual level; 2) socially stipulated and regulated at the level of organization and recruitment; and 3) ritually effected through the process of performative enactment" (1997). This model is significant insofar as it situates possession as a uniquely sociocultural event rather than one embedded within psychological states; possession experiences are "effected through the power of its constituent ritual procedures rather than through the psychologies of individual practitioners" (1997). The notion of formalized possession corresponds with my emphasis on the culturally bound structures of possession rituals that engender efficacy in terms of purificatory catharsis and healing.

Another aspect related to embodiment involves how traditional healers view the physicalities of afflicted patients. When sick people visit healers to report localized bodily symptoms, such as gastrointestinal or *gastrik* problems, chronic bodily pains, or symptoms related to viral and bacterial infections, rice or ginger divination is performed to determine if a physician is to be consulted due to a "natural" (in Nepali, *prākṛtika*) sickness. While this may be the case, it is also often the case that these symptoms are diagnosed as resulting from harmful witchcraft, contamination by harmful spirits, or offending nature spirits such as *śikārī*. The presence of benevolent devas or *devīs* who mediate within this person's body for various reasons may also cause this; these *deutā* enter their bodies to protect the patient from harmful entities, or to initiate them as potential healers. Mental ailments such as listlessness, depression, and anxiety, often generalized as the English word "tension," as well as symptoms relating to madness, are almost always diagnosed as resulting from *boksī* or malignant entities such as *pret* or *bhūt*. Pumpha Regmi Mātājī discussed these recurring themes while expanding on diagnoses among her patients: "People get sick because of the powers of the gods and goddesses [*daivik śakti*]. Sometimes children get scared and their *sāto* [consciousness] gets subdued. In homes where Devīs are worshipped, the people sometimes falter in their worship. They make mistakes in puja and they also realize that they have faltered or made a mistake. This thought itself creates a feeling of unwellness and they fall sick. We heal them through the wisdom that we derive from our books."

In this manner, pharmaceutical medicines are seen as ineffective for bodily symptoms that are not purely physiological as the term is understood within the mechanistic lens of localizing Western biomedical diagnoses. The human body is conceived of as more than the viscera composing the material body—it also intersects unseen and incorporeal domains, vulnerable to the wills of capricious terrestrial spirits. Pumpha's main technique is to intone powerful healing mantras derived from texts such as the *Bhagavad Gītā*, the sonic presence of which is strong enough to extract malignant influences from the bodies of afflicted patients. It must be reiterated that the *sonic presence* of the intonations is what affects magical change, rather than the semantic meaning of the literary contents—hence her last statement about the "wisdom derived" from these sacred texts. She expanded on this point:

> The Śakti of the Devī enters my body when I invoke Her through the mantras in the books [*Caṇḍī, Gītā, Vedas*]. Our *sādhanā* is through mantras. We too can, through the mantras and chants in our books, put harmful spirits on their path to peace. The book we use is the Bhagavad [*Gītā*]. Restless spirits [*pret*], *bhūt* and troublesome spirits can all be warded off through the mantras in the book. I heal [in Nepali, *upakār*] through mantras and also āyurveda. We make these medicines potent through our mantras and the divine powers of Devī.

Pumpha Mātājī's description of the healing effects of mantra demonstrate her unique adoption of folk Tantra. Rather than approaching the *Gītā* and other foundational Hindu texts as guides to ultimate liberation, her orientation is quite pragmatic, drawing upon mantras within these texts for their sonic ability to heal. Such mantras are powerful enough to physically draw in and embody the presence of *devīs*. They also directly empower āyurvedic medicines employed for healing. "Our *sādhanā* is through mantras"—her main healing practice, shared with *mātās* in her use of first-person plural, is chanting healing mantra. It is the sonic pulsation of the mantra itself, the vibratory essence which flows into the afflicted patient's body, that catalyzes the healing process. Harmful and parasitic entities such as *bhūt* are consequently released by the sonic presence of these mantras. Mantra can thus be intoned as a powerful form of sonic healing, as described to me by an initiatory guru, Lakṣmī Mātājī: "Mantras and knowledge come to me instantly. Once I chant, the mantra is so powerful that it instantly heals the body. I also use [the sound of] instruments (e.g., conch, *ḍamaru*) at the same time."

Reflections on Folk Tantric Healing

Proceeding diagnosis, *jhākris* and *mātās* release embodied sicknesses by appeasing harmful spirits, the former often giving offerings of chicken blood to satisfy the hungry spirits. If an ill patient has offended natural spirits, the patient may be required to give their own offering to natural sites to reestablish any lacking reciprocity. Healing pujas are not isolated, individual events; they are often highly public, with an array of local villagers and family members attending these intensive sessions. This illustrates the socially integrative aspect of healing in Nepali traditional healing arts: healing as reintegration is not isolated from the greater community and is directly connected to the web of relationships existing between individuals and their local community.

While *jhākris* are described by villagers as those who apply "Tantra-mantra" and are sometimes even referred to as *tāntrikas* due to their association with charnel-ground practice and contact with spirits, the *mātās* I interviewed distanced themselves from this set of practices. As healing practitioners who undergo spirit possession, often for the benefit of afflicted patients, I regard *jhākris* and *mātās* as practitioners of "folk Tantra," a pragmatic, localized, and village-based approach to healing, which integrates Hindu and Buddhist devas and *sādhanā* unique to Himalayan cultural and religious confluences. Folk Tantra includes the South Asian phenomenon of *āveśa,* or merger with a spirit or tutelary deity by a ritual specialist, which is more prevalent in rural, village-based healing modalities wherein affliction by spirits requires the exorcistic abilities of a healer. Pragmatic necessity regarding a local health-care system is crucial, as many villagers in rural Himalayan areas cannot afford hospital or physician care or are too remote to access such facilities during emergencies. Healing is an inherently embodied process, requiring a release of malignant entities that have created a disruption in one's bodily states.

I am thrilled to contribute these ethnographic reflections to this current work. This volume's dedication to the ethnography of Tantric traditions is particularly relevant in gaining even a remote understanding of the multivalent plurality of South Asian Tantric praxis in situ. Relying strictly on textual analysis to extrapolate what kinds of Tantric praxis are applied by modern practitioners proves especially confusing and problematic. Among the research participants in this chapter, esoteric praxis and mantras are primarily transmitted orally, and *śāstra* are approached uniquely, as a basis for powerful magical spells that can engender healing and the removal of malignant substances or entities.

As Monkumari Tamang Jhākri told me in her home adjacent to the Takdah Tea Estate, allopathic medicine and Western biomedical treatments can assist some illnesses—but these are most effective when taken in addition to healing pujas. Her work is eminently practical, as those who visit her for treatment often have few options: "Medicines work well alongside pujas. People come to me because there aren't other options. . . . We *jhākris* are practical and we help!"

Notes

1. There is no consistent English translation of this term. It is generically translated as "healer" and rather inaccurately translated as "shaman." I choose to retain the original Nepali term without attempting to translate it.

2. This mysterious half-human, half-animal hybrid is famous as a shamanic initiatory being in Nepali mythological lore. The *ban jhākri* reputedly takes children to be trained and later leaves them in the exact spot where they were taken—hours, days, or even years later. As a master healer, the *ban jhākri* lives in the wilderness and trains those individuals who are destined to be *jhākris*.

3. Malignant practitioners of harmful magic often translated—with certain semantical issues—to the English word "witch."

Bibliography

Anzaldúa, Gloria. 2012. *Borderlands / La Frontera: The New Mestiza*. San Francisco: Aunt Lute Books.

Cook, Patricia Moffitt. 1997. "Sacred Music Therapy in North India." *The World of Music* 39, no. 1: 61–83.

Csordas, Thomas J. 1990. "Embodiment as a Paradigm for Anthropology." *Ethos* 18, no. 1: 5–47.

Gonzales, Patrisia. 2012. *Red Medicine: Traditional Indigenous Rites of Birthing and Healing*. Tucson: University of Tucson Press.

Gurung, Dristy, Deepa Neupane, Santosh K. Shah, Hanna Kienzler, Laurence J. Kirmayer, and Ram P. Sapkota. 2014. "A Village Possessed by 'Witches': A Mixed-Methods Case–Control Study of Possession and Common Mental Disorders in Rural Nepal." *Culture, Medicine, and Psychiatry* 38, no. 4: 642–68.

Dinnell, Darry. 2017. "Can Tantra Make a Mātā Middle-Class? Jogaṇī Mātā, a Uniquely Gujarati Chinnamastā." *Religions* 8, no. 8: 1–23.

Erndl, Kathleen M. 2000. "A Trance Healing Session with Mātājī." In *Tantra in Practice*, edited by David Gordon White, 97–115. Princeton: Princeton University Press.

Freeman, John Richardson. 1997. "Possession Rites in the Tantric Temples: A Case Study from Northern Kerala." *DISKUS Internet Journal of Religion* 2, no. 2.

Jones, Rex L. 1976. "Spirit Possession and Society in Nepal." In *Spirit Possession in the Nepal Himalayas*, edited by John T. Hitchcock and Rex L. Jones, 1–11. Warminster: Aris and Phillips.

Kirmayer, Laurence. 1992. "The Body's Insistence on Meaning: Metaphor as Presentation and Representation in Illness Experience." *Medical Anthropology Quarterly* 6, no. 4: 323–46.

Kirmayer, Laurence. 2003. "Reflections on Embodiment." In *Social and Cultural Lives of Immune Systems*, edited by James M. Wilce Jr., 282–302. London: Routledge.

Kovach, Margaret. 2021. *Indigenous Methodologies: Characteristics, Conversations, and Contexts*. Toronto: University of Toronto Press.

McDaniel, June. 2004. *Offering Flowers, Feeding Skulls: Popular Goddess Worship in West Bengal*. Oxford: Oxford University Press.

Mastromattei, Romano. 1989. "Shamanism in Nepal: Modalities of Ecstatic Experience." In *Shamanism: Past and Present*, edited by Mihály Hoppál and Otto von Sadovszky, 225–51. Budapest: Ethnographic Institute, Hungarian Academy of Sciences.

Redfield, Robert. 1957. *The Little Community: Viewpoints for the Study of the Human Whole*. Chicago: University of Chicago Press.

Samuel, Geoffrey. 2007. "Spirit Causation and Illness in Tibetan Medicine." In *Soundings in Tibetan Medicine*, edited by Mona Schrempf, 213–24. Leiden: Brill.

———. 2017. *Tantric Revisionings: New Understandings of Tibetan Buddhism and Indian Religion*. London: Routledge.

Sidky, Homayun. 2008. *Haunted by the Archaic Shaman: Himalayan Jhākris and the Discourse on Shamanism*. Lanham, MD: Lexington Books.

———. 2010. "Ethnographic Perspectives on Differentiating Shamans from Other Ritual Intercessors." *Asian Ethnology* 69, no. 2: 213–40.

Smith, Frederick M. 2006. *The Self Possessed: Deity and Spirit Possession in South Asian Literature and Civilization*. New York: Columbia University Press.

———. 2011. "Possession in Theory and Practice: Historical and Contemporary Models." In *Health and Religious Rituals in South Asia*, edited by Fabrizo Ferrari, 3–16. London: Routledge.

Trawick, Margaret. 1990. *Notes on Love in a Tamil Family*. Los Angeles: University of California Press.

White, David Gordon. 2000. *Tantra in Practice*. Princeton: Princeton University Press.

———. 2003. *Kiss of the Yogini: "Tantric Sex" in Its South Asian Contexts*. Chicago: University of Chicago Press.

Wujastyk, Dominik. 2009. "Interpreting the Image of the Human Body in Premodern India." *International Journal of Hindu Studies* 13, no. 2: 189.

———. 2013. "Perfect Medicine." *Asian Medicine* 8, no. 1: 15–40.

Zysk, Kenneth. 1991. *Asceticism and Healing in Ancient India: Medicine in the Buddhist Monastery*. New York: Oxford University Press.

6

Songs for *Siddhi*

An Ethnographic Analysis of Bāul Fakiri *Sādhanā*

Keith Edward Cantú

In this chapter I introduce a new perspective on ethnography for the study of Bengali Fakirs (male) and Fakirānis (female) with regard to yoga and Tantra,[1] as well as their participation in the broader umbrella of the Bāuls of Bengal. More specifically, I aim to use songs, recorded interviews, and textual data I have accumulated over the past eleven years to describe the way in which participation in Bāul Fakiri *sādhanā* ("ritual," "effort," and "practice," among other meanings, also often rendered without the final long vowel as *sādhan*)[2] can constitute a new method of ethnography as inspired by Bengali practitioners' perspectives. I am convinced that such a methodical lens can be usefully extended to other contexts—not just vernacular Yogic and Tantric traditions across South Asia for which the term *sādhan* is salient, but also esoteric communities or "secret societies" as more broadly construed.[3] In this chapter I first show how Bāul Fakirs often participate in the same social networks as sadhus (in Sanskrit, *sādhaka*, and by extension the feminine *sādhikā*) and practice a related but nevertheless distinct form of *sādhanā*. I then proceed to summarize my own ethnographic engagement with Bāul Fakiri *sādhanā* and the unique data such engagement provides when considered in conversation with secondary scholarship. I conclude the chapter with some observations on how ethnography could benefit from the application of a kind of participatory *sādhanā* alongside a philological analysis of Bāul Fakiri songs, notebooks, and early modern source texts, as well as reviews of secondary literature.

Throughout this chapter I interweave perspectives gathered from two interviews, recorded in high-definition video using my Android smartphone, conducted in Bengali of a Bāul Fakiri couple from Bangladesh I have known for over ten years and been close friends with for seven years, even before my academic interest in this topic began. This couple was selected on account of the details they were able to provide given their trusted relationship with me as well as their espousal of a kind of *sādhanā* that engages material of direct relevance to the study of Tantra. I wanted to make a general record of how this couple chose to publicly speak for themselves with their full knowledge that these answers would be used to assist international researchers in better understanding the beliefs and practices of Bāul Fakirs. One interview was conducted with only Nusrat Fakirani, the other with her husband the late Alam Fakir (with Nusrat present and interjecting).[4]

While this may be a formal interview with only a single couple, the trust and access that facilitated its acquisition is a culmination of the greater part of a decade (end of 2010 to the present) of sustained musical, academic, spiritual, affective, and emotional engagement with communities of Bāul Fakirs, the personal experience of which I will outline in the next section.[5] As James Clifford has indicated (1986, 2), it is possible—and today I would think desirable—for anthropologists to "assume that academic and literary genres interpenetrate and that the writing of cultural descriptions is properly experimental and ethical." Michael Fischer has also more recently pointed out the critical importance of constant experimentation in ethnography, noting its function in helping to dynamically "relay experiences in one place to other places" (2018, 2). This is the perspective of ethnography I have adopted for this chapter, as I think the constant "experimental" approach is necessary when attempting to understand Bāul Fakiri *sādhanā* and relay perspectives on it that are salient in the regional fields in which it originates and is most dominant; namely, certain areas of Bangladesh and West Bengal, India. As for the ethics of writing that Clifford alludes to, in this case I consider willful attempts to sensationalize and/or exoticize their *sādhanā* to be highly irresponsible since this would directly play into historical genealogies of othering and oppression (such as colonial-era campaigns against Tantra) that have historically marginalized their communities—unfairly—as heterodox (Lorea 2018b; Cantú 2019; Urban 2003). At the same time, the ethics of the ethnographer should be able to adapt, to some extent, to relationships as they change and evolve, and as new information is shared. This seems especially the case in esoteric contexts in which secretive behaviors are sometimes contrary to or transgressive of normative discourse, as well as when these behaviors or the worldviews that inform them may have severe material consequences when expressed publicly. Additionally, there are cases when the marker "esoteric" does not refer to intentional secrecy on the part of the practitioner, but to a kind of hermeneutics that favors multiple interpretations of texts, teachings, and songs, the public expression of which can have social consequences. In other words, conducting ethnography on esoteric topics, and especially Tantric ritual, does naturally require a great deal of sensitivity and adaptability on the part of the ethnographer.

While I make no secret about the fact that my academic training is in religious studies and not in anthropology, the cultural descriptions in this chapter will nevertheless attempt to approximate these experimental and ethical anthropological approaches to simultaneously integrate and transcend the world of the written text. My primary source material from this period of engagement accordingly includes not just notebooks of transcribed songs in Bengali (i.e., traditional primary source material), but also an intimate understanding of the material culture of musical instruments and other items, numerous contact numbers and addresses, analyses of terminology, a wealth of audio and video recording, YouTube videos of performances I physically attended, my inheritance of many handwritten papers and manuscripts of Carol Salomon (a prominent scholar of Bengali literature and Bāul songs, who translated over a hundred songs by Lālan Fakir based on her sustained engagement with communities in both Bangladesh and West Bengal), my correspondence and meetings with other scholars who also were immersed in the world of Bāul Fakirs, recorded phone calls, and published newspaper articles, as well as records of participation in multiple events and lectures, ritual festivals, and other events of relevance to Bāul Fakirs. I do not claim that the sum of this experience constitutes a reflection of a singular "authentic" Bāul Fakiri tradition, nor am I seeking to legitimize or reify a new or any other extant tradition. My aim instead is to experimentally relay my experience and the primary experiences of practitioners who are largely if not wholly unaware of debates in scholarly discourse around Tantra and yoga. This warrants further research into how their own conclusions are reached and how widely they are shared by others in these and related traditions. In this way I hope to start a discussion on the methods by which one can make the *sādhanā* of these Bāul Fakirs be more adequately heard in conversations in these fields. By comparing both my field experiences and their formal answers to interview questions with established consensus in current scholarship, I think much could potentially emerge of interest to both anthropologists and scholars of religion as they profitably work together on these and other topics.

A further point is that Alam and Nusrat's answers were usually in the context of my own relationship with this couple—they refer to me using my Bengali name, "Kiron"—and answers to questions are almost always directed not at a general audience but specifically to my situation in life, so to some extent they must be considered with my subjective position in mind. Their impression of me was undoubtedly informed by their view of me as an American non-Bengali white (*sādā*) male (*puruṣ-lok*) foreigner (*bideśi*) with Hispanic (*spenīẏa*) roots, but this impression of being an "outsider" should also be considered in the context of their knowledge of my fluency in Bengali and sincere "insider" interest in their songs and musical tradition that celebrates common humanity and largely de-emphasizes cultural difference (see McCutcheon 2005 for classic writing on this dichotomy).

Further, at the time of conducting these interviews I had not yet formally taken initiation into any chain of guru succession (*guru paramparā*) in the tradition (literally, *ghar* "house") of Lālan Fakir. However, upon their visit to Chennai in September and October 2019, they did confer an initiation upon me and shared new details about their rites, which I largely omit in this chapter, mostly since it reflects what they called a confidential "matter between teacher and student" (*guru-śiṣyer byāpār*). It is in these terms that secrecy surrounding certain practices is largely based; "secrets" are predicated on an individual relationship and are seldom static but negotiated in dialogue and practice between student and teacher and, in certain cases, with an additional partner and the "guru-mother" (*guru-mā*, or the guru's wife or partner). The one exception to this may be mantras and sacred "sayings" (*kalmā*; in Persian, *kalimat*) that are recorded in a guru's or murshid's personal notebook to be recited on certain occasions, which are thus relatively static formulae that are passed from teacher to student.[6] Nusrat's own reasons for encouraging Alam to visit me with her and confer this initiation, as I found out later, were inextricably intertwined with her personal feelings of attraction toward me that I did not share, and it soon became clear that this attraction was also combined with a desire for sustained financial and medical support. Her expression of these feelings in Chennai, which she had also made known to Alam, was contrary to my desire to obtain instruction (*śekhā*) in a more objective sense. I therefore stopped requesting more instruction when I realized that pursuing my own intention to learn further would not only be insensitive to her feelings but also contrary to my own personal motivations for further instruction in and for ethical writing on esoteric rites.[7]

Finally, two further developments should also be mentioned that transpired later in the time between submitting this manuscript and revising it for publication: First, Alam Fakir died between January 22 and 23, 2021; and second, Nusrat introduced me to Nasrin Ruponti, her niece, in May 2021; we fell in love and got married. My perspective on this couple's family relations and personal involvement has further expanded since the initial time of writing.

Bāul Fakir as Sādhu

Bāul Fakiri communities are directly and inextricably connected to a broader South Asian phenomenon, that of the sadhu (*sādhu*; male *sādhak(a)*, female *sādhikā*) of South Asia, some of whom live an itinerant life and some of whom are more established in hermitages (*āśram* or *ākhṛā*) (Hausner 2007). The Bengali scholar Sudhīr Cakrabartī in his book *Bāul phakir kathā* was probably the first to merge the category "Bāul" with "Fakir" (*phakir*) to delineate a more widely encompassing category that spans related milieus in both Bangladesh and West Bengal, India: "Bāul Fakir" (Cakrabartī 2001). Various scholars (Urban 1999; Openshaw 2002, 5, 113–17; Knight 2011, 143–53) have framed distinctive Bāul attitudes toward renunciation in different ways. The category "Fakir" (*phakir*, via Persian *faqir*, "poor") is also relatively tenuous and fluid, but it gains some specificity when understood in conjunction with "Dervish" (*darbeś*) and Vaiṣṇava attitudes toward renunciation (Cantú 2019, 136–38). In the confusion of categories, however, it is easy to overlook the fact that both Bāul and Fakiri identities are inextricably connected to another much more general social category, that of the sadhu in its many forms and social manifestations (Knight 2011, 143–46). When understood in this way, questions of categorization become less relevant than a determination to the extent possible of what *sādhanā* (understood as what sadhus do) means to these Bāuls and Fakirs within the local Bengali contexts in which they operate.

Many Bāul Fakirs I have met during my time in the field used or still use the title "sadhu" interchangeably with their name as a title of respect, such as Sadhu Humayon Fakir (1958–2017; see Cantú 2019, 122–27), who was most commonly addressed or spoken of simply by his title "Sadhu" (e.g., "Go ask Sadhu," "Sadhu wants to meet you"). Alam Sai was also referred to endearingly as "Sadhu" by his wife Nusrat, and Nusrat's younger sister also has referred to him as "Sadhu," stressing a folk etymological connection with *śuddha*, "pure." Additionally, many recurrent events in the life of Bāul Fakirs are marked by consistent references to the term, such as *sādhu-sebā* (in Sanskrit, *sādhu-sevā*); literally, "service to (or by or for) the sadhu," which refers to more or less formal meals shared in the company of a sadhu (or sadhus). The term is also frequently used in the compound *sādhu-saṅga*, "company of sadhus," which refers to formal gatherings of sadhus, their partners, and their extended relations, sometimes lasting several days, with elevated contextual rules for interacting, eating, performing music, talking with followers, and so on. These facts alone show that, especially prior to Partition, communities of Bāul Fakirs were undoubtedly part of an interconnected web of relationships that also spanned regions outside Bengal; such conceptions of *sādhu-sebā* and *sādhu-saṅga* are not unique to Bangladesh, as they are also found in other regions across India as well as Nepal.

A sadhu by simplest definition is someone who does *sādhanā*; both terms derive from the common Sanskrit root *sādh*/*sadh*, or "succeed" (Whitney 1885). Indeed, much of what I also describe in the next section "Bāul Fakiri Sādhanā and Tantra" will be applicable to Pan–South Asian "Sadhuism," a term first coined by John Campbell

Oman, a colonial-era author, to describe overlapping but disparate commonalities between groups of sadhus and "other strange sectarians" (Oman 1905). The perceived commonality between sadhus is a compelling idea and finds support on account of their networks of travel and exchange beyond borders (Hausner 2007). However, the "-ism" suffix is problematic as the consistency inherent to *sādhanā* that I describe is not one of doctrines, which often vary greatly from guru to guru, but of the general method of committing long amounts of time and effort to succeed in a goal of self-exploration and bodily and mental cultivation. These are efforts that are usually—but not always—at odds with or marginal to the constraints of conventional worldly life and include ascetic practice (*tapas*) and techniques of Haṭhayoga (Bevilacqua 2017).

Lālan Fakir (d. 1890), who is often considered the most famous Bāul Fakir among a host of other important personalities and poets such as Bhaba Pagla, Raj Khyapa, Panju Shah, and his student Duddu Shah—and arguably even the most important figure in Bengali folk literature as considered more broadly (Salomon 1991)—was himself intimately familiar with the concept of *sādhanā*. The term even explicitly occurs in the opening line of several songs attributed to him, such as "*Samaẏ gele sādhan habe nā*" ("If time passes then the practice [*sādhan*] will not happen"), which forms a pun on general success and the symbolism of sexual rites regarding the full moon (*pūrṇimā*, or the Supreme in semen) and the new moon (*amābasyā*, or a woman's menstrual period; see Salomon 2017, 32–35, 112–15; Jhā 1995, 74–76). The term also occurs in the *sthāyī antarā*, "permanent verse" (i.e., the chorus), of a Lālan song I learned from Sadhu Humayon Fakir: "*Āmi ki tāi jānile sādhan siddhi haẏ*" ("What is 'I'—when that is known the practice is accomplished [*sādhan siddhi*, one variant has *sādhan siddha*]" (Cantú 2019, 137–38, 157–58). The Bengali *tatsama* term *siddhi* in Sanskrit literature most commonly refers to power(s) obtained through the practice of yoga and alchemy (Vasudeva 2012), and the alternate *siddha* can also refer to a siddha, or person who either possesses those *siddhi*s or is accomplished in *sādhanā*. Yet, in Bengali it has a wider semantic range, and in Bāul Fakiri contexts *siddhi*, as a derivative from the above meaning, also commonly refers to the mixture of cannabis and tobacco (*tāmak sebā*, Skt. *sevā*) ritually smoked either alone or in the company of other sadhus or followers as kind of a "reward" of properly engaging *sādhanā* under the guidance of a guru or murshid.

While *sādhan* can therefore imply a technical practice, method, or meditation that results in a specific *siddhi,* in this song there is an explicit link between *sādhanā* and the general process of self-exploration; that is, intensified self-reflexivity, which is of course also an important part of any ethnography and a quality that can lead to communal reciprocity within one's social circle of engagement (see Gay y Blasco and Hernández 2020, 170–71).

Another important aspect of the latter song's use of *sādhanā* is that it is told in an Islamic Sufi frame, which demonstrates that *sādhanā* is not exclusively Hindu but is relevant to other religious contexts; in this case, Islam as practiced in South Asia. The concept also occurs frequently in Indian Buddhist Tantric medieval literature. While these religions all contribute to Bāul Fakiri *sādhanā,* I would argue that the perspectival lens of a given religion, when taken singularly, fails to fully appreciate the Bengali humanism of Bāul Fakirs that eschews any single religion.[8] For example, it may be tempting to equate them with Vaiṣṇavas, which is somewhat understandable given their roots, but they cannot be reduced as such since describing them as something like "Vaiṣṇava sadhus" does not sufficiently account for their Islamic Sufi, Buddhist Tantric, or even "materialist" (*bastubādī*) inspired song lyrics or ritual practices (Salomon 1995, 187–208; Knight 2010). A stock response when confronted with material that does not fit a dominant religious category in question is to view it as a folk accretion or syncretism, as Ernst (2005) has pointed out. While I think syncretism can be a fair descriptor when used critically, there is also the danger of using it to dismiss rather than identify and celebrate a combination of threads that do not fit dominant scholarly narratives on religious history or practice.

Bāul Fakiri Sādhanā and Tantra

Bāul Fakirs also are intertwined in the hybridity and eccentricity of Tantra, a world that on the ground is full of intersecting, overlapping, interpenetrating, and trans-sectarian practices and doctrines (Padoux 2017, 2010). While I find Hindu Tantra, Buddhist Tantra, or even subcategories like Śākta Tantra to be convenient for delineating a general scope of study, such categories when rigidly applied have a tendency to negate the way Bāul Fakirs fluidly—and most often consciously—

occupy a musical and doctrinal site in between the neat contours of religious establishments as defined either by scholars of religion or by the orthodox adherents to such religions themselves. This problem is especially brought to the forefront when considering the Islamic aspects of Bāul Fakiri practices that intersect with Tantra. The principal mode of their interstitial occupation that transcends religious categories is *sādhanā*, which is not demarcated by a religious category but by the connection between the guru (and often guru-mother as well) and student(s). Certain gurus certainly have discernible religious persuasions or familial backgrounds (e.g., toward Vaiṣṇavism, Sufism, or Śaivism), but none of the Bāul Fakirs I have met have ever indicated that the student must adhere to any formal set of doctrines or rituals beyond what the guru deems necessary for one's *sādhanā*. The lack of emphasis on caste affiliation in favor of the guru-disciple model is at least partially inspired by the Jāti-Vaiṣṇavas (O'Connell 1982), although in Bangladesh this phenomenon also derives from universalizing tendencies in local Sufi traditions in which all castes are welcome. As Openshaw has noted, in many cases multiple gurus are also considered, such as a *dīkṣā guru* ("guru for initiation," albeit for householders), a *bhek guru* ("guru for *bhek*," a kind of renunciation prevalent in Vaiṣṇava-inspired contexts), and a *śikṣā guru* ("guru for instruction"). Partners in one's *sādhanā*, especially the female, are also considered to be a guru, adding multiple possible interpretations to the mention of "guru" in Bāul songs.

Bāul Fakirs are additionally considered by at least some scholars to be a survival of a medieval Tantric or Haṭhayogic tradition (White 2006, 77, 82; Mallinson 2018, 199n59). On one hand, this is completely understandable; their sexual rituals do resemble instructions that are provided in manuals of Tantra, such as the circa fifteenth-century *Śivasaṃhitā*, which was also an important text for Haṭhayoga, and it is believed to have first been developed in a Buddhist Tantric milieu (Birch 2019; Mallinson 2020).[9] On the other hand, I was surprised to learn that many Bāul Fakirs do not usually use the Bengali word *tantra* as an operative word to denote the practice of sexual rites, but they use the term *sādhanā* instead. Tantra instead refers to the teaching of mantras as well as adherence to the guru's commands and, in a more controversial sense, to those mantras that are thought to bring about powers of control and subversion, which incidentally are perceived of as negative in most Bāul Fakiri circles. Established Bāul Fakirs also sometimes possess handwritten notebooks that contain initiatory formulae such as these mantras, and some were known to compose independent works and instructional materials. These written sources preserve an early modern and contemporary manuscript record of various practices in a vernacular Indic language that are also of direct relevance to yoga and Tantra. Tracing the genealogy of Bāul Fakiri texts, beliefs, and practices in terms of Tantra is a relevant task for yoga and Tantric studies since it directly connects the world of a given text with worlds of living attitudes and dispositions that helped inform the text, even if such worlds have been constantly changing. Understanding the way Tantra is still lived on a daily basis can shed light on missing pieces in the historical record and show how ritual innovations have been introduced in the wake of modern developments. Additionally, from a spiritual point of view the Bāul Fakiri emphasis on *dehatattva*, "the doctrine (or reality, truth) of the body," and body-centered practice (*dehakendrik sādhanā*) is intrinsically related to the way Tantra was embodied elsewhere in India, as well as in Tantric Buddhist (Vajrayāna) contexts in Nepal, China (especially Tibet), and elsewhere in Asia (Wallace 2001; Cantú 2023). Many bridges still are waiting to be built between the world of vernacular Indic sources and the texts celebrated in the Sanskrit-dominated disciplines of yoga and Tantric studies, not to mention Indology more broadly. This is not only true in the context of Bengali but also in Tamil and Hindi/Urdu/Hindustani, where critical analyses of vernacular texts of relevance to yoga and Tantra, both manuscripts and printed works, remain scarce. I find that there is often a general tendency for vernacular-language printed or manuscript textual sources to be overlooked by anthropologists as tangential to "lived religion," while Indologists for their part often overlook Indic vernacular-language texts as tangential to more established Sanskrit or Persian texts that treat on these same subjects, albeit sometimes in a very different mode. As a consequence, Bāul Fakirs seldom receive focused treatment using combined philological and ethnographic methods, although there are exceptions (see concluding remarks). I find that one solution to overcome this tendency is to focus on a primary thematic lens that directly intersects the worlds of both vernacular and Sanskrit sources, including oral and written (see fig. 6.1). The focus on *sādhanā* that I am proposing in this chapter is just one example among many other possibilities.

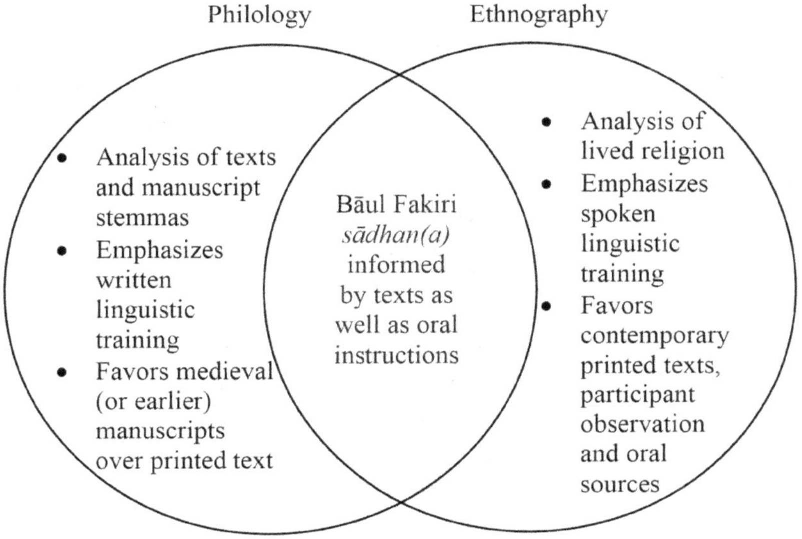
Philology
Ethnography
• Analysis of texts and manuscript stemmas
• Emphasizes written linguistic training
• Favors medieval (or earlier) manuscripts over printed text
Bāul Fakiri sādhan(a) informed by texts as well as oral instructions
• Analysis of lived religion
• Emphasizes spoken linguistic training
• Favors contemporary printed texts, participant observation and oral sources

Figure 6.1. A visual depiction of how a theme like Bāul Fakiri *sādhanā* cuts across a few of the general modes of ethnography and philology as currently operative in fields related to yoga and Tantric studies. *Source*: Photograph by the author.

A Journey to Find Sādhanā: Work in the Field before "Fieldwork"

In the ethnographic sections that follow I will recount portions of my own personal immersion in the world of Bāul Fakirs in which *sādhanā* became a guiding concept. While I had first read of *sādhanā* as a college student in the writings of John Woodroffe and the Arthur Avalon collaboration (see Strube 2022), my own personal introduction to the Bāul Fakir cosmos and its particular *sādhanā* was in Dhaka, Bangladesh, in 2010 while pursuing a Fulbright teaching fellowship. I met Binod at a photography exhibition, and he invited me to bring my harmonium to play with him at a section of Suhrawardy Udyan opposite the art college of the University of Dhaka (Charukala) in Shahbagh. I was already familiar with the area from my visits to a former temple to Kali (Ramna Kali Mandir) that had been razed to the ground during the Bangladesh Liberation War in 1971; a few months prior to meeting Binod I had made contact there with Shyama Devi, a self-proclaimed Śaiva *sādhikā* who was highly knowledgeable about devotional music, visual arts, dancing, and the Ten Goddesses of Great Wisdom (*Daś Mahābidyā*; Skt., *Daśa Mahāvidyā*). Yet Binod practiced a kind of *sādhanā* that I didn't expect. People came around to sit on the grass and enjoy some silence and a smoke of cannabis mixed with a special kind of tobacco leaf (*tāmak sebā*; Skt., *sevā*, or "serving of tobacco") out of Binod's clay chillum (*bā̃śi*). Periods of silence were often followed by songs by Binod with his ektara (a one-stringed lute) and his duggi.[10] As time passed I started to devote all of my free time to learning the songs of Lālan Fakir, whom I had only heard of a few months previously thanks to discovering a DVD of the eponymous film of his life *Lalon* (Mokammel 2004), released six years prior to *Moner Manush* (Ghose 2010), today a more famous film on Lālan. Binod helped me record several of these songs in my notebooks, starting with a typical "introductory" song for new singers and children entitled "I say that he/she is gracious" (*Dhanya, dhanya o bali tāre*).[11]

Binod invited me to begin spending the days and nights at a rooftop site in Dhanmondi 27, formerly a halfway house between two of Dhaka's most prominent Sufi shrines (*mājār*), where he and other Bāul Fakiri artists were welcomed to stay and pursue their *sādhanā* free of cost. Binod proceeded to open up his world of other Bāul Fakiri artists for me, including, among many others celebrated and unknown, the late Abdur Rob Fakir, Anu Fakir, the late Liberation War veteran Boduruddin Shah, and a couple named Alam Fakir and Nusrat Fakirani, whom I would go on to spend much time with and even interview together and separately. The afternoons, weekends, and numerous hartal or strike days were free for exploration, and explore we did: we not only stayed in Dhaka, but he also took me on my first visit to Lālan Fakir's *ākhṛā* in Kushtia as well as on a memorable trip to the annual festival for "Naked Father" (Leṃṭā Bābā, a Sufi *pīr*) in the environs of Comilla. We even spent at least one night at a cremation ground (*śmaśān ghāṭ*) associated with the syncretic religious figure Loknāth, where we stayed awake all night amid dances, drums, and smoke. He also took me to visit his guru, the late Sadhu Humayon Fakir, whose *ākhṛā* was in the environs of Narshingdi, and where I would later stay on numerous occasions and even perform at his annual festival. Sadhu Humayon Fakir had a contrasting presence (*bhāb*) from the relative quietism of his own gurus, Daulat Shah (1928/1929–September 24, 2015) and his partner the late Kishori Fakirani (dates unknown), whose *ākhṛā* is in the environs of Meherpur, and with whom I also had the opportunity to stay on a few occasions. Humayon Fakir publicly expressed his interest in the songs of Lālan that presented Islamic esoteric teachings on the Prophet Muhammad (*nabir gān*), yet at dawn he—like many other Bāul Fakirs—would usually rise at dawn to play an invocatory song to the guru, followed by a sequence of songs for the cow pasture (*goṣṭher gān*) that contain metaphors about the boyhood of Krishna (Kṛṣṇa) and the relationships with his mother Yashoda (Yaśodā) and his brother Bolai (Balarāma).

Contrasting Definitions of *Sādhanā* among Bāul Fakirs

My relationship with Binod continued to develop remotely and through subsequent visits, such as a memorable trip I took in 2012 with him and a close American friend, Zeke, to Ajmer, Rajasthan, to the shrine of the Sufi *pīr* Moinuddin Chishti. In 2013 my ex-wife Margaret, another American artist who took the name Sanatan, and I traveled to Dhaka and met with Binod with the intention to stay permanently. Binod took us to Kushtia and found a place for us to stay at a Sufi shrine run by one Bhanai Guru adjacent to Lālan Fakir's former *ākhṛā* and the present Lalan Academy. The shrine and its interior, blue-tiled room (see figure 6.2) holds special prominence at Lālan festivals, such as Dol Purnima, a major Vaiṣṇava festival held on the full moon that at Lālan's *ākhṛā* is celebrated with days of constant music, busy crowds and festivities, and sincere seekers looking to connect with Bāul Fakiri *sādhanā*.

We began to have a falling out with Binod, however, as we became more aware of his interpretation of *sādhanā* as a practice that essentially forbade or at the very least strongly discouraged any romantic activity between unmarried males and females. Frustration with Margaret's and my relationship led him to eject us from his life and accept Sanatan instead, which forced the two of us to find a new place to stay in Bangladesh, feeling like rather foolish white foreigners (*bideśi lok*) with dwindling money, limitations on visas, and broken dreams of pursuing a life of spiritual music. We initially gravitated

Figure 6.2. The blue-tiled room, part of a Sufi shrine complex adjacent to Lālan Fakir's historical *ākhṛā* in Cheuriya, a village near Kushtia, in which Bāul Fakiri music of exceptional quality was most often performed. *Source*: Photograph by the author.

toward Sadhu Humayon Fakir, who visited us during his stays at the rooftop of Dhanmondi 27 in Dhaka, where we were allowed to stay privately in a small room beneath the rooftop structure where other Bāul Fakirs stayed as a group and where there was usually a constant flow of people (see figure 6.3). Unlike Binod, Humayon accepted us and our lifestyle, and even formally claimed in front of him and others that while he didn't currently practice "pair practices" (*yugal-sādhanā*), he certainly knew of Fakirs and Fakiranis who did, and he publicly disagreed with Binod's position that such a lifestyle is incompatible with *sādhanā*. I renewed contact with Binod, who is an extremely talented artist-sadhu now active on social media, in early 2021, and he apologized and expressed that his understanding has changed and evolved as he spent more time in West Bengal and elsewhere in India.

Although at first we were discouraged from visiting their house on account of what was perceived to be their loose moral behavior, we eventually visited and stayed with the couple Alam and Nusrat (see

Figure 6.3. Our room just below the rooftop of Dhanmondi 27, Dhaka, where we were allowed to stay free of charge for several months in the summer of 2013. *Source*: Photograph by the author.

fig. 6.4, 6.5, 6.6), whom I had first met at Dhanmondi 27 in Dhaka in 2011. I had renewed contact with them while staying at the Sufi shrine adjacent to Lālan's *ākhṛā*, but they always remained somewhat on the margins even of Bāul Fakiri society. Alam and Nusrat had a different take on worldly and familial life (*saṃsār*; Skt., *saṃsāra*) since they made a crucial distinction, on the one hand, between those who are celibate sannyasis (*sannyāsī*) and brahmacharyas (*brahmācārī*) and, on the other hand, noncelibate sadhus and fakirs. His assertion that sadhus are noncelibate and distinct from sannyasis and brahmacharyas probably indicates a different conception of sadhu that remained salient in Bangladesh, or alternatively a shifting of the definition to bring the sadhu category closer to that of the fakir as defined by towering figures like Lālan Fakir in the nineteenth century. In any event, the category of brahmacharya which he contrasted with that of the sadhu can in some contexts still be applied to those who have an active sexual life but who have become committed to locking the *bindu*, as Carola Lorea has asserted is salient in the lineage of the Bhaba Pagla, a celebrated

Figure 6.4. Part of an old (ca. 1980s) and weathered magazine-like photo of Alam Fakir and his *dotārā* in front of the *mājār* ("shrine") at Lālan Fakir's *ākhṛā* (now Lalon Academy). From the surviving library of Alam Fakir. *Source*: Photograph by the author.

Bāul Fakir who was understood to have kept his Brahmacharya status (Lorea 2016, 172). In any case, Alam's response does seem to indicate that the category of sadhu seems explicitly tied to the practice of *sādhanā* rather than a stock category for any renunciate, and that this is the kind of data that either deep ethnographic immersion and/or participatory involvement in *sādhanā* can help nuance. The narrative of the "sadhu" as exclusively a renunciate, celibate male appears to have been greatly assisted by the biases of colonial modernity, perhaps indirectly assisted by Oman's seminal work on "Sadhuism" in which

Figure 6.5. Alam and Nusrat's *ākhṛā-bāṛi* or "hermitage-house," with Alam Fakir's *mājār* under construction as of 2021. *Source*: Photograph by the author.

Figure 6.6. Nusrat Fakirani's bed inside Alam Fakir's *mājār*, where she sleeps on occasion and greets visitors. *Source*: Photograph by the author.

considerations of female ascetics ("Sadhvis"; Skt. *sādhvī*) figure only about five pages (Oman 1905, 242–47), unless one counts a separate section on fictional accounts in which a low-caste woman disguises herself as a "*jogi*" to dupe a prince into sexual favors (90–91). Oman's legacy is important to consider since most subsequent authors have all but ignored the question of sexual activity among sadhus, including nonheterosexual orientations, which I have personally encountered in at least one context. He also omits consideration of consecrated sadhu "couples," which appears to have at one point been quite normal but is today usually subsumed into more conventional forms of marriage. An exception to this trend is Hausner's work, which does insightfully include consideration of sadhu couples who "argued that their experience of family structures was so different from lay experience that they legitimately inhabited an alternative universe" (2007, 39–41).

"The Practice of Yoga": *Sādhanā* among Bāul Fakirs

As we became closer to Alam and Nusrat while staying at their *ākhṛā* toward the end of 2013, Nusrat started to warm up to us and be comfortable with sharing information on the details of their *sādhanā,* some of which I will not repeat here since as mentioned previously it was material demarcated as a confidential matter between guru and student (*guru-śiṣyer byapār*). When I met back up with them several years later in Kolkata to assist them with obtaining medical care, they clarified some of their positions in an interview that they knew would be shared with interested academic scholars. Alam described that the "ritual" (*sādhan*), paired with "worship" (*bhajan*) to make *sādhan-bhajan,* is entirely a "matter of the body" (*deher biṣay, deher bhed*). The connection between all of these concepts is made clear in his following point: "They who take a guru, who take a mantra [and by extension Tantra], who have initiation (*dīkṣā*), who are initiated, who unite (*mile*) as husband and wife—among them there is a binding (*bandhan*) and expansion (*biśār*) [or trust (*biśvās*)]. This concourse between selves (*ātmasaṅgam*) is the 'practice' (*sādhan*)."[12]

This practice is made even more explicit under the rubric of "practice of yoga" (*yog sādhan*), which refers directly to sexual practices and not to modern postural practice.[13] Alam was in fact taught various postures (Skt. *āsana*) known to Haṭhayoga by his guru that he demonstrated to me on one occasion late at night in Santiniketan, but he referred to these as "exercises" (*byām*), not as yoga; I have also heard *prāṇāyāma* qualified as *yog byām* (not *yog* alone). At the same time, Nusrat was explicit in noting that *yog sādhanā* is for two people, usually a husband and a wife but also open to any two people who are compatible partners, and that the Yogic element is intended to create in the body an internal "posture" (*āsan*) within which the Supreme (Īśvara) can dwell. The above expressions of *sādhanā* when considered in the light of contemporary scholarship could be seen as an expression of Tantric practice, while the term *tantra* itself appears to be considered differently among Bāul Fakirs. Nusrat appeared taken aback when I asked her what *tantra* meant to her, but she eventually revealed that she viewed it as very similar to one's dharma, which she mentioned in connection with "knowing oneself" (*nijeke cenā*). Alam gave a much more direct response: "Tantra? Tantra is to take a mantra from a guru. Okay? One takes a mantra from them, and the guru gives an instruction/explanation. You have to go according to the instruction. That is what one calls 'Tantra.'"[14] When I repeated his use of "mantra" to note that I understood the main point of his response, he elaborated further: "Yes, mantra then Tantra. This means to receive explanation and instruction from the guru. Let's say I were to give you an instruction, Kiron, such as follow this, do this, or move that, alright? This is Tantra."[15] In other words, he understood Tantra as receiving and implementing practical instruction from a guru, which when enacted for accomplishment (*siddhi*) or in order to be accomplished (*siddha*) becomes *sādhanā*. Its practical nature relates to the suffix *-tra* as denoting a kind of "means to an action" and implies a kind of participation in "Tantric Culture," as described by Lorea and Singh in the introduction to this volume.

This exchange exemplifies a more general observation that the word "Tantra" on its own does not carry a negative stigma among Bāul Fakirs in Bangladesh, but rather it has a range of meanings and acquires specificity depending on the context, such as the importance of mantra and its connection with *sādhanā*. Although many Fakirs at least publicly distance themselves from what are perceived to be the more transgressive (*atikramaṇīẏa*) practices of Śākta Tantra, which prior to Partition would have been as prevalent as they are still today in West Bengal and Assam, even these practices are not commonly understood under the term "Tantra" (at least without any clarification such as the compound "mantra-Tantra" or *sādhan*). In other words, the term "Tantra" used on its own to denote a specific category of practice, whether stigmatized or not, is much less prevalent than other more general definitions like "system" or "science"; an entry for the word "Tantra" in the 1937 edition of Jñānendra Mohan Dās's *Bāṅgālā bhāṣār abhidhān*, for example, yields as many as twenty-eight distinct definitions, only a handful of which relate to "Tantra" as understood in modern English. Furthermore, evidence suggests that Lālan himself understood the Sanskrit and Bengali term "Tantra" as a class of scripture and not a practice, as in at least two songs he encouraged devotees to read the Tantras "whose essence is the Śakti" (*śakti sār*). Lālan is believed to have met Śivacandra Vidyārṇava, who was the guru of John Woodroffe (1865–1936) and who lived near Lālan's *ākhṛā* in Kumārkhāli, Kushtia (Salomon 2017, 178; Strube 2022, 166–67). At the same time, there is no evidence that Lālan himself actively participated in debates that would lead to the construction of Tantra as a global discursive category. Similarly, most Bāul Fakirs in Bangladesh remain remarkably aloof and distant from global discussions of Tantra despite the undeniably Tantric nature of their *sādhanā,* and aspects known to scholars or practitioners of Tantra are more often discussed using Islamic esoteric terminology or using the range of terms Lālan used in his songs (Cantú 2009; Hatley 2007).

Concluding Thoughts: Toward an Ethnography of Sādhanā as Tantra

The chief importance that at least some Bāul Fakirs place on yoga or sexual *sādhanā,* even as far to consider it a defining feature of sadhus or fakirs, should give us pause to consider potential distinctions between sadhus and sannyasis in regional contexts that may have since been elided in contemporary scholarship. A prevailing tendency in some previous academic treatments of Bāul Fakirs, such as that by Rahul Peter Das, who largely subsumed Fakirs into his description of Bāuls, has been to evaluate the practices of this "religious group" not in terms of its definition of *sādhanā* but by means of extensive references to extant secondary scholarship on Bāuls and their wider cosmology (Das 1992; see especially 388, 389n6). This method is highly valuable and useful on account of its encyclopedic engagement with an extensive range of secondary sources, especially sources in the Bengali language that are often ignored by surface-level summaries of the Bāuls. However, as Das himself admits, to dig through all the secondary material is to discover much that "is confusing and contradictory, much that is unclear, and much that is unknown" (422). Das's scholarly pessimism, based on his comprehensive overview of secondary material, was even recently quoted by Mallinson, who obliquely referenced Das's assertion, which Das himself had quoted from R. M. Sarkar and Sudhīr Cakrabartī, that Bāuls are known for "deliberately misleading enquirers" (1992, 395; Mallinson 2018, 119n59).

It is natural to be pessimistic about trying to understand the dizzying and divergent array of secret practices and esoteric symbolism when it comes to Bāul Fakirs, and skepticism is healthy wherever enterprising sadhus and gurus are concerned. For many of them, being a Bāul Fakir is an entrepreneurial career and is very similar to being an "artist" in North America or Europe with all the starving and struggle that may entail. Gurus and "guru-ma"-s as human beings therefore will often have motivations, desires, and needs that are not always in accord with a student's vision, or in other cases they will be more focused on their own economic livelihood or physical needs than the needs of the student. At the same time, every relationship is unique, and there are Bāul Fakirs whose creative passion, series of life experiences, and genuine teachers have allowed them to cultivate an intricate understanding of many practices and how the symbols connect with one another.

As to the confusion in secondary sources, part of the difficulty is that every scholarly source must to some extent be secondary in the sense that it is a mediated view; that is, if for the present we omit consideration of scholar-practitioners, whether Bengali or not, who may claim to represent emic perspectives from a "religionist" (i.e., a perspective claiming that the academic study of religion should conform to the specific lens of a given religion or sect) rather than an "empirical" (or even loosely "objective" or "historical") point of view (see Hanegraaff 1995, 102, for this distinction). However, I would argue that this pessimism expressed by Das can be at least partially mitigated by a willingness to approach the Bāuls from methods that are more directly engaged in the field, such as an experiential method that seeks to comprehensively understand their practice as a kind of *sādhanā* in itself. A fantastic push in this direction has been attempted in recent decades by means of both the textual exegesis of the lyrics of Bāul songs themselves, by ethnographic observer-participation, or by a combination of both. As alluded to previously, the late Carol Salomon's annotated and exegetical treatments of the songs of Lālan Fakir as primary literary sources (Salomon 2017), which also made use of ethnography, are an important example. Equally important are the extensive anthropological treatments of Openshaw (2002) and Carola Lorea (2016). To these approaches could also be added the ethnographic focus of women's experiences as engaged by Kristin Hanssen (2018), Lisa Knight (2011), and Rudrani Fakir née Anne-Helène Trottier (2007) as well as focuses on other poetic traditions that bear a similarity to the songs of Bāul Fakirs, such as that of Kabir (Hess 2002). An important further step in the context of Bāul Fakirs could include a more rigorous textual analysis of physical notebooks and compositions that contain their songs, instructions, and prose accounts (e.g., Openshaw 2010). These perspectives show that the path of *sādhanā* is full of twists and turns and encompasses a veritable universe of teachings, opinions, and humor; even the dead ends lead to something new that was previously unforeseen.

I believe this multifaceted approach to ethnography on topics relevant to Bāul Fakiri *sādhanā* also echoes the general indication by anthropologists as to how an earlier, more rigid ideology about the ethnographer and fieldwork being somehow different from the process of writing has all but "crumbled" (Clifford 1986, 2). In other words, the participants in the writing process begin to also be an intrinsic part of and partaker in the "object" of study. Once one's participation in the "object" is consciously considered as ethnography and written records are more consistently kept, such "ethnography of *sādhan*"—or, "ethnography as *sādhan*," but also "*sādhan* as ethnography"—can turn into a powerful tool that can be harnessed as an academic method in its own right, and one which reinforces trust within one's circle of confidants who perceive the ethnographer to be on the same path and to inhabit the same worlds. This kind of responsible ethnography as *sādhanā*—in which informants are respected as fellow human beings who are, like the ethnographer, also daily expressing virtues and flaws—may provide an important bridge not just to parrot back practitioners' responses, but to relay relevant information to individual fields like yoga and Tantric studies, as well as between religious studies and anthropology more broadly.

Notes

1. Throughout this chapter I have elected to use capital letters as in "yoga" and "Tantra" when I am referring to these words as proper concepts and/or collections of texts that are studied and analyzed in scholarship. I have kept them lowercase when translating the words "yoga" and "Tantra" directly from Bengali (*yog* and *tantra*).

2. Unless otherwise noted, all italicized terms are Bengali and transliterated according to academic conventions (ISO 15919, except for vowel-strengthening markers) that show phonetic relationships with Sanskrit (in this chapter abbreviated Skt.).

3. For the question of Bāul Fakirs and their historical relationship to (principally Islamic) esotericism, see Cantú (2019, 109–65) and Irani (2016) for sources of their esoteric Sufi cosmology. For the related question of their secrecy, see Lorea (2018, 1–24).

4. Throughout this chapter I have changed the names of living Bengali Bāul artists and Fakirs whom I have met and interacted with to protect their identity and help preserve them from public harassment. Some have expressed that they want to be contacted by sincere and interested scholars or practitioners, however, and as of the time of writing I am willing to provide their contact information to interested individuals with experience in spoken Bengali. I have also changed the names of other living relations whom I mention in this chapter.

5. I am very grateful to Carola Erika Lorea (personal correspondence, April 15, 2020) for providing me with contemporary sources on ethnographic theory that were very useful in the reframing of this chapter for publication.

6. The term "murshid" (Bengali *murśid*), a kind of Sufi "guide," is most often used synonymously with "guru" (and in some cases the *sādhikā* or female practitioner) in Lālan Fakir's songs, especially those that contain Islamic esoteric symbolism. See Salomon (2017, 8, 53–4, 67n18, 68, and throughout).

7. Although in my initial view one could separate feelings of love from *sādhanā*, in her view they could not be so easily separated. She demonstrated this by showing me an empty glass of water and filling half with water and half with oil, each representing *sādhanā* and love (*prem*). The water and oil naturally separate, but shaking the glass brings them into temporary contact with each other, and the glass needs to be continually shaken for the two to stay together. In this case I expected that esoteric instruction could be given separate from the cultivation of feelings of love, which was probably naïve.

8. The humanism of the Bāul Fakirs, idealized by Rabindranath Tagore, is centered on a conception of the human being (*mānuṣ*) as the principal object of devotion and the human body (*deha*) as the "primal Mecca"; see Salomon 2017, 52–59.

9. For a brief analysis as to how some of the *Śivasaṃhitā*'s teachings on sexual *mudrās* appear to resemble teachings of Bāul Fakirs, see Cantú (2019, 127–30).

10. The duggi is a miniature version of the left tabla drum, in a common configuration played in the lap with one hand while the ektara is played in the other hand. For more on the musical aspects of Bāul Fakirs, see Capwell (1986).

11. The pronoun *tāre,* synonymous with *tāke,* can be either masculine or feminine since gender is almost always unmarked in Bengali. For ambiguity of gender in Lālan's lyrics, see Jeanne Openshaw's introduction to Salomon's *City of Mirrors* (2017).

12. "*yārā guru dhare, yārā mantra neẏ, yārā ei dīkṣā, dīkṣita haẏ, tārā svāmī-strī mile, tāder madhye ektā bandhan āche, biśār* [or *biśvās*] *āche, ātmasaṅgam-i āche, sādhan. ṭhik āche*?" A few words (e.g., *biśār* or *biśvās*) in this part of the interview were not pronounced clearly.

13. For the different trajectory that so-called Modern Postural Yoga (a phrase coined by Elizabeth De Michelis) took toward physical exercise, see Singleton 2010.

14. *tantra? tantra gurur kāche eṭā mantra nite haẏ. ṭhik āche? guru tār kāche mantra nite haẏ, guru eṭā byākhya deẏ. ṭhik āche? byākhyā anuyāẏi calṭi haẏ. oiṭāi hacce tantra kaẏ.*

15. *hyā̃, mantra erpar tantra. māne guru byākhya niẏe, ādeś niẏe. haẏta tomār eṭā ādeś karlām* [*yeman*] *kiraṇ tumi eṭā mānbā tā eṭā karo eṭā calo, ṭhik āche? eṭā hacche tantra.*

Bibliography

Primary Sources

Interview with Alam Fakir and Nusrat Fakirani. In Bengali. August 15, 2018. Video and audio recording.

Interview with Nusrat Fakirani. In Bengali. August 15, 2018. Video and audio recording.

Secondary Sources

Bevilacqua, Daniela. 2017 "Let the Sādhus Talk. Ascetic Understanding of Haṭha Yoga and Yogāsanas." *Religions of South Asia* 11, no. 2–3: 182–206.

Bhaṭṭācārya, Upendranāth. 1981. *Bāṅglār bāul o bāul gān*. Calcutta: Orient Book Company, 1981.

Birch, Jason. 2019. "The Amaraughaprabodha: New Evidence on the Manuscript Transmission of an Early Work on Haṭha- and Rājayoga." *Journal of Indian Philosophy*, no. 47: 947–77.

Cakrabartī, Sudhīr. 2001. *Bāul phakir kathā*. Kolkata: Loksaṃskṛti o Ādibāsī Saṃskṛti Kendra.

Cantú, Keith Edward. 2019. "Islamic Esotericism in the Bengali Bāul Songs of Lālan Fakir." *Correspondences* 7, no. 1: 109–65.

———. 2020. " 'Don't Take Any Wooden Nickels': Western Esotericism, Yoga, and the Discourse of Authenticity." In *New Approaches to the Study of Esotericism*, edited by Egil Asprem and Julian Strube, 109–26. Supplements to Method & Theory in the Study of Religion. Leiden: Brill, forthcoming.

———. 2023. *Like a Tree Universally Spread: Sri Sabhapati Swami and Śivarājayoga*. New York: Oxford University Press.

Capwell, Charles. 1986. *The Music of the Bāuls of Bengal*. Kent, OH: Kent State University Press.

Chatterji, Suniti Kumar. 1926. *The Origin and Development of the Bengali Language Part I: Introduction. Phonology*. Vol. 1. Calcutta: Calcutta University Press.

Clifford, James, ed. 1986. *Writing Culture: The Poetics and Politics of Ethnography*. Berkeley: University of California Press.

Das, Rahul Peter. 1992. "Problematic Aspects of the Sexual Rituals of the Bāuls of Bengal." *Journal of the American Oriental Society* 112, no. 3: 388–432.

Dāś, Matilāl, and Pīyūṣkānti Mahāpātra, eds. 1958. *Lālan-Gītikā*. Calcutta: Calcutta University.

Ernst, Carl. 2005. "Situating Sufism and Yoga." *Journal of the Royal Asiatic Society, Third Series* 15, no. 1 (April): 15–33.

Fakir, Rudrani. 2007. *La déesse et l'esclave: sagesse tantrique et pauvreté perdue des fakir du Bengale*. Paris: Maisonneuve et Larose.

Fischer, Michael M. J. 2018. *Anthropology in the Meantime: Experimental Ethnography, Theory, and Method for the Twenty-First Century*. Durham: Duke University Press.

Gay y Blasco, Paloma, and Liria Hernández. 2020. *Writing Friendship: A Reciprocal Ethnography*. Cham, Switzerland: Palgrave Macmillan.

Ghose, Gautam. 2010. *Moner Manush*. Dhaka and Kolkata: Impress Telefilm and Rose Valley Films.

Hanegraaff, Wouter J. 1995. "Empirical Method in the Study of Esotericism." *Method & Theory in the Study of Religion* 7, no. 2: 99–129.

Hanssen, Kristin. 2018. *Women, Religion, and the Body in South Asia: Living with Bengali Bauls*. Routledge South Asian Religion Series 9. London: Routledge.

Hatley, Shaman. 2007. "Mapping the Esoteric Body in the Islamic Yoga of Bengal." *History of Religions* 46, no. 4: 351–68.

Hausner, Sondra L. 2007. *Wandering with Sadhus: Ascetics in the Hindu Himalayas*. Bloomington: Indiana University Press.

Hosen, Phakir Ānoyār. 2000. *Lālan-saṅgīt*. Second Edition. Vol. 1. Cheuṛiyā, Kuṣṭiyā: Lālan Mājār Śarīph o Sebā-Sadan Kamiṭi.

Irani, Ayesha. 2016. "The Prophetic Principle of Light and Love: Nūr Muḥammad in Early Bengali Literature." Edited by Wendy Doniger. *History of Religions* 55, no. 4: 391–428.

Jhā, Śakti Nāth. 1995. "Cāri-Candra Bhed: Use of the Four Moons." In *Mind, Body, and Society: Life and Mentality in Colonial Bengal*, edited by Rajat Kanta Ray, translated by Jeanne Openshaw, 65–108. Calcutta: Oxford University Press.

Kabir, Linda Hess, and Śukadeva Siṃha. 2002. *The Bijak of Kabir*. Oxford: Oxford University Press.

Knight, Lisa I. 2011. *Contradictory Lives: Baul Women in India and Bangladesh*. New York: Oxford University Press.

Knight, Lisa. 2010. "Bāuls in Conversation: Cultivating Oppositional Ideology." *International Journal of Hindu Studies* 14, no. 1: 71–120.

Lorea, Carola Erika. 2013. "Playing the Football of Love on the Field of the Body: The Contemporary Repertoire of Bāul Songs." *Religion and the Arts* 17 (4): 416–51.

———. 2016. *Folklore, Religion, and the Songs of a Bengali Madman: A Journey Between Performance and the Politics of Cultural Representation*. Leiden: Brill.

———. 2018a. "Pregnant Males, Barren Mothers, and Religious Transvestism: Transcending Gender in the Songs and Practices of 'Heterodox' Bengali Lineages." *Asian Ethnology* 77, nos. 1–2: 169–213.

———. 2018b. "Sectarian Scissions, Vaiṣṇava Deviancy, and Trajectories of Oral Literature: A Virtual Dialogue between the Bengali Songs of Bhaktivinod Thakur (1838–1914) and Duddu Shah (1841–1911)." In *Zeitschrift für Indologie und Südasienstudien*, edited by Hans Harder and Ute Hüsken, 83–114. Vol. 35. Studien zur Indologie und Iranistik. Bremen: Hempen Verlag.

Mallinson, James. 2018. "Yoga and Sex: What Is the Purpose of Vajrolīmudrā?" In *Yoga in Transformation: Historical and Contemporary Perspectives*, edited by Karl Baier, Philipp A. Maas, and Karin Preisendanz, 183–222. Vienna: Vienna University Press.

———. 2020. Mallinson, James. "The Amṛtasiddhi: Haṭhayoga's Tantric Buddhist Source Text." In *Śaivism and the Tantric Traditions: Essays in Honour of Alexis G.J.S. Sanderson*, edited by Dominic Goodall, Shaman Hatley, Harunaga Isaacson, and Srilata Raman, 409–25. Leiden: Brill.

McCutcheon, Russell T., ed. 2005. *The Insider/Outsider Problem in the Study of Religion: A Reader*. Reprinted edition. Controversies in the Study of Religion. London: Continuum.

Mokammel, Tanvir. 2004. *Lalon*. Laser Vision.

O'Connell, Joseph. 1982. "Jāti-Vaiṣṇavas of Bengal: 'Subcaste' (Jāti) without 'Caste' (Varṇa)." *Journal of Asian and African Studies* 17, nos. 2–3: 189–207.

Oman, John Campbell. 1905. *The Mystics, Ascetics, and Saints of India: A Study of Sadhuism, with an Account of the Yogis, Sanyasis, Bairagis, and Other Strange Hindu Sectarians*. London: T. Fisher Unwin.

Openshaw, Jeanne. 1998. " 'Killing' the Guru: Anti-Hierarchical Tendencies of the 'Bāuls' of Bengal." *Contributions to Indian Sociology* 32, no. 1: 1–19.

———. 2002. *Seeking Bāuls of Bengal*. Cambridge: Cambridge University Press.

———. 2010. *Writing the Self: The Life and Philosophy of a Dissenting Bengali Baul Guru*. Oxford: Oxford University Press.

Padoux, André. 2010. *Comprendre Le Tantrisme: Les Sources Hindoues*. Paris: Albin Michel.

———. 2017. *The Hindu Tantric World: An Overview*. Chicago: University of Chicago Press.

Salomon, Carol. 1991. "The Cosmogonic Riddles of Lālan Fakir." In *Gender, Genre and Power in South Asian Expressive Traditions*, edited by A Appadurai, F Korom, and M Mills, 267–304. Philadelphia: University of Pennsylvania Press.

———. 1995. "Bāul Songs." In *Religions in India in Practice*, edited by Donald Lopez, 187–208. Princeton: Princeton University Press.

———. 2017. *City of Mirrors: Songs of Lālan Sā̃i*. Edited by Keith Cantú and Saymon Zakaria. South Asia Research. New York: Oxford University Press.

Singleton, Mark. 2010. *Yoga Body: The Origins of Modern Posture Practice*. Oxford: Oxford University Press.

Strube, Julian. 2022. *Global Tantra: Religion, Science, and Nationalism in Colonial Modernity*. Oxford University Press.

Tagore, Rabindranath. 1930. *The Religion of Man: Being the Hibbert Lectures for 1930*. New York: Macmillan.

Urban, Hugh B. 2003. *Tantra: Sex, Secrecy Politics, and Power in the Study of Religions*. Berkeley: University of California Press.

Urban, Hugh B. 1999. "The Politics of Madness: The Construction and Manipulation of the 'Baul' Image in Modern Bengal." *Journal of South Asian Studies* 22, no. 1: 13–46.

Vasudeva, Somadeva. 2012. "Powers and Identities: Yoga Powers and the Tantric Śaiva Traditions." In *Yoga Powers: Extraordinary Capacities Attained Through Meditation and Concentration*, edited by Knut A. Jacobsen, 264–302. Leiden: Brill.

Wallace, Vesna A. 2001. *The Inner Kālacakratantra: A Buddhist Tantric View of the Individual*. New York: Oxford University Press.

White, David Gordon. 2006. *Kiss of the Yoginī: "Tantric Sex" in Its South Asian Contexts*. Chicago: University of Chicago Press.

Whitney, William Dwight. 1885. *The Roots, Verb-Forms, and Primary Derivatives of the Sanskrit Language*. Leipzig: Breitkopf and Härtel.

7

Serving the Divine Element in Humans

Everyday (Tantric) Vaiṣṇavism and What Begging Means to Bāuls

KRISTIN HANSSEN

Bengali poet-singers known as Bāuls bear a number of traits in common with other marginal groups belonging to the Tantric rubric. They divinize the body through mantras and receive initiation into their guru's lineage, after which they learn sexo-yogic practices where the ultimate aim is to vanquish death and acquire liberation from the cycle of rebirths (*saṃsāra*). Yet, Bāuls do not identify as Tantrics. Most consider themselves Vaiṣṇavas or Muslims, though some are also Śākta-worshippers.[1] Begging is their primary means of subsistence. They sing their songs in train cars, holding out their begging bags (*āslās*) for passengers to donate alms. Some couples sing together, but male Bāuls whose partners do not sing perform their songs alone, while women often beg with other women singing on the trains or going door-to-door in neighborhoods away from home. Begging is a commonplace activity, yet little attention has been given to the subject. To the extent that it is broached, it is mainly to argue that begging should not be viewed as an inherent feature of the Bāul path.[2]

One reason why begging has been understudied is because scholars writing about Bāuls tend not to highlight everyday activities like begging. Scholarly work is often multi-sited, based on interviews and conversations rather than on observations of social interaction involving day-to-day concerns. The poverty of village studies addressing social interactions between Bāuls and others is perhaps also tied to middle-class imaginaries of Bāuls as solitary minstrels, an image celebrated by the poet and Nobel laureate Rabindranath Tagore. In these imaginaries, Bāuls are typically portrayed as free and unattached, following a country road or walking by a river, with the instrument called *ektārā* raised into the air, while singing enigmatic songs about the heart-mind (*maner mānuṣ*). Since Tagore's time, scholars have argued against the view that Bāuls are unattached, pointing out that the majority of Bāuls, including those initiated into *sannyās*, have homes and children to support (see, e.g., Hanssen 2002, 365; Knight 2011, 50–51). The binary "renouncers versus householders" concept South Asianists commonly employ is therefore not entirely applicable (Sarbadhikary 2020, 169). Even so, Bāuls are often portrayed as inhabiting the fringes of society or as located outside society. The wider social context—their relatives, their neighbors, and the laypeople who give them alms—has largely gone unnoticed. In exploring practices of begging (*bhīkṣā*), I make the point that begging is more than a source of sustenance: it is a vocation. Those with whom I lived were adamant when claiming that they were not ordinary beggars. Like the Nath performers Ann Gold describes, they did not beg for "reasons of the stomach" (2011, 92). Rather, they described singing as a service (*sebā*) they perform for the divine element in humans (DeNapoli 2014, 274–75). Singing requires them to breathe life (*prāṇ*) into a melody, which empowers those who listen, and the alms they receive in return are signs of laypeople's affection. The exchange marks and facilitates the making and unmaking of relations where singers constitute themselves not as passive, destitute, and needy, but as pious conduits of a sacred power. Emphasizing piety through their manner of comportment and the clothes associated with renunciation, they show that singing merits a return (Mahmood 2005, 31). Clara Devlieger describes a similar situation among disabled beggars in DR Congo, who by modeling their begging practices on nongovernmental organization (NGO) activities "try to present their relationship with donors as reciprocal" (2018, 456).

The following chapter examines begging and what it means for Bāuls from the heterodox Vaiṣṇava community. It is based on fieldwork carried out in a rural, low-caste neighborhood in West Bengal, where I lived with a family of four, sharing their one-room hut for a period of nine months.[3] Aside from traveling with family members to perform the songs they taught me at festivals and village celebrations, I took part in everyday activities in order to experience first-hand what Branislaw Malinowski has referred to as "the imponderabilia of actual life" (1922, 18–19). The examples he cites include descriptions of how people care for their bodies, the meals they cook, their individual ambitions and vanities, their interactions with others, friendships formed, and hostilities expressed. Access to these minutiae, he writes, cannot be obtained through conversations, but requires an immersion in the everyday (18–19). In a similar vein, Carole McGranahan recently observed, "ethnography is both something to know and a way of knowing" (2018, 3). It allows us to acquire information, but it also enables us to note the rhythm and logics by which people make sense of the world they inhabit. The point is not to pit interviews and conversations against participant observation, but to show that the sacred enters into extraordinary as well as ordinary realms. Myths, rituals, and festivals contain the sacred in condensed form, but as I note below, the sacred is also found in routine practices like cooking and sharing a meal (Hinsely 1983, 57). Activities that may seem trivial or insignificant, such as cleaning the floors with dung or begging, are not unequivocally utilitarian but related to the sacred in complex, unexpected ways. Not only does a holistic approach emphasizing social context highlight the relationship between various domains, pointing to the ways in which, for example, dietary habits are linked to begging and sexo-yogic practices—it also brings to light the ways in which people are related. It was by sitting in the roadside or in the courtyard, watching mendicants and other people come and go, week by week, month by month, listening to their arguments and conversations, and getting to know their friends, relatives, and gurus that I realized that Bāuls do not constitute a separate *sampradāẏ* (religious community), which is how many scholars have described them (see, e.g., Capwell 1986; Dasgupta 1967; Salomon 1995). Rather, Bāuls turn to the same gurus whom (non-Bāul) mendicants and laypeople seek out to learn body-centered practices. Gurus, who specialize in these practices regularly meet with other gurus—Vaiṣṇava, but also Muslim and Śākta—to engage in spiritual discussions (*hari-kathā*) and share a meal (*sādhu sebā*). Indeed, body-centered practices are what these marginal communities bear in common; they also constitute the main subject matter of Bāul songs.

Because I was interested in esoteric knowledge, family members encouraged me to undergo initiation into *śikṣa* (learning). An arrangement was subsequently made where the senior member of the family, Muni Baba, assumed the role of a guru. He was not reputed for his knowledge; he had no other students. As far as I was able to ascertain, the step was a formality, carried out according to convention, to legitimate my learning esoteric knowledge—but I quickly realized there were strings attached. Muni Baba seemed to think that his taking on a foreign student would enhance his standing in the eyes of others and that his esteem would rise if I provided lavish gifts. The ceremony was a simple procedure. A youngish-looking, white-clad Vaiṣṇava sādhu, Dhiren Baba, bestowed the mantras known as *dikṣā* (initiation) and *śikṣā* (training), while Gita, his wife, tied a string of beads around my neck, after which I took the dust off Muni Baba's and his wife Sunita's feet. A few days later, friends and neighbors began to slip into the courtyard. Smiling sheepishly, they seated themselves on the edge of the porch. Then one man spoke up, noting that Muni Baba was my guru, and suggested I buy a platform bed and supply his house with electricity. Perturbed, Sunita countered that I had given them a lot. I chipped in with expenses for meals and clothing and replaced their torn mosquito nets. But deciding the amount and how often I should give was a delicate issue. His daughter Tara warned me, "My father has no limits."

A couple of days later, Dhiren Baba made another visit. Seated before me, legs crossed, he said, "Imagine that you gave me five thousand rupees and I asked you for another five thousand, I would show desire [*kām*]. Then imagine that you gave me five rupees, after which you offered me another five, and I responded saying, 'what you gave me is sufficient,' I would show no desire [*niskām*]." His point was that gurus should not seek to extract donations by exerting their influence, as Muni Baba did; they should show moderation. Ideals of modesty were evident in Tara's and in her husband's and her sister-in-law's behaviors. Before setting off from home, they put their wristwatches away. The women tied their hair into a bun, removed the dot between their eyes, and dressed in simple cotton clothing. Tara wore a sari dyed an earthy pink (*geruyā*) while her sister-in-law wore white—both colors associated with renunciation.

Origins

Although the circumstances of their origin remain obscure, it is likely that the spiritual techniques practiced by this heterodox and largely lower-caste Vaiṣṇava community, of which Bāuls constitute a part, have Buddhist roots. Buddhist and Hindu Tantra emerged in the region of Bengal and Orissa, where the worship of the female principle as *śakti* embodied by the goddesses Kāli and Tārā has its origin (Bannerjee-Dube 2000, 71). Glen Hayes points out that detecting their exact links with Tantric Buddhism is difficult; however, there is no existing evidence to support this view (2011, 507).[4] What evidence we have suggests that the community emerged in northeast India during the medieval period following the demise of the saint Kṛṣṇa Caitanya (1483–1533). Work by Carl Ernst highlights the interaction that took place between Sufi and Hindu yogis; his findings indicate that yogis from the rural lower-caste Vaiṣṇava communities in the Bengali-speaking region possibly engaged in similar exchanges of knowledge and ideas with yogis who practiced different sets of spiritual techniques: some Śaiva, some Śākta, and some Sufis and Vaiṣṇavas (Ernst 2005; Hatley 2007). That Tantric modes of worship, involving sexual *sādhanā,* were combined with love and devotion for Kṛṣṇa and his beloved Rādhā is not unlikely (Hayes 2000, 311).[5] Bengali Vaiṣṇavas, including those with whom I worked, believe the saint Caitanya is an avatar or incarnation of the divine pair Rādhā and Kṛṣṇa. Those from the Vaiṣṇava community, known by scholars as *Sahajiẏās,* claim that the saint Caitanya was a follower of *sahaj,* and some also trace their lineage to him.

The word *sahaj* derives from Sanskrit. It is composed of the prefix *saha,* meaning "together," and *ja,* meaning "to be born," which when joined connotes "together-born," as well as "cosmic unity" and "bliss." In colloquial Bengali the word means "simple" and "natural," which reflects the view that body-centered practices come easily and naturally (Bose 1930, 209; Hayes 2000, 308). The name *Sahajiẏā* is a scholarly term, established in order to distinguish practitioners of esoteric rites from other Vaiṣṇavas. The subjects themselves, however, simply call themselves Vaiṣṇava and identify each other in terms of levels of initiation: *dīkṣā* (initiation), *śikṣā* (training), and *sannyās* (also known as *bhek,* which means "Vaiṣṇava renunciation"). Training is regarded as essential, but taking *sannyās* carries more prestige insofar as it involves commitment.

Once, when I visited Tara's guru at his ashram—a vigorous, commanding man in his early fifties—he leafed through the pages of a clothbound book to show me a drawing made in ink of a human figure seated in a yogic posture. The body's interior had cakras that had been drawn in a diagram fashion as lotus flowers, each one bearing a different set of petals, with channels (*nāḍīs*) running through them. The top-most lotus, hovering just above the cranium, known as the *sahasrār* bearing a thousand petals, had a pool of water made of seed that contained a pair of swans, which I later learned are identified with breathing (*śvās-niśvās*). On meeting up with Dhiren Baba after I returned, I told him of the cakras, *nāḍīs*, and swans. Smiling, he began to demonstrate techniques of breath control used when raising male and female seed up into the head.

As I stated at the outset, singers of Bāul songs and Vaiṣṇava Sahajiẏās share features with other marginal communities considered Tantric. Techniques of breathing and the terminology of cakras and *nāḍīs* are prominent (see Padoux 1990, 140–43; Flood 2006, 157–62). Women are considered absolutely necessary in religious discipline (*sādhanā*). They also share sexual practices with certain Tantric groups that involve the ingestion and retention of body substances (Flood 2006, 164–65; White 2003, 68–122). Yet, despite these similarities, Vaiṣṇava Sahajiẏās, including Bāuls, are more inclined to highlight differences, such as that Tantrics worship goddesses and ritually ingest alcohol and meat as part of their religious practice, in contrast to Vaiṣṇavas who ideally at least strive to maintain a cooling diet made of vegetables and fish and who value milk and curds identified with Kṛṣṇa and the milkmaid Rādhā. Their most distinguishing feature, however (and one that sets them off from other Tantric groups), is their emphasis on love (*prem*). While Tantrics practice sexual *sādhanā* in order to acquire strength of will and power (*śakti*), Vaiṣṇava Sahajiẏās do so to acquire beauty, happiness, and love. Love is an essential quality of the Supreme, and since humans emanate from the Supreme "the way a spark emanates from fire," they reason that love is also a defining quality in humans (Bose 1930, 209). Love inheres in semen identified as Kṛṣṇa's essence, and it is also inherent in female fluids, menstrual blood, and sexual secretions, identified as Rādhā's essence. Hence, to lose a portion of one's fluids is to lose a portion of one's love (Hanssen 2018, 96). Other substances emitted by the body also carry beneficent traits, which means that to ingest them leads to the body's regeneration. Harmony and balance are key in one's attempt to keep the body beautiful and healthy, though as I note in the next section, begging for alms (*bhīkṣā*) can sap the body of its strength.

Everyday Practices

One day Tara and I traveled to another town, and upon finding that Bara Ma, the woman we had come to visit, was gone, we struck up a conversation with two other women living in a small house next door. The mother and her daughter managed to survive by stitching clothes for the market, supplementing their income by frying *muṛi* (puffed rice) they sold to neighbors. After chatting for a while we took our leave, and as we headed toward the station, Tara remarked, "They lead the lives of householders," implying that she felt they should follow the ideals of Vaiṣṇava renunciation through begging, adding fervently, "You don't have to be a singer; you can beg for alms without knowing how to sing." Her attitude toward doing rounds (*madhukarī*) was somewhat sentimental. Despite the fact that singing on the trains yields a larger income than doing rounds, she nevertheless insisted that she disliked boarding trains to sing, that she would much rather beg in villages. She and others used the term *madhukarī* (collecting honey) when they spoke of begging door-to-door. Because images of honey, bees, and flowers frequently occur in Sahajiẏā literature, songs, and oral discourse, the term *madhukarī* lends an air of sanctity to begging, framing it as a sacred Vaiṣṇava practice and allowing subjects to connect begging with body-centered worship (*sādhanā*). The dark jewel Kṛṣṇa is likened to a black bee, and the milkmaids too are compared to bees, drawn to Kṛṣṇa as bees are drawn to honey-dripping flowers (see Kinsley 1975, 24, 43). Tara's attitude toward begging may also have been linked to Bara Ma's appealing, graceful manner. A woman in her sixties, she had lived with Tara and her parents for a year or so during her childhood. Now, whenever she came by to visit, she made sure to do a round. Once, upon showing us the contents of her begging bag (she was only gone about an hour), I counted an eggplant, a banana, some coins, and a few handfuls of grains. But Tara recognized that people's willingness to give was perhaps linked to her charisma.

Begging could be tiring. In fact, the mendicants I knew, such as Dhiren Baba and his wife, were often gone for hours. Still, Tara insisted that singing was more taxing on one's system. I could barely make them out as they passed me on the porch leaving in the dark morning. Returning home six or seven hours later, Tara and her husband lay upon the mats, looking utterly exhausted as I fanned them and offered them a drink of water to recuperate. What made them weak (*durbal*) was singing. It required them to breathe life (*prāṇ*) into the melody, which depleted them of energy and upset their balance. Their means of restoring it was eating different kinds of foods classified as heating (*āmiṣ*) or cooling (*nirāmiṣ*). Because Tara tended to grow overheated, she avoided onions and garlic, which were viewed as hot. After singing on the trains, she also rubbed her scalp with coconut oil in the hopes that it would counteract the heat she believed might cause a stroke. Her husband's constitution was the opposite of hers. In an effort to invigorate him, Tara heated up some cloves of garlic fried in mustard oil and rubbed this on his chest and back. As a further remedy, he always heated up the water he would use for showering, no matter the season. At times, her husband would remark that he would take his urine, but he shook his head uneasily when I inquired whether he had done so. Occasionally, I saw him press his hand against his forehead, looking faint, and once I asked, "Why don't you take your body substances?" Tara explained, "They are poisonous if taken when you're weak. They must be cooled through eating cooling foods." She added, "But only those who beg in villages are able to get by on cooling foods. Since we sing we need heating foods to replace the loss of life [*prāṇ*] we suffer when expending breath."

Keith Cantú writes of Fakir Bāuls in Bangladesh that *prāṇ* is homologized with semen; the two bear different functions but are actually identical (2019, 127–28; see also Hyman 2019, 309). The Vaiṣṇava Bāuls with whom I lived similarly believed that *prāṇ* is embedded in semen, but they also said it inheres in female sexual secretions and menstrual blood. Singing involves being able to control the rhythm of one's breathing (*śvās-niśvās*), and these techniques are also crucial when you control your flow of body substances. When I practiced singing in the evenings, they watched me closely, urging me to moderate my flow of breath, for if I were to sing too quickly, my vitality or *prāṇ* would ebb, and as a result the song would also die. Their explications and experiences of how these entities are linked resonate with widespread South Asian understandings of sound as charged with transformative healing powers. Mantras used in ceremonies of initiation where novices are born anew involve a guru's whispering seed mantras through the ears and through the forehead, enabling their rebirth (Hanssen 2018, 35; Hess 2015, 33; Openshaw 2002, 127; Östör 1980, 57). In a related vein, Jarrod Hyam notes that the mantras used by Nepali healers are imbued with female power (*śakti*) employed to alleviate imbalances that render people ill (2019, 305).

Watching them, however, I wondered whether the reason they felt so weak could also be because they suffered disrespect when singing on the trains. At times, passengers would voice their disapproval. When Tara and her sister-in-law went singing together, they were sometimes told, "You seem like nice and decent women, why do you beg, why don't you stay at home, doing chores and caring for your family." Tara's father spoke of a similar experience. After returning home one day, I overheard him tell his daughter of how he had been mocked. Seated on a stool, shaking his right leg anxiously, he looked pained as he described the way a group of young men had humiliated him, urging him to sing one song after another, but then only giving him a single coin as a token of his efforts. "They disrespected you," said Tara.

Their experiences echo what Abhishek Basu calls attention to when he writes that many Bāuls are ashamed of begging. He also notes that many passengers, albeit for different reasons, dislike the practice, too, and that they openly express disdain. This set of circumstances is perhaps surprising insofar as Bāuls are widely viewed as icons of Bengali regional identity. Basu writes, however, that many people from the middle classes "do not like the idea of an able-bodied person begging on the trains." He often heard passengers exclaim, "Cannot you work to earn your own bread" (2011, 232–33). What the middle classes cherish are the songs and the image of the poet-singers as symbols of Hindu-Muslim unity. That they increasingly wear readymade patchwork coats, that some play synthesizers when they perform on stage, that they are invited to perform abroad, that the singer Paban Das recorded his music in France—these are things the middle classes do not entirely approve of. They prefer them to remain unchanged, roaming the countryside, untethered by family relations: an image that resonates with middle class romanticized imaginaries, and which also serves as a reminder of a rural, pristine Bengali past (Basu 2011, 234–45; see also Krakauer 2015, 356, 364).[6]

But even as the Bāuls I worked with suffered disrespect, they also claimed that begging is a positive endeavor. In fact, Tara told me that some passengers, including those from the middle classes, grew fond of them and would miss them sorely if they didn't go. She called them intimate relations, comparable to kin (*ātmīya matan*). They were *āpan* (own), signifying close, opposed to *par* (other), signifying distant. To exemplify this, she said they were occasionally invited into people's homes to "do *sebā*" (*āpni sebā karben āmār bāṛite*), meaning that they were asked to "share a meal of rice," a gesture evidencing loving care. Sharing food is supposed to generate relatedness. Intriguingly, the meal should be followed by the gift called *dakṣinā*, consisting of a small sum of money that dissolves the ties created. In answer to my question as to the meaning of this sum, Tara's guru said, "If you withhold the *dakṣinā* your guests will not be able to depart." In other words, the ceremonial language of begging, involving *sebā* and *dakṣinā*, serves to create and regulate relations, an understanding that differs sharply from that of Jain nuns and monks who seek to cancel and obliterate relations with the laity (Laidlaw 2000; Vallely 2006).

In his discussion of Buddhist transactions, Nicolas Sihlé calls for a conceptual clarification of reciprocity, which he claims has been uncritically accepted by anthropologists as universal (2015, 377). He notes that the alms given to Buddhist monks should give rise to merit, but he suggests that because merit is generated automatically on a systemic level, rather than by a particular monk, the reciprocity is weak. By contrast, strong reciprocity requires a long-term relationship between lay benefactors and a monastic recipient. Yet, this latter set of circumstances is something he finds lacking in the Buddhist material he examines (2015, 365). What he finds instead is the performance of religious services in return for remunerations, which are "misrecognized" or euphemized as gifts (2015, 35–36).

In response to Sihlé's call for clarity, I should point out that the alms Bāuls receive are not gifts, as Marcel Mauss defined them, insofar as passengers do not feel obliged to donate alms. They may give what they deem fit, but if nothing is forthcoming, the singer moves away. Still, from the perspective of the mendicants, the goal is to forge long-term ties of patronage marked by strong reciprocal relations (Devlieger 2018, 456). Songs performed for the sacred element in humans should be followed by an invitation to a meal, serving to establish feelings of relatedness, which in turn is followed by a sum of money (*dakṣinā*), allowing visitors to take their leave. I should note that the same patterns of exchange take place when Bāuls perform their songs during village celebrations, as well as when they visit one another's homes. Consonant with Sihlé's insights, the economic dimension of the exchange is softened or euphemized, clothed in a ceremonial language that presents begging as a pious practice that benefits the donor. Still, their sense of having been depleted of their life force (*prāṇ*) when singing songs for alms was real. As will become clear, however, Tara's claim that begging is a pious practice is, I believe, also tied to ideals of Vaiṣṇava renunciation (*bhek*), a ritual with strong emotional appeal where begging may be viewed as the "pivotal action that creates the true renouncer" (Gold 2011, 92).[7]

Vaiṣṇava Renunciation

Tara had reached the age of fifteen when she underwent the ceremony marking her rebirth as a renouncer. She was secluded in a room, which symbolized a womb, for three days and was given boiled rice with salt to eat. Her hair was ritually "shorn," though in reality she only cut a few strands; to remove it all would have been upsetting in that long, thick hair is a mark of beauty in a woman. On emerging from the room she received a novel set of parents. In giving her a seed-mantra, her guru became her father, while an older woman became her mother, known as *bhīkṣā-mā* (begging mother). She gave Tara pudding made from rice, representing sustenance, and a plate of brass, after which her guru tied a loincloth around her forehead before giving her a new name. She wore a new sari, blouse, and petticoat, all of which were dyed an earthy pink (*geruẏā*). She received a begging bag (*āslā*), a pair of wooden sandals, and a pot filled with Gangā water. These, too, were associated with renunciation (*sannyās*). Finally, rice grains were placed into the palm of her hand, which her guru forcefully shook; this caused the grains to scatter, at which point she was told to call, "give me alms" (*āmāke bhīkṣā dāo*), a gesture signifying that she would henceforth beg for alms (Openshaw 2007, 324–25; see also Knight 2011, 141; and Hanssen 2018, 34–35).

The ritual of renunciation serves as an emotionally charged model where begging is portrayed as positively valued. What is particularly moving is the expression of innocence a novice has if she takes *bhek* when young, dressed in the clothes of a renouncer, not fully conscious of the gravity of the occasion. People weep when they see the ceremony. It is a life-cycle ritual, which if undergone in adolescence marks not one but two transitions: the novice leaves her childhood behind, but she also leaves the comforts and security associated with the householder realm to embark upon a path of asceticism. Tara said, "my guru, and my parents, everybody cried. They knew I wouldn't leave them, but they *imagined* I would leave, and this is why they cried." What she said recalls Michael Jackson's insights of ritualization as capable of stirring one's emotions because it changes our perception of the world; our beliefs are forever altered, and new ways of understanding are instilled (2017, 53).

In her description of the initiation rituals she observed, Jeanne Openshaw notes that "with their emphasis on loss, death, and renunciation, the ceremonies were intensely moving"; however, she adds that weeping is expected (2007, 325). A woman crying inconsolably at one ritual she witnessed seemed unperturbed when she participated in another (325). While her ethnography is similar to mine, her analysis does not attend to the emotional dimensions, such as why the ceremony moves people to tears and why parents often want their children to take initiation. She writes that what is striking regarding Vaiṣṇava renunciation is that couples may renounce together, as well as that women are considered indispensable in religious worship. She interprets this in light of Bengali gender categories, where women are construed as soft, liminal, and malleable as opposed to men, who are conceived as hard and permanent, and that in taking *bhek,* men are feminized. Their clothes dyed an earthy pink, associated with the blood of a newborn infant, which will fade back into white, evidences the transcendence of hard, male, patrilineal structures (2007, 328).[8] She further notes that *bhek* is taken for strategic reasons. Low-caste men and women use it as a means of garnering respect, to keep social judgement or disapproval at bay, to loosen ties with relatives, and to legitimize their begging practices (2002, 136–37; 2007, 329). Lisa Knight similarly points to the instrumental value of renunciation; namely, that the Bāul path allows women to loosen society's hold on them. The robes of a renouncer and the taking of a *bhek* mantra give women a protective cloak, allowing them to move about in public without having to be chaperoned (2011, 152).

But perhaps another reason why renunciation is significant lies in its symbolic value as a model. As Drew Westen notes, people draw on cultural models, such as sacred narratives and rituals, to make their lives meaningful. He adds, however, that such models are only meaningful if laden with emotion at the level of the individual (2001, 39). Following Westen, I suggest that Tara found the ceremony of renunciation meaningful in part because it called forth values inculcated in her childhood. To her, initiation into *bhek* evokes feelings of humility, a quality Vaiṣṇavas seek to cultivate when singing songs for alms or when begging door-to-door. Her father taught her how to sing in train cars when she was a child, and he in turn learned the practice from his second partner Bara Ma, who lived with them during Tara's childhood. Bara Ma taught her sacred narratives and songs and started doing rounds (*madhukarī*) when she grew too old to sing on trains.

As I stated at the outset, begging, just like singing, is perceived as a vocation. It can also be enjoyable; there were times when they came home telling of a passenger who had been captivated by the lyrics. Moreover, singing on the trains allowed them to promote their talents, which in turn might lead to being asked to sing at village religious celebrations (pujas), an endeavor more materially rewarding than begging on the trains. It was also more prestigious. They wanted me to come along, and they taught me songs so I could join them. A group of lay musicians would be assembled, often relatives or friends of theirs. But other Bāuls were also invited to perform with them; their earnings would be split between them.

When singing during village pujas, they would dress in costumes they reserved for stage performances in brighter shades of orange, pink, and yellow. Singing for larger audiences created extraordinary events. The everyday seemed flat in comparison. As Jackson notes, festivities disrupt the daily grind, the predictable and tedious. By contrast, the intensity of feeling that occurs during celebrations frequently gives rise to a blurring of boundaries between one's self and others, an "identity fusion" similar to what Emile Durkheim describes as an emotional effervescence that occurs when the social order is suspended (in Jackson 2017, 26). Consonant with Jackson's insights, I found that the unfolding of village celebrations and fairs (*melā*) would easily lead to a sense of chaos and disruption. We never knew how things would turn out—whether villagers would meet us at the station, what food would be given, whether the audience would drink excessively, and whether they would treat us with respect. Curious as to how our performance had unfolded, neighbors and relatives greeted us on returning home, asking us about the events of the night. Begging never roused their curiosity.

Tara said, "All day long people go about their daily chores, enmeshed in trivial affairs. Not once do they stop to think of Kṛṣṇa." She said that Bara Ma, the woman who had lived with them, would rise at dawn and walk around the village, playing her cymbals while softly singing songs appropriate for daybreak, literally rousing villagers to the presence of the Supreme. Ann Grodzins Gold describes similar sentiments among singers and bards called Naths in Rajasthan, where collecting grains door-to-door is described as an awakening. When they come to the door of a householder, they make their presence known by crying *alakh, alakh* (Unseen, Unseen), alerting people to an imperceptible, higher spiritual reality and reminding them not to be distracted by unimportant everyday concerns (Gold 2011, 91). Like the ritual of renunciation (*bhek*), the following narrative features begging as a practice associated with religious piety.

Feeding Narayan

Tara learned this tale from Bara Ma, and she emphasized that this had actually happened in the past. There was once a Brahman couple. Both were poor. The god Narayan decided that he too would take the form of a Brahman, and so he came to their doorstep and asked them whether he could have some grains (*cāl sebā*). But because they were poor, they had nothing to offer. Rather than disclose their situation, they told the Brahman to sit down. Meanwhile, the husband slipped out, going around the village begging door-to-door. On returning home emptyhanded, his wife decided she would try to beg in a different area. She crossed the river and continued until she reached a town, where she found a store. Stepping up to the counter, she asked the storekeeper if she could have some grains, promising to pay him back as soon as she was able. He offered her some but insisted that she would have to leave something valuable behind. "Cut off one of your breasts," he said. "You can have it back when you return the loan." Having done so, she started back to cook the meal, but as she served it, a drop of blood fell on the rice. The mendicant inquired where the blood had come from. She refused to tell him: "Finish your meal, I will tell you later." But he insisted, "Ma, Ma, first tell me, then I'll eat." When she told him what had happened, he put some money into her hands (he actually gave her cowry shells, used as money in the days of yore) and told her to turn back. She reached the store and gave the money to the shopkeeper (he was really the god Narayan), who in touching her body restored it—but not entirely. Tara explained, "This is the reason why women's breasts are not identical. One is always slightly smaller than the other."

Apart from the explanation Tara offered, I suggest there is a moral embedded in the story, one consonant with the meaning of the tales Gold recorded, where listeners are warned of the risks involved in being miserly. Because the mendicant arriving at your doorstep could be the Imperceptible, refusing to give grains may have dire consequences, which is why a person should be generous (2011, 91). Generosity is the theme of Tara's story, too. The mendicant in her tale was indeed the god Narayan, taking the shape of a humble beggar, and the woman's gift to him—her breast—was one of boundless generosity, not only in the sense that her sacrifice must have been extremely painful, but because the female breast is understood to be a mark of motherhood and feeding. Here, as with the Nath stories Gold recounts, mendicancy centers on ideas of commensality in that sharing food establishes a sense of unity, something Vaiṣṇavas commonly refer to by the name of *sebā*. The word is usually defined as "self-less service," an act of humbling one's self by putting others first. Typical examples might include showing devotion and respect by oiling and massaging the limbs of an elderly relative, or by feeding and caring for the icons of one's shrine (Lamb 2000, 60; Hanssen 2018, 150). Doing *sebā* expresses the humility and "love that devotees share with the divine and with each other" (DeNapoli 2014, 274). That it also signifies the sharing of a meal (*bhāt*) puzzled me at first, but the significance of this is clearer when viewed in light of widespread understandings of sharing food as a means of channeling affection.

Helen Lambert writes that "who eats and drinks with whom" does not only serve to mark differences of purity, but also that the sharing of food and water is a means of establishing relatedness that cuts across differences of caste. Within this framework, food is understood to be a medium of love (2000, 73, 84). Margaret Trawick makes a similar point when she notes that in the Tamil Brahmin household where she lived, "love was often at odds with the demands of physical cleanliness and purity. It was not that love was intrinsically impure, but rather that in the presence of love, conventional purity did not matter" (1992, 104–5). Sharing a meal is a universal means for celebrating joy and togetherness. But in this Vaiṣṇava community, sharing food (*sebā*) is considered a sacred practice, often referred to as *bartamān* (based on direct experience), as opposed to *anumān* (based on inference). Significantly, too, food shares qualities with body substances in that both are sources of affection. Because love is embedded in male and female seed, a loss of seed signifies a loss of love, while its retention will ensure a healthy loving body. As I have noted, Rādhā's essence inheres in a woman's flow, while Kṛṣṇa's essence inheres in semen. The two emerge from the head visualized as Māthurā—the place of Kṛṣṇa's birth, from where they flow through the body to the genital region, called Vṛindāvan, or the moonlit forest where Kṛṣṇa meets with Rādhā and where they carry out their love play (*līlā*).

The ethnography Sukanya Sarbadhikary offers is strikingly similar. She conducted fieldwork among heterodox Vaiṣṇava Sahajiẏās near Navadvip, who related that they carry Vṛndāvan within their bodies and who referred to the practice of ingesting body substances as *sebā*. To be seated before one's bodily emissions, and to contemplate and ingest them, allows one to recognize the fundamental sameness in all humanity. Citing Openshaw, she further notes that "ingestion practices dissolve boundaries between self versus non-self," and in so doing, the practice generates affection (2015, 137). Their attitudes toward bodily emissions are consonant with my observations concerning food framed in terms of *sebā*, where sharing a meal constitutes a celebration of equality and togetherness. Also, as I have noted elsewhere, Tara and others believed that the food one ingests and the substances one emits both carry seed, looked upon as sacred sources of regeneration, which is why they are ingested (2018, 93–94). As with the sharing of a meal (*sebā*), ingestion practices dissolve distinctions, an activity serving to engender love. Yet, to ingest one's body substances is clearly an exclusive practice, one reserved for the initiated. Knowledge about body substances is not supposed to be transmitted widely, since noninitiates would be disgusted (*ghṛṇā kare*) if they knew. Sarbadhikary points out that because they found their practices disgusting, people from neighboring Vaiṣṇava communities urged her not to associate with Vaiṣṇava Sahajiẏās. They also disapproved of the begging bags (*āslās*) they carried, claiming that these should be reserved for "respectable" renouncers (2015, 108–9, 123). But one wonders whether the low-caste poor living in the area also viewed Vaiṣṇava Sahajiẏās with disdain.

Indeed, those who gave them alms or arranged a program were mostly poor like the mendicants themselves; they were landless laborers and peasants. In addition to the income they would get through begging, they received some help from music students, as well as from fixers or mediators, or local politicians, able to navigate the bureaucracy, who would assist them with documents and subsidies. In return, Bāul singers showed their loyalty by performing songs at public events to honor and support them. As with the Bāuls Knight has worked with, the singers I lived with were invited to perform at functions arranged by the middle classes to raise awareness about leprosy and tuberculosis, as well as caste-based discrimination, and the importance of learning how to read and write (2011, 40, 130). Their earnings were scant; the bulk of their income stemmed from begging, yet the ties they forged with patrons were still perceived as valuable and might prove useful in times of stress. To be an isolated, disconnected person without material resources is to be destitute.

Conclusion

One might argue that Bāuls and mendicants are subject to exclusion from mainstream society due to their ingestion practices. According to this reasoning, because Bāuls and Vaiṣṇava mendicants practice esoteric rites, initiation into *śikṣā* or *bhek* (Vaiṣṇava renunciation) does not ameliorate their social difficulties, as Khandelwal and Hausner argued (2006, 5). Rather, the taking of these mantras and their engaging in body-centered practices only serves to marginalize them even further (see Sarbadhikary 2015, 123). In this light, their efforts to befriend the laity would appear to be in vain insofar as their deviancy excludes them. And yet, I would venture to suggest that their religious practice is perhaps not the only reason why many orthodox Vaiṣṇavas as well as some people from the middle classes choose to keep apart. My evidence suggests that those who view them with disdain find their poverty offensive; they also fail to appreciate their calling, dismissing Bāuls and Vaiṣṇava mendicants as poor and undeserving, as low-class, low-caste riffraff who only beg to fill their stomachs

(Basu 2011, 232–33; Gold 2011, 106–7). In describing Nath performers, Gold (2011, 106–7) notes that singing for alms is increasingly difficult; people no longer give as lavishly as they did in former times, and in consequence some Naths have ceased doing rounds. Begging is becoming increasingly difficult for Bāuls and mendicants, and because they are often treated with disdain, they feel ambivalent about the practice, which is not to say that begging is conceived as unimportant. As I have shown, it is a religiously sanctioned activity. Begging is perceived in terms of a ritual idiom that confirms and validates the practice as an act of humility and piety that benefits the laity through their offering of *prāṇ* embedded in words and music. Ideally, their practice is reciprocated through the gifting of alms as well as through invitations to share a meal (*sebā*). Sharing food (*sebā*) establishes a sense of unity and joy. In contrast, *dakṣinā* establishes a sense of separation. In ritual terms, the two are linked. Together they mark the flow of social interaction between mendicants and others.

Bāul songs have been described as windows into a system of beliefs where human beings are portrayed through metaphors and tropes as carriers of a divine essence (Salomon 1995). Their songs have also been shown to voice resistance against injustices of caste (Knight 2011, 129; Lorea 2016, 2n5; 2018, 88). In attending to the ritual language of mixing and separation, I add another wrinkle to this discussion. The ritual idiom of *sebā* and *dakṣinā* situates singers and mendicants at the center of a ceremonial exchange, a religious transaction that allows them to connect and disconnect from others. Esoteric training and their views of singing involving *prāṇ* are clearly borne out of Tantric practices of discipline and bodily control. David Gordon White defines *Tantra* as the beliefs and practices involving the ability to harness sacred energy, equated with the Supreme that gives rise to and upholds the universe, through processes of appropriation and by adopting techniques enabling adepts to control the Supreme energy within the body (White 2000, 9). Bāuls seek to transfer this sacred energy to others. The tale of the divine Narayan, taking the form of a humble beggar who comes to the door of a Brahman couple, bears resonance in part because they see themselves as vessels transmitting life (*prāṇ*). Like the Brahman woman offering up her breast, a source of life, to nourish Narayan, Tara and her family members would offer up their *prāṇ* when singing on the trains. That begging is important and considered part of their vocation was brought home to me quite early in my fieldwork. The first gift I received was a patchwork-begging bag, and the first task I was taught was how to carry it and open and close it by tying the strings into a special knot.

Notes

1. Lorea's work (2016) is a study of the Bāul *śākta* worshipper called Bhaba Pagla and a number of the songs he composed.

2. Knight argues against essentialist perceptions of begging as comprising an intrinsic feature of the Bāul path and a means for gauging the authenticity of Bāuls (Knight 2011, 151).

3. Additional six months of fieldwork preceding this was carried out for my master's thesis in 1994, a two-month follow-up study was carried out in 2006, and an additional brief visit was made in 2012, which when taken together amount to eighteen months in all.

4. Shashibusan Dasgupta is of the view that their beliefs and practices clearly predate Buddhist and Hindu Tantric cults (1969, 116).

5. It is interesting to note that Tara's guru claimed he was well acquainted with all the major creeds, including Buddhism, Islam, and Christianity—a remark that serves as a reminder of the competition that occurs between yogis with different religious orientations, an issue Ernst addresses, though he notes too that many yogis were in sympathy with one another (2005, 36).

6. Knight similarly writes that the middle classes regard the singers, particularly female singers, with ambivalence, romanticizing them as saintly persons unfettered by conventions, while on the other hand rebuking them for their nonnormative behavior (2011, 25, 49; see also Capwell 1986; Salomon 1995; Openshaw 2002).

7. Gold (2011, 92) notes that it is particularly the act of begging from one's family relations, particularly one's mother or sister, that renders one a real or true renouncer. Knight's (2011, 141) findings indicate that this is also true for Vaiṣṇavas and Bāuls.

8. Rather than the blood associated with birth, my findings indicate that the colors red, pink, and orange stand for menstrual blood (see Hanssen 2006, 95).

Bibliography

Bannerjee-Dube, Ishita. 2011. "The Influence of the Naths on Bhima Bhoi and Mahima Dharma." In *Yogi Heroes and Poets: Histories and Legends of the Naths*, edited by David N. Lorenzen and Adrián Muñoz, 63–76. Albany: SUNY Press.

Basu, Abhishek. 2011. "The Baul Workplace: Towards a Review of the Icon." In *Poetics and Politics of Sufism & Bhakti in South Asia: Love, Loss and Liberation*, edited by Kavita Panjabi, 223–42. Hyderabad: Orient Black Swan.

Bose, Manindra Mohan. 1930. *The Post-Chaitanya Sahajiyā Cult of Bengal*. Calcutta: University of Calcutta.

Cantú, Keith. 2019. "Islamic Esotericism in the Bengali Bāul Songs of Lālan Fakir." *Correspondences* 7, no. 1: 109–65.

Capwell, Charles. 1986. *The Music of the Bauls of Bengal*. Kent, OH: The Kent State University Press.

Carsten, Janet. 2000. *Cultures of Relatedness: New Approaches to the Study of Kinship*. New York: Cambridge University Press.

Dasgupta, Shashibhushan. 1962 [1946]. *Obscure Religious Cults*. 2nd ed. Calcutta: K. L. Mukhopadhyay Publishers.

DeNapoli, Anotinette Elizabeth. 2014. *Real Sadhus Sing to God: Gender, Asceticism, and Vernacular Religion in Rajasthan*. New York: Oxford University Press.

Devlieger, Clara. 2018. "Contractual dependencies: Disability and the bureaucracy of begging in Kinshasa, Democratic Republic of Congo." *American Ethnologist* 45, no. 4: 455–69.

Ernst, Carl W. 2005. "Situating Sufism and Yoga." *Journal of the Royal Asiatic Society* 15, no. 1: 15–43.

Gold, Ann Grodzins. 2011. "Awakening Generosity in Nath Tales from Rajasthan." In *Yogi Heroes and Poets: Histories and Legends of the Naths*, edited by David N. Lorenzen and Adrián Muñoz, 91–107. Albany: SUNY Press.

Hanssen, Kristin. 2002. "Ingesting Menstrual Blood: Notions of Health and Bodily Fluids in Bengal." *Ethnology* 41, no. 4: 365–79.

———. 2006. "The True River Ganges: Tara's Begging Practices." In *Women's Renunciation in South Asia: Nuns, Yoginis, Saints, and Singers*, edited by Meena Khandelwal, Sondra Hausner, and Ann Grodzins Gold, 95–123. New York: Palgrave Macmillan.

———. 2018. *Women, Religion, and the Body in South Asia: Living with Bengali Bauls*. London: Routledge.

Hayes, Glen. 2000. "The Necklace of Immortality: A Seventeenth Century Vaiṣṇava Sahajiya Text." In *Tantra in Practice*, edited by David Gordon White, 308–26. Princeton: Princeton University Press.

Hatley, Shaman. 2007. "Mapping the Esoteric Body in the Islamic Yoga of Bengal. *History of Religions* 46, no. 4: 352–68.

Hess, Linda. 2015. *Bodies of Song: Kabir Oral Traditions and Performative Worlds in North India*. Oxford: Oxford University Press.

Hinsley, Curtis. 1983. "Ethnographic Charisma and Scientific Routine: Cushing and Fewkes in the American Southwest, 1879–1893." In *Observers*

Observed: Essays on Ethnographic Fieldwork, edited by George W. Stocking Jr., 53–69. Madison: University of Wisconsin.

Hyam, Jarrod. 2019. "The Transformational Body: Bāul and Jhākri Approaches to Embodied Healing." PhD diss., University of Sydney.

Jackson, Michael. 2017. *How Life Worlds Work: Emotionality, Sociality and the Ambiguity of Being*. Chicago: University of Chicago Press.

Khandelwal, Meena, and Sondra Hausner. 2006. Introduction to *Women's Renunciation in South Asia: Nuns, Yoginis, Saints, and Singers*, edited by Meena Khandelwal, Sondra Hausner, and Ann Grodzins Gold, 1–36. New York: Palgrave Macmillan.

Kinsley, David R. 1975. *The Sword and the Flute: Kāli & Kṛṣṇa, Dark Visions of the Terrible and Sublime in Hindu Mythology*. Berkeley: University of California Press.

Knight, Lisa I. 2006. "Renouncing Expectations: Single Baul Women Renouncers and the Value of Being a Wife." In *Women's Renunciation in South Asia: Nuns, Yoginis, Saints, and Singers*, edited by Meena Khandelwal, Soundra Hausner and Ann Grodzins Gold, 191–222. New York: Palgrave Macmillan.

———. 2011. *Contradictory Lives: Baul Women in India and Bangladesh*. New York: Oxford University Press.

Krakauer, Ben. 2015. "The Ennobling of a 'Folk Tradition' and the Disempowerment of the Performers: Celebrations and Appropriations of Baul-Fakir Identity in West Bengal." *Ethnomusicology* 59, no. 3: 355–79.

Lambert, Helen. 2000. "Sentiments and Substance in North Indian Forms of Relatedness." In *Cultures of Relatedness: New Approaches to the Study of Kinship*, edited by Janet Carsten, 73–89. New York: Cambridge University Press.

Lamb, Sarah. 2000. *White Saris and Sweet Mangoes: Aging, Gender, and Body in North India*. Berkeley: University of California Press.

Lorea, Carola Erika. 2016. *Folklore, Religion and the Songs of a Bengali Madman: A Journey between Performance and the Politics of Cultural Representation*. Leiden: Brill.

Lorenzen, David N., and Adrián Muñoz. 2011. *Yogi Heroes and Poets: Histories and Legends of the Naths*. Albany: SUNY Press.

Mahmood, Saba. 2005. *Politics of Piety: The Islamic Revival and the Feminist Subject*. Princeton: Princeton University Press.

Malinowski, Bronislaw. 1961 [1922]. *Argonauts of the Western Pacific: An Account of Native Enterprise and Adventure in the Archipelagoes of Melanesian New Guinea*. Long Grove, IL: Waveland Press.

Mauss, Marcel. 1996 [1950]. *The Gift: The Form and Reason for Exchange in Archaic Societies*. London: Routledge.

McGranahan, Carole. 2018. "Ethnography Beyond Method: The Importance of an Ethnographic Sensibility." *Sites: New Series* 15, no. 1: 1–10.

Openshaw, Jeanne. 2002. *Seeking Bauls of Bengal*, Cambridge: Cambridge University Press.

———. 2007. "Renunciation Feminised? Joint Renunciation of Female-Male Pairs in Bengali Vaishnavism." *Religion* 37, no. 4: 319–32.

Östör, Ákas. 1980. *The Play of the Gods: Locality, Ideology, Structure, and Time in the Festival of a Bengali Town*. Chicago: University of Chicago Press.

Padoux, André. 1990. *Vāc: The Concept of the Word in Selected Hindu Tantras*. Translated by Jacques Gontier. Albany: SUNY Press.

Panjabi, Kavita. 2011. *Poetics and Politics of Sufism & Bhakti in South Asia: Love, Loss, and Liberation*. Hyderabad: Orient Black Swan.

Raheja, Gloria Goodwyn. 1988. *The Poison in the Gift: Ritual, Prestation, and the Dominant Caste in a North Indian Village*. Chicago: University of Chicago Press.

Salomon, Carol. 1995. "Baul Songs." In *Religions of India in Practice*, edited by Donald S. Lopez Jr., 267–304. Princeton: Princeton University Press.

Sarbadhikary, Sukanya. 2015. *The Place of Devotion: Siting and Experiencing Divinity in Bengal-Vaishnavism*. Oakland: University of California Press.

———. 2020. "Sahajiya Text of Nadia: Beyond Reform and Revival." In *The Legacy of Vaiṣṇavism in Colonial Bengal*, edited by Ferdinando Sardella and Lucian Wong, 167–84. London: Routledge.

Stocking Jr., George W. 1983. *Observers Observed: Essays on Ethnographic Fieldwork*. Madison: University of Wisconsin.

Travick, Margaret. 1992 [1990]. *Notes on Love in a Tamil Family*. Berkeley: University of California Press.

Vallely, Anne. 2006. "These Hands Are Not for Henna." In *Women's Renunciation in South Asia: Nuns, Yoginis, Saints, and Singers*, edited by Meena Khandelwal, Sondra Hausner, and Ann Grodzins Gold, 223–45. New York: Palgrave Macmillan.

Westen, Drew. 2001. "Beyond the Binary Opposition in Psychological Anthropology: Integrating Contemporary Psychoanalysis and Cognitive Science." In *The Psychology of Cultural Experience*, edited by Carmella Moore and Holly F. Mathews, 21–47. Cambridge: Cambridge University Press.

White, David Gordon. 2000. "Introduction: Tantra in Practice: Mapping a Tradition," edited by David Gordon White, 3–38. Princeton: Princeton University Press.

———. 2003. *The Kiss of the Yogini: "Tantric Sex" in its South Asian Context*. Chicago: University of Chicago Press.

Part III

Institutions and Individuals in the Making of Tantric Traditions: To Be or Become Tantric

8

The Cremation Ground, the Battlefield, and the Path of Compassion

or, What Makes the Fabric of an Individual's Tantric Encounter?

Nike-Ann Schröder

In this chapter, I will briefly discuss how the Tibetan Buddhist Tantric *chöd* (*gcod*) practice is represented in academic discourse. I will then suggest a situated approach that draws on ritual descriptions, ritual texts, and philosophy as well as on anthropological fieldwork, including the documentation of practitioners' biographies. To understand the complexity of the *enacted* dimension of Tantric practice—its lived reality—I propose that we have to consider it as unfolding from an interplay of Tantric ritual techniques on the one hand, and the motivations, experiences, and skills the practitioner brings in on the other. It is this interplay from which a Tantric *encounter*[1] arises, and I will trace the complexity of such a Tantric encounter for an individual by describing Pema Wangchuk, a Tibetan Buddhist Tantric *chöd* practitioner in Ladakh, North India. My description and analysis rely on data and experience gathered during fieldwork stays in the extended Himalaya region from 2010 to 2018 and is one of the many mosaic pieces of my ethnographic research on the *chöd* practice as a healing ritual in Ladakh.[2]

Tibetan Buddhist Tantric *Chöd* Practice

Chöd (cutting)[3] is a Tantric Tibetan Buddhist ritual practice with a simultaneously conducted meditation. According to Tibetan traditional history, the origins of this ritual can be traced back to Machig Labdrön, a Tibetan yoginī who lived during the eleventh and twelfth centuries in Tibet, and her teacher Padampa Sangye, a wandering yogin who was a mahāsiddha of South Indian origin. He was the main proponent of a corpus of techniques known as "Pacification of Suffering" (*sdug bsngal zhi byed*). *Chöd* is practiced in different places. However, due to the lifestyle of its founding figures, iconographic depictions, ritual instruments, and ritual contents, it can be conceptualized as a cremation-ground practice. Tantric practice has developed in different historical phases, and the cremation-ground practices seem to originate from the first period.[4]

Representations of *Chöd* in Description and Analysis

The cremation-ground aspects of *chöd*—and the ritual procedure that involves the practitioners in their meditation visualizing cutting their own body into pieces and offering it to the ritual guests—has been the focus of early descriptions by Western authors. To give an impression: Bleichsteiner (1937, 178) attests *chöd* to be a "dreadful rite which despite its Buddhist surface is a gruesome mystery of a more primitive era" (my translation). He described—relying on David-Néel's description of the *chöd* ritual (2007 [1932], 121–22) and Evans-Wentz's translation of ritual *chöd* texts (1958 [1935], 301–34, see esp. 311)—its core as follows: "The power of meditation evokes a goddess brandishing a naked sword; she springs at the head of the sacrificer, decapitates him, and hacks him into pieces; then the demons and wild beasts rush on the still-quivering fragments, eat the flesh and drink the blood" (in Eliade 1974 [1964], 436). The authors reported of a gruesome and bizarre ritual. It may add to this assessment of the *chöd* ritual that one context of its practice is the sky burial in which the corpse is hacked into pieces and fed to vultures, and that the *chöd* practitioners' ritual instruments are made from human skulls and bones. In summary, it can be stated that *chöd* here appears as an exotic ritual, without a meaning that intersects with the authors' own cultural backgrounds.

However, most of the scholarly works on *chöd* are not centred on its ritual performance or living performers but rather on its scriptural sources, and thus they place it into a trajectory that paints a very different picture: it is pointed out that the philosophical basis and theoretical premises of *chöd* can be found in the *Prajñāpāramitā* (Perfection of Wisdom) *sūtras* and literature (a.o. Gyatso 1985, 324; Edou 1996, 6; Allione 2000, 167; and Orofino 2001 [2000], 399). This is not a new conclusion but an approach already explicit in historical Tibetan works.[5] This close relationship is also obvious since not only the Heart Sūtra (Prajñāpāramitāhṛdaya)'s *dhāraṇī* is included into various *chöd* practices, but also *Prajñāpāramitā* as a female deity (Gyatso 1985, 324; Orofino 2001 [2000], 399). The authors mentioned above situate *chöd* as relying on the view outlined in the *Prajñāpāramitā Sūtras* and conceptualized in Buddhist philosophy, and thus as a specific means to apply this in practice. Scholars have worked on translating *chöd sādhana* texts,[6] *chöd* lineages,[7] and hagiographies of Machig Labdrön.[8] Other than the ritual accounts, these works tend to present *chöd* as an "object" of scriptures, which is ordered and classified according to Tibetan Buddhist philosophical concepts, versions of hagiographies, and other structures such as *chöd* lineages.

Diverging Representations: Possible Reasons

By comparing these two diverging representations, we find two different answers to the question of what the Tantric *chöd* technique actually *is;* namely, a *script* in one trajectory and a *ritual* in the other. Furthermore, the former trajectory speaks of methodical classification and collocation, while the latter adheres to exotic practices and transgressive behavior. These diverging representations can be explained by examining the respective authors' conditions of research and writing. Lopez (1995, 1–13) traces the history of Buddhist studies, showing how scriptures were taken as the "real source" and representation of a "classical" and "pure" Buddhism in contrast to both acts and words of contemporary practitioners and ethnographic accounts. The availability of Tibetan texts sent to Europe by colonial civil servants were taken as a basis for early European scholars, as Tibet was largely inaccessible due to geographical and political reasons. At the same time, the quest to re-find a primordial Buddhism in old scriptures while the current era was taken as suffering from decline led to a strong tendency of privileging texts and "focussing on doctrinal, philosophical, and historical issues rather than lived religious experience or ritual context" (Gutschow 2001, 187–88). On the other hand, we have the reports of colonialist officials and missionaries who had direct access to the persons in India and the Himalayas, and their descriptions found entrance into the works of early anthropologists. The travelogues of David-Néel might be sorted to this side in regard to the author's Orientalist stance of taking herself as being more capable to represent the local practitioner than themselves, and at the same moment constructing them as "the other."[9] It is not astonishing that her descriptions portray the exotic (and the bizarre) with particular emphasis.

However, I argue that pointing to the extremes of either "bizarre ritual" or exclusively to scriptures and philosophy (and privileging these) is not merely an invention of Western academics, but rather finds predecessors in Tibetan (and Indian) history with the monastic institutionalization of Buddhist Tantric practices. During the time of the second dissemination of Buddhism in Tibet from the eleventh century onward, the Tantric practices that were introduced by Buddhist Indian teachers were more closely amalgamated with scholarly Buddhist philosophy and adjusted to fit into monastic ritual practice and curricula. One major actor in the field of initiating and supporting the second dissemination, the Tibetan King Yeshe Ö, promoted (re) installing a "pure Buddhism" in Tibet. This is supported by historical sources such as the Chronicles of Ngari' (see Vitali 1996, 214) and King Yeshe Ö's ordinance (see Snellgrove 2013 [1987], 170), relying on Karmay 1998 [1980], 9–16). What needed to be counteracted according to this view were mainly Tantric ritual practices that were portrayed as transgressing ritual ("liberation through sexual union, meditation on corpses") and the direction that was initiated supported monastic institutions with ordered hierarchies, scriptures, and philosophy. The split into these two sides and the definition of "proper Buddhism" still echo in academic works of the twentieth and twenty-first century: the origins of *chöd* are often interpreted in "non-Buddhist" terms,[10] and this claim is supported by describing the practitioners' dress, lifestyle as wandering ascetics, and their behavior as differing from that of monastic practitioners[11] (who are apparently taken as "standard Buddhists").

Toward an Approach near to the Practitioners

It is time to ask—not as a rhetorical question but with a real epistemological interest—to what extent the academic enterprises referred to previously match with a practitioner's perspective and with the reality of *the enacted practice*. All mentioned academic works offer valuable insights, descriptions, and explanations of the *chöd* ritual and have granted access to manifold sources essential to the understanding of *chöd*. The accounts of *chöd* practices and practitioners by David-Néel can be taken as early and pioneering ethnographic descriptions of *chöd* and reveal fascinating details. However, they treat the Tantric *chöd* practice within their own frame of reference and as part of their own enterprise. For example, in David-Néel's accounts, *chöd* becomes a token of the researcher's adventurous journeys, and in philology, *chöd* is likely to be equated with its *sādhana* texts. In other words, the lived, enacted practice of *chöd* and its Tantric encounter runs the risk of becoming "colonized" in varying ways.

I suggest that a decolonized approach to Tantric Tibetan Buddhist *practices* first needs to overcome Orientalist attribution. However, it also needs to overcome a fixation on either text and philosophy only, or on only ritual, including the quest to collect the most exotic tokens. The division between the diverging representations of Tantric practice in Tibetan Buddhism needs to be scrutinized, and both sides reconciled, to come nearer to the practitioner's reality. Finally, the practitioners' voices need to be heard and involved in both research procedures and descriptions. Furthermore, I suggest a second movement toward the reality of the practitioner and propose that the *lived dimension* of Tantric practice unfolds from ritual techniques, performances, scripts, and philosophy on one side, and from what the practitioners brings in on the other. So, it is the interaction between both the practice and the practitioner that constitutes the *enacted* practice and with it the Tantric encounter.

To grasp these enacted and lived realities of this ritual practice, I see the need for a multidimensional methodological approach inclusive of ethnographic perspectives.[12] In my larger research, this entails first the restoration of the practitioners' own voices and their own accounts on *their* modes of practice. Second, I follow an ethnographic approach in my research to trace actual, embodied, and performed practices. Third, I am working on reintegrating ritual scripts into practice situations and environments to trace what unfolds from the texts and performances during ritual practice. Fourth, I consider the importance of experience that follows the yogi's perspective. Finally, I look at life events and conduct biographical work to gain a contextual understanding of the situated ritual practice. My research relies on fieldwork conducted with various *chöd* practitioners—Ladakhi, Nepali, and Tibetan—mostly in Ladakh but also in Himachal Pradesh, Uttarakhand, and Nepal.

The way of conducting fieldwork determines both the collecting of data and the approach to understanding and thus analyzing the findings. Thus, it needs to be reflected in terms of positionality—and critically examined in terms of ethics. Both enterprises are, in my opinion, less a matter of quoting the right literature and more one of actually living and working in relationships of mutual interest, respect, and concern. In this view, positionality and ethics are entwined, and to clarify my position in this combined field, I will provide a brief sketch of it. In order to understand the *chöd* practice from within, as the technique and as a participant of its religious and social networks of practice, I have practiced it myself as an initiate. My "fieldwork" has involved living in Tibetan lay practitioner families and in monastic institutions, sharing daily life and practice, and participating in numerous rituals. In 2010, while living with a Tibetan family, we experienced the devastating flood disaster in Ladakh together in the refugee settlement. In the following, I have used the privileges of my passport and networks in Europe to first set up numerous disaster-relief projects on the spot and since then to conduct other aid work for those in need in the fieldwork regions I live and work in.

Here, the positionality of the *chöd* practitioner described in this article, Pema Wangchuk, also comes in. After watching my said activities in 2010 and carefully examining my conduct, he entrusted me with his life story, which led to many shared hours of biographical interviews. These interviews took place in the contexts of life in the refugee settlement, practicing *chöd* and other rituals and going on various pilgrimages together, so that my interview transcripts are in company with numerous descriptions written down while sharing daily life and attending lengthy rituals, yet also while being en route, staying in tents, or encircling holy places. Publishing the outcome accords with his wish to share his biography, decisions, and transformation with a public audience.

In this chapter, I will mainly follow the first and fifth methodological points[13] outlined previously: restoring the practitioners' own voices and conducting biographical work. The focus will be on the often exoticized practice at the cremation ground. The *chöd* practitioner I describe is Pema Wangchuk, a Tibetan refugee living in India. Back in Tibet, he was a member of the Tibetan armed resistance. In this respect, this chapter can be read in two trajectories: first, in the sense of tracing lived realities of a Tantric practice, and second, as a negotiation with political turmoil. It is significant that the biographies of members of the Tibetan armed resistance movement did not find their way into the grand narratives of the past, resulting in what McGranahan (2010) calls "arrested histories." Against this background, we can read Pema Wangchuk's Tantric practice as his unique path to integrate the past, with all its sufferings and deeds, into the present.

I will start with a description of a cremation-ground practice by David-Néel, followed by a description of Pema Wangchuk practicing in the cremation ground. Then I will look at this Tantric ritual practice against the background of the practitioner's biography to understand what he was actually doing there. To trace this, I will first describe the circumstances in which he decided to become a Tantric practitioner. Next I will trace three of his affiliations to Tantric practice, and then I will discuss the motives and aims of his practice—which I argue all imbue his specific Tantric encounters.

At the Cremation Ground

In the early literature, we find descriptions of a Tibetan practitioner's ritual performance of *chöd* near a corpse or in a cremation ground. In most cases, David-Néel's report (2007 [1932], 120–134) served as a template. In her account, the cremation ground[14] disappears behind the practitioner's exotic outlook and his dramatic performance of the *chöd* ritual:

> One of the lama's disciples [. . .] performed chöd near the corpse. [. . .] He wore his usual ragged *naljorpa* dress, [. . .] the monastic toga was thrown over it and, though as shabby as the rest of the clothes, its folds imparted a dignified and impressive mien to the tall, emaciated monk. When I

> arrived, the young ascetic recited the mantra of praise to the *Prajñāpāramitā*. [. . .] The man stood in challenging attitude, as if defying some invisible enemy. [. . .] Apparently agitated by disturbing thoughts, the lean ascetic looked at the pieces of corpse scattered on the ground and then turned his head as if inspecting the surroundings [. . .]. Then, shaking himself as if summoning his courage, he seized his *kangling*, blew loudly a number of times, [. . .] and entered the tent. [. . .] The excited ascetic blew furiously [. . .], uttered an awful cry and jumped on his feet so hastily that his head knocked against the low roof of the tent and the latter fell on him. He [. . .] emerged with the grim, distorted face of a madman, howling convulsively with gestures betokening intense physical pain. [. . .] No doubt that the man felt the teeth of some invisible ghouls in his body.

David-Neél's description undoubtedly paints a vivid picture of a dramatic ritual performance; however, in her exoticizing report, the practitioner does not emerge as a person with their own personality, history, and agency. I will now describe a *chöd* practice at the cremation ground without the use of dramatizing exoticism.

On a late summer evening, I accompanied Pema Wangchuk on his way through a deserted area at some distance from the Tibetan Refugee Settlement located in Ladakh. No other people were to be seen, and it was rather difficult to imagine that there had ever been any in this place amid a mountain desert. Pema Wangchuk carried a red suitcase and a small rug. He looked around to find a place suitable for the ritual he wanted to perform. A frame made from iron bars had curled up into a twisted formation (see figure 8.1.), due to the many fires that had been lit to burn the corpses on it. The only people to come here were those who brought their deceased relatives.

The only noise to be heard was that of faded rows of flags—hung one on top of the other—flying in the harsh wind, which swept across a plain dotted with rocks and covered with sand. The wind blew the sand into our eyes and noses. Some wild dogs watched us from afar, waiting to see whether something interesting was about to happen.

Not far off in the distance, a rock of enormous size carried a huge *maṇi*[15] inscription, with letters exceeding the size of a human.

Figure 8.1. Cremation ground near the Tibetan Refugee Settlement Choglamsar in Ladakh, 2011. *Source*: Photograph by the author.

The sun desiccated the ground and inexorably shone on rocks, the dogs, and the two of us—the only humans present in this deserted land. Pema Wangchuk meanwhile had put down his suitcase at a place that was as good as any other here, spread his small rug, and sat down. After having arranged his ritual instruments from his suitcase carefully, he started to sing his invocations; his closed eyes and all facial expressions showed an orientation inward. He only came back to the visible reality to place a richly ornamented hat of brocade on his head and to reach out for his ritual instruments; he held the colorfully ornamented, double-faced drum ready for use, and with his other hand he brought his bone trumpet to his mouth. Squeezing a deep breath into the hollowed human femur bone with all his strength, he educed an unusual sound from his instrument—elongated, plangorous, and calling.

Adopting Tantric Practice: A Biographical Contextualization

Life circumstances of misery and despair led Pema Wangchuk to adopt the Tantric *chöd* practice. Several years after he had escaped from Tibet and arrived in India, he received a letter from Tibet: "In that letter it said that my mother, one of my uncles, and thirteen other elderly people had died all at the same time from starvation. The letter also said: 'you are in a safe place where dharma can be practiced, so please do the prayers and rituals for those who have passed away. Here we cannot do anything.' "[16] The immense shock of the news that his mother and other relatives had died struck him deeply. It was compounded by the traumatic memory of the last time he had seen her before he fled to India; that time he had been on the run and feared to be arrested or killed by soldiers. His mother had urged him to leave quickly and try to escape to India. He had been terrified and had not been able to even say goodbye. Now hearing not only about her death but also its awful circumstances—she died of starvation—shed light on her former miserable condition. He fell into the deepest misery.

A further dimension of shock was added when he was struck by the great fear that his mother would be reborn in hell to repay the karmic debts for the deeds he had carried out during his time as a member of the Tibetan armed resistance. His fear assumed that his mother could share a fate that is described in a part of the Gesar Epic, which he knows by heart. In the part called *dmyal gling*, it is described how Gesar's mother—due to the deeds her son had performed in war—was reborn in hell.

> I reflected that in my former life [in Tibet] I had carried out numerous non-virtuous deeds. Especially when I had been a Chushigangdruk [Tibetan armed resistance] soldier, I had killed many Chinese: how many did I kill? It had been such a great sin. I could not even remember how many people I had killed. I thought that the karmic result of those dreadful deeds could be transferred to my mother as it happened in the story of King Gesar, when his mother was reborn in hell.

When Pema Wangchuk assumed that his mother stayed in hell due to the karmic consequences of his own deeds, his despair grew into horror. Since the mother's sufferings were said to be caused by *his* karma, past deeds, and decisions, he had no choice but to confront his former actions and decisions. This was a deeply painful process since many memories were unlocked and came back with all their emotional power.

Battlefields

Pema Wangchuk was young when the Chinese People's Liberation Army had invaded Eastern Tibet and the soldiers had killed his father. He was separated from family members and forced to work under the harsh regime of a communist commune where he was always hungry. During famine he saw many people die of starvation, and he was consumed by the desire for revenge. When he got a chance to escape, he joined the armed resistance. "Since we were very few, we had to fight day and night. There was no time to rest. [. . .] We did not even have time to eat. [. . .] We had to run away when the planes flew over us. Sometimes they mistook animals for our people and dropped bombs on them. [. . .] So many of us died. [. . .] And we killed a lot of Chinese, but it was no use." Pema Wangchuk's exposure to war also included imprisonment by PLA soldiers, interrogations, and torture: "After they arrested us, some were taken away and executed, others were buried alive. They put a rope round some peoples' necks and told them to run before killing them. [. . .] [When they arrested me,] they took away my protection amulet. They tore off all my clothes and bound me with a rope. [. . .] They asked how many people I had killed. Those who confessed were killed immediately." After being arrested, he spent almost nine years in various forced-labor camps.

> The work in the mines was extremely dangerous. There was always the risk of your fingers, or your foot being cut off. Thousands of us were working in dreadful conditions. I don't know the exact number. [. . .] We had to work all day and also at night. It smelt terrible and there was almost nothing to eat or drink. [. . .] We got just one bowl of *tsampa* and one cup of water per day. [. . .] That is why many people died. [. . .] Every day between three to six people died. After a few months, the death toll was about 700 people.

Pema Wangchuk had been exposed to various circumstances in which he had fought and had been threatened to be killed. Most of the settings he had encountered back in Tibet after the violent death of his father had turned into sites of death.

Karma

Until he received the letter that told of his mother's death, Pema Wangchuk had viewed his own position in war and violence solely as exposure to the aggression of the Chinese army. His decision to fight was based on the desire to avenge his father's death, the killing of family and clan members, and the destruction and expropriation of their herds and properties, as well as to join the struggle to regain freedom. Returning to the story of King Gesar as summarized by Kapstein (2007, 362), the Lord of Death allows Gesar to catch sight of his mother: "His mother *is surrounded by all the heroes and warriors Gesar and his armies have slaughtered in battle,* and if he wants to liberate her, he must free them first. Though Gesar may be a Buddha, the wars fought by Ling have purposelessly brought death to many, who have fallen into hells or have continued to wander in the bardo between lives. Owing to such conditions, mother Gokmo has also fallen into hell" (emphasis added).

When Pema Wangchuk applied Gesar's encounter on his own biography and evaluated his own deeds accordingly, the impact was enormous: he was confronted with his own actions, for being responsible for the death of people during the war. The dimension of his shock was fueled by the loss of his mother and the inability to have helped her, her suffering due to his deeds, and the sudden shift in the interpretation frame that forced him to take responsibility for the consequences of his actions. Pema Wangchuk told me he was so desperate, he cried continuously for several days. The exposure was so unbearable, he had to do something.[17]

He went to seek advice from a high Buddhist teacher who lived in the neighborhood. He was told to take up the Tantric chöd practice to purify his deeds.[18] When consulting the *chöd sādhana* "A Dharma Instruction Revealed in a Dream," one of his ritual texts which he had kindly shared with me, concerning the issue of purification, it said (translated from the Tibetan original):

> In the spacious sky, the realm of Great Bliss [Mahāsukha], [there are] the glorious blood-drinking Heruka, the assembly of the deities of the four [main] branches of the Kagyu-lineage and the *dākas* and *dākinis* of the twenty-four [sacred

> power] places: to you I offer a Tantric feast, [consisting of my] body [with all its] flesh and blood, through this I [seek to] complete the accumulations [of merit and wisdom] and purify non-virtuous deeds and obscurations; please bestow the conventional *siddhi* and the ultimate *siddhi* within the time of this life!

In this *chöd* practice, to "purify non-virtuous deeds" is mentioned as a possible result (among others) of conducting the Tantric feast offering. We can imagine how much relief this statement has offered to Pema Wangchuk: it proves that it is possible to purify non-virtuous deeds (and thus help his mother) by practicing *chöd*.

A Threefold Affiliation with Tantric Practice

Pema Wangchuk began his Tantric Tibetan Buddhist practice based on different but interconnected affiliations. I will outline three of them in the following subsections. Each tells of and brings about a different interaction between Tantric ritual and former life events in the wake of political turmoil.

First Affiliation: Tantric Teacher, Preliminaries, and Temple Service

The first affiliation was the enterprise of karma purification: the trajectory that originated from the despair over his mother's death and the reflection on the karmic impact of his own deeds led Pema Wangchuk to becoming a Tantric disciple and entering a *guru-chelā* relationship. Before he could start to learn and practice *chöd*, he first served his teacher as an assistant during rituals and promised to complete the "preliminary practices" [*sngon 'gro*].

These practices must be repeated 100,000 times—which is taken literally; these are conducted by both monastic and serious lay practitioners who wish to take up Tantric practice. Along with this enterprise, Pema Wangchuk got involved in regular Tibetan Buddhist ritual service in a nearby Buddhist temple. For five years, it was his task to conduct the daily offerings. All in all, he was placed firmly into

Tibetan Buddhist structures by assisting his teacher in rituals, conducting regular practice, and being the caretaker of the small temple in the refugee settlement.

Second Affiliation: Tso Pema's History as a Template for Tantric Agency in the Face of Death

A second affiliation with Tantric practice opened when Pema Wangchuk visited Tso Pema (the Lotus Lake) in Rewalsar, associated with the Tantric *mahāsiddha* Padmasambhava and princess Mandāravā. He and I had already worked intensively on his biography, but it was only later, when I joined him on his second pilgrimage to Rewalsar, that I realized the very significance this site holds for the yogin. The first thing he had turned to right on arrival at the lake was a little board describing the events that took place at the site. According to Tibetan religious history,[19] the lake is the result of a display of Padmasambhava's Tantric power: the king of Mandi, finding out that his daughter had become the Tantric consort of the *mahāsiddha,* tried to kill the Tantric master. However, Padmasambhava had performed a miracle, turning the pyre, which had been piled up to burn and kill him, into a lake.

The yogin had stood motionlessly at that board for a long while, reading about the king's attempt to burn the *mahāsiddha* on a pyre. I saw the anguish and the pain in his eyes. We shared intense moments of silence. Based on the knowledge gathered in our interviews and the time we had spent together, I felt how this situation unlocked memories of his father's death back in Tibet. When the Chinese People's Liberation Army had invaded Eastern Tibet, his father refused to cooperate with the Chinese forces. The soldiers then killed him to set a warning example. The circumstances of this had been horrific—after a public "struggle session" his father had been burned alive, and his family had been forced to watch.

In Rewalsar, Buddhist history reports how the *mahāsiddha* showed another ending to a violent attack on his life, and by emerging unharmed on a lotus flower that grew from the lake, he displayed his Tantric power. This also changed the attacking king's attitude, who became Padmasambhava's devotee. The similarity that connects Pema Wangchuk's life story to the hagiography of Padmasambhava in the pilgrimage site of Rewalsar is that of exposure to a life-threatening attack, which in the case of Pema Wangchuk's father led to death and thus ensuing misery for the family. However, Rewalsar was the site in which the attack had been successfully counteracted with Tantric power by Padmasambhava. The (historical, in Tibetan perspective) figure of Padmasambhava served as both a source of blessing for the yogin and a role model for transformation: he demonstrated that even in a situation of exposure to deadly attack, agency was possible. Pema Wangchuk undertook a pilgrimage to a site that holds him in deep relation to intense suffering in his own life story; it also holds significance as a place of Tantric agency, power, and potentials of transformation.[20]

Third Affiliation: Helping the Dead

When we recall the various circumstances in Pema Wangchuk's biography in which he had fought, been arrested, and seen people dying, we find manifold experiences with sites of death and the loss of many people around him. According to Tibetan Buddhist understanding, the consciousnesses of the dead may roam around in despair—especially when they died a violent death.

When Pema Wangchuk had changed his life after receiving the letter that reported his mother's death in Tibet, he had also adopted another practice besides the preliminary practices for *chöd*: he inscribed *maṇi* mantras into stones, which he then brought to *maṇi* walls. "When I came from my work, I used to inscribe *maṇis* into stones, especially for my parents and for all other sentient beings, too. [. . .] If we simply inscribe letters into stone, it will not help. But since it is the *mantra* of Chenrezig [*Avalokiteśvara*], the bodhisattva of compassion, it can help." Pema Wangchuk relies on Buddhist practice and the Buddhist pantheon to regain agency and the ability to help his deceased parents. Soon, he extended his practice of inscribing *maṇi* mantras into stones by choosing rocks at the cremation ground to inscribe the *maṇis* to help the consciousnesses of the deceased. The cremation ground became a place to remember them and where one can act to help. We see from his quote that Pema Wangchuk takes for granted that the impact of his activity reaches out to his parents, crossing boundaries of place and time.

His *maṇi* inscriptions and other ritual activity are not restricted to the people involved in Tibet in the past but are affiliated with recent developments, too:

> In these days people in Tibet are doing self-immolation. I am not as brave as them. I escaped from Tibet since I feared to die. The only thing I can do now for the cause of Tibet is inscribing *maṇis*. [. . .] It was decided by all people here in the camp, to make the *maṇi* stones for these people [who immolated themselves for the Tibetan cause]. [. . .] I inscribed [the mantras] for them and for all living sentient beings and for the dead.

The three affiliations I outlined above show different entanglements between biographical events and Tantric practice. The first led from despair into the structures of Tibetan Buddhist practice: a teacher-student relationship, continuous practice, and visits to the temple for ritual community work. The second affiliation led him from the powerlessness of his father's death toward a path of Tantric power, with religious history providing a template of potential agency in the face of death. The third led Pema Wangchuk to the cremation ground as a place of practice to reach out to the deceased to help them. All three affiliations to different aspects of Tantric practice are closely entwined with incidents and people of his past.

Pacification of Suffering and Beyond

So far, we have seen how Pema Wangchuk's affiliations to Tantric Buddhist practice serve to negotiate his past, including terrifying events in his biography, and to regain agency to help the people left behind, living and dead. An assessment of his Tantric practice as a means to "cope with suffering" seems to be obvious. However, I began this chapter with an enumeration of colonizations of Tibetan Buddhist Tantric practice, and "psychologization" would just be another one. The "pacification of suffering" as practiced in *chöd* is not primarily designed as a coping strategy but rather for healing, and, even more essential: it entails and serves as a Tantric Buddhist *path to enlightenment*. It is in this regard that Tibetan Buddhist philosophical texts are relatable to the practice, with *chöd* as their enactment, or as a skillful means to bring forth a transformation of attitudes and perception, which is systematically and thoroughly described in Buddhist philosophy.

Chöd practitioners are usually introduced into the practice and its frameworks through a teacher who has mastered the practice and holds the lineage. This introduction (like in all institutionalized Tantric Tibetan Buddhist practices) entails the threefold set of initiation into the *maṇḍala* and empowerment [*dbang*], reading transmission of the *sādhana* text [*lung*], and oral instructions [*khrid*] in which the teacher introduces the student into the doctrinal backgrounds and practical application of a technique. For the Tantric *chöd* practice, an additional traditional way of learning is suggested or demanded from the disciple; namely, to set out and perform the ritual in specific places.

The enterprise of exchanging the safe environment of a temple or a monastery with the exposure of a wandering hermit and practice at the cremation ground is a heritage of the Mahāsiddha tradition and the founders of the *chöd* practice: Machig Labdrön, the founder of *chöd*, and the practice itself have this affiliation, as do the *mahāsiddhas* such as Machig Labdrön's teacher and Padmasambhava.[21] The topic of exposure already emerged in Pema Wangchuk's second affiliation. During his *chöd* education, both, institutionalized Buddhist structures and exposure merged when his teacher sent him to practice *chöd* 108 times in different village households at springs and in the cremation grounds.

Pema Wangchuk had already created his own affiliation to the cremation ground by inscribing *maṇis* in that area. However, conducting *chöd* there at dusk and nighttime meant a different level of practice. Before he set out, he asked other *chöd* practitioners about their experiences: "Many *chödpas* said: 'When you practice *chöd* for the first time in the cremation ground area, you will see lots of spirits. You will also see lots of skeletons. And wolves and many different animals will also appear.' So, I was afraid about what would come." He then turned to his teacher for advice: "When I asked my lama about performing *chöd* in the cremation ground, he said: 'When you perform *chöd* there, it will help all sentient beings living in the three realms, any being alive or dead. If you see a spirit, then remember me, then it will disappear. After this, you pray for all sentient beings. Then all the merit [generated through your practice] will bless them.' " So, after he had stabilized his practice, he set out to practice in the cremation ground:

> When I practiced [there] the first time, this all [what they had talked about] appeared. Then I remembered my lama's face. Then that all disappeared. This is exactly what he had told me before. It is a matter of "emptiness of phenomena."

> When you meditate about emptiness, your mind will become calm and happy. When you see lots of these different animals and spirits, you need to practice compassion. When strong storms appear, you need to practice fearlessness. You need to meditate on your guru, Machig Labdrön, Guru Rinpoche [Padmasambhava] and Jetsun Dolma. When you see all those animals, then you meditate on compassion and think of them as spirits who have not got a physical body due to their karma.

These statements show that the *chödpa* must deal with spirits, the dead, wild animals, storms, and one's fear.[22] The Tantric practitioner thereby evokes the presence of the guru and Buddhist deities and identifies with a Buddhist deity herself. The two Buddhist core practice concepts of "emptiness of self and phenomena" and compassion are implemented by relying on former meditation practice and by identifying with deities and their qualities. In addition to developing and stabilizing the views and perceptions that unfold from the practice concepts "emptiness" and "compassion," both serve to develop resilience and to be able to act under difficult conditions.

The cremation-ground practitioners meet adversary conditions and enormous challenges. These are illustrated by Pema Wangchuk's reports:

> Once, three Tibetans who now live in Choglamsar went on pilgrimage to Mt. Kailash to practice *chöd* at a sky burial ground which is a very good place for practicing *chöd*. When they arrived there, two of the pilgrims saw many wolves roaming around the area. The third, the leading *chödpa*, saw beings big as mountains and he sat down and practiced the *chöd* meditation. Then [through that,] the beings became smaller and smaller and finally disappeared. The two others became distracted and scared by the wolves. These two *chödpas* with lesser experience were so frightened that they were not able to practice and realize emptiness, and so they died.

We see here how *chödpas* themselves, by circulating such reports, believe in and cultivate a picture of the ritual practitioner facing enormous dangers, which either lead to death or—through endowment with sufficient skill and power—can be transformed. The shaping and stabilizing of meditation skills takes place under conditions of extreme exposure that puts the practitioner at risk but also grants an intensification of practice, as well as a potential enhancement of agency: according to the yogin's understanding, the Tantric ritual and meditation not only transcends perception but also affects the environment and its inhabitants.

Now recalling Pema Wangchuk's affiliations to Tantric practice, he practices at the cremation ground because he assumes that there are many beings and spirits who need help, and the *chöd* ritual is the appropriate means to turn to the consciousnesses of the dead and at the same time purify his own and their karma.[23] Within the *chöd* ritual, he conducts a Tantric *gaṇacakra* and invites all invisible beings at the cremation ground to partake so that he can pacify their sufferings. For the ritual invitation, he uses the *rkang gling*, a trumpet made from a human femoral bone. During my fieldwork, I repeatedly heard whispered statements that a *rkang gling* of the best quality was one made of the femur of a young woman of seventeen years who had died while giving birth to a stillborn child.[24] Such attributions contribute to the ambivalent reputation of *chöd* practitioners as *tāntrikas* who possibly possess mysterious powers, perform secret nighttime rites in cremation grounds, and use materials such as blood from victims of murder. However, if we follow the trajectory so far outlined in this chapter, I argue that such a femur bone can also be conceptualized as originating from—and telling of—a situation of *extreme suffering*.

It is a common reaction to avoid exposures to suffering and death as prominent in Pema Wangchuk's life story and to turn away from such traumatic memories. However, in his biography, intense suffering and Buddhist practice have been closely entwined: his despair when hearing of his mother's death in Tibet and the "karmic framing" of his deeds with the urgent need for purification led him to turn to those sufferings that otherwise would have been avoided. Tantric practitioners may use "disgusting materials" to overcome disgust and to realize that there is nothing impure. *Chöd* practitioners who approach the ritual similarly to Pema Wangchuk seek neither the community of monastics in a comfortable assembly hall nor the comparison or the recitation of as many *chöd* texts as possible. Rather, they *seek the exposure*, and they engage with suffering and the spirits of the dead and other troubled beings to pacify their sufferings.[25] Thereby, the trumpet made of a femur bone with its suffering context stored in the material itself serves to *relate* and *call them in* to be present in the ritual—and to partake in the performed Tantric *gaṇacakra*.

To perform this kind of ritual work, the practitioner must be able to deal with suffering and fear and to confront situations of danger and even death. The practitioner is required to apply the double and interrelated approach of emptiness of self and phenomena on the one hand, and compassion on the other. From the perspective of Tibetan Buddhist frameworks, they rely on each other to transcend *saṃsārik* perception and to develop the needed resilience to be able to conduct the "pacification of suffering." Both become inevitably entwined, and the ritual practice thereby encompasses techniques to transform the practitioner's perception of—and the way of her being in—the world profoundly. As such, *chöd* is a specific approach to pursue the Buddhist quest of realizing "emptiness of self and phenomena" and, with that, "ultimate truth" (to go back to *Prajñāpāramitā*) and great compassion. For Pema Wangchuk, these are not abstract philosophical ideas recited as a text or performed as a ritual duty; rather, they are practiced with a deeply rooted commitment born from intense despair—and thereby they become endowed with both a personal and a practical meaning.

Conclusion

When I asked Pema Wangchuk what the very essence of *chöd* in his view was, he had said:

> The [purpose and the benefit of the] teaching and practice of Machig Labdrön is first to benefit all sentient beings in the world, and to bring down the harming influences and to pacify them. Furthermore [it also serves] to increase everything which brings benefit to the sentient beings. It [serves to] pacify people's suffering, to alleviate their worries and to help the sick. *Chöd* is a skillful method which creates benefit within all these [conditions of suffering]. [This is achieved through] Machig Labdrön's teaching and her [ritual] *gaṇacakra* [Tantric feast offering] which is practiced by meditating [her] *sādhana*.

We can read his statement in two ways. A common reading identifies the "four activities [*las bzhi*]" of Tibetan Buddhist Tantric practice in his statement and may end with this recognition. However, if we read this statement against the background of Pema Wangchuk's biography and specific practice, it tells of complex negotiations of political turmoil and opens numerous doors not only to Tantric practice but also to various chapters of a political biography. The entanglements show that Tantric lives and ritual agency may emerge as a choice that is profoundly personal, political, and affective, as well as religious. The adoption of Tantric practice may (or for a proper integration, one could argue must) include individual applications and possibly adaptions.[26] The dimensions of the processes involved can foremost be revealed through ethnographic work with ritual practitioners.[27]

I conclude this chapter with the note that Buddhist Tantric practice embedded in biographical perspective offers insights into the very depths of its transformative agency, and I argue that the unique lived space of it arises from an interplay of its ritual formula, including meditation *and* what the ritual practitioner brings in: their own biographical experience. *Together* they unfold as the actual Tantric practice. Every ritual practitioner brings in their own unique pattern as they practice *chöd*, and in this chapter I have introduced one.

As an impulse to the study of ritual in Tibetan and Tibetan Buddhist studies, I suggest taking a third major field into account in addition to text and doctrine as well as performance; namely, that of personal involvement, reception, and enaction—and, ultimately, encounter. This move adds a "lived" dimension to traditional text-based works; it counteracts exoticizing perspectives on the ritual performance; it traces pathways of how Buddhist philosophy is "translated" into life; and, ultimately, it deepens the understanding of Tantric Buddhist *practice*.

Notes

1. I use the term *encounter* in the sense of the German term '*Begegnung*,' which refers to both the act and the experience of being exposed to, meet, or take part in a situation, incident, or event with people or other beings.

2. See Schröder (2018).

3. *Chöd* [*gcod*] is a Tibetan term with the meaning of "cutting" or "severing," and in this context it refers to a multitude of meanings and activities,

mainly carried out in meditation (among others)—it refers to severing or cutting through ego clinging, *māras*, afflictions, identification with the body (and personality of) "this life," and conventional (*saṃsārik*) perception. However, it can also refer to dismembering corpses in preparation for sky burials with an accompanying *chöd* ritual.

4. See White (1998, 172–73, relying on Sanderson (1988, 660–704), for more detailed descriptions for the development of *Śaiva* Tantric practices in India in three historical periods. According to Samuel (2008, 328), a similar transformation of Tantric Buddhist practices occurred simultaneously. The Indian and Tibetan Buddhist contexts, however, differ in their relationship to (and involvement in) a scholarly monastic environment. The first period of *Śaiva* Tantric practices—"Clan–Practice" (*kula–dharma*)—began in about the sixth century CE, and its practices were carried out in cremation grounds and centered on "terrifying" worship of *Śiva-Bhairava,* his consort and *yoginīs,* and the worship of *Kālī.*

5. See Stott (1989, 222, relying on Roerich) for the Tibetan historian 'gos Lotsāva (1392–1481) interpreting *chöd* as "the Prajñāpāramitā cutting the demons."

6. For the titles of various *chöd sādhana* texts, commentaries, and other works in Tibetan and Sanskrit related to the *chöd* practice, see Edou (1996, 220–25) for the Tibetan-Buddhist tradition; see Gyatso (1985, 340, n105) for an overview of Tibetan literature on *Bon chöd;* and see Edou (1996, 224–25) and Chaoul (2009, 79) for annotated bibliographies of *Bon sādhana* texts and commentaries.

7. Academic works which include charts or enumerations of *chöd* lineages are (among others) Lauf (1970, 89–95), Gyatso (1985, 331–40), Kollmar-Paulenz (1993, 221–88), Edou (1996, 79–94) as well as Chaoul (2009, 27–28) and Nicoletti (2013, 39–41) for *Bon chöd.*

8. See, for example, Gyatso (1985); Kollmar-Paulenz (1993); Edou (1996); Allione (2000); and Harding (2003).

9. For Orientalism and its implications, see Said (1998) and Gutschow (2004, 9).

10. See, for example, David-Néel (2007 [1932], 106), Evans-Wentz (1958 [1935], 284), Bleichsteiner (1937, 178); and Eliade (1974 [1964], 436), especially his classification of *chöd* as being "clearly shamanic in structure," which has been repeated many times.

11. See, for example, David-Néel (2007 [1932,1965],121–34); Bell (1968 [1931], 72); Gyatso 1985, 321); Edou (1996, 7); and Samuel (2009 [2008], 130).

12. For one of very few more recent ethnographic descriptions of (Bon) *chöd,* see Nicoletti (2013). For the more recent popularization of Throema Nagmo (khros ma nag mo) *chöd,* especially among female lay practitioners,

see Pommaret (2015, 124–29); and Joffe (2019, 230–33), who also mentions the recent global dissemination of *chöd*.

13. To elaborate on all five points thoroughly fills many pages; I will present a detailed ethnography of *chöd* as a healing ritual among Tibetan refugees in Ladakh in my forthcoming monograph.

14. The term "cremation ground" should not be taken too literally in the context of *chöd*—the Tibetan term *dur khrod* rather refers to a place where dead bodies are taken and then treated. See Stoddard (2009) for different practices of disposal of the dead in Tibetan culture, as well as possible links between the *chöd* practice and the introduction of sky burial. See Harding (2003, 47–49) for practicing *chöd* in "charnel grounds or cemeteries" (*dur khrod*) and "haunted places" (*gnyan sa*).

15. The term *maṇi* refers to the six-syllable mantra *oṃ maṇi padme hūṃ*, which serves to evoke, relate to, or identify with the Bodhisattva of compassion Chenrezig (*spyan ras gzigs, Avalokiteśvara*).

16. All interviews were conducted in Tibetan, and thus all quotes are translations.

17. I use the term "exposure" according to the meaning the German terms "*Ausgesetztsein*" (exposedness) and "Preisgegebensein" (abandoned, unprotected, be held to be exposed to) convey, to denote the situational sense of "being placed into a situation and facing particular conditions and/or scenario."

18. To the attentive reader with a background in Tibetan Buddhism, it will be clear that there are parallels to the life story of the yogin Milarepa. Pema Wangchuk knows about these, and it might have served as a template. Yet, Pema Wangchuk rarely mentions him in this context; King Gesar is by far the more important reference point for him.

19. For a traditional account, see Kunzang (1993, 45–46). For the late identification (not before the late eighteenth or early nineteenth century onward) of the Mandi district as Zahor and the Rewalsar Lake as the place where the king tried to burn Padmasambhava, see Huber (2009, 240).

20. For a detailed description and analysis of this pilgrimage with its outer and inner journeys, see Schröder (2019).

21. For Machig Labdrön and *chöd*, see Edou (1996, 7) and Harding (2003, 48–49); for Padampa Sangye, see Molk and Wangdu (2008, 50–51); and for Padmasambhava, see Kunsang (1993, 38–40).

22. For *chöd* as a practice that draws on working with fear, see Harding (2003, 55). Sheehy introduces *chöd* under the heading of "severing the source of fear" and describes that the *chöd* practitioners seek out adversity to directly work with fear and terror (Sheehy 2005, 41). Allione concludes: "the direct encounter with one's fears and the transcendence of them through

understanding of the true nature of demons is the essential point of the Chöd practice (Allione 2000, 171).

23. See Mills (2003, 227–28) for monastic purification rituals for clearing obstacles, inauspiciousness, and (karmic traces of) non-virtuous deeds of the deceased as part of the death rituals.

24. Cf. to Scheidegger (1998, 23–24), who mentions three special types of bones suited best for a *rkang gling*—including the *bam rkang* from a dead woman who was pregnant. See also Beer (2003, 110) on this topic.

25. There are many more ways and motivations to practice *chöd*: it can be applied in order to overcome *māras*, to cut the attachment to *saṃsārik* perception and the identification with the conventional body, to subdue and tame local gods and spirits, to generate Tantric power, to pacify particular places, or to offer the body of a deceased to the birds and other animals, just to name a few. The way of approaching gods, spirits, *māras*, and so forth naturally also depends on whether the *chöd* practice that is performed is a peaceful or a wrathful practice.

26. For an ethnographic account and analysis of the adaption of Tibetan Tantric ritual for social contexts, see Sihlé (2018).

27. For a brilliant description and analysis on Tibetan Buddhist ritual agency in and after times of political turmoil, relying mainly on textual sources (private correspondences) embedded in ethnographic work, see Gayley (2016).

Bibliography

Allione, Tsultrim. 2000. *Women of Wisdom*. Ithaca, NY: Snow Lion.

Beer, Robert. 2003. *The Handbook of Tibetan Buddhist Symbols*. Chicago: Serindia.

Bell, Sir Charles. 1968 [1931]. *The Religion of Tibet*. Oxford: Oxford University Press.

Bleichsteiner, Robert. 1937. *Die Gelbe Kirche: Mysterien der Buddhistischen Klöster in Indien, Tibet, Mongolei und China*. Wien: Josef Belf.

Chaoul, Alejandro. 2009. *Chöd Practice in the Bön Tradition*. Ithaca, NY: Snow Lion.

David-Néel, Alexandra. 2007 [1932, 1965]. *Magic & Mystery in Tibet. The Classic Account of a Woman's Extraordinary Journey to Tibet*. London: Souvenir Press.

Edou, Jérôme. 1996. *Machig Labdrön and the Foundations of Chöd*. Ithaca, NY: Snow Lion.

Eliade, Mircea. 1974[1964]. *Shamanism: Archaic Techniques of Ecstasy*. Bollingen Series LXXVI. Princeton: Princeton University Press.

Evans-Wentz, Walter Y. 1958 [1935]. *Tibetan Yoga and Secret Doctrines*. London: Oxford University Press.

Gayley, Holly. 2016. *Love Letters from Golok: A Tantric Couple in Modern Tibet*. New York: Columbia University Press.

Gutschow, Kim. 2001. "What Makes a Nun? Apprenticeship and Ritual Passage in Zangskar, North India." *Journal of the International Association of Buddhist Studies* 24, no. 2: 187–215.

Gyatso, Janet. 1985. "The Development of the gCod Tradition." In *Soundings in Tibetan Civilization*, edited by Barbara Azis and Matthew Kapstein, 74–98. Delhi: Manohar.

Harding, Sarah, ed. and trans. 2003: *Machik's Complete Explanation. Clarifying the Meaning of Chöd*. Ithaca, NY: Snow Lion.

Huber, Toni. 2008. *The Holy Land reborn. Pilgrimage & the Tibetan Reinvention of Buddhist India*. Chicago: University of Chicago Press.

Joffe, Ben P. 2019. "White Robes, Matted Hair: Tibetan Tantric Householders, Moral Sexuality, and the Ambiguities of Esoteric Buddhist Expertise." PhD diss., University of Colorado.

Kapstein, Matthew T. 2007. "Mulian in the Land of Snows and King Gesar in Hell: A Chinese Tale of Parental Death in Its Tibetan transformations." In *The Buddhist Dead: Practices, Discourses, Representations*, edited by Bryan I. Cuevas and Jaqueline I. Stone, 345–77. Honolulu: University of Hawai'i Press.

Karmay, Samten G. 1998 [1987]. *The Arrow and the Spindle: Studies in History, Myths, Rituals and Beliefs in Tibet*. Kathmandu: Mandala Book Point.

Kollmar-Paulenz, Karenina. 1993. *'Der Schmuck der Befreiung': Die Geschichte der Zhi byed-und gCod-Schule des tibetischen Buddhismus*. Wiesbaden: Harrassowitz.

Kunsang, Erik P., trans. 1993. *The Lotus-Born: The Life story of Padmasambhava*. Boston: Shambala.

Lopez, Donald S., Jr., ed. 1995. *Curators of the Buddha: The Study of Buddhism under Colonialism*. Chicago: Chicago University Press.

McGranahan, Carole. 2010. *Tibet, the CIA, and Memories of a Forgotten War*. Durham: Duke University Press.

Mills, Martin A. 2003. *Identity, Ritual, and the State in Tibetan Buddhism: The Foundation of Gelukpa Monasticism*. London: Routledge Curzon.

Molk, David, and Lama Tsering Wangdu Rinpoche (trls.). 2008. *Padampa Sangye: Lion of Siddhas*. Ithaca, NY: Snow Lion.

Nicoletti, Martino. 2013. *The Nomadic Sacrifice: The Chöd Pilgrimage Among the Bönpo of Dolpo*. Kathmandu: Vajra Publications.

Orofino, Giacomella. 2001. "The Great Wisdom Mother and the Gcod Tradition." In *Tantra in Practice*, edited by David. G. White, 396–416. Delhi: Motilal Banarsidass.

Pommaret, Françoise. 2015. "Empowering Religious Women Practitioners in Contemporary Bhutan." *Revue d'Etudes Tibétaines*, no. 34: 115–38.

Said, Edward W. 1978. *Orientalism*. London: Routledge and Kegan Paul.

Samuel, Geoffrey. 2009 [2008]. *The Origins of Yoga and Tantra: Indic Religions to the Thirteenth Century*. Cambridge: Cambridge University Press.

Sanderson, Alexis. 1988. "Śaivism and the Tantric Traditions." In: *The World's Religions*, edited by Stewart Sutherland, Leslie Houlden, Peter Clarke, and Friedhelm Hardy, 660–704. London: Routledge.

Scheidegger, Daniel A. 1988. *Tibetan Ritual Music: A General Survey with Special Reference to the Mindroling Tradition*. Opuscula Tibetana, 19. Rikon: Tibet Institut.

Schröder, Nike-Ann. 2018. *Belonging, Encountering and Transformation: An Ethnography of Suffering and its Negotiation through Ritual Gcod Healing in and around Tibetan Refugee Settlements in Ladakh*. PhD diss., Heidelberg University.

———. 2019. "Journey, Ritual and Lived Spaces: Encounters on a Pilgrimage." In *Ritual Journeys in South Asia: Constellations and Contestations of Mobility and Space*, edited by Christoph Bergmann and Jürgen Schaflechner, 85–118. London: Routledge.

Sheehy, Michael R. 2005. "Severing the Source of Fear: Contemplative Dynamics of the Tibetan Buddhist Gcod Tradition." *Contemporary Buddhism* 6, no. 1: 37–52.

Sihlé, Nicolas. 2018. "Assessing and Adapting Rituals That Reproduce a Collectivity: The Large-Scale Rituals of the Repkong Tantrists in Tibet." *Religion and Society: Advances in Research* 9, no. 1: 160–75. https://doi.org/10.3167/arrs.2018.090112.

Snellgrove, David. 2013. "The Rulers of Western Tibet." In *The Tibetan History Reader*, edited by Gray Tuttle and Kurtis J. Schaeffer, 166–82. New York: Columbia University Press.

Stoddard, Heather. 2009. "Eat it Up or Throw it to the Dogs? Dge 'dun chos 'phel (1903–1951), Ma cig lab sgron (1055–1153) and Pha dam pa Sangs rgyas (D. 1117): A Ramble Through the Burial grounds of Ordinary and 'Holy' Beings in Tibet." In *Buddhism Beyond the Monastery: Tantric Practices and their Performers in Tibet and the Himalayas*, edited by Sarah Jacoby and Antonio Terrone, 9–36. Leiden: Brill.

Stott, David. 1989. "Offering the Body: The Practice of Gcod in Tibetan Buddhism" *Religion* 19: 221–26.

Vitali, Roberto. 1996. *The Kingdoms of Gu.ge Pu.hrang According to mNga'.ris rgyal.rabs by Gu.ge mkhan.chen Ngag.dbang grags.pa*. Dharamsala: mTho lding gtsug lag khang.

White, David G. 1998. "Transformations in the Art of Love: Kāmakalā Practices in Hindu Tantric and Kaula Traditions." *History of Religions* 38, no. 2: 172–98.

9

The Spectrum of Eclecticism and Conservatism within Kerala's Tantric Traditions

A Case Study of Meppaṭ *Sampradāya*

Maciej Karasinski

This chapter investigates both conservative as well as eclectic tendencies within Tantric traditions of modern Kerala. Several studies (see, e.g., Sarma 2009; Karasinski 2020a) have shown the syncretistic nature of Kerala Tantrism and mutual interdependence of its many currents. To limit the scope of the study, I have chosen a Tantric tradition of a Nāyar caste, the Meppaṭ *sampradāya* (tradition) of Kannur district.[1] I will show how the Meppaṭ *sampradāya* integrates various elements of Śākta and Tantric traditions of Kerala within its ritualism. Moreover, I intend to indicate several similarities between the ritual praxis of Meppaṭ and the so-called Śākta Brahmans of Kerala.[2] In what follows, I want to show that the idea of belonging to the Tantric, Kaula, Śākta, or Śrīvidyā tradition—which is inherently tied to notions of identity and alterity, or to a differentiation between *us* and *them*—is itself a multifaceted and stratified phenomenon within Keralan communities.

In my research, conducted in Kannur and Kozhikode districts of Kerala, I mostly used a mixed method that combines oral sources and oral exegeses, in-depth semi-structured interviews with Nādānta (the current guru of Meppaṭ *sampradāya*), and participant observations of Tantric rituals. Additionally, I made an attempt to compare and contrast this ethnographic material gathered during fieldwork in Kerala with textual sources in Sanskrit and in Malayalam that define Keralan Tantrism and discuss its ritualism. The fieldwork was conducted during my doctoral research (2009–2013), which focused on texts and practices of Śākta communities in Kerala. In my research I also attempted to highlight issues surrounding safeguarding the intangible cultural heritage of Tantric traditions and the importance of preserving endangered archives, such as palm-leaf manuscript collections of Brahman families in Kerala.

The Meppaṭ tradition, as I intend to show in this paper, is unique and worth researching as it marries existing Tantric currents of Kerala within a tradition of a Nāyar clan and hence represents current eclectic tendencies of Keralan Tantrism in general and Śāktism in particular. Interestingly, while following the path of their ancestors' religious heritage, this Nāyar family welcomes new disciples who do not need to belong to any particular caste or creed. Moreover, the followers also learn spiritual practices from other Tantric gurus and Śākta Brahmans.[3] Thus, I would like to show how the case of the Meppaṭ tradition illustrates a general tendency of many Tantric communities in Kerala that modify, reinterpret, and adapt their ritualism to mould their multifaceted identity and open their tradition to a wider public.

Positionality and Keralan Śākta Communities

When interacting with Tantric practitioners I introduced my position as both academic researcher and spiritual seeker, and it was within these limits that I accessed information included in this study. As a foreign academician enrolled at an Indian university and interested in traditional practices, I was generally welcomed to attend Tantric rituals. In many Brahman houses (*illam*), the Śrīvidyā stream of Śāktism forms an esoteric path within Tantric ritualism of a particular family. In other words, to receive such an esoteric knowledge, one should be an *adhikārin*—a deserving student who necessarily belongs to a particular Tantric family. Therefore, I remained an outsider and observer rather than a participant of the "family-only" rituals. Nevertheless, in time, my position within the communities changed with my progress in learning Malayalam and becoming a practitioner. The study here includes data from participant observations of the rituals of Śākta communities. "Active participation" (Spradley 1980, 62) allowed me to document and interpret the observed rituals. I attempted to study the communities empathetically and bridge the gulf between insiders and outsiders' views with utmost respect for the traditional values upheld by the practitioners. For example, I am preparing an edition of a Tantric manuscript from a Śākta family collection with a commentary of practitioners, but, as requested by the family, without elaboration on the construction of their secret mantras. At times, the power struggle among Brahman and Tantric communities restricted my access to rituals and temples. Several Śākta temples are in fact under control of Devasom boards, government of Kerala–controlled socioreligious trusts that appoint the chief temple priests (*kṣetra tantri*), usually a Nambudiri Brahman, but they allow the Śākta family to perform their special rituals and organize ritual routines. The senior member of the family also remains the main ritual expert and the head priest (*kṣetra melśānti*). To enter a Śākta temple in Central Kerala,[4] I first sought permission from a *melśānti*. He agreed but recommended consulting also the temple's *tantri*. Having received their permission, I attempted to enter the temple but was at once approached by an overzealous officer from the Devasom Board who vehemently disagreed, stating that he was, in fact, in charge. Ultimately, the conflict was resolved and I could attend the temple ceremonies, but the incident points to the power relations and hierarchical tensions between Brahmans, temple officers, and the Śākta Tantrics, which also affected my research.

Mascarenhas-Keyes (2004), commenting on her research on Goan communities, observes that the anthropologist's dialogue with the local communities should not terminate upon the conclusion of fieldwork. She concludes her essay by saying that apart from academic feedback, scholars should solicit and analyze native feedback to "reduce the dangers of ethnocentrism" of researchers-outsiders. My research on Śākta tradition began with my fieldwork for my PhD dissertation, and in time it morphed into an ongoing project that draws together both textual and ethnographic data I have collected in Kerala. The research would not be possible without the help and constant encouragement from the members of the local Śākta communities, especially Mūssat and Meppaṭ.

Tantra and Śākta Traditions in Kerala: An Introduction

It has been proposed (Goodall and Isaacson 2011, 122–37) that by around 1000 CE Tantric theory and practice began to have observable effects on the mainstream Hindu religions of Śaiva, Śākta, and Vaiṣṇava currents. Thus, one may say that Tantrism or Tantra stands for a complex Asian system of esoteric practices and philosophies that made a considerable impact on various sects of Hinduism (Brooks 1990, 3). The word *tantra* may also mean a practical treatise on religion and esoterism. These ritual handbooks provide courses for developing the hidden, dormant power of human beings (White 2000, 8). In fact, one can define a Tantric spiritual exercise as a secret, systematic quest for salvation and mystical powers. The aims are to be attained by means of strict spiritual discipline (Rao 2019b, 4).

In the Keralan context, meanwhile, the term *Tantra* often refers to the public temple rituals standardized in the *Tantrasamuccaya* treatise and performed by Nambudiri (Nampūtiri) Brahmans (Ajithan 2018, 166–71). However, this contribution focuses on Tantric (Śākta) practice that is followed within a Keralan family of a Nāyar caste. In fact, several studies have shown the syncretistic nature of Kerala Tantrism and mutual interdependence of its many currents. Indeed, the very expression "Tantra of Kerala" means much more than just temple ritualism, and it spins out a whole universe of ancient sacrality, symbols, rituals, and texts. The custodians of these Tantric traditions are in most cases Nambudiri Brahmans, Śākta Brahmans, and Nāyars by caste.

M. S. Nair (2000, 32–33), in his study of Maṭayi Kāvu, one of the prominent Śākta temples of Kerala, divides Tantric priesthood into three categories: (1) the Nambudiris of the Vaidika Tantric tradition;[5] (2) the traditions of *Mantravāda*; and (3) the Śākta or Śākteya Brahmans (e.g., Mūssats, Piṭārars, and Aṭikals). This division of the priesthood is made according to social status and the purity-power relations between castes. Nair's distinction between Mantravādins and Tantrics is also noteworthy, even if questionable, as it points to complex relations between Tantra and Mantravāda. The latter has retained in modern Kerala its pejorative connotation with black magic (*abhicāra*), while the first term is used to name temple-related rituals and techniques of spiritual development (Ramavarma 1910, 636). However, it is undeniable that in Kerala, Mantravāda remains as a personal practice restricted usually to members of certain families and does not form any religious institution or cult that can be followed by devotees. On the other hand, Mantravāda can simply mean a technique of using mantras. Therefore, any expert on mantras, especially the mantras employed for exorcisms, is called—by the majority of devotees—a *mantravādin*. In this respect, even a Nambudiri Brahman, whose religious practice is usually not associated with any form of magic or violence (Vidal, Tarabout, and Meyer 1994, 211) is sometimes called a *mantravādin* when they act as a magician or exorcist dealing with malevolent spirits. However, Sadasivan (2000, 321), in his study on the social history of India, states that Brahmans, who came to Kerala from the West Coast and dominated the native tribes, learned magic from the Indigenous communities. Therefore, he also calls them *mantravādins*.[6]

The Mūssats (*Mūssatu*) and Piṭārars are well-known representatives of Śākta Tantrism in Kerala.[7] They form one Śākta Tantric community. Both castes claim to follow the nondualistic Śākta-Śaiva tradition of Kashmir;[8] that is, Krama.[9] Their temple complexes, with groves and attached shrines, are inherited from one generation to the next, and their existence is perpetuated through the care and agency of the senior heads of the clans, usually called *Mūtta Piṭārar* (literally, senior Piṭārar) assisted by *Iḷaya Piṭārar* (literally, junior Piṭārar). There are indeed various legends and myths about the Śākta Brahmans, and the members of these communities differ in their opinions about the origin of their tradition. When asked how Kashmirian Krama rites could potentially have been transplanted into essentially Keralan ritualism, some Piṭārars of Maṭayi Kāvu suggest that their tradition might have been brought to Kerala by Kālī worshippers from Bengal. However, this claim is pure speculation, and we have no evidence or reason to accept it. Conversely, the Mūssats see their tradition as a Kashmirian Krama cult of the goddess Kālī Kālasaṃkarṣiṇī, worshipped together with Tripurāsundarī, and I have thus hypothesized that Śrīvidyā[10] could have been a vehicle of transmission of at least some of their ritualistic practices (Karasinski 2010, 18).

However, a Mūssat priest of Vaḷayanāṭ Kāvu (see figure 9.1) questioned the connection of his tradition with the Kālī of Bengal and

Figure 9.1. Vaḷayanāṭ Kāvu temple in Kozhikode, 2018. *Source*: Photograph by the author.

other Śākta traditions of South Kerala. For him, the Krama rituals are the heritage of Kashmirian itinerant ascetics who, according to legend, visited Kerala in ancient times. A Piṭārar[11] who was the main priest of Mannampuṟattu Kāvu agreed with the Mūssat priest's view and stressed in the interview that all temples of Mūssats and Piṭārars are devoted to the warrior goddess, imagined as a divine heroine defeating demons,[12] and that their rituals include Krama and Kaula forms of worship. Special pujas with offerings of liquor, meat, and fish can be found in these so-called Śākta temples, together with an adoration of *śrīcakra* (installed either in the temple or the house of the chief priest).[13]

The goddesses of those holy groves or *kāvus* (often invoked as Caṇḍi, Kālī, Caṇḍayogeśvarī, or Rurujit[14]) are worshipped with an entourage of Divine Mothers and Śiva. This peculiar system of a collective worship of these fierce divinities is better known as *Rurujidvidhāna*. It is described in an authoritative text of the Kerala Brahman tradition entitled *Śeṣasamuccaya* (Pasty-Abdul Wahid 2017, 79).

Interestingly, *Śeṣasamuccaya* belongs to the Nambudiri tradition—it was written by Śaṅkara, the son of Nārāyaṇa, author of *Tantrasamuccaya* (Sarma 2009, 335). However, the Mūssat priests accepted the text as describing their *Rurujidvidhāna*. It seems that the Śākta tradition might have been powerful and influential in the time of

Śaṅkara (the fifteenth century CE), as he mentioned this belief system in his treatise (Karasinski 2020a, 561).

As I have suggested in this brief introduction, the various traditions of Keralan Śāktism and Tantrism have acted on and reacted against each other but also influenced the ritualism of other religious communities in Kerala. An interesting example of this influence and of Tantric eclecticism in Kerala is the Meppaṭ tradition of Kannur. Drawing on my ethnographic data, I will now shed some light on the elements of Meppaṭ ritualism and explain how the modern gurus of this clan integrated various Tantric systems within their religious practice.

Nāyars of Holy Groves and Martial-Arts Temples

My first encounter with the Keralan Śākta tradition was during my field research on Keralan rituals in a Tantric temple of Kozhikode. The temple was built on the outskirts of the town where narrow, crooked lanes wind around ancient Hindu shrines, forming an impenetrable labyrinth. At the time, I was assisted by a local scholar, a professor at the University of Calicut. Once we were greeted at the entrance of an *illam* (Brahmans' household), the wife of the main priest requested that we sit on the veranda and wait for her husband to return from a temple. The request caused a considerable surprise to my assistant who, because of his slightly inferior social status, as he later explained, had never been allowed to sit on a veranda of a Brahman house in his early childhood days in Thrissur. Indeed, as noted by Fuller (1976, 44), the gate, the courtyard, and the veranda of the Nambudiri Brahman house may still function as a pollution threshold that divides clans, castes, and temple communities. However, the *illam* we visited in Kozhikode was owned by a family of Śākta Brahmans who followed their own rules of purity and ritualistic practice that integrated local communities within the sacred space of their holy grove. I stayed with the Brahmans to observe and learn about the spiritual practices. Once, after a late puja, I wandered off pondering the ritual practice of the Brahmans. I soon found myself in the vicinity of a wooden Bhagavatī temple where only few hours before priests had concluded their daily routines. The leftovers of ritual offerings were cleaned up, and only one altar ghee lamp was flickering in the wind. To my surprise, inside the temple two Brahmans (my hosts) were pray-walking, circumambulating the tiny chamber of the temple in a dervish-like fashion. The priests, visibly energized by their spiritual exercises, whirled between goddess images (*mūrtis*) in a religious ecstasy. With each whirl, the Brahmans' repeated motions were becoming smoother and faster; they expertly moved around, constantly spinning, touching the images, and exchanging sacrificial vessels between themselves in an almost playful manner. My observation was abruptly interrupted by the main priest who, suddenly fast awake, pointed at me and shouted to a young helper, "Take him away, he is not supposed to see that!" I stayed with the Brahmans for a few more days, but they were reluctant to discuss the nocturnal rites. They explained, however, that those acts were performed to invoke their Śākta-Śaiva gurus who guide them from the beyond. To trace the roots of the Keralan Śākta-Śaiva tradition, I traveled north to Kannur district. There, in Kaḷarivātukkal Temple, I met other Śākta Brahmans and a Nāyar Tantric guru, Nādānta, who shared with me his knowledge of Śākta Tantrism and the ritualism of the Nāyars.

The origin of the Nāyars is still uncertain, but it is hypothesized that they could have originated from a matrilineal hill tribe that migrated to the plains and coastal regions of Kerala in the fourth century CE, possibly fleeing invasions (Gough 1961, 303). In Kerala, they became settled agriculturists and warriors who, in the course of time, made alliances with the Nambudiri BrahmanBrahmans but were always ranked inferior to them (Stone 2013, 138–39).

However, Gough (1961, 298) has suggested that the name *Nāyar* can be used as an umbrella term to name a category of higher castes in Kerala that were subdivided into smaller units and allied to other ethnic groups.[15] The complexity of the caste system of Kerala has been discussed in many anthropological studies, and, as suggested by Freeman (1999, 282), virtually every community in Kerala exhibits shifting strategies of marital alliance, both at the intra-caste level or in clan alliances. That, in turn, provoked exchanges in ritual praxis and customs between castes and clans. Thus, for example, according to Nambudiri law, the land of a Brahman family should be inherited by the eldest son. To avoid the partition of the inheritance, younger brothers generally did not marry but had permanent liaisons with women from matrilineal castes. These nonmatrimonial alliances (*sam-*

bandham) were usually formed between the Nambudiris and women from the Nāyar community (Fuller 1975, 284).

In Northern Kerala, the matrilineal households of the Nāyars (*taravād*) were granted rights by the Nambudiris over lands and forests. Nāyars had their own shrines in local holy groves (*kāvus*), where they worshipped warrior goddesses, ancestral deities, and Brahmanical deities. In some cases, for instance at the time of festivals, Nāyar rituals involved worshipping *śrīcakra* and offering liquor or animal flesh to the tutelary gods. In fact, on one of my visits to Nādānta's family house, I was shown a traditional room of the *kāraṇavan* (the head of the *taravād*) where *śrīcakra* used to be worshipped in olden times. Such practices were strikingly similar to those that can still be observed within the communities of Piṭārars and Mūssats.

In the past, many Nāyars were warriors and mercenaries. They created their own martial arts (*kalariapayattu*) that were further developed and taught in their family gymnasia (*kalari*). These *kalari*s had their own training regimen, rites of passage, and divine patrons—the fierce goddesses (Zarilli 2000, 131). Indeed, for many Nāyars, *kalaris* were not only gymnasia but holy places consecrated with daily and occasional rituals and graced by the presence of spiritual masters of the art called *gurukkal*s or *pannikar*s (Bayly 1984, 177–213). *Kalaris* were sanctuaries where martial exercises were practiced side by side with spiritual ones. The training began with prayers for protection addressed to the clan's divine patrons. Further, the goddesses were often invoked with an entourage of ferocious imps (*piśāca*) or spirits (*bhūta*) and honored with offerings of intoxicating drinks (*vīrapāṇa*), traditionally consumed by warriors before going to the battlefield. The goddess of *kalari*, usually an incarnation of Kālī, was associated with the hot season (the month of *mīnam*); she remained unmarried and heated with passion. In fact, according to contemporary Meppaṭ priests I have interviewed, the *abhiṣeka* of various types is performed for their ferocious deities to literally cool them down and pacify them. Moreover, the daily worship involved offerings for Bhairava and Bhairavī. Bhairava represents the *raudra* (ferocious) aspect of Śiva, whereas Bhairavī is the terrifying goddess who embodies the power of death (Zarilli 2004, 70–71). Interestingly, even though the Tantric spiritual practices of Meppaṭ can be followed by both men and women, the temple duties are traditionally entrusted to the male priests, and, as noted above, their warrior deities are predominantly female.

Moreover, the followers of the Meppaṭ tradition call their family temple *kalari* or *māntrika-kalari*—a sacred space where Tantric practitioners hone their spiritual skills. The members of the Meppaṭ family call themselves Māntrika Nāyars, the appellation once ascribed to legendary religious specialists and *mantravāda* experts of Northern Kerala. In fact, in the Meppaṭ parlance, the term *māntrika* is preferred over *mantravādin*. While the latter may refer to a black magician, the former designates a practitioner who uses magical techniques only for protection or the fulfillment of wishes. According to Nādānta, the current guru of the Meppaṭ order, the term *kalari* has a broader spectrum of meaning—it not only refers to a place of martial training but also denotes the threefold system of Nāyars' training: Hindu education, physical training, and the knowledge of mantras (Karasinski 2021).

As with the households of Nāyars and Brahmans, *kalaris* are often associated with, or built close to, a holy grove (*kāvu*). As observed by Freeman (1999, 261), the modern *kāvu* is a garden or forest land dedicated to particular deities. Therefore, the groves usually adjoin or are a short distance from a shrine, though sometimes a temple complex may be built within the confines of a *kāvu* itself. Some Brahman interviewees expanded this definition of *kāvu* by calling it an ecofriendly sanctuary that should necessarily be located near a river or a brook.[16] However, these sacred spaces within forested territories are defined both as a metaphysical domain and a terrestrial realm that belongs to a particular familial tradition. Deities of *kāvus* are believed to dwell on a different plane of existence and need to have their presence manifested within the holy space of rituals to be accessed and propitiated properly. Furthermore, the idea of *kāvus* being ecofriendly sanctuaries implies that the identities of the worshippers and their gods are intricately linked through the power of nature—a power that, in turn, is apotheosized and worshipped as a goddess: the embodied divine *śakti*.

On the other hand, *kāvu* stands for a place of cultural synthesis, integrating castes and creeds within the context of its festive rites.[17] Some practitioners suggested that the original system of worship in the Śākta groves was in time reformed to conform to the liturgy of the Brahman temples (*kṣetras*) that was taught in *Tantrasamuccaya* (Unni 2006, 227–56). However, many *kāvus* were also aligned with specific (Nāyar) *taravāds*, who indirectly imposed the interdependence of castes by requesting members of each community to contribute to temple festivals and rites. This interplay between the ritualistic traditions of *kṣetras, kalaris,* and *kāvus* underline the complexity of Hindu (Tantric) traditions in Kerala.

Traditional, Progressive, or Eclectic? The Story of Meppaṭ

According to family legends as told by the Mūssat priests, the sacred groves of the Śākta Brahmans were hermitages established by spiritual masters from the Kashmir Śaiva tradition who came to ancient Kerala in search of new converts. On the other hand, some Keralan scholars like P. Narayanan also claim that the Śākta Brahmans were brought from Kashmir by the Keralan king Kōlattiri Rāja to officiate in the royal temples (Viju 2017). In addition, some goddesses of Śākta *kāvus* were worshipped by members of royal families.

Similarly, legends concerning the Meppaṭ tradition, as recounted by members of the clan, refer to siddhas and warrior ascetics (*Brahma Kṣatriya*) who came down to the northern regions of Kerala and built hermitages in the Kannavam forest (presently near Thalassery in Kannur district), where they worshipped their family deity Śrī Porkali (Caṇḍikā) (Unni 1972, 94). These legendary figures are therefore regarded as the progenitors of the Meppaṭ tradition. This tradition was revived in modern times by Arjun Karunakaran Nair, known to his disciples as Gurukkal Nādānta Anandanatha. Nādānta received spiritual teachings from his mother, who was from a traditional Nāyar family of Putiyavīṭṭil of Tallicherry, and was initiated into the ritualistic practice of his grandfathers, the Meppaṭ. Nādānta's grandfather, Kammaran Gurukkal, initiated him into the practice of Śrīvidyā and inspired him further to follow the spiritual path. The revival of the tradition led to its adoption by the wider public—Nādānta became a full-time guru and started accepting disciples interested in spiritual training. The tradition was also influenced and enriched by the Tantric experience of Nādānta and his Śrīvidyā practice. I therefore wish to turn to this unique Tantric system practiced by modern Meppaṭ followers. The Meppaṭ case shows how some Tantric traditions in Kerala change their ritualism and adapt elements of other systems to form their new identity.

To understand the multifaceted problem of Tantric identity in Kerala, it is worth considering the terminology used by the practitioners to name their *sampradāya*. While Mūssats and Piṭārars call their tradition Kashmiri Sampradāya, Raudra (the Ferocious One), and Mahārtha (Great Meaning), the Meppaṭ Nāyars prefer different epithets, like Vīra, Śākta, or Kula (Kaula). The Kashmiri Sampradāya refers to elements of Krama and Trika ritualism that is known from Kashmirian Śaiva sources and remains a core of ritual practice among the Śākta Brahmans. Mahārtha is another appellation of the Krama tradition and a name of the goddess Kālī who, in this tradition, is worshipped as Kālī Kālasaṃkarṣiṇī, the Destroyer of Time. Mahārtha is also the aim of the spiritual practice of Krama devotees—the realization of the ultimate nonduality of the world. Conversely, the epithets used to describe the Meppaṭ tradition indicate the mode of ritual practice and the code of conduct followed by the clan. *Vīras* (literally, heroes) in Tantric traditions are Tantric practitioners who have gained mastery over the senses and have reached a high level of spiritual development through strict discipline and rituals deemed inappropriate for all other adepts (Wenta 2015, 114–36), which might include ritualized sexual intercourse. Regarding the term *kula*, Muller-Ortega (1997, 55) argues that it should not be seen as the name of a school of thought but a lineage or a preceptorial line that shares theological affinities with esoteric yogic movements. The early Tantric Kula traditions were originally followed by small communities of ascetics who had their own rules of conduct (*kula-dharma*) and revelation (*kaula-jñāna*) (White 1998, 173). It is hypothesized that the Kula tradition belonged primarily to ascetic groups who lived near cremation grounds. Their rites involved violations of customary laws of purity and ritual sanctity to realize both nonduality and supernatural abilities. Thus, a Kula ritual was an interplay of taboos, conventions, and integration of sacred and profane realities that led one into a realization of oneness with the divine (Gupta 2005, 79). *Kaula* is sometimes defined as a reformed version of Kula liturgy, which became suitable for householders. This involved a structural inversion of ritual paradigms that led to the substitution of impure offerings with their symbolic representations (*pratinidhi*) (Dupuche 2000, 6). However, Dupuche (2000, 38) adds that in ordinary parlance *Kaula* is often used interchangeably with *Kula*, even though the former has a broader spectrum of meaning.

In the context of Kerala, *kaula* is usually understood as a method of ritual practice (*kaula-prakriyā*), which is centered on the worship of fierce goddesses and *yoginī*s who require "impure" offerings. Generally, Kaula Tantric traditions refer to the five "Ms": the five offerings of wine, meat, fish, parched grain, and sexual intercourse or sexual fluids (Kinsley 2005, 30).

As per historical sources, the ancient Kaula developed four transmissions, each with its own set of deities, mantras, and ritual practices, as follows: the Eastern or the Earliest, whose chief divinity is Kuleśvarī; the Northern transmission, where the Twelve Kālīs are worshipped; the Western transmission, whose chief divinity is Kubjikā; and the Southern transmission, with the main goddess Tripurāsundarī (Dupuche 2000, 17). Thus, in the case of Śākta Brahmans and the Meppaṭs, Kaula rituals are conducted mostly for the Tripurā (Śrīvidyā) goddess and Kālī of Krama. Nādānta introduces himself also as a follower of the Kaula path (*mārga*) of Śrīvidyā and Kālī Krama.

We can therefore conclude that the terms *vīra* and *kaula* describe the nature of Śākta ritualism that is found in the Meppaṭ *kalari*. Furthermore, the Meppaṭ practitioners accept *Kulārṇavatantra*, a well-known Kaula treatise, as one of their authoritative texts. Nādānta explains to his disciples the need for them to follow spiritual discipline according to their natural disposition, which is either *paśu* (beastly), *vīra* (heroic), or *divya* (divine), the distinction known from many Tantric sources (Kripal 2008, 515–16). According to *Kulārṇavatantra*, the heroic path with its transgressive rites and strict discipline is not suitable for the *paśus* and may lead them to commit sins, ultimately causing their damnation (*Kulārṇavatantra* chapter 2, verse 124). Similarly, *Tantrāloka* (chapter 29, verse 1) informs that the Kula mode of worship is a secret technique meant for those who are spiritually qualified. However, as explained by Nādānta, the *paśus'* perception of the world is limited by their ignorance, and therefore they need the spiritual practice and guidance of a guru until they reach a higher state. Thus, in the Meppaṭ tradition, the *paśus* start their spiritual journey with an initiation (*dīkṣā*, known also as *śākta-abhiṣekam*) and spiritual exercises prescribed by the guru. The *vīras*, on the other hand, have a different rite of passage that is called *kaula-abhiṣekam*. The more spiritually inclined and talented adepts may receive a *karma dīkṣā* that leads to the so-called *divya* stage of spiritual practice, where no external rituals are required and in which one must focus solely on meditation.

I have met several gurus of Kaula traditions in Kerala who recommended their neophytes read the *Kulārṇavatantra*'s section on gurus and *kula-dharma* but who would not practice any rites prescribed in that treatise. However, these disciples were asked to read the authoritative texts of Śrīvidyā (e.g., *Yoginīhṛdaya* and *Paraśurāmakalpasūtra*) to understand the basics of ritual practice before they were admitted into the inner circle of the *vīras*. Therefore, the Kaula path of Śrīvidyā has been instrumental in shaping current ideas about Tantrism within the Śākta communities of Kerala.

Meppaṭ Kalari: Daily Rituals for Warrior Goddesses

In this section, I will present some observation and analyses of daily rituals based on fieldwork I conducted with members of the Meppat community. As mentioned earlier, while the temple of the Meppaṭ tradition is called *Meppaṭ kalari* by the gurus and devotees, another name, *Meppaṭ mantra-śālā* (literally, The Hall of Mantras), is also used. The sacred space of the Kalari temple grounds consists of the main temple complex: *gau-śālā*, a cowshed where cows are kept and fed; and *yāga-śālā*, a sacrificial space where fire oblations and sacrifices are performed.

The daily rituals in the Meppaṭ temple start at 4:30 a.m. with water satiation (*abhiṣeka*) for the goddess Durgā, the protector of the tradition (as shown in figure 9.2). The priests invoke her first as Mother of the World (Jagadambā) and afterward visualize and honor her as Śrī Porkali, the war goddess of the Meppaṭ and Śūlinī, the Spear-Bearer. The fierce goddess Porkali is referred to also as Caṇḍikā (the fierce one), represented in the temple in a form of a mirror. Then, the main priest worships *guru-paramparā* (the lineage of spiritual teachers) and Tripurāsundarī, the goddess of Śrīvidyā tradition, with her retinue. *Abhiṣeka* is performed for *bindu* (the center) of *śrīcakra* and then for *śiva-liṅga*, both installed in the main temple. Afterward, the same satiation is offered to the Five Divine Representations (*pañca-mūrtis*). The group of five gods who have been worshipped by generations of Meppaṭ Nāyars (see figure 9.3) include: Yogi Bhairava, Bhairavi, Kuṭṭi Cāttaṉ (Karim Kuṭṭi), Guḷikan, and Cāmuṇḍī. Of these, Kuṭṭi Cāttaṉ and Guḷikan are local Keralan spirits invoked as wish-bringers in various Tantric and Mantravāda traditions (Tarabout 2003).

Afterwards Anandabhairava, Anandabhairavi, Śakti Gaṇapati,[18] and Bhadrakālī are honored. Jagadambā is visualized as the universal mother holding a conch (*śaṅkha*), a disc (*cakra*), a bow (*dhanu*), and an

Figure 9.2. An image of the goddess in Meppaṭ Kalari temple in Kannur district, 2010. *Source*: Photograph by the author.

arrow (*bāṇa*) in her four hands. She is seated on the lion that stands on the elephant called *Gajāsura* (literally, elephant-demon). The Meppaṭ priests interpret her mount (*vāhana*) as a symbol of mental power that can be controlled and used with divine help. The bow and arrow symbolically represent the goal of *sādhana*: *samādhi*, the final liberation.

The worship of the goddess Śūlinī is not restricted to the Meppaṭ temple, and in the Keralan tradition Śūlinī she is often invoked as Asuramardinī (the slayer of demons), Vindhyāvāsinī (the one who lives on the Vindhya mountains), or Yuddha-priyā (the one who enjoys battle). Also, *Mātṛsadbhāva* (138–48) narrates the story of a goddess who fought against demons and killed their army with a spear, after which the spear was glorified and worshipped as a symbol of her victorious battle.

Figure 9.3. *Homa* (fire oblations) at Meppaṭ Kalari, 2020. *Source*: Photograph by Arjun Karunakaran Nair.

Interestingly, Śūlinī is also worshipped as the goddess of medicine of Meppaṭ Kalari.[19] For healing purposes, she is visualized as an elderly woman who removes all diseases by sweeping them out with her broom. Thus, she is also called Dhūmāvatī Śūlinī and invoked with other gods and mythological patrons of medicine and healing—Vaidyanatha and Dhanvantari. The priests at Meppaṭ perform Śūlinī *abhiṣeka* with water, milk honey, ghee, curd, fruit juice, and sandal water to please her and to obtain her healing powers.

Śrī Porkali is a war goddess worshipped by Śākta Brahmans (Mūssats and Piṭārar) and invoked in many Śākta temples of Kerala, including the famous Piṣāri Kāvu near Koyilandi in Kozhikode district. Interestingly, Porkali is also venerated in many *kalaris*. Anandabhairava and Anandabhairavī, the deities worshipped in Meppaṭ Kalari, are reminiscent of theological concepts behind the ritual practice of Kashmirian Śaivism. According to Śaivism, the body of a Tantric practitioner should be spiritually transformed into the cosmic body of Śiva, who appears in the male-female form of Anandabhairava and Anandabhairavī (Werner 1993, 189).

The presence of the goddess Tripurāsundarī and her entourage is also vital for understanding Śāktism in Kerala in general and the peculiar eclecticism of the Meppaṭ tradition. The many aspects of Śrīvidyā are present in almost all Śākta traditions of Kerala; *śrīcakra* (the main yantra of this tradition) is venerated by Tantric practitioners of Brahman and non-Brahman lineages, and Śrīvidyā mantra is often given at the time of initiation as the most secret Tantric formula (Karasinski 2020a, 549). In Meppaṭ Kalari, Śrīvidyā is regarded by the guru and his disciples as an individual spiritual path that requires initiation and strict discipline. However, it is also a mode of practice that has been integrated into the temple ritualism and its daily and festive rites.

Next in the sequence of ritual activities, a *malar nivedyam* (a type of puffed rice) is given as an offering to all images Afterwards Bhadrakālī is worshipped outside the temple in a grove—she is invoked near an old jackfruit tree. With these rites, morning worship is over, and the temple usually closes by 8:00 a.m. However, certain special, secret rituals called *śakti-samārādhana* (adoration of *śakti*) may be conducted later, at 10:00 a.m. At this time, the puja for Bhadrakālī is performed and she is invoked into Durgā's image. This is followed by *guruti* (*gurusi*) *tarpaṇa* (satiation with bloodlike liquid) in front of Bhadrakālī *pīṭha*. *Guruti* is usually a red liquid composed of turmeric and lime in imitation of blood (Pasty-Abdul Wahid 2020). In the Kaula rites I observed in Kannur, the actual blood of sacrificed roosters mixed with wine was offered. The sacrificial rooster was first hypnotized with mantras, and later the person for whom the ritual was performed had to move the bird above their head in anticlockwise motion several times (they were supposed to meditate and repeat mantras mentally while doing so). Finally, the rooster was given to a priest who sacrificed it and poured its blood into the pots of *guruti*. In fact, in Kerala, the *guruti tarpaṇa* is performed generally for wrathful deities, demon-slaying goddesses, or deities of Teyyam ritual performance (see figure 9.4).[20]

In some temples, *guruti* is performed as an exorcism to banish evil spirits and protect devotees against inimical spiritual influences. In the Meppaṭ temple, the satiation with *guruti* not only forms an obligatory act of worship but also functions as a rite of protection and empowerment. Following these rites, the priests perform Śrīvidyā *śrīcakra pūjā* in the temple as part of a ceremony known as *śakti-samārādhana*. Interestingly, at the time of *śakti-samārādhana*, the ritual is performed not only for the Tripurā of Śrīvidyā but also for the Kālī Kālasaṃkarṣiṇī of the Krama tradition. This suggests that Śrīvidyā may function as a link between various Tantric elements that Meppaṭ gurus creatively combined.

Figure 9.4. Teyyam in Kannur district, 2011. *Source*: Photograph by the author.

During temple festivals, special observances are also performed for another god installed in the temple: Yogi-Bhairava. The deity is worshipped, during special festivals or rites, by a representative of another caste—Yogi–Gurukkaḷs. Regarding the origin of this caste, Freeman (2015) points to the influx of Yogi-Bhairavas of Bhairava Śākta cult, who went to Kerala from Mangalore and in time transformed themselves into the settled caste known locally as Cōyis. Yogi-Gurukkaḷs are the senior Cōyis, who govern their community and temples. Traditionally, they worship Bhairava and various fierce goddesses with blood sacrifices, meat, and alcohol. The community has its own Śākta rites that include *śrīcakra* adoration, and Yogi-Gurukkaḷ are often invited to perform ceremonies of other communities, such as Nāyars, Tiyyans, or Mukkuvans (Thurston 2001, 12)

The morning pujas of the Meppaṭ temple end with the light ceremony performed by a waving of the sacrificial lamp. The leftovers of the puja are given to so-called leftover deities, usually Ucciṣṭa Bhairava.

Interestingly, the main goddess changes her forms depending on the time of the day. During the midday ritual she is worshipped as Caṇḍikā and Kāmeśvarī; in the evening she is honored as Auṣadhīśvarī Śūlinī, the goddess of medicine. She is also worshipped as Pratyaṅgirā Śūlinī at midnight, along with Tripurā of Śrīvidyā, and Kālasaṃkarṣiṇī of the Krama tradition. Thus, Śūlinī can be understood as an epithet used to describe and invoke any fierce warrior goddess who helps devotees with her healing and protective powers.

In conclusion, we should stress that Śrīvidyā and Krama form the core of private, esoteric, and exterior dimensions of Meppaṭ ritualism. It was through Śrīvidyā that Nādānta found his way into the spiritual domain and revived the temple rituals of his family with the inspiration he got from the Śrīvidyā practice. As observed in the scheme of temple rituals shown previously, the adoration of *śrīcakra* and the honoring of Tripurā goddess are integrated into ritual routines prescribed by Nādānta's ancestors in family manuscripts. Nādānta found his Śrīvidyā guru in Amṛtānandanātha of Devipuram (Andhra Pradesh).[21] Arjun Karunakaran Nair received *pūrṇa-dīkṣā* (full initiation) of Śrīvidyā from Amṛtānandanātha, and with it a new name (Nādānta-ānandanātha), which indicates that he is fully initiated in the Śrīvidyā path. Nādānta's family tradition has its own Śrīvidyā rites that are still followed, but the practice is enriched with mantras and rituals of Amṛtānandanātha's lineage. It is worth mentioning that in some Tantric families, a Śrīvidyā mantra (the mantra of Bālā Tripurāsundarī)[22] is given to children during *saṃskāra*s, Hindu rites of passage. The initiation to this mantra, considered as the first stage of Śrīvidyā worship, is a prerequisite for any *śrīcakra* rituals. Thus, paradoxically, Śrīvidyā is a secret spiritual doctrine followed by advanced practitioners from traditional Tantric houses, but it is also a system that can be followed by anyone who is accepted by a Śrīvidyā guru.

The second stream of spiritual inspiration, the Krama, came from Nādānta's study of family manuscripts, visits to the Kaḷarivātukkal temple, the guidance of its Śākta priests, and a revelation he said he had received directly from the goddess at Kaḷarivātukkal. After the revelation and study of ritual manuals, Nādānta continued his Śrīvidyā worship and combined it with Kālī-Krama ritualism, the tradition that is otherwise perpetuated by the Piṭārars. It is also visible in the spiritual aim of the followers of Meppaṭ, which is envisioned as merging with the divine, nondual reality of *anākhyacakra*. The Krama's Kālī Kālasaṃkarṣiṇī and her emanations represent the Wheel of the Nameless (*anākhyacakra*), a spiritual dimension that encompasses all other cakras of that system (Dyczkowski 1992, 30). Thus, the goddess of Meppaṭ, with her many avatars, iconographic representations, moods, and personalities, incorporates several Śākta-Śaiva traditions that are present in Kerala.

Concluding Remarks: The Composite Identity of a Contemporary Tantric Lineage

The Meppaṭ *sampradāya* incorporated and adapted religious beliefs and rituals of Kashmirian Śaivism, the Kaula path of Śrīvidyā, and the mode of worship followed by the Nāyar clan.

When discussing the eclecticism of this tradition and temple rituals of Meppaṭ, one should remember that, in contrast with many temples in other parts of India, those in Kerala cannot be divided into Śaiva, Vaiṣṇava, or Śākta. In Keralan temples, many different gods are worshipped and invoked on various occasions, and, for instance, a temple dedicated to Viṣṇu can conduct ceremonies for Śiva (Narayanan 2011, 187). Similarly, a particular Tantric goddess can have various avatars and be ferocious or calm, depending on the rituals or the time of day.

The idea of identity and belonging, or whether one is affiliated with the Tantric, Kaula, Śākta, or Śrīvidyā tradition, is multifaceted and stratified within Keralan communities. Thus, a scholar conducting research on Keralan Tantra should avoid attributing clear-cut identities based on prestigious textual traditions. As I have tried to show, living practitioners do not ascribe to single identities: these categories in reality are always overlapping and stratified in complex ways that only long-term empathetic ethnography within Keralan communities can reveal. Interestingly, the Meppaṭ constitutes, and represents, its identity at several levels: by referring to the authority of the clan (Nāyar), the esoteric knowledge of the Krama tradition of Kashmir, and the Śrīvidyā tradition of Amṛtānandanātha. Thus, paradoxically, we can call the tradition of Meppaṭ gurus traditional and eclectic at the same time.

The Śākta tradition present within various communities of Kerala has remained relatively unexplored in academic debates. This chapter has examined how Meppaṭ gurus create an identity both of and for themselves. Closely tied to this construction of identity and notion of belonging is the way in which the followers of this tradition relate to their goddesses and sacred spaces (*kalari*s or *kāvu*s) and the myths they create around them. I visited the Meppaṭ temple many times in the years 2010 to 2012 and observed how the place had changed and grown into a Tantric center with followers, disciples, and devotees going there to pray, study Tantric paths, or discuss spiritual matters. The Meppaṭ tradition, like its goddess, has many faces. Meppaṭ is at once traditional and progressive—it links various Tantric currents and represents a path followed by members of a particular clan, but it is also open to spiritual seekers from outside.

The case of the Meppaṭ tradition exemplifies tendencies that can be found within several Tantric traditions of modern Kerala. During my research in Kerala, I met with and interviewed various Tantric practitioners and gurus who expressed a need to conduct deeper research into their traditions, reread the family manuscripts, or even embark on a spiritual search to find new gurus to help them to gain in-depth insight into Tantric philosophy. This trend is observable within Brahman and non-Brahman communities of modern Kerala, and one of its effects is the proliferation of new Tantric institutions, ashrams, and training and research centers (Karasinski 2020a, 555–58). Some traditions are opening up to admit new devotees and disciples, but there are also Tantric *sampradāyas* followed only by certain families within the sacred space of their holy groves and temples. Thus, these tendencies of opening, reviving, or in some cases reinventing Tantric traditions require new research on Tantric identities in Kerala. This necessitates a closer examination of hitherto scantly explored living Tantric traditions. Scholarly inquiry into this underresearched field may help to redefine notions of tradition and orthodoxy within Keralan Hinduism as well as notions of continuity and change within Tantric traditions in general.

Notes

1. I would like to express my sincere gratitude to Arjun Karunakaran Nair (Nādānta Ānandanātha) for discussing his family tradition with me and for sharing his knowledge of Tantric ritualism.

2. The complexity of Śākta traditions in Kerala has been investigated by several scholars. Van Brussel (2020) and Pasty Abdul-Wahid (2017) discuss the worship of fierce goddesses in Kerala and traditional ritualistic art forms devoted to them. Caldwell (2003) provides a useful introduction to the cult of

goddess Kālī in Kerala and her manifold representations in rituals and *teyyam* performances. Also, Menon (2015) discusses folk traditions, rites, customs, and taboos related to the Kālī worship in Keralan temples. Sarma (2009), Ajithan (2018), and Karasinski (2020b) indicated textual sources of early Śākta ritualism and reflected on Tantric temple rituals in modern Kerala. On the other hand, Freeman's (1999) groundbreaking research on Śākta rituals and their holy groves provoked more academic interests in the ritualism of the *kāvus*. Nair (2000) and Vijayaraghavan (2007) represent two in-depth studies on Śākta groves written by Keralan scholars. Similarly, readers interested in Śākta temples of Southern Kerala may consult Gentes (1992) and Elayath (2003), two anthropological studies on the Kodungallur temple and its priests, the Aṭikals. Finally, for an academic study on *mantravāda* and its links with Tantra and magical practices in Kerala, one may consult Tarabout (2003).

3. They are also called Śākteya Brāhmana or Madhu Brāhmana (The Intoxicated Brahmans) by other communities in Kerala because their *sādhanā* (spiritual discipline) supports the empowerment generated by the ritual use of wine.

4. In several temples of Kerala, foreigners are not allowed to enter the inner sanctum without permission from the temple authorities.

5. As indicated by Unni (2006, 10), the ritualism of the Kerala temples of the Nambudiris is known as *Vaidika-Tantrika* because it has two components: *Vaidika* (i.e., rites that include Vedic elements such as Vedic mantras and fire ceremonies), and *Tantrika*—the ritual use of non-Vedic mantras and Tantric offerings.

6. While analyzing Tantra in Bengal, Ondračka (2020) suggests a possibility of existence of what he calls "vernacular Tantra." He further hypothesizes that in the Bengal Tantric milieux, two streams of Tantra might have coexisted, one "more normative and elite, expressing its ideas in Sanskrit," and the other "less privileged and educated, in Bengali." Similarly, in the context of complex and intertwined Keralan Tantric cults, one may observe an analogous interplay between Sanskrit and Malayalam mantric traditions. Several informants claimed that in Mantravāda practices, the "Malayalam mantras" were supposed to be more effective and powerful. This claim raises another interesting point of divergence between Tantra and Mantravāda: while Tantric practices in general are based on Sanskrit sources, Mantravādins often combine Sanskrit and Malayalam mantras, invoking both Tantric deities and local Mother Goddesses, or *genii loci*, who reside in their family shrines.

7. Freeman (1994) explains that the Piṭārars preside as the priests of certain royal temples. They study and employ Sanskrit texts in worship, are endowed with sacred threads, and undergo other Brahmanical life-cycle rites. However, they also eat animal flesh and drink liquor, and offer these items to their gods. Freeman suggests also that they represent either a group

of Brahmans who were degraded to serve in such temples or a lower caste elevated to serve as priests.

8. The term Kashmirian Śaivism, sometimes referred to as Kashmirian Śaiva-Śākta tradition, is often used in reference to the nondualistic schools of philosophy that flourished in Kashmir starting around the tenth century CE. Among these traditions, Trika and Krama are considered the most notable (Furlinger 2009, 1). The Trika was primarily a cult of three goddesses (Parā, Aparā, and Parāparā). On the other hand, Krama concepts, as confirmed by Abhinavagupta and other Śaiva thinkers, were seen as the very basis of Trika (Sanderson 2005, 102). The term *Krama* literally means a sequence or a lineage (*Tantrāloka* 3.129), and the tradition was known for its pantheon and for its spiritual practices organized in complex sequences. Krama is regarded as one of the Kālī cults of the Northern Transmission (*uttarāmnāya*) of the Kula school of Tantrism (Padoux 1998, 59).

9. Among important Śākta centers of the tradition in Northern Kerala (Kannur-Kasargode) are Māṭāyi Kāvu (*kāvu*, meaning a sacred grove), Kaḷarivātukkal, and Caṇḍayogeśvarī Mannampuṟattu Kāvu.

10. Śrīvidyā, often regarded as the Southern Transmission of Kaula, is a tradition of the goddess known as Tripurā. The goddess is worshipped as a personification of the highest Śakti, the supreme power and principle of the universe, and her worship includes rituals of *śrīcakra* and the use of secret mantras (Hirmer 2020).

11. A Piṭārar priest of Mannampuṟattu Kāvu, 2009, personal communication, fieldwork notes.

12. Many scholars confirm that in Hindu traditions the fearsome and dangerous goddesses are often depicted as lonely warriors. The peaceful and maternal goddesses of the Hindu pantheon are those who are married and who have "transferred control of their sexuality to their husbands" (Wadley 1977, 118). Similarly, Sax (1991) points out that in South India "it is believed that women have more śakti than men and therefore men must control women's dangerous and excessive sexuality." Yet, in the Śākta traditions of Kerala, we often find mother goddesses praised as fearless warriors known for their lone battles against demonic armies.

13. My reading of the Mūssat family manuscripts reveals elements of Krama ritualism in the religious observances of the clan. For more on this subject, please see Karasinski (2020b).

14. In Śākta temples of Kerala, the goddess is often depicted as fighting against demons Dāruka (Dārika) or Ruru, thus she is called Dārukajit (The One Who Killed Dāruka) or Rurujit (The One Who Killed Ruru). On the Keralan rituals and ritual theatrical performances inspired by the legend of the goddess' fight against Dāruka, see Van Brussel (2020).

15. The word *Nāyar* is traditionally derived from the Sanskrit term *nāyaka* (leader) or *nāga* (snake). However, even though Nāyars were often warriors

with their own martial-art gymnasia and, like many people in Kerala, worshipped snakes, there were many subgroups and communities of Nāyars who had a lower social status and various occupations. See Sadasivan (2000, 327).

16. A Brahman priest, 2011, Vadakara, personal communication, fieldwork notes.

17. Menon (1994, 44–45) observes that *kāvus* were of various kinds, but generally the focus of worship of a community of lower and upper castes within a region defined by the sphere of overlordship (*melkoyma*) of the dominant family or families managing the shrine.

18. For detailed descriptions of Śakti Gaṇapati, see Bühnemann (2008, 47–50, 75–76).

19. According to Nādānta (private communication, November 2010, Kannur), Śūlinī protects from enemies and provides all imaginable wealth and assets, in addition to curing mental problems and blessing her devotees with children.

20. *Teyyam* can be defined as a form of worship of the local deities of northern Kerala through costumed spirit possession and ritual dance (Freeman 2003, 307).

21. On Devipuram and its guru, see Rao (2019a).

22. Tripurā is adored in three aspects: Tripurā bālā, Tripurā sundarī, and Tripurā bhairavī (Kinsley 1998, 43).

Bibliography

Primary Sources

Kulārṇavatantra. Avalon, Arthur. 2001. New Delhi: Motilal Banarsidass.

Mātṛsadbhāva, MSS. no. 1017a, 13377. The Oriental Research Institute & Manuscripts Library (ORI & MSS) Trivandrum.

Tantrāloka. 1987. *The Tantrāloka of Abhinavagupta: With the Commentary of Jayratha*. Edited by R. C. Dwivedi and Navjivan Rastogi. New Delhi: Motilal Banarsidass.

Secondary Sources

Ajithan, P. I. 2018 *Tantric Rituals of Kerala Temples: Texts and Traditions*. New Delhi: DK Printworld.

Brooks, Douglas R. 1990. *The Secret of the Three Cities: An Introduction to Hindu Śākta Tantrism*. Chicago: University of Chicago Press.

Bayly, Susan. 1984. "Hindu Kingship and the Origin of Community: Religion, State and Society in Kerala, 1750–1850." *Modern Asian Studies* 18, no. 2: 177–213.

Bühnemann, Gudrun. 2008. *Tantric Forms of Gaṇeśa According to the Vidyārṇavatantra*. New Delhi: DK Printworld.

Caldwell, Sarah. 2003. "Margins at the Center: Tracing Kālī Through Time, Space, and Culture." In *Encountering Kālī: In the Margins, at the Center, in the West*, edited by Rachel McDermott and Jeffrey Kripal, 249–73. Berkeley: University of California Press.

Dupuche, John R. 2003. *Abhinavagupta: The Kula Ritual, as Elaborated in Chapter 29 of the Tantrāloka*. Vol. 5. Delhi: Motilal Banarsidass.

Dyczkowski, Mark. 1992. *The Stanzas on Vibration*. New York: SUNY Press.

Elayath, Kunjikuttan. 2003. *Koṭuṅṅallūr Kṣetretihāsaṃ: Kālīkṣetraṃ oru caritra paṭhanaṃ*. Kodungallur: Devi Book Stall.

Freeman, Rich. 1994. "Possession Rites and the Tantric Temple: A Case-Study from Northern Kerala." *Diskus Online Journal of International Religious Studies* 2, no. 2. Accessed September 7, 2019.http://jbasr.com/basr/diskus/diskus1-6/index.html.

———. 1999. "Gods, Groves and the Culture of Nature in Kerala." *Modern Asian Studies* 33, no. 2: 257–302.

———. 2003. "The Teyyam Tradition of Kerala." In *The Blackwell Companion to Hinduism*, edited by Gavin Flood, 307–26. Oxford: Blackwell Publishing.

———. 2015. "Śāktism, Polity and Society in Medieval Malabar." In *Goddess Traditions in Tantric Hinduism*, edited by Bjarne Wenicke Olesen, 153–85. Oxford: Routledge.

Fuller, Christopher John. 1975. "The Internal Structure of the Nayar Caste." *Journal of Anthropological Research* 31, no. 4: 283–312.

———. 1976. *Nayars Today*. Cambridge: Cambridge University Press

Gentes, M. J. 1992. "Scandalizing the Goddess at Kodungallur." *Asian Folklore Studies* 51, no. 2: 295–322.

Goodall, Dominic, and Harunaga Isaacson. 2011. "Tantric Hinduism." In *The Continuum Companion to Hindu Studies*, edited by Jessica Frazer, 122–37. London: Continuum.

Gough, Kathleen E. 1961. "Nāyars: Central Kerala." In *Matrilineal Kinship*, edited by David M. Schneider and Kathleen E. Gough, 298–385. Berkeley: University of California Press.

Gupta, Sanjukta. 2005. "The Domestication of a Goddess." In *Encountering Kali: In the Margins, at the Center, in the West*, edited by Rachel Fell McDermott and Jeffrey J. Kripal, 60–79. Delhi: Motilal Banarsidass.

Hirmer, Monika. 2020. "'Devī Needs those Rituals!' Ontological Considerations on Ritual Transformations in a Contemporary South Indian Śrīvidyā Tradition." *Religions of South Asia* 14, nos. 1–2: 117–49.

Karasinski Maciej. 2010. "Orthodoxy Resignified: Peripheries and Centres of Tantra in Kerala." *Journal of Sukrtindra Oriental Research Institute* 12, no. 1: 1–18.

———. 2020a. "A Goddess Who Unites and Empowers: Śrīvidyā as a Link between Tantric Traditions of Modern Kerala—Some Considerations." *Journal of Indian Philosophy* 48, no. 4: 541–63.

———. 2020b. "Śākta Tantric Traditions of Kerala in the Process of Change: Some Notes on Raudra-Mahārtha Sampradāya." *Religions of South Asia* 14, nos. 1–2: 150–75.

———. 2021. "When Yogis Become Warriors—The Embodied Spirituality of Kaḷaripayattu," *Religions* 12, no. 5: 294. https://doi.org/10.3390/rel12050294.

Kinsley, David, R. 1998. *Tantric Visions of the Divine Feminine: The Ten Mahāvidyās*. New Delhi: Motilal Banarsidass.

———. 2005. "Kālī." In *Encountering Kali: In the Margins, at the Center, in the West*, edited by Rachell Fell McDermott and Jeffrey J Kripal, 23–38. New Delhi: Motilal Banarsidass.

Kripal, Jeffrey. 2008. "The Roar of Awakening: The Eros of Esalen and the Western Transmission of Tantra." In *Hidden Intercourse: Eros and Sexuality in the History of Western Esotericism*, edited by Wouter J. Hanegraaff and Jeffrey Kripal, 479–520. Leiden: Brill.

Mascarenhas-Keyes, Stella. 2004. "The Native Anthropologist: Constraints and Strategies in Research." In *Methodology and Fieldwork*, edited by Vinay Kumar Srivatsa, 421–35. Oxford: Oxford University Press.

Menon, Chelanattu Achutha. 2015. *Keraḷattile Kāḷīseva*. Trichur: Sahitya Pravarthaka Co-operative Society.

Menon, Dilip. 1994. *Caste, Nationalism and Communism in South India: Malabar, 1900–1948*. Cambridge: Cambridge University Press.

Muller-Ortega, Paul. 1997. *The Triadic Heart of Śiva*. New Delhi: Motilal Banarasidass,

Nair, M. S. 2000. *Māṭāyikkāvŭ oru Paṭhanam*. Calicut: Calicut University Press.

Narayanan, N. 2011. "Purnatrayisa Temple—A Centre for Arts and Culture." In *Royal Family of Cochin and Sanskrit Studies*, edited by K. K. N. Kurup, C. M. Nīlakaṇṭhana, and K. A. Ravindran, 175–202. Cochin: Centre for Heritage Studies.

Ondračka Lubomír.2020. "Vernacular Tantra? An Analysis of the Bengali Text The Garland of Bones." *Religions of South Asia* 14, nos. 1–2: 63–86.

Padoux, André. 1998. *Vāc the Concept of the Word in Selected Hindu Tantras*. New Delhi: Sri Satguru.

Pasty-Abdul Wahid, Marianne. 2017. "'She Doesn't Need Muṭiyēttu There': The Interplay of Divine Mood, Taste and Dramatic Offerings in South Indian Folk Hinduism." *Religions of South Asia* 11, no. 1: 72–98.

———. 2020. "Bloodthirsty, or Not, That Is the Question: An Ethnography-Based Discussion of Bhadrakāḷi's Use of Violence in Popular Worship, Ritual Performing Arts and Narratives in Central Kerala (South India)." *Religions* 11, no. 4.

Ramavarma, R K. 1910. "The Brahmans of Malabar," *The Journal of the Royal Asiatic Society of Great Britain and Ireland* 42, no. 3: 625–39.

Rao, Mani. 2019a. "The Experience of Śrīvidyā at Devipuram," *Religions* 10, no. 1: 14. https://doi.org/10.3390/rel10010014.

———. 2019b. *Living Mantra: Mantra, Deity, and Visionary Experience Today.* Palgrave Macmillan.

Sadasivan, S. N. 2000. *A Social History of India.* New Delhi: APH Publishing Corporation.

Sanderson, Alexis. 2005. "A Commentary on the Opening Verses of the Tantrasāra of Abhinavagupta." In *Sāmarasya Studies in Indian Arts, Philosophy and Interreligious Dialogue in Honor of Bettina Baumer*, edited by Sadananda Das and Ernst Furlinger, 89–148. New Delhi: DK Printworld.

Sarma, S. A. S. 2009. "The Eclectic Paddhatis of Kerala." *Indologica Taurinensia. The Journal of the International Association of Sanskrit Studies* 35: 319–39.

Sax, William S. 1991. *Mountain Goddess: Gender and Politics in a Himalayan Pilgrimage.* Oxford: Oxford University Press.

Spradley, James P. 1980. *Participant Observation.* Orlando: Harcourt.

Stone, Linda. 2013. *Kinship and Gender: An Introduction.* Philadelphia: Westview Press.

Tarabout, Gilles. 2003. "Magical Violence and Non-Violence: Witchcraft in Kerala." In *Violence / Non-Violence Some Hindu Perspectives*, edited by Vidal D. Tarabout and G. Meyer, 219–54. New Delhi: Manoharlal.

Thurston, Edgar. 2001. *Castes and Tribes of Southern India.* Vol. 5. Madras/New Delhi: Asian Educational Services.

Unni, N. P. 1972. *Kokilasandeśa of Uddaṇḍa.* Trivandrum: College Book House.

———. 2006. *Tantra Literature of Kerala.* New Delhi: New Bharatiya.

Van Brussel, Noor. 2020. "Tales of Endings and Beginnings: Cycles of Violence as a Leitmotif in the Narrative Structure of the Bhadrakāḷīmāhātmya," *Religions* 11, no. 3: 119. https://doi.org/10.3390/rel11030119.

Vidal, Denis, Gilles Tarabout, and Éric Meyer. 1994. "On the Concepts of Violence and Non-violence in Hinduism and Indian Society." *South Asia Research* 14, no. 2: 196–213.

Vijayaraghavan, K. 2007. *Kollam Śrī Pīṣārīkāvu Kṣetram.* Calicut: Calicut University Press.

Viju. B, 2017. "Who Are the Moosaths—Second-Class Nambuthiris or Elite Brahmans? Accessed June 12, 2020. https://timesofindia.indiatimes.com/blogs/Second-Nature/caste-away/.

Wadley, Susan. 1977. "Women and The Hindu Tradition." In *Women in India: Two Perspectives*, edited by Doranne Jacobson and Susan Wedley, 113–39. New Delhi: Manohar.

Wenta, Aleksandra. 2015. "Between Fear and Heroism: The Tantric Path to Liberation." In *Emotions in Indian Thought-Systems*, edited by Purushottama Bilimoria and Aleksandra Wenta, 114–36. London: Routledge.

Werner, Karel. 1993. *Love Divine: Studies in Bhakti and Devotional Mysticism*. Durham Indological Series. New Delhi: Curzon Press.

White, David Gordon. 1998. "Transformations in the Art of Love: Kāmakalā Practices in Hindu Tantric and Kaula Traditions." *History of Religions* 38, no. 2: 172–98.

———. 2000. Introduction to *Tantra in Practice*, edited by David Gordon White, 3–38 Princeton: Princeton University Press.

Zarilli, Philip. 2000. *Kathakali Dance-Drama: Where Gods and Demons Come to Play*. London/New York: Routledge.

———. 2004. *When the Body Becomes All Eyes—Paradigms, Discourses and Practices of Power in Kalarippayattu*. New Delhi: Oxford University Press.

10

Tantric Lives in Bengal and Bali

Toward a Comparative Ethnography

June McDaniel

Hindu Tantra has been a difficult area to explore ethnographically, both because of its controversial reputation and because of practitioners' hesitation to open up to outsiders. Of course, access to practitioners has always been a challenge for anthropologists and religionists. Some have negotiated the role of "insider" to explore the lives and experiences of practitioners. For example, Antoinette DeNapoli (2019) spent six years with the guru Mataji (Trikal Bhavanta Saraswati) and her community. She writes that Mataji claims to have learned the Vedas "without reading them," because she "embodies the Vedas" through her charisma, conduct, and character. DeNapoli acted as a community member and biographer, observing the dynamics of the group. We can also see this close ethnography in Angela Rudert's (2017) work on a female guru from the Punjabi Sikh tradition. Rudert's ethnography shows a good example of a scholar who was able to gain close access to the guru Anandmurti Guru Maa and her community in India and America. This guru, like many other modern female gurus, emphasizes the primacy of personal experience over formal study of Vedic texts and ritual traditions to construct her alternative authority and to critique social problems.

Mani Rao (2019) worked with Śrīvidya tantrikas (Sanskrit *tāntrika*) and mantra practitioners in South India. Her interviews and narratives showed depth and sensitivity to her informants' concerns and an extraordinary ability to enter into their lived experiences. Her project strived toward an "anthropology of mantra," learning about the spiritual lives of Tantric practitioners of mantra meditation through participant observation and embodied research. We also see this sort of careful ethnography in the work of Sukanya Sarbadhikary (2015), who explored Bengali Vaishnava groups in the Navadvipa/Mayapur area of West Bengal. She observed different, competing Vaishnava groups in the same region, with detailed fieldwork and extraordinary access to groups that are difficult to interview. Her observations on the Vaishnava Sahajiya Tantric groups were the most valuable for the field of Tantric studies. We have many descriptions of Sahajiya texts in the literature on Vaishnavism, but few narratives from living practitioners. Hugh Urban has moved from historical studies of Tantra in colonial Bengal to ethnographic fieldwork in Assam, especially in Kamakhya, a *śākta pīṭha* or center for Shakta Tantra (Urban 2008). He is interested in power relationships, especially between Sanskritic, Brahmanical rituals and the indigenous rituals of Assamese folk religion.

The above scholars show the modern rise of ethnography as a methodology for the study of Indian religion, especially valuable for Tantric studies. In this chapter, I discuss the lives of Hindu tantrikas in the state of West Bengal, India, and on the island of Bali, Indonesia. While these areas differ in size and population, both have traditions of Tantra that have lasted over 500 years and living practitioners who perform traditional rituals. Both have a background in which Tantra has been related to Shaivism, Shaktism, and Vajrayana Buddhism, and both have developed different strategies for legitimacy and survival. The two cases present interesting similarities as well as differences, offering us a worthwhile comparative ground for exploring issues like authenticity, legitimacy, social expectations, and varying interpretations of *sannyāsa,* or renunciation, within the context of diverse historical and ethnographic settings.

In terms of fieldwork, there were both colleagues and informants who were incredibly helpful.[1] I did not enter devotee groups as a way to overcome the "outsider-insider" problem, but I have done yogic meditation and had visions with Tantric imagery. This turned out to be very useful during fieldwork, for many of the priests and renunciants with whom I spoke would have an initial period of gazing deep into my eyes to ascertain my worthiness for sharing life stories and ecstatic experiences. When we could share experiences of deep yogic states, they were then willing to share their stories as well.

As a note on positionality, being a white woman in the field had both advantages and disadvantages. I am small with long dark hair, and in India strangers generally thought I was there to study Indian dance, which was an acceptable role for a Westerner. I wore saris every day, and I was eventually assumed to be a light-skinned Bengali woman. The advantage to this was easier access to rituals and temples. The disadvantage was that I was ignored. Being foreign gets attention, and people are willing to answer questions and explain the reasons for their actions to somebody from the USA. Local researchers might be seen as having a lower status, and questions might go unanswered (or practitioners might think the researcher is crazy for questioning something so obvious). Whenever I asked questions (and managed to get the attention of participants), I identified myself as a visitor from the USA who was interested in their experiences. Many were impressed that I would travel all the way around the world to learn about them.

While my fieldwork in West Bengal was conducted in the 1990s, my fieldwork in Bali is more recent (2010s). In India, as a woman I found it easier to speak with female renunciants than with male ones. In Bali the high priests are married, and the issue of gender was not as important. I traveled with a male Balinese colleague who knew the special etiquette, language, and schedules of the *pedanda*s. I was thus not just a foreigner traveling alone, but I was working with someone who was considering becoming a *pedanda* himself. In both countries, the questions on religious experience interested my informants, and most said that they had never been asked such questions before. Most visitors to holy people were not interested in their inner lives; rather, they just wanted gifts or counseling or help of various sorts. Though their religious experiences had motivated their life choices, my informants were unaccustomed to thinking about their own life stories in this way.

As we look at Bengali and Balinese cultures, we may note that the lifestyles of practicing tantrikas are quite different. These initial notes toward a comparative ethnography of Tantric traditions can be useful to examine the effects of different understandings of Tantra on the lived experience of practitioners. We shall focus here on the different understandings of renunciation, or *sannyasa,* as a major contributing factor to the different styles of Tantric lived experience.

West Bengal

Hindu Tantric practices were widely known by the seventh century, flourished between the eighth and fourteenth centuries, and slowly declined in popularity with the rising prominence of bhakti devotional movements. The development of Tantra in medieval India came with the rise of many new kingdoms across the subcontinent after the breakdown of two major dynasties, the Guptas in the north and the Vakatakas in the southwest. Many rulers were drawn to Tantra's promise of power, and public temples often incorporated Tantric deities as guardians. From the Hindu Tantric perspective, all material reality is animated by Shakti (*śakti*)—unlimited, divine feminine power. This inspired the dramatic rise of goddess worship in medieval India.

In West Bengal, the major Tantric goddess was Kali. She was portrayed as a destructive yet compassionate Mother by Bengali poets like Ramprasad Sen (1718–1775); like nature, she would both create and destroy. Ramprasad Sen's verses became popular during a time of crisis in Bengal, intensified by the rise of the British East India Company. Devotion to Kali as an all-powerful deity increased, and there were poems (*śyāmā saṅgīt*) and large festivals (*melās*) dedicated to her. Kali was regarded by many British officials as threatening to the colonial domination of India in the nineteenth century, and Bengali revolutionaries exploited these fears and portrayed her as a symbol of political resistance.

Despite the popularity of Kali as a devotional goddess in many areas, Tantric practice developed a bad reputation. In early Sanskrit literature Kali is portrayed as negative and devouring. In Bhavabhuti's popular eighth-century play *Mālatīmādhava,* Kali is a terrifying goddess who is dark and violent (*ugra*), and her temple is in a burning ground. Her worshipper is an evil tantrika who kidnaps the innocent heroine to sacrifice her to the goddess (Dasgupta 1985, 66). The image of tantrikas who kidnap people for sacrifice has remained in Indian literature and was later adopted by colonial writers. As David Gordon White notes in his book *Sinister Yogis*, tantrikas and yogis were often equated as sorcerers and people with dangerous powers, such as hypnosis and raising the dead (White 2009). However, their emphasis on mantra, mudra (ritual hand positions), mandala (sacred diagrams of the universe, often geometrical), and *nyāsa* (ritual purification and placement of deities and/or mantras within the body) continued and was absorbed within many forms of Hindu deity worship, thus showing a positive side to the tradition. But the negative image of tantrikas continues, for even in recent years Bengali informants told me of their mothers' threats when they were young—that the evil tantrika would come out of the jungle and punish and kill them (this was a convincing argument for children to behave well).

Tantra also has a devotional side for some tantrikas, in which ritual practice is a way to get close to the goddess and show dedication to her. As goddess of life and death, she can control rebirth and can send the soul to a positive next life, or to a joyous eternity in the lap of the Mother. Tantra gives knowledge of the supernatural worlds, as well as supernatural powers and paths to liberation. But the Mother is a jealous goddess and places great demands on her devotees.

An additional problem for tantrikas is the fact that many are renunciants, having taken vows of *sannyāsa*. In India, this means that they have renounced ordinary social life; they are "dead to the world," vowing to spend the remaining part of their lives in meditation. In Bengal there are a number of interpretations and manifestations of the concept of *sannyāsa*. Some heterodox lineages practice what they call coupled renunciation (*yugala sannyās*), a form of asceticism taken by a man and a woman together as a consorted (not necessarily married) couple (see Openshaw 2007). Some (particularly low-caste) communities practice a form of *saṁsāre sannyās*, being spiritually engaged like an ascetic while being active as a household member and pursuing one's worldly duties (Lorea 2016, 2020). Reformist Vaishnava leaders have proposed a form of *sannyāsa* that is not escapist but rather engaged rationally in social and political life (*yukta vairagya*; see Sardella 2013). While these alternative conceptualizations of *sannyāsa* are widely practiced, the mainstream understanding of renunciation in lay society remains closer to the orthodox Hindu paradigm; hence, *sannyāsī*s are expected to be detached from material goals, having abandoned passions and desires. They may be seeking liberation from rebirth, supernatural powers (*siddhis*), or a good afterlife, but they are considered to be no longer part of society. Because of this perspective on *sannyāsa,* they have been condemned from many sides. For many modern Hindus, they are viewed as street people—homeless transients who have no jobs (except for those with side jobs as astrologers). For Marxists, they waste the money of the workers and are lazy hangers-on who exploit the working class. For scientists and "guru busters" (especially the Rationalist Association, which emphasizes "scientific skepticism"), they prey on the superstitious and make false claims. While I was in rural West Bengal, I was frequently told that Rationalist representatives had been telling local children to throw stones at tantrikas who entered their villages, because the tantrikas wanted them to stay poor and hungry.

During my research in the 1990s, I interviewed many people on their attitudes toward tantrikas: taxi drivers, cooks and waiters, poets and writers, artists, Bengali academics, even a grant administrator or two. But salespeople had some of the widest social networks, and the best stories. I found that bargaining for food in the market was an excellent way of starting conversations.

In Gariahat Market in Kolkata, vegetable and fruit merchants had many stories of tantrikas in their extended families. These stories were mostly about how the tantrikas had upset them. One told of his father's brother, Uncle Tantrika, who would sometimes visit their house in his wanderings. He would scream horribly in the night, frightening the children. When the merchant was young, his mother would threaten him with giving him away to crazy Uncle Tantrika—this threat was enough to stop all bad behavior. Others complained of Tantric relatives not doing their duty to the family: not bringing sons and wealth for the household. Tantrikas were selfish, weird, and even strange as children. Most people did not wish to have tantrikas in the family.

For these reasons, there is some hesitation about adopting a public Tantric identity. The decision to become a tantrika is not an easy one. The person must leave society and become bound by a variety of vows and obligations. In Bengali Shakta Tantra, the serious practitioner is generally imagined as a renunciant who wanders, sleeping at temples or under trees, or who lives in an ashram. The tantrika tends to experience initial ecstatic states, which begin as spontaneous events and are slowly controlled by meditation and bound to ritual. Leading a worldly life becomes more and more difficult, while leaving home and going off alone to lead a renunciant life is generally discouraged by family members. This creates a situation of great inner conflict, especially for female tantrikas, as it is shameful for families to have an unmarried daughter.

There are varying levels of commitment in Bengali Tantra. For those who have it as a side interest, Tantra generally means hanging out and smoking bidis with renunciant *sādhus* at the burning ground, learning some mantras to give magical abilities, and scaring each other with ghost stories. It may be a phase for rebellious teenagers instead of running away from home or joining a traveling theater troupe, or it may be a side practice for engineers, doctors, Indian Administrative Service officers, and bureaucrats. People may have a living guru (often employed in the secular world) or they may learn through tapes, CDs, and websites made by distant Tantric gurus. It allows for a great deal of individual variation—one engineer interviewed in Kolkata worshipped a Tantric Shiva whose manifestation on his altar was three red lights, representing Shiva's incarnation as Marx, Lenin, and Stalin. Singers may dress as tantrikas with matted hair and red-orange clothes to play songs (*śyāmā saṅgīt*) by famous Tantric poets like Ramprasad and Kamalakanta. This aspect brings religion closer to entertainment, as has been noted in village religious festivals by Frank Korom in "To Be Happy" (Korom 1992).

The lives of more committed tantrikas generally follow a series of events, which also tend to appear in the hagiographies of Shakta saints (e.g., see the saint biographies in Dasgupta 1985). There are generally religious or visionary parents, who could interpret the child's early ecstatic experiences as being religious ones. Without such parents, children with intense religious experiences would be called insane and exorcists would be called in, or the child might be sent for Ayurvedic treatment or Western psychotherapy (in more urban areas). The child had to have the strength to resist the treatments, and many tantrikas with whom I spoke told horror stories of the ways they were treated as children and teenagers when they shared their experiences. One woman showed me the thick scar tissue on the inside of her legs, which she said came from being tied down for a week by an exorcist her family had called. He had lit a fire between her legs to chase out the evil spirit that pretended to be a god, yelling at her and threatening her. When she still insisted on the legitimacy of her experiences after a week of torture, he gave up and said that it probably was a god calling her after all. With that, the parents allowed her to go off after the god.

Some parents tried to settle the teenagers down by marriage, and such arranged marriages were rarely successful. The spouses had no idea how to deal with mates having visions of Shiva and Shakti, and the future tantrika often left the marriage to go wandering, looking for a path in life and a guru to give guidance. Some future tantrikas avoided marriage but still ended up wandering, as their experiences were not accepted in their hometowns.

Along with illness, homelessness, and starvation, wandering future tantrikas often had visions, trances, and supernatural encounters. Some described bodily distortions—mantras and pictures suddenly appearing on their skin, arms and legs expanded and contracted, limbs dismembered and then put back together, faces changing into other people and deities. There were also the classical ecstatic bodily changes or *sāttvika bhāvas* (which include skin color change, hair standing on end, etc.). These were described not only by the tantrikas involved (who tended to be rather vague on the details), but especially by their devotees. They are important because they are understood as supernatural evidence of a spiritual state, most often bhakti devotion, but Tantric realization as well. There is a wide literature of biographies of Bengali saints written by disciples that includes such events. Hagiographies of Ramakrishna Paramahamsa and Chaitanya Mahaprabhu were very influential for Shakta tantrikas, for they legitimized ecstatic experiences. Sometimes the tantrikas found gurus to initiate them, but others had visionary initiations, or initiated themselves.

The result of such ecstatic states was often a new identity, temporarily as a child (especially as a child of the goddess Kali) and more permanently as a renunciant who rejected his or her past life. Such renunciants who had received this sort of revelation would wander until they were accepted by a person or group, usually as a result of a miraculous healing or by finding a lost statue or other valuable object. Once they had a disciple, they would then be Tantric gurus: you only need one disciple to be a guru, as you only need one child to be a mother. This new social identity would be strengthened by performance of ritual, thus maintaining the link with the relevant deity and taking on a traditional social role. When there are disciples to feed them, renunciants no longer have to beg. However, they might still wander—along the pilgrimage routes for festivals, or to see their own gurus.[2]

Some tantrikas were unable to move into a new identity, and they could be found at Kali temples and cremation grounds wandering distractedly. I was told by local Shakta priests of several potential tantrikas who went mad, unable to stand the *savasādhanā* corpse ritual (when the person sits on a corpse at night, and all of the person's fears are believed to rise at midnight) or the vision of the goddess Kali. One such mad tantrika passed by as we spoke, walking erratically. The priest said he would eventually return to sanity, but only when the goddess willed it.

Such behavior is generally understood as either divine madness (*divyonmada*) in which an ordinary mind has trouble reacting to a deity's presence, or *pāglāmi* (ordinary madness, which could mean anything from crazy behavior that is "cute," to violent and irrational behavior that is a serious problem). Sometimes a third category of possession (*bhar*) is added, especially in rural Bengal, where angry ancestors and spirits are believed to torment the person until they are propitiated. In divine madness, the person is able to remember their experiences, while in possession trance (*bhar*) there is no memory of events. When asked about experiences of possession, tantrikas I interviewed typically referred me to their disciples.

Female tantrikas in West Bengal faced an even more difficult choice than male ones. There is much pressure in India for women to marry and have children. Staying unmarried was bad enough, but to be a tantrika on top of this—there were dark suspicions of immorality, orgies, impurities of all sorts. Even if the family was poor and could not afford a dowry, this was a shameful situation. Though social pressures impeded women from becoming tantrikas, still they could not compete with the power of the dreams and visions that called them.

One response to this negative image was choosing a celibate life, becoming a tantrika who would follow the life of a *brahmacārī* (or *brahmacārinī*). Tantra could be recast as yoga or bhakti devotion, and esoteric practices could be largely hidden. This was necessary because of social disapproval. One woman interviewed, Jayashri Ma, was unmarried and lived with her brother. She said that she would lose her job as a teacher if people knew she led a secret Tantric circle with male devotees. She would be possessed by both Kali and Shiva during chakras.[3] She understood herself to be an incarnation of Adya Shakti Kali, with her soul shared with the goddess. She was initiated at nine years old by an officer of the Indian Administrative Service who was secretly a Tantric practitioner. They sat on matching seats with five skulls beneath them (*pañcamuṇḍir āsan*), chanting and doing visualizations, and he transferred his power into her. She never married, and she used her meditative powers for healing and prophecy. She did not take money from members of her Tantric circle, and they attended because they were interested in her divinatory and mediumistic abilities. She looked deeply into my eyes and concluded that Adya Shakti Kali was also living in me, so we could discuss her.

Some Tantric holy women got married, but then left their husbands and families. These were *gṛhī sādhikās*, who had children and household responsibilities but had later received a call from the goddess in a dream command. Some were discontented in their married life, but this was not a sufficient reason to leave. They too felt they had no choice and were called to be tantrikas. This was their destiny, written on the forehead at birth, and they embraced their new identities.

Lakshmi Ma had visions of the goddess from childhood, and her marriage was arranged by her husband's guru, Naga Baba. She would see Shiva, Durga, and Kali and run to their temples. Her in-laws called exorcists to stop the visions, but the exorcisms did not work. She could see the goddess Tara spontaneously without performing any ritual, but over time she learned to limit and control her experiences through mantras and visualizations she learned from dreams, and she became known as a healer and devotee.[4] Ritual practice allowed her to be a *strī guru*, a guru who was female, respected by devotees and observers.

Often this initial call is resisted, and both male and female tantrikas spoke of periods of madness when they denied the goddess. They spoke of their worlds falling to pieces, and they felt compelled to wander alone, trying to figure out what to do with their lives. They meditated under trees and in caves, going from one guru to another, begging along the way. Sometimes they were led by dreams and visions to Tantric centers like Tarapith and Bakreshwar, and they would meditate in the burning grounds. Such wandering is particularly difficult for *sadhikas*, because they are without social defenders and may be attacked, both by householder men and by male *sādhus*. Some female tantrikas I interviewed carried large staffs, ostensibly as ritual objects sacred to Shiva, but also for help in walking and for self-defense. They were *sannyāsinīs*, female renouncers, but there was suspicion by local people as to whether they really meant it.

Many practicing male tantrikas also described problems. They spoke of hunger, lack of money, difficulty in finding or keeping a home if they were householders. But becoming a tantrika was not done to gain benefits or have a comfortable life—it was done out of obedience to a divine command. One Kali priest did Tantric meditation, and his major ritual was feeding skulls kept in his temple to gain meditative power. Tantra was part of his family tradition; his grandfather was a temple priest and Tantric sādhu, and his father was a priest who taught him ritual procedures. In town he did traditional worship, but up in the mountains he performed Tantric ritual, as his grandfather did. He also described himself differently depending on my companions when I came for interviews (if they looked high caste, he said he was only a devotee or Kali bhakta). He called his dead grandfather his main Tantric guru, who gave him instruction in dreams. But he said he did not want his own son to be a tantrika—it was too hard a life. The goddess was very temperamental and would get angry over trivial actions (or sometimes, for no reason that he could find), and then he would have illness and bad luck. He wanted his son to work in an office, to become an engineer or a government official, and to have an easier life than his father. But he himself had no choice: the goddess had called him, and he had to obey.[5] He was able to make extra money by intervening in politics, when Communist politicians would come to him secretly at night to get the goddess' blessings and win upcoming elections.[6]

Most tantrikas did not discuss caste, but it was implied by the forms of Tantra they performed. I found that the more educated type of Tantra, what I have called in my books "classical Tantra," tended to be performed by tantrikas with a Brahmin background.[7] Such "pandit tantrikas" were often interested in literature and answered questions about their lives by quoting from Sanskrit texts. The goal of practice was *brahmajñāna*, or deep knowledge of brahman (often in the form of Shakti). Sometimes classical tantrikas would obscure the Tantric side of their knowledge and emphasize devotion or bhakti, as several heads of ashrams did. Some of these tantrikas marry, some remain celibate. While several Western writers have expressed skepticism about the seriousness of tantrikas whose goal was liberation through the classical Tantric practices of mantra, mudra, and mandala and understood this to be a "sanitization" of what was "really" going on, I found that these practitioners were serious about their practice, though it is possible that for some classical tantrikas the focus on academic knowledge and justifying their practices got in the way of the goals they were seeking.[8]

Folk or popular Tantra tends to be followed by non-Brahmins, for it does not involve Sanskrit texts, or even Sanskrit mantras (most are in Bengali). Its goals tend to be supernatural powers (*siddhis*), especially those involved with health, wealth, and fertility. There was little talk of liberation or immortality. Folk Tantra also gives instructions for encounters with spiritual beings, such as *yoginīs*, ancestors, and ghosts. Often, rituals focus on death, and sometimes nontraditional sexuality is included; such rituals tend to be understood literally. Many folk tantrikas interviewed had little education, learning about Tantra through oral tradition, visions, or dream initiation. They were often anti-caste and anti-text; if they did use a text, it was usually the *Kulārṇava Tantra,* which emphasizes direct experience over book-based learning. We may note that some tantras emphasize personal experience, while others focus primarily on ritual practices.

There is no hard and fast line between folk and classical Tantra, although their motivations for meditation and their interpretations of the Tantric texts (literal vs. symbolic) do tend to separate them. There are occasionally class distinctions visible, in the bemoaning by classical tantrikas about folk practitioners who cannot interpret texts properly, and the folk tantrikas who look down on classical tantrikas for their focus on texts and lack of direct experience.

This distinction is similar to David Lorenzen's (2002) types of Tantra as narrow and broad. According to his narrow type, Tantrism, or "Tantric religion," is elite and directly based on the Sanskrit texts called tantras, *saṁhitās,* and *āgamas*. Lorenzen's broad type includes such elite knowledge and extends this to include "magical beliefs and practices." I have found that Bengali folk tantrikas rarely have knowledge of Sanskrit, let alone read Sanskrit texts, and have more focus on local and tribal deities than Pan-Indian ones. Many are non-Brahmin and do part-time work for tribal communities (indeed, I found in interviews that there is often a "continuing education" in which folk tantrikas share their knowledge with tribal practitioners and healers, like *ojhās, guṇins,* and *deẏāsīs*). I found more classical tantrikas in urban settings and in universities, while there were more folk tantrikas in the villages.

Many tantrikas are aware of the difficulties of surviving in an India that is becoming westernized, where people were more skeptical of Tantric practices and unwilling to buy astrological gems to change their luck or support them in other ways. Those who married also commented on the irony that their own children were not interested in Tantric religion, but Westerners were. We see similar anxieties over legitimacy and authenticity among Tantric specialists in Bali.

Bali

Various theories describe how Hinduism first came to Indonesia. One popular theory is that it came around the first century, generally through traders, sailors, scholars, and priests. From the sixth century onward, Buddhist ideas were mixed into Hinduism. There were many Hindu-Buddhist kingdoms in Java and Bali, for the developing religion merged Hindu and Buddhist Tantric ritual practices with preexisting Javanese culture. This religion influenced Indonesian kings and warriors, and there were both Hindu and Buddhist kingdoms on the major Indonesian islands (Sumatra, Java, Bali, and Kalimantan). The most influential Hindu kingdom was the Majapahit empire, which reached its peak in the fourteenth century. However, Hinduism lost its status as the dominant religion during the fifteenth and sixteenth centuries, when the Majapahit empire was conquered by the Muslim sultanates. As the Majapahit kingdom disintegrated, many of its priests, artists, musicians, and leaders fled to the island of Bali, which remains the only Hindu island in Indonesia (though there are Hindu communities in Lombok, Sulawesi, and Kalimantan).

Foreign merchants were attracted by the spice trade (primarily pepper, nutmeg, and cloves), especially Portuguese and later Dutch traders. Dutch seamen came to the islands of Bali and Lombok in the sixteenth century, and in the following centuries the Dutch East Indies Company came to dominate much of Indonesia. When Indonesia gained official independence from the Dutch in 1949, the island of Bali was integrated into the Republic of Indonesia.[9]

However, religious problems became apparent. Balinese religion was classified by the independent Indonesian government as "tribal" or uncivilized, and thus not an agama or legitimate religion. To be accepted by the government, Balinese Hinduism had to change in order to fit the rules of the *pancasila*, as well as the requirements of the

Ministry of Religion. Hinduism in Indonesia went through extraordinary effort to fit the criteria delineated by the government and to ultimately become an accepted religion.

Indonesia currently has the world's largest Muslim population, and while Indonesian Islam is tolerant, it influences the governmental requirements for a legitimate religion. An accepted religion needs a monotheistic god, a messenger or prophet who brings a revealed sacred text, and a morality that is universally applicable, not limited to a specific ethnic group. So, a group of high priests and Balinese intellectuals got together to adapt Hinduism to these requirements, for an accepted religion is immune to pressure from proselytizing by larger religions, such as Islam and Christianity (see Bakker 1993). In 1959 they formed a council, today called the Parisada Hindu Dharma Indonesia, to reformulate Hinduism to fit the criteria set down by the government. One god was called the Almighty God (the others were demoted to angels); the Vedas, Ramayana, and the Bhagavad Gita became the equivalent of the Qur'an or the Bible; and the Vedic sages or rishis became the prophets. Philosophy and theology were developed, with a strong emphasis on ethics and national identity, and the Parisada promised to emphasize texts and theology and to simplify ritual. Hinduism was accepted by the Indonesian government as an official religion in 1958. Perhaps the biggest change was the adoption of a monotheistic deity, named Sanghyang Widhi Wasa, a god unknown to Indian Hinduism but often equated with Shiva (see McDaniel 2013)

In modern Indonesian Hinduism, there are now three Hindu prayers a day (the *trisandhya*), as well as devotion to the four teachers or gurus: God, parents, schoolteachers, and the government. There are also five pillars of belief (in brahman, atman, karma, moksha, and reincarnation) and five pillars of practice or *yadnya* (offerings to God, to ancestors, to people and society in the life-cycle rites, offerings to propitiate destructive spirits, and offerings to sages in the rites of ordination). Balinese Hinduism is now a compulsory topic taught in Balinese schools, with a heavy emphasis on ethics and obedience to authority, and children must attend classes for six years. True religion is understood to be revealed by God, the sign of a "religion of heaven," as opposed to ethnic "religions of the earth," which are manmade. Thus, Balinese Hinduism is legal in Indonesia, and gaining that legality involved much theological innovation.[10]

Balinese Hinduism has two levels: the traditional and the governmental. The governmental form emphasized ethics, ritual, and prayer to a monotheistic god, and the traditional form maintained the ancestors, local spirits, and mystical traditions. *Pedandas*, the Brahmin high priests, must walk a fine line between these two levels. The schools teach the government-approved form of Balinese Hinduism, while the people practice the traditional religion in their homes and seek the ritual expertise of the *pedanda*s.

*Pedanda*s are *sannyāsīs*, and in Bali the understanding of *sannyāsa* is quite different than in India. This greatly influences attitudes about becoming a Tantric practitioner. Balinese Hinduism developed before the rise of bhakti devotion in India, and the idea of love of the deity as primary in worship was not present. Worship in Bali emphasized proper social behavior and ethics. *Sannyāsa* in Bali means dedicating oneself to the community, staying with the family, counseling people about problems, and practicing with mantra and mudra as a way of ensuring blessings. According to one *pedanda, sannyāsa* means embodiment or becoming, showing the presence of the god.

In the case of Balinese high priests or *pedandas*, Tantric meditation (using mantra, mudra, mandala, *nyāsa*, and *bhūtaśuddhi*) is part of daily ritual (see figures 10.1 and 10.2). Each morning, they identify with the god Shiva, mystically merging with him in the *suryasevana* ritual to create the holy water needed for all rituals in Bali. This ritual includes visualization of lotuses within the body and the visualization of the *nava-saktis* (eight goddesses at the points of the compass and one at the center). As the energy of the god Shiva flows through him, the priest fully embodies the god.[11]

High priests using Tantric meditation create the most valuable type of holy water, to be used by the community for important rituals. *Pedanda* clans and families not only support the decision to become a practitioner, but they also often pressure retired couples to enter the priesthood (both husband and wife become *pedandas* together). Three gurus are required in the training and initiation process, as well as public testing, witnesses, and registration. The process is generally a harmonious one, supported by family and community.

While Balinese priests use palm-leaf manuscripts called *lontars* rather than Sanskrit texts called tantras, we may call them Tantric practitioners because of their rituals. These make use of Sanskrit and Kavi seed (*bīja*) mantras, as well as mudras and mandalas, which

Figure 10.1. Balinese priest, 2018. *Source*: Photograph by Jim Denosky.

Figure 10.2. Balinese priest chanting, 2018. *Source*: Photograph by Jim Denosky.

are found in Tantric practices worldwide. Purification rituals like *bhūtaśuddhi* and *nyāsa*, the placement of deities within the body, are also important. Balinese ritual links macrocosm and microcosm and involves visualization of deities and their emanations. The high priest undergoes a secret initiation by a guru and becomes the mediator between natural, supernatural, and divine worlds, following an esoteric Hinduism based on the god Shiva. The priest ritually unites with the god to bring divine power down to earth.

There are other forms of priest in Bali, and they come from different castes. There are *pemangkus, rishi bhujanggas*, and *empus* or *jabas*, all of which are non-Brahmin ritual specialists. However, the Brahmin *pedanda* has the highest status and has learned the esoteric mantras and mudras and visualizations to create the highest and most effective type of holy water.

In Bali, not only are Brahmin families amenable to their older members becoming priests, but they often encourage it. As an example, a female *pedanda* interviewed mentioned that she did not want this vocation at all—it involved too much work, and people come over in the middle of the night for blessings or counsel and they cannot be refused. But her son's business was going badly, and he thought it would improve if his parents became *pedandas*. So, the couple became *pedandas*—and his business actually did improve.[12] Being part of a priestly family adds prestige, for priests are understood to be highly ethical and honest. This is a good family for a businessman.

Only one Balinese priest out of the fifteen interviewed did not specifically mention family pressure as a reason for taking this job (the remaining one mentioned an inner call to help others). There is an obligation to family, both living and dead, and the person must fulfill "*pedanda* DNA," as one priest said in English. There is a desire for an unbroken lineage in priestly families; many had great-great-grandfathers who were priests, and the family felt that their sons and descendants should fulfill their ideals. Male *pedandas* undergo initiation and training with their wives and often practice together. In 2018, there were about 450 *pedanda* couples in Bali, and 600 couples total in Indonesia.[13]

Becoming a *pedanda* requires three gurus. The guru *nabe* is the *dīkṣā* guru, who begins the process. He gives the initiation mantra, and a new name. He is usually in the same *griya* or clan group as the novice priest. The student is humble, and will not look the guru in the eyes, but keeps their face bowed. The guru *waktra* is the guru who gives practical teaching (similar to the role of the Vaishnava *śikṣā* guru in Bengali Vaishnavism). He gives puja (worship) details, how to perform ceremonies at their various levels of complexity, how to find good dates for events (Bali uses three calendars), and how to do *suryasevana* meditation on the god Surya / Shiva and create holy water. He can be from a different clan (*griya*). The guru *sakshi* is the witness guru, who makes sure that the novice is worthy and has understood the teachings.

Usually the husband and wife study together to become *pedanda* couples, and at the end they take the public exam together. She can take over his duties when the husband dies, but primarily it is the husband who must know how to organize all rituals, while his wife must know how to make *banten* or ritual offerings. Both must know the required literature and be able to interpret it for others. The major job of a *pedanda* is as a counselor, to harmonize the heavens and the earth and to bring peace to families and communities. At the final public exam, there is a big crowd—usually the whole town plus invited religious and political figures. A public feast is sponsored by the new *pedanda* couple. None of the *pedandas* interviewed could think of a situation where one member of the couple passed the test and the other did not.

Priests must follow ethical rules: they must not travel alone, or handle money; they must wear white clothes and a topknot; and they must not go to plays or films or restaurants. They must eat only pure *sāttvik* foods, like duck or egg. Pork, chicken, or flesh of wild animals are not allowed. They must learn some Sanskrit (called by some informants "archipelago Sanskrit") to read the older *lontar* texts—today often from more practical paper xeroxes—as well as Old Javanese, theology, astrology, meditation, philosophy, mantras, mudras, and mandalas. They must learn how to bless and purify the soul, both before birth and after death. Recently, some *pedanda* committees have been interested in standardizing ritual knowledge and have developed some optional classes for future *pedandas*. These classes have about ten to twenty students and are six months long. Students can repeat the class if they fail. The classes are intended to homogenize ritual practices on the island.

Training is both outer and inner. We have the outer layer of training in different levels of ritual (*uttama, madhya, nishta*), and styles of public interaction with the community. This training can be learned from books. We also have the inner training, which includes *bīja* mantras, mudras, mandalas, *bhūtaśuddhi* or purification of the elements in the body, and *nyāsa* or placing deities in the body, as well as visualization of the god Shiva and his emanation forms, including Ardhanarishvara. These techniques can only be learned through direct interaction with a guru. The background philosophy is Shaiva, with an official state emphasis on Shiva as the single, monotheistic god Sanghyang Widhi Wasa, but Shiva is a creative god and has many forms. These forms are used in Tantric meditation and visualization.

Most *pedanda*s interviewed had direct experiences of the god, especially during the daily *suryasevana* ritual, in which they mystically unite with Shiva. As Hinduism in Bali is pre-bhakti, there is no Balinese version of the complex devotional theology of *bhava* or *rasa* as we see it in Indian Vaishnavism. However, some *pedanda*s spoke of a relationship between Shiva and the soul that was like that of a father and son, characterized by love and respect. Shiva enters the heart and gives blessings; he is the guru, and in meditation the priest is born from him and returns to him. He merges spiritually with Shiva and gains realization when he fully identifies with the god.[14]

Such experiences were not required, and some *pedandas* stated quite clearly that they had never had supernatural experiences. They saw the role of *pedanda* as primarily social and ethical. But these sorts of experiences show a special depth of awareness. Some Western writers have compared the *suryasevana* ceremony to the communion ritual in Catholicism for its centrality to the religion (see Hooykaas 1966).

As Ida Pedanda Gde Putra Tlabah phrases it: "Here we practice Shiva/Buddha Tantra. The vision of Shiva is like a shared cosmic smile. We have the search for *moksha* as a part of daily life; there is no terminology for renunciation. We have temporary separation during prayer, and we seek to become a part of the huge cosmic soul which is Shiva. The only real separation that we have is at death, when the soul flows out of the body like a river."[15] We may note that the early form of Tantra that came to Bali from Java-combined Shaiva and Buddhist rituals, which later separated out.

Classical Tantric practice can be found in the daily Hindu ritual of *suryasevana*. As Ida Pedanda Putra Yoga describes it:

> In Saiva meditation, the body is equated with the universe, and we recognize that gods live in parts of the body. Using visualization and *bija* mantras, gods come to dwell in every part of the body. We learn these mantras through oral

> tradition, they are given at *diksa* and then there are later teachings by the guru. They are secret, and not written down—mantras are only oral. The bodies of the gods are made of mantras. One has *bhakti* towards the guru, through serving him [*seva*] and showing compassion [*karuna*].[16]

Ida Pedanda Gde Tarukan emphasizes the feelings that accompany this practice: "Shiva is felt inwardly, when the priest visualizes a figure to represent the god, through yogic meditation. This helps him to focus on Shiva or Sanghyang Widhi. Shiva becomes his guru, and the priest is born from him and returns to him; the priest must manifest Shiva. There is the feeling of Shiva's presence; he is found through shakti, siddhi, mantra, and mudra."[17]

Ida Pedanda Made Paketan comes from a line of royal pedandas who performed rituals and gave advice to kings, acting as *puri yajamana*. Each generation needs at least one priest, and his is the sixth generation from the Klungkum area. Earlier in life he was a contractor in Jakarta, and he became a pedanda at the age of seventy, partly due to family obligation (his brothers were dead, and a priest was needed). He noted that priests need to know the Balinese language, as well as ethics, Sanskrit and Kawi languages, meditation, mudras, astrology, and politics (especially the *Nitisastra* text). Different lineages (*griyas*) have different policies, and in his, female priests (*kanya pedandas*) can create holy water.

On his experiences, he says, "One feels Shiva inwardly—in deep puja, there is a sense of presence; it is empty, *niskala, sunya,* but peaceful and full of light." Shiva is not seen as a person, but rather sensed as a presence. Sometimes one can sense other deities, but they are all really Shiva. Some priests can see ancestors, and they can guide souls after death, using rituals to free the soul from the body. They can die consciously through jnana moksha, and if they died the high death (*adimoksa*) there is only ash left at death. "For those who have attained the state of *paramamoksha,* there is nothing left at death," said Ida Pedanda Made Paketan. "The best part of the *pedanda* role is doing the morning puja, when one feels clean and pure; the worst part of it is when the people forget to worship their ancestors, and they ruin their own lives."[18]

We also see folk Tantra practiced by some *pedanda*s. In Balinese Hinduism, bodies can hold many deities, localized through rituals of *nyāsa* and *bhūtaśuddhi*. There are also bodily deities who are there spontaneously: the *kanda empat* spirits. These are bodily guardians who can evolve into gods if they are treated correctly and worshipped. They originate at birth, emerging from the placenta, the amniotic fluid, and the layers of fat and blood that brought life to the newborn baby. There are ritual ways to deal with these at birth and through life, and the guardians or "elder siblings" develop through different names and forms as the person grows. Each form has its own special powers. If the *kanda empat* spirits are worshipped, they bring blessings, but they may also grow dark through neglect and bring evil and misfortune. There are some *pedandas* who focus on the *kanda empat* spirits as a specialization; as one *pedanda* stated, "They grow along with the child, starting out bodily, developing souls, eventually becoming gods and accompanying the soul to the heavens. They protect the person through life, from illness and evil spirits, if they are invited during ceremonies and honored. They are very important."[19]

Another area of folk Tantra among *pedandas* involves the guidance of souls, both before birth and after death. Tantric practices can purify the *atma,* and some *pedandas* give afterlife *diksha,* with an empowered mantra and a set of directions for the soul when it is no longer embodied. Other *pedanda*s are understood to contact both distant ancestors and the souls of the recently dead, and this helps in learning what sort of soul will be born to pregnant women (souls are understood to generally reincarnate within the family).

We also see a form of folk or popular Tantra in the lives and practices of balians, the non-Brahmin Hindu shamans of Bali. Here I will include two stories. Jero Sushum is a balian *tenung* who heals people from black magic spells and who tells people what chants, offerings, and sarong colors they should use to help spirits in the afterlife. Her life as a balian began when she spontaneously fell into a trance at a Shiva temple and a god spoke through her. She learned Tantric mantras and mudras in trance, which she said helped her to defend herself against black magicians. She later took *ekajati diksha,* where a balian guru wrote mantras on her tongue, forehead, shoulders, and every joint. The guru used honey as ink, and he applied it with a special leaf. Rituals came to her spontaneously, using Balinese mantras, mudras, and *vajra* symbols. She also learned from a vision how to perform a version of *suryasevana.*

She works with the dead; she said death is like a courtroom, and she can get you a better lawyer due to her abilities at mantra and *banten* offerings.[20] She emphasized that becoming a balian was not her choice—she had been chosen by the god Ida Sanghyang Sinun. Her husband is also a balian, but he acts as her assistant, instructed by his wife. During the interview, she spoke, and he served snacks to the long line of people waiting for her. She has eleven brothers and sisters, and eight of them are balians or *pemangkus* (lower, non-Brahmin ritual specialists); for spiritual power runs in bloodlines.

The balian Mangku Teja Kandel said that Tantra for balians involves both light and dark clasped together, like hands. Light protects and saves, whereas dark creates danger for others; however, many of the forms that look terrifying are actually protective and defensive. He eventually took *mewinten diksha* to become a *pemangku* priest, but his early self-determined initiation made him into a balian. He had read about Tantric *sādhana* in religious texts, and he wanted to become a tantrika. He went to the local death temple (*pura dalem*) to perform rituals to the death deities, Durga and Prajapati. He offered them a black chicken and its blood at midnight, chanting the Durgastava, and wore a Durga *poleng* (black-and-white-checked sarong). Durga appeared to him in frightening form and gave him mantras and mudras to practice. These involved his ancestors, so he had to gain their permission to practice the rituals, and they agreed to communicate with him at special shrines. This gave him skills at healing, purification, foreseeing the names of babies and their future spouses, and fortune-telling.

But he said that mostly people come to him for success in business, to become beautiful, and for love magic. He noted that balians come from an ancient Tantric lineage, structured by the Rishi Markandeya and King Airlangga. This lineage is changing now with Indian influence, adopting new practices like the use of skulls and bones, and adding more focus on magic.[21] His family accepted the practice, as he had many balian relatives. He hopes that his son will become a balian after him, as it is a good business, and it helps the community.

Discussion

Comparing the ethnographic data gathered in West Bengal in the 1990s and then in Bali in the late 2010s, one is struck by the different styles of Tantric life in these two areas, as well as the motivations for becoming a tantrika. In West Bengal, the traditional emphasis on ritual purity and the legacy of colonial repulsion had made Tantra an underground practice, hidden from the community and only told to a trusted few. It was also a personal set of rituals learned from dreams, a guru, or books, and performed alone. Few tantrikas had Tantric practice as their public profession.

On the other hand, in Bali the *pedanda*s are community leaders, bringing the best holy water to purify and heal people, and giving counseling and advice to the many people who request it. Even balians, who practice folk Tantra, are proud of their lineage and practice. Tantra is something one can discuss with confidence, for the religion has been made legitimate, and its practices help and support others.

The ethnographic data presented in this chapter suggests that the different practices and lifestyles of tantrikas in Bengal and Bali arise primarily from the different understandings of renunciation, but also from different levels of institutionalization and recognition from central authorities, social expectations from the lay society, and a different emphasis on the relevance of hereditary priesthood and bloodline transmission. In the Bengali case, the society expects that Tantric *sannyāsa* involves renouncing the world and living in poverty, looking toward a transcendent goal of union with Shiva and Shakti. The Bengali Tantric practitioner is expected to be separated from the community; indeed, it is part of the long war between dharma and moksha, worldly success and spiritual liberation, as the major goal of life. The practitioner is supposed to seek a transcendent freedom, and society is left behind. Society does not react to this in a positive way—thus, the necessity of having the practices secret or underground. This also makes interviewing tantrikas more difficult for scholars; networks of informants need to be created to even find practitioners. I found that visiting burning grounds, temples, *śākta pīṭhas* (sites sacred to goddess worship), and puja supply stores was the most effective way to find practitioners (as well as speaking with local academics who had an interest in Tantric practice). But I recognize that the situation might have changed, and at present, a few decades after my main ethnographic fieldwork, scholars as well as tantrikas likely face new challenges.

In the Balinese case, the problem was not finding practicing tantrikas, but rather going through the etiquette required for talking to them.[22] *Pedandas* led a family life, living in compounds with the extended family. They did not maintain social secrecy, but there were many ritual requirements and complex offerings that were needed that were a part of their Tantric training, and not revealed to uninitiated people. Many only spoke the obscure language of High Balinese. They also tended to be very busy, both as ritual specialists and as family counselors, and some had lines of people waiting to speak with them. I found them quite willing to talk about their lives and experiences, though they would not speak of Tantric ritual details, which required initiation. *Sannyāsa* did not require isolation or secrecy; it only required giving up worldly pleasures like movies, restaurants, and travel alone. The *pedanda* performing Tantric rituals can bestow Shiva's worldly blessings on those who visit and remain within the community. However, the *pedandas* cannot really enjoy the worldly blessings, for they should be dedicated to the god. In that way, they are much like Weber's (1968) "inner-worldly ascetic."

The interpretations of renunciation are particularly interesting as they are contrasted between these groups. The issue of *sannyāsa* shows a major difference in the understandings of Hinduism in India and in Indonesia. In India, it refers to a stage in a person's life in which the *sannyāsī* renounces material possessions and dedicates their life to achieving *mokṣa,* which is liberation from the cycle of death and rebirth. In English, the term *sannyāsa* translates to "abandonment," "to put down everything," or "renunciation of the world." This is the final of the four life stages (*āśrama*) in Hindu philosophy: a permanent seclusion from ordinary social life. The traditional *sannyāsī* lives a celibate life of meditation and is considered to be both socially and legally dead. A ritual death is part of the process of becoming a *sannyāsī,* and they leave their family behind to live a homeless life. They are no longer considered to have a caste, or a family. In the shared social imagination as well as in the scriptures, a *sannyāsī* must live an austere and ascetic life, relinquish all property, abstain from sensual enjoyment, and wander alone (except during the rainy season). Patrick Olivelle notes that *sannyāsa,* along with the *āśrama* system, gained mainstream scholarly acceptance around the second century BCE (see Olivelle 1993). The Upanishads mention King Janaka and Yajnavalkya, who renounced worldly life and retired to forests for liberation. The texts describe that when a person entered *sannyāsa,* they had to undertake an oath by performing one last fire sacrifice to give up all attachments and social identities, such as his name or family name, and they could not maintain any active relationship with their family or friends. Because they had renounced the world by performing their own funeral and abandoning all claims to social or family standing, the *sannyāsī* is not cremated but rather buried in a seated posture of meditation.[23]

This is quite different from the understanding and the connotations of *sannyāsa* in the Balinese Hinduism of Indonesia. In this case, the *sannyāsī* lives in the family home with his wife and children. Indeed, the couple is composed of two renunciants living together, acting as high priest and priestess for the community. There is no statement of legal or social death, no emphasis upon solitude or wandering. Not only do relationships continue with family and friends, but the renunciant becomes the center of the community, a counselor and helper to the neighborhood.

We might compare the situation to Catholicism. Seeing a priest married to a nun, living together as a family and still performing communion for the congregation, would be a very surprising thing in Catholic-majority countries. This might give insight into the Indian view of married *sannyāsī*s.

In both West Bengal and Bali, Tantra appears in many aspects of life and practice. In academia, there is scholarly debate about the proper categorizations and definitions of Tantra. Recognizing that there is a continuum, we can say that in Bali there are two major types of Tantra, similar to the types in West Bengal. One is classical Tantra, which requires textual training and knowledge of the Sanskrit and Kavi languages, and which focuses on the god Shiva. This is what we see in the case of the *pedanda*s or high priests. The other is popular or folk Tantra, which does not require shastric knowledge or languages, and which focuses on nature deities, bodily spirits (the *kanda empat*), and ancestors. This is primarily done by balians—local shamanic healers who have not gone through a priestly education—though some high priests will include folk Tantra in their repertoire. In general, Tantra requires esoteric knowledge, learned only after initiation, of mantra, mudra, mandala, visualization, and entrance into supernatural and divine worlds. While these worlds may be metaphysically continuous, as all are created by Shiva, they are experientially distinct.

Though both forms of Tantra are practiced today, the classical form studied by *pedanda*s is more authoritative for the Balinese and is institutionally recognized. Folk Tantra, especially as practiced by balians, is generally understood as less traditional and historically accurate, and it focuses on lower levels of gods and ancestors. Some balians have adopted New Age ideas and magical practices, which *pedanda*s have resisted. This is why Western tourists tend to visit balians as healers and trance mediums and know little about *pedanda*s. In the recent American bestselling novel *Eat, Pray, Love*, the healer the main character visited was a balian (see Gilbert 2006).

In these cultures, both forms of specialist are important—they just tend to have different audiences. The difficulties in study are also similar, though in a sense they are reversed. In West Bengal, most Indologists study Tantric texts, often with Indian Sanskritists, but they tend to avoid the folk tantrikas at the margins of society. In Bali, anthropologists of religion study balians in rural surroundings, but they rarely study the high priests, who are shielded by ritual complexity and language use. Thus, in the field of Tantric studies, the work on Bengali Tantra has been primarily textual, while the study of Balinese Tantra has been primarily anthropological.

However, there has been some fine research on the topic of Tantric texts in Indonesia, especially by Andrea Acri (see Acri 2015, 2019). We also see valuable research from the field of anthropology and art history, especially by Michele Stephen (2005). Some of the most detailed scholarship on Balinese Tantric language and ritual among pedandas can be found in the works of Christiaan Hooykaas (1966, 1973, 1974). There are no other studies, to my knowledge, that include the lives and practices of the Tantric high priests of Bali.

In terms of social acceptance of tantrikas, the central issue for both West Bengal and Bali is renunciation (*sannyāsa*) and how it is to be understood. Does *sannyāsa* mean leaving society, or does it mean being detached while in the midst of society? Granted that there is no single and unequivocal interpretation of this complex concept in the stratified societies of both West Bengal and Bali, the answer to this question will likely tell us much about the status and social acceptance of Tantric practitioners, and their different understandings of renunciation can be explored through comparative ethnography.

In this chapter, I have attempted to summarize both the role of traditional Tantric knowledge and lived experience in the tantrikas of West Bengal, and the *pedandas* and balians of Bali. The goal, as noted in the introduction to this volume, is to connect distant shores of Tantric scholarship and lived Tantric practices using ethnography as the most suitable material to build this bridge.

Notes

1. I would like to thank the American Academy of Religion for their International Collaborative Grant, which I received with my colleague Dr. Andrea Acri. It provided the funding for this research. I would also like to thank my Balinese colleague Dr. Ida Bagus Putu Suamba for his help in facilitating the interviews with *pedandas*. His collaboration was very important to this research.

2. For more details on this life pattern, see McDaniel (1989).

3. Interview, Jayashri Ma, Birbhum, May 1984.

4. Interview, Lakshmi Ma, Calcutta/Kolkata, March 1994.

5. Interview, Tapan Goswami, Bolpur, April 1994.

6. He noted that sometimes he would do puja to the goddess for both opposing candidates for office.

7. For more on the distinction between classical and folk Tantra, see McDaniel (2004).

8. For more on the "sanitization" discussion, see Urban (2009).

9. For more details on history, see Howe (2001).

10. For more details on how this occurred, see McDaniel (2013).

11. For further details on the ritual, see Hooykaas (1966) and Stephen (2015).

12. Interview, Ida Pedanda Istri Sthiti Yogi, Denpasar, August 2018.

13. Interview, Dr. Ida Bagus Putu Adriana, Denpasar, August 2018. He is currently a teacher of pedandas for the Parisada Hindu Dharma Indonesia (HPDI), and formerly he taught religion (Agama) at Hindu University in Denpasar.

14. Interview, Ida Pedanda Putra Yoga, Tabanan, August 2019.

15. Interview, Ida Pedanda Gde Putra Tlabah, Denpasar, July 2012.

16. Interview, Ida Pedanda Putra Yoga, Tabanan, July 2012.

17. Interview, Ida Pedanda Gde Tarukan, Tabanan, August 2018.

18. Interview, Ida Pedanda Made Paketan, July 2019.

19. Interview, Ida Pedanda Putra Yoga, Tabanan, August 2018.

20. Interview, Jero Sushum (Jero Mangku), Bangli, August 2018.

21. Interview, Mangku Teja Kandel, Bangli, August 2018.

22. This involves special types of gifts and formal use of language. For this I thank my colleague Dr. Ida Bagus Putu Suamba.

23. For further data on early Upanishadic ideas about renunciation, see Olivelle (1992).

Bibliography

Acri, Andrea. 2015. "Revisiting the Cult of 'Siva-Buddha' in Java and Bali." In *Buddhist Dynamics in Premodern and Early Modern Southeast Asia*, edited by D. Christian Lammerts, 261–82. Singapore: ISEAS.

———. 2019. "Becoming a Bhairava in Nineteenth Century Java." *Indonesia and the Malay World* 47, no. 139: 285–307.

Bakker, Frederick Lambertus. 1993. *The Struggle of the Hindu Balinese Intellectuals: Developments in Modern Hindu Thinking in Independent Indonesia.* Amsterdam: Vrije University Press.

Bapat, Jayant Bhatchandra, and Ian Mabbett, eds. 2017. *Conceiving the Goddess: Transformation and Appropriation in Indian Religions.* Melbourne: Monash University Press.

Dasgupta, Shashibhushan. 1985 [1393 BS]. *Bhārater Śakti-sādhanā o Śākta sāhitya.* Calcutta: Sahitya Samsad.

DeNapoli, Antoinette. 2019. "A Female Shankaracharya? The Alternative Authority of a Feminist Hindu Guru in North India." *Religion and Gender* 9, no. 1: 27–49.

Flood, Gavin. 2006. *The Tantric Body: The Secret Tradition of Hindu Religion.* London: I.B. Taurus.

Gilbert, Elizabeth. 2006. *Eat, Pray, Love: One Woman's Search for Everything across Italy, India and Indonesia.* New York: Penguin Books.

Gray, David B. 2016. "Tantra and the Tantric Traditions of Hinduism and Buddhism." *Oxford Research Encyclopedias, Religion.* Oxford: Oxford University Press. https://doi.org/10.1093/acrefore/9780199340378.013.59.

Harper, Katherine Anne, and Robert L. Brown. 2002. *The Roots of Tantra.* Albany: SUNY Press.

Hooykaas, Christiaan. 1966. *Surya-sevana: The Way to God of a Balinese Siva Priest.* Amsterdam: Noord-Hollandsche Uitg. Mij.

———. 1973. *Religion in Bali.* Leiden: Brill.

———. 1974. *Cosmogony and Creation in Balinese Tradition.* The Hague: Martinus Nijhoff.

Howe, Leo. 2001. *Hinduism and Hierarchy in Bali.* Santa Fe: School of American Research Press.

Korom, Frank.J. 1999. "'To Be Happy': Ritual, Play, and Leisure in the Bengali Dharmarāj *pūjā*." *International Journal of Hindu Studies* 3, no. 2: 113–64. https://doi.org/10.1007/s11407-999-0001-4.

Lorea, Carola E. 2016. *Folklore, Religion and the Songs of a Bengali Madman: A Journey Between Performance and the Politics of Cultural Representation.* Leiden: Brill.

———. 2020. "Religion, Caste and Displacement: The Matua Community." *Oxford Research Encyclopedia of Asian History.* Oxford: Oxford University Press. https://doi.org/10.1093/acrefore/9780190277727.013.428.

Lorenzen, David N. 2002. "Early Evidence for Tantric Religion." In *The Roots of Tantra*, edited by Katherine Anne Harper and Robert L. Brown, 25–36. Albany: SUNY Press.

McDaniel, June. 1989. *The Madness of the Saints: Ecstatic Religion in Bengal.* Chicago: University of Chicago Press.

———. 2004. *Offering Flowers, Feeding Skulls: Popular Goddess Worship in West Bengal.* New York: Oxford University Press.

———. 2013. "A Modern Hindu Monotheism: Indonesian Hindus as 'People of the Book.'" *The Journal of Hindu Studies* 6, no. 3: 333–62.

Olivelle, Patrick, 1993. *The Ashrama System: The History and Hermeneutics of a Religious Institution.* New York: Oxford University Press.

———. 1992. *The Samnyasa Upanisads: Hindu Scriptures on Asceticism and Renunciation.* New York: Oxford University Press.

Openshaw, Jeanne. 2007. "Renunciation Feminised? Joint Renunciation of Female–Male Pairs in Bengali Vaishnavism." *Religion* 37, no. 4: 319–32. https://doi.org/10.1016/j.religion.2007.06.007.

Rao, Mani. 2018. *Living Mantra: Mantra, Deity and Visionary Experience Today.* London: Palgrave Macmillan.

Rudert, Angela. 2017. *Shakti's New Voice.* Lanham: Lexington Books.

Sarbadhikary, Sukanya. 2015. *The Place of Devotion: Siting and Experiencing Divinity in Bengal-Vaishnavism.* Berkeley: University of California Press.

Sardella, Ferdinando. 2013. *Modern Hindu Personalism: The History, Life, and Thought of Bhaktisiddhanta Sarasvati.* New York: Oxford University Press.

Stephen, Michele. 2005. *Desire, Divine & Demonic: Balinese Mysticism in The Paintings of I Ketut Budiana and I Gusti Nyoman Miriana.* Honolulu: University of Hawai'i Press.

———. 2015. "Sūrya-Sevana: A Balinese Tantric Practice." *Archipel* 89: 95–124.

Urban, Hugh. 2009 *The Power of Tantra: Religion, Sexuality and the Politics of South Asian Studies.* London: I.B. Tauris/ Palgrave MacMillan.

———. 2008. "Matrix of Power: Blood, Kingship and Sacrifice in the Worship of Mother Goddess Kāmākhyā." *South Asia* 31, no. 3: 500–39.

———. 2011 "The Womb of Tantra: Goddesses, Tribals and Kings in Assam." *Journal of Hindu Studies* 4, no. 3: 231–47. https://doi.org/10.1093/jhshir034.

Weber, Max. 1968. "Asceticism, Mysticism and Salvation." In *Economy and Society; An Outline of Interpretive Sociology*, 541–56. New York: Bedminster Press.

White, David Gordon. 2009. *Sinister Yogis.* Chicago: University of Chicago Press.

———. 2000. *Tantra in Practice.* Princeton: Princeton University Press.

Afterword

Geoffrey Samuel

It is a pleasure to write an afterword to this stimulating collection of ethnographic studies from India, Bangladesh, and Indonesia, all of which fall in one way or another within the ambit of that ever-enticing if often opaque term *Tantra*. These studies are impressive both for their high level of scholarly accomplishment and for the theoretical sophistication of many of the contributions. Much work on Tantric topics still shows limited awareness of contemporary work in postcolonial studies, gender studies, or other areas of critical scholarship. Most of the authors here, by contrast, are fully aware of the issues of representation and narration that have shaped and continue to shape the existing Western-language literature on Tantric studies, and of the complex relationships of power and inequality within which much Tantric research takes place. The critical perspective offered by contemporary theory is a vital tool for making sense of what has gone on in the field of Tantric studies in the past and an essential guide for current and future work.

The editors of the volume, Carola Lorea and Rohit Singh, have provided an overview of the individual chapters in their excellent introduction. Lorea and Singh rightly point to the volume's contribution in highlighting "the individuals, communities, and institutions that constitute living Tantric traditions as located in particular sociocultural environments . . . the multifarious life of vernacular Tantric practices and livelihoods across South Asia, Southeast Asia, and

Himalayan regions" (Lorea and Singh, this volume, 3–4). As their words suggest, the move to a focus on "living Tantric traditions" uncovers a more varied and complex picture than can be found in many studies of Tantra. The collection however also raises a question: What is gained by considering studies such as those gathered in this volume as a group? Is "Tantric" a meaningful analytic category for understanding these various ethnographic accounts? In this afterword, I discuss some of the ways in which this collection shows how useful it is to look at this material through a "Tantric" frame.

Certainly, "Tantra" is not the only possible category under which the research presented here might be studied. While this is, as far as I know, the first collection specifically dedicated to the ethnography of Tantra as such, there already exists a substantial body of ethnographic work in anthropology and religious studies in which Tantra has had a significant role. Restricting ourselves to English-language work on South Asia, we could note works such as Robert I. Levy and Kedar Rāj Rājopādhyāya's study of the social and ritual life of the Newar city of Bhaktapur (Levy 1992), David Gellner's (1992) analysis of Newar Buddhism, or Frédérique Apffel Marglin's (1985) book on the rituals of the Devadasis of Puri, not to mention William Sax's own earlier books and articles on the people of the Garhwal Himalaya (e.g., Sax 2009), June McDaniel's *Offering Flowers, Feeding Skulls* (2004), or the work on Bāuls and related groups from authors such as Jeanne Openshaw (1998, 2004) or Carola Lorea herself (2016). If one were to include Tibet and the Himalayan plateau (represented by one chapter here), and the substantial body of scholarship in other European languages, particularly French and German, there would be many more works that might be included. But this collection asks us to consider: What specifically might we learn from a group of ethnographic studies whose common feature is defined as "Tantra"?

One starting point might be to engage with the various ways in which the term "Tantra" or its derivatives are used in the chapters collected here, both by the authors and by the people they are talking about. To borrow our editors' intriguing neologism, what kinds of "Tantricking" do we see described here? Lorea and Singh introduce this term (8–10) as a way of moving away from ideas of Tantra or "Tantrism" as a single category, noting that such approaches have been largely been abandoned by "modern, largely Western scholarship" (Lorea and Singh, this volume, 9). In its place they suggest Tantra as "an ever-changing and complex array of things people do: actions, practices, and disciplines (*sādhana*) rather than any static or essentialized category." Thus, "Tantricking" creates a space within which we can ask how these actions, practices, and disciplines might, or might not, fit productively within a single frame.

Not all of our ethnographic subjects see the "Tantric" label as applying to their activities. Pumpha Regmi Mātājī, in Jarrod Hyam's chapter (this volume), comments that "the *jhākris* work through Tantra and Tantric ways, whereas we [*mātās*] work through Devīs like Mahā-Kālī and Śakti. Tantric practices pertain to magic [black magic] and *masāns* [restless ghosts]. *Jhākris* derive their power from these sources. We instead derive our powers from the divine goddesses like Durga, Kālī" (177). In other words, she does not see what she does as "Tantric." I am not sure how far the Bāul Fakirs discussed by Keith Cantú or the Vaiṣṇavas in Kristin Hanssen's study would identify with the "Tantric" label either. As for Bali, as Annette Hornbacher asks in her chapter in this volume, "How can one investigate 'Tantra' in Bali if the term does not even exist?" (Hornbacher, this volume, 91).

I do not hold the view, sometimes found in contemporary religious studies, that our only job as scholars is to provide a description as congruent as possible to that of our informants, to give as perfect a translation as possible of the concepts they themselves use. The two disciplines mainly represented in this collection, anthropology and religious studies, are analytic enterprises; they aim at understanding, not just translation. At the same time, if there is a mismatch between our analytic categories and the categories of our informants, this suggests that something significant is going on that needs our attention. Such issues are particularly complex when, as in several of the studies here, the scholarly analyst may also be a committed participant, and may also be a member of the society being studied. The emic/etic distinction, inspired by Kenneth Pike's work in linguistics (Headlund et al. 1990), gave an earlier generation an initial take on such situations, but it has increasingly come to be seen as problematic. It is particularly so for societies, such as most of those here, where we are dealing not just with casual lay understandings but with sophisticated (and often competing) models developed by scholars within those societies over many centuries. Likewise, as Lorea and Singh note (28, 39), the complexities involved in "insider" and "outsider" roles have become increasingly evident (see also McCutcheon 2005), and any simplistic distinction between the two is unviable.

However, if we are to see ourselves as scholars who are doing more than simple translation and conceptual clarification, we need to keep a distinction between Tantra (Tantric, etc.) as the analytic category, real or potential, around which this collection is built, and *tantra* (or equivalents in local languages) as a term deployed, positively or negatively, by the people we study and with whom we work. Pumpha Regmi Mātājī communicates something significant when she defines her own activity as non-Tantric, just as Pandit Paboch is saying something meaningful (Sax, this volume, 78–79) when he insists that Tantra refers to the material basis used for a healing ritual, rather than to a set of teachings or practices. It is at least part of our job to work out what they mean by these statements, as Hyam and Sax both recognize. This is also implied by Hornbacher's endorsement, which I imagine we would all share in one way or another, of "an anthropological research ethos that tries to take other epistemic traditions and terms seriously rather than projecting the assumptions and categories of the researcher" (Hornbacher, this volume, 91).

Simultaneously respecting both the analytic frame and the views of those within it is not always a straightforward matter. Lorea and Singh take us some way toward it in their introduction, where they give a list of eleven "salient characteristics that emerge from ethnographic engagements with contemporary communities" (17). They present this list as a supplement to Doug Brooks's suggestion some years ago (1990, 52–72) of a "polythetic" approach to the study of ("Hindu") Tantra, though, wisely I think, they do not directly endorse Brooks's solution. Their list simply summarizes regular features of scholarly definitions of Tantra such as that advanced by Brooks, while adding other aspects generally omitted from such definitions but which an ethnographic approach might see as equally or more significant.

A polythetic definition of a phenomenon consists of a variety of features, and any specific instance of the phenomenon does not need to possess them all. In anthropology the concept goes back to a 1975 article by Rodney Needham, who was arguably mainly concerned with the philosophical deconstruction of anthropological categories rather than an endorsement of polythetic approaches (Needham 1975). The polythetic approach was later popularized in religious studies by Jonathan Z. Smith (1982), who illustrated his argument with a sketch of how one might go about replacing a "monothetic definition of early Judaism" by a "polythetic classification of Judaisms" (Smith 1982, 18). Smith, like Needham, seems mostly interested in destabilizing simplistic assumptions. People might have defined themselves as Jewish in a variety of ways in Roman and Hellenistic times, and their intentions in doing so were not necessarily all the same (Smith 1982, 8–18). Brooks's more positive endorsement of a polythetic definition followed on from Smith. One can see why Brooks felt it might provide an escape from the somewhat confused tangle of definitions of and approaches to Tantra, Tantric, and Tantrism that were around at the time. As Brooks notes (1990, 53), a polythetic definition could allow a phenomenon to be referred to as "Tantric" even if it has only some of the features included within the definition; indeed, "a Tantric phenomenon need not call itself 'Tantric' to be Tantric."

Brooks was writing primarily as a textual scholar of Śrīvidyā Tantra, if one who had studied at length in India and was well aware of Tantra's changing presence within Indian society and the different ways in which it may be perceived by contemporary South Asians.[1] His own perspective on Tantra is, for all of the "polythetic" structure, relatively conventional. Tantra, for Brooks, is a spiritual discipline, entered by initiation and, it would seem, primarily textually defined. It involves internal yogic practices (*kuṇḍalinī* yoga is specifically mentioned), employs mantras and yantras, along with antinomian practices, and is regarded as both dangerous and efficacious. Hindu Tantra, he notes, involves both male and female divine polarities, but it "does not differ significantly from Purāṇic Hinduism in how it conceives of the world and God" (Brooks 1990, 66). Notably, only one of his ten points (number four) suggests that Tantra may be practiced for worldly as well as soteriological aims (Brooks 1990, 60). While Brooks' definition is presented in terms of Hindu Tantra, one could find similar Western characterizations of the Buddhist Tantra (Vajrayāna Buddhism) of Tibet or Mongolia, which take it for granted that "Tantra" is primarily a spiritual discipline, and which treat non-soteriological aspects of Tantric practice as secondary and marginal.

Lorea and Singh's listing (eleven characteristics rather than Brooks's ten points) is not presented as a definition, polythetic or otherwise, but more modestly as a "conceptual map" for those "new to Tantric studies." Their list mentions many of the same points as

Brooks, but it also involves shifts in emphasis, extensions into new areas, and a stronger emphasis on pragmatic and this-worldly results. That is certainly reflected in the contents of this collection, where the material, the pragmatic, and the this-worldly play significant roles in practically every chapter. Three specific additions in Lorea and Singh's listing are also notable: healing, confronting death, and divine possession (21–22).

Certainly, pragmatic and this-worldly rituals can be found in the work of textual scholars. David Gordon White, in an article cited in both Sax's and Hornbacher's chapters, demonstrated that many of the practices reported on by William Sax for contemporary Garhwal can already be found in the *Netra Tantra* (White 2012). Similar practices are also included in Indian Buddhist Tantric texts such as the *Hevajra Tantra* (e.g., Farrow and Menon 1992, 25–36), and in very large number in the Tibetan tradition. Possession (cf. Frederick Smith 2006), healing (Hofer 2014; Samuel 2017), and death (e.g., Lati and Hopkins 1979) can also be found.[2] But these issues have been often ignored or marginalized by a textual tradition that has focused on the soteriological aspects of Tantra, on Tantra as a path of spiritual development. It is mainly from the anthropological accounts that we see more of these aspects. While there have been, as I suggested previously, a number of such anthropological works—particularly for the Newars and Tibetans, but also for Indian societies such as Orissa or Kerala—they have tended not to be categorized primarily as "Tantric studies."

In any case, Lorea and Singh's "conceptual map" suggests a particular phrasing of the material—in terms of both a series of techniques, traditions, or practices, and the way in which they are employed in contemporary life—that might be characteristic of an ethnography of Tantra. In the remainder of this chapter, I consider some specific themes that might arise out of this general approach. I hope this will demonstrate what is gained by looking ethnographically, as this book does, across a wide range of material that might in one way or another be considered as "Tantric."

The Tantric Career through the Ethnographic Lens

I begin with the whole question of Tantra as a path for personal spiritual development. This remains present within Lorea and Singh's introduction, but in a less central role than it usually has in studies of Tantra. Our authors vary in how much recognition they give to this dimension. Sax is perhaps the most negative about Tantra as a spiritual path, though his conclusions are phrased in the regional context of "Tantra in the Western Himalayas." This, he says, "looks more like a system of practical rituals for dealing with life's problems than a system for spiritual advancement" (Sax, this volume, 82). Other chapters here, such as Sarbadhikary's or Borkataky-Varma's, are focused primarily on pragmatic issues so they have relatively little to say directly about Tantra as a spiritual path. Sarbadhikary nevertheless notes how the practical understandings of her Bengali conch- and bangle-makers echo formulations from theoretical and philosophical texts that are indeed related to Tantra as a spiritual path. I shall return to this later. Similarly, Borkataky-Varma's study of the online mediation of Bagalāmukhī rituals still allows for something that, she suggests, can validly be called "religious experience" (153–57).

In many of the other chapters, Tantra as a path, technique, or set of practices for something that might be called "spiritual development" undeniably remains important. However, seeing this path through an ethnographic lens complicates the picture found in more conventionally textually based approaches. Here it is useful to distinguish between Tantra as a *spiritual path* and Tantra as a *spiritual career*. By a "spiritual career," I mean that involvement in Tantra operates as a way of making a living, full or part-time. Such spiritual careers exist at a variety of levels from extreme poverty to considerable opulence. Intriguingly, the fact that Tantra is something people might do to earn a living does not appear to be included at all within the ten components of Brooks's polythetic definition—though it figures in several of Singh and Lorea's categories—nor does it occur in most other textually based studies.[3]

Now, whether one is involved in a spiritual *career* is a different question from whether one is on a spiritual *path*. The two are compatible, but the spiritual career does not, in and of itself, guarantee personal commitment to a spiritual path, and it certainly does not guarantee that the Tantric teacher may not exploit their situation for personal gain, financial or other.

The marginality of the spiritual career in Western academic studies perhaps reflects the personal orientation of Western scholars toward Tantric practice. While many scholars may themselves be involved in yogic and Tantric practice, they are unlikely to be earning their income through providing Tantric services (as opposed to building a career around being an academic specialist in Tantric studies). To the extent that Tantra outside its traditional Asian contexts involves finance (which it certainly does, as evidenced by the very substantial amount of real estate around the world that has been converted to Hindu or Buddhist retreat centers in recent years), such issues tend to be presented primarily in spiritual terms. What is significant is that the Tantric ashram or Dharma center provides the basis for pursuing a spiritual path, rather than that it provides a commercial opportunity for a Tantric guru (Asian or Western).

In South and Southeast Asian ethnographic studies such as those in this volume, the material processes that underlie the situation tend to be more evident. This is not only a question of the Tantric guru, lama, or teacher, or the Tantric ritual expert (who these days, as Borkataky-Varma reminds us, may be selling their services to an international clientele via the Internet). We should also bear in mind the substantial population of residents and ancillary staff who may be supported by a Hindu *math* or a Tibetan *dgon pa*, and the considerable number of artisans and technicians who are involved in producing paraphernalia for Tantric rituals.[4]

In fact, at least nine out of the ten studies in this collection (or ten out of eleven studies, if we count the Bengali and Balinese components of McDaniel's chapter separately) describe people for whom Tantra is in some sense at least a career, and in most cases a full-time one.[5] This points to a major feature of all of these studies: Tantric practice is socially embedded; it is part of a wider social context, even when the Tantric practitioner may be regarded as socially inferior or having a polluted identity or occupation. Also, and here McDaniel's comparison between West Bengal and Bali makes the point in a particularly dramatic way, Tantric careers are determined in many ways by that wider social context.

In any case, in these chapters we find a variety of careers as Tantric specialists, generally with a matter-of-fact acceptance of the fee for service. Some of these careers are hereditary, as with the *sāñcā vidyā* specialists of the Garhwal Himalaya, the *pedanda* of Bali, and the Tantric priests of Kerala. Such hereditary Tantric specialists may have to negotiate a changing social context and identity, as with McDaniel's example of the need to reconstruct the *pedanda*'s role so as to be compatible with definitions and constructions of a "proper" religion imposed by the modern Indonesian state (309–10). This may again have an impact on whether someone wishes to be seen as associated with the often heavily loaded term "Tantric."

More generally, making a living may involve a lot of work that is only tangentially related to the spiritual path, such as forming relationships with local patrons or government officials, or acquiring new ritual techniques that help in building a clientele. I was reminded, particularly in Karasinski's chapter and the two Balinese studies, of the complex social and marital alliances and teaching linkages that one can find in Tibetan hereditary lama families. These alliances and linkages may reflect personal predilection and practical opportunities, but they are also very much entangled with the ongoing question of how to construct a successful Tantric career (see, e.g., Samuel 2022). There is nothing particularly new about such situations, but the field can undoubtedly use a clearer focus on how Tantric spiritual paths are intertwined with more practical considerations. Alexis Sanderson moves some way in this direction in his long essay from 2009, and there are some good recent examples from the Tibetan context, such as Hildegard Diemberger's discussion of the relationship between the discovery and "opening" of "hidden lands" (*sbas yul*) by visionary lamas and the need by Tibetan states for specific economic resources (Diemberger 2021). In the case of the "hidden lands," we also have good historical material to demonstrate how a Tantric guru in sixteenth-century Tibet might work himself into a job with a local ruler through appropriate prophecies and revelations (Sardar-Afkhami 2001, 67–89; Samuel 2021, 63–67).

All this may seem obvious when one points it out, but it is notable how little of it one sees in many standard discussions of Tantra, even those focused on the present day. Even that early anthropologist of Tantra, Agehananda Bharati, who tells us quite a lot in passing about the contexts of Tantric practice in his various writings (e.g., Bharati 1962, 1965, 1976), is capable of extended descriptions of Tantric practice that reveal little or nothing about the lives of those who are performing the ritual, let alone who is getting paid for it.

Seeing that someone is being paid for Tantric services, or is begging support from the local community, as in Kristen Hanssen's chapter, does not mean that one should reduce the Tantric career to a purely pragmatic undertaking. Even where it is a hereditary profession rather than one that is personally chosen, it may be and often is a role involving considerable skill and knowledge. For some, this may just be the family business, but others may take it on with pride and develop it with care and creativity. Consider the Meppaṭ guru in Maciej Karasinski's chapter, who has expanded his hereditary repertoire through study with a highly respected but apparently non-hereditary Śrīvidyā guru (287). Being a *pedanda* in Bali, as in Hornbacher's and McDaniel's chapters, is also an occupation that brings status and respect, as does being a hereditary *sāñcā vidyā* specialist in the Garhwal Himalaya.

In other cases, people without any hereditary connection may have chosen to adopt a Tantric career for a variety of personal reasons. This is the case for some of the Bāul Fakirs and Vaiṣṇava sādhus discussed in this book, while others are born into the Bāul context. Keith Cantú's and Kristen Hanssen's chapters are illuminating as to the social context. It is clear from Hanssen's chapter that the Bāuls she studied are a low-status community. While a few Bāul musicians have achieved enough fame for their singing to make a decent income, most Bāuls make a modest and marginal living as mendicants and itinerant performers. However, the sense of a secret, hidden inner knowledge, of the possession of something of great value, runs through the songs and conversation in Cantú's and Hanssen's chapters. One can see some of it, too, in Sarbadhikary's account of a community of conch- and bangle-makers resettled in West Bengal from Bangladesh and having, despite what seems like a quite modest economic situation, evident pride in the skill and the spiritual significance of their work.

In some of these contexts, the spiritual dimension can be a way of coping with a social role regarded by society as of low value. There are parallels with, for example, the way in which low-status birth attendants in South Asia see their role as of spiritual value, even if they are given little respect by their clients (e.g., Rozario 2002, 141–44). As Cantú's and Hanssen's narratives make clear, ethnography with such groups can be difficult on a personal level. Whatever the emotional closeness and goodwill, the distance in material circumstances and social standing between the two sides can be hard to resolve. But it can also be possible through such relationships to gain real understanding of what it means to live as a spiritual practitioner in these difficult and marginal situations.

One should be wary anyway of being too reductionist about spiritual careers. One of the most striking chapters in this collection is

Nike-Ann Schröder's, which is also the only study here from a Tibetan Buddhist context. There has been a fair amount of ethnographic writing on Tibetan Buddhism, but accounts of why people might be motivated to take up a spiritual career are often formulaic, perhaps because a standard set of motivating factors for the spiritual life (the value of being born as a human being, the need for awareness that death can come at any time, and so on) is so well known among Tibetan Buddhists. In her chapter, Schröder breathes life into these doctrinal formulations by showing what they might mean for Pema Wangchuk, a refugee who had been forced, while still in Tibet, to watch his father being publicly humiliated and then burned alive for refusing to cooperate with the invading Chinese forces, and whose mother and other family died from starvation during the Chinese occupation. After leaving Tibet, he eventually became the attendant at a charnel ground in Ladakh, in North India. Schröder discusses what his specific spiritual practices (*chöd*, also carving ritual inscriptions on stone) and his visit to the pilgrimage center at Tso Pema (Rewalsar) might mean to him in relation to his personal life experiences. This is also not easy research, and it needs a kind of sensitivity very different from that of the textual scholar. It gives an insight, however, into the meaning of Tantra for some of its practitioners that is difficult to gain in other ways.

Schröder's chapter reminds us that Tantric practice can be a way in which individuals come to terms with and even transcend very difficult and challenging life situations. In this case, Pema Wangchuk might be said to have a Tantric "career" that emerged from his commitment to practice (he served as a caretaker of a temple in a Tibetan refugee settlement), but Schröder rightly places the emphasis elsewhere in how his practice reflected "a deeply rooted commitment born from intense despair" (262). Much of the work of a good ethnographer is to understand the significant contexts and meanings for the people they study.

The Tantric Client and the Question of Tantric Ethics

I have focused thus far on the Tantric career as a way of making a living. Here I move to the other key role that such a view implies: the clients of the Tantric practitioner. Here too our collection provides a series of revealing examples and shows the advantages of employing an ethnographic approach.

The Tantric clients provide the funds and other resources to support the Tantric career. They vary from the wealthy patrons behind some of the massive property purchases for Hindu gurus or Tibetan lamas, to people whose financial position is much more modest, such as the village families who offer meals to Hanssen's Bāuls. There are many other client relationships that we can find in the ethnographic literature here and elsewhere. They include long-term and even hereditary relationships (as with, say, Newar Tantric priests), or more temporary and occasional encounters, as might be involved in a pilgrimage to a Tantric site or a one-off commissioning of a Tantric ritual. Other examples in the present essays include, for example, Borkataky-Varma's online patrons; Sax's Garhwali villagers who employ Tantric experts for a variety of calendrical, healing, and other rituals; and the clients of the various healers and specialists described in Hyam's chapter, or in Hornbacher's and McDaniel's accounts.

Such relationships tend not to figure in textually based descriptions except in an idealized way (e.g., the "four modes of gathering disciples" described in Tibetan teaching manuals such as Tsong-kha-pa 2004, ii, 225–31). In part, this is perhaps because the texts take for granted a network of social institutions (such as the mendicant ascetic) with which Western scholars are unfamiliar, along with a set of services provided by such institutions that might provide a regular income stream.

One issue that is raised by several studies in this collection is the use of Tantra for aggressive and violent ends. There is a long history of negative stereotyping of Tantra and an understandable desire, which I have certainly shared myself, to present Tantra in a more positive way: as a sophisticated spiritual and cultural accomplishment oriented toward the betterment of humanity and indeed of other living beings. Many Tantric traditions, particularly perhaps on the Buddhist side, place great emphasis on ideas such as the compassionate motivation (*bodhicitta*) necessary for successful Tantric practice. I do not mean to suggest that this emphasis may not be genuine. Yet, as our studies illustrate, the picture is clearly more complex. Sax notes that in the Western Himalayas, Tantra refers to "a set of practices one might call 'black magic' or 'sorcery': love magic, rituals of possession by local gods and goddesses, and techniques to cause harm to others via supernatural means'" (64–65). These rituals may have positive aims, and Sax goes on to discuss healing rituals, but as he makes clear, Tantric experts can be and are commissioned to perform rituals "to harm or even kill their clients' enemies" (69). Much the same is true of the online rituals discussed by Borkataky-Varma; one of her examples involves the commissioning of what is at least intended to be an act of murder through Tantric ritual (154).

Tantra in such contexts appears as an amoral power. It can cause harm as well as healing, and it does not seem difficult to find practitioners who will use it for destructive purposes. This double-edged nature of Tantric action is found elsewhere too, and the edge between legitimate and problematic employment of Tantric power is not always clear. Katherine Anne Harper argued some years ago that what may be our earliest evidence of Tantric ritual refers in effect to state sorcery, utilizing the fearsome Saptamātṛkā deities for purposes of defending the Gupta state (Harper 2002). By the seventh century, both the Chinese and the Korean states were using Tantric ritual for military purposes (cf. Samuel 2008, 311–12). Historically, both individual Tantric priests and Tantric colleges were often maintained by states as part of their control over violence. One can see elements of that in contemporary material on Newar and Tibetan state ritual, and also in Maciej Karasinski's Keralan material, where hereditary traditions of Tantra are linked to the Nayar warrior caste and the temple doubles as a location for martial arts practice.

We can see a similar relationship between Tantra and warriorship in nineteenth- and early twentieth-century Bali, for example in Margaret Wiener's (1995) work, and this involvement of Tantra in the management of aggression continues into the contemporary period. The Balinese balian Jero Sushum, in McDaniel's chapter, heals people from black-magic spells, and she herself had to learn to defend herself against the attacks of black magicians as part of her training (317–18); another balian discussed by McDaniel, Mangku Teja Kandel, performed rituals to the death deities, Durga and Prajapati, at the local death temples (*pura dalem*) (318). Some years ago, the anthropologist Linda Connor discussed another balian who had meditated at the local *pura dalem* and been gifted with invisible strength and invulnerability (*kemasukan kekuatan*) by the spirits. He trained local people in these techniques, initially gaining a clientele during the political upheavals of the early to mid-1960s, when "supporters of all parties reputedly sought him out to obtain invulnerability to the threats of their political opponents" (Connor 1995, 128). By the late 1970s, his clients were more likely to include soldiers about to be posted to East Timor; some were policemen, and others were merchants seeking protection against sorcery. Almost all were male.

Such situations are reminiscent of quasi-Tantric practices found in mainland Southeast Asia, such as the Shan protective tattoos discussed by Nicola Tannenbaum (1987, 1991). The Shan tattoos, one of several widespread Southeast Asian traditions of protective tattooing, could "give the bearer magical protection and invulnerability to weapons" (695). To be effective, they required that the bearer kept one of the five basic Buddhist precepts. However, as long as one was maintained, the bearer was free to break other precepts. "Often people with tattoos use them as a license to engage in a life of crime" (699). A tattoo could also cause others to believe you, and thus help you deceive and cheat them (699).

My intention here is not to reinstate the demonization of Tantra of a previous age, but rather to suggest that Tantra can be part of wider discourses and practices about the legitimate use of violence and aggression.[6] At one level, Tantra is a part of everyday life, and like everyday life it can include a fair share of selfish, aggressive, and destructive orientations. Fortunately, human beings are for the most part more concerned with getting on with their lives than attacking others, but Tantra as a practical art can be used in either way, and both states and powerful people have and do employ aggressive and destructive power in the covert mode of sorcery as well as in more overt ways.

Put otherwise, Tantra can be a highly sophisticated enterprise, but it also has something real in common with the more widespread use of defensive and aggressive ritual in many human cultures and situations.[7] The negative reputation of Tantra in many lay contexts in South Asia is a reflection of this. This is also, presumably, why Pumpha Regmi Mātājī in Hyam's chapter says what she does about her own practice *not* being Tantric, and why the altruistic motivation of *bodhicitta* is such a central issue in Tibetan Tantra. People might not be so concerned about asserting the virtuous and socially constructive nature of their own ritual practice if there was not a sense that similar rituals might be used in less altruistic ways.

The Question of "Folk Tantra": Possession and Multiple Contexts

Pumpha Regmi Mātājī's statement, and her use of mantras drawn from respected texts such as the Bhagavad Gītā, point toward another issue occurring in many of our studies that is useful to consider in an ethnographic frame. Some versions of Tantric practice have close links to formal, scholarly, and literal traditions, while others appear less formal and more related to the folk and village context. We do not have a uniform approach among our studies to this issue. McDaniel, for example, speaks of "folk Tantra" and opposes it to "classical" or "scholastic" Tantra (321); Sarbadhikary notes her discomfort with the opposition and clearly prefers a more fluid and less categorical approach (this volume, 116).

Possession is often seen as a sign of folk Tantra, but here, as elsewhere, the ethnographic material can complicate the folk-scholastic dichotomy. The idea of possession in the negative sense, where an individual's mind and body are taken over by some sort of malevolent and destructive spirit entity, is widespread in South and Southeast Asian societies. It is a common form of explanation for illness, particularly psychiatric illness, and generally leads to some kind of healing that can also involve a shift in the patient's self-understanding and in the wider group's relationship with them (cf. Kapferer 1979; Tambiah 1970; Dwyer 2003). However, possession, in the sense of a person's body and speech being understood to be taken over by a spirit entity of some kind, is not always seen as negative. People may be recognized as spirit mediums—as channels for the communication and healing power of the spirits providing a culturally valued service to the community. While some anthropologists classically recognized a distinction between a situation where the individual remains in active control and one where the individuality is submerged by the possessing deity (often phrased as shamanism versus spirit mediumship), this distinction is also not necessarily straightforward to draw, particularly in the South and Southeast Asian context. Shamans can also incorporate healing spirits within their bodies, and spirit mediums may have more conscious control over their "possession" state than is explicitly recognized.

Tantra can be seen as something quite different from possession, but it can also be seen as related to it. A key operation in formal textual

Tantra is often taking on the identity of a deity, and this may involve elements of possession-type behavior (Gellner 1992, 277–78; see also Samuelson 2011; cf. Aziz 1976; Sumegi 2010). The same issues are involved in ritual dance, which can involve a variety of possibilities, from "performing" a deity to "being possessed by" a deity (Samuel 2008, 315–22; Samuel and David 2016). One can approach this in typological terms and construct a series of distinct categories in which to locate, say, a Tibetan lama meditating on himself as Cakrasaṃvara; a Newar *vajrācārya* (Tantric priest) dancing the role of Cakrasaṃvara in a formal initiation context; a Tibetan *sku rten* ("oracle priest") through whom the protective deity Pe har is speaking; a *teyyam* dancer in Kerala acting out the role of a form of Kālī; and so forth. In reality things may be more fluid and more complex. The mimetic process, in which the identity of another being (real or envisioned, human or animal or divine, etc.) is adopted, is a basic human ability, which we all have in varying degrees. Tantra, spirit mediumship, shamanic practice, and the like are not so much rigid and closely defined modes of activity as symbolically constructed frames which individuals need to find their own way to inhabit. Certainly, my experience of Tibetan lamas is that there are many differing ways to occupy or instantiate the role of Tantric lama.

Another issue regarding the folk-scholastic division is the need to bear in mind both the central ritual participants and the wider context of the lay participants and audience. Folk and scholastic can coexist, not only as different elements present within a single situation, but also as different interpretations by different participants. I remember my own surprise during an elaborate fire offering that was being carried out in full and precise liturgical style by a mixed Tibetan and Bhutanese Tantric community in Kalimpong, West Bengal. The offerings made into the fire were a complex array of different offering substances. They were laid out on a table, brought to the presiding lamas and officiants for consecration, and then offered by their ritual assistants into the fire with evident care and precision and, as far as I could tell, full conformity to the ritual manuals. After a while, however, local villagers and townspeople, including small children, started coming up to the ritual fire and throwing various offerings of their own into it, without any particular ceremony. The ritual assistants did not seem at all disturbed, and it was evident that these additional unprescribed lay offerings were in fact normal and expected.

I did not have an opportunity on that occasion to interview the lay participants who made personal offerings, but the way in which the ritual fire could in effect be repurposed—or perhaps more accurately, multiply purposed—indicates the difficulty in being too categorical about what is going in a complex situation such as this. There was certainly a specific and technical purpose for the fire ritual laid out in the extensive textual material (liturgical texts, commentaries, ritual manuals) employed by the lamas and their community of ritualists. I think it would be misleading, nevertheless, to say that their understanding was correct and the villagers' understandings were ignorant or mistaken. The ritual was the sum of *everyone's* actions and understandings—including those of the visiting ethnographers, who also became incorporated into the situation in a variety of ways (some intended, others less so). To put this in a different way, the ritual was perhaps effective and meaningful precisely *because* it had been incorporated into the many, inevitably slightly idiosyncratic, idioms and understandings of the several hundred or so people participating in different ways and at different levels of understanding.[8]

Sarbadhikary's chapter also bears on this issue of the multiple meanings and purposes of Tantra, as well as the possibilities of missing some of the subtler undertones of knowledge among the supposedly unscholarly. She describes a situation where the boundary between the everyday practice of the community of conch- and bangle-makers she studies and the world of scholastic or classical Tantra seems far from absolute. Here, concepts from the scholastic Tantric context, such as the mystic number of 3½, form part of the technical knowledge of the artisans (118–20), 126–32). A somewhat similar example is found in Janet Chawla's work on the traditional knowledge of some Indian birth attendants (*dai*), which includes ideas of "internal energy" closely related to the subtle body concepts of *prāṇa* (Chawla 2002, 2013).

Considerations of this kind lead me to feel that contrasts between folk and classical/scholastic Tantra can only have a limited and provisional value. Perhaps rather than trying to cram all available options into a polythetic definition of Tantra, we might be better off recognizing that in any given situation, multiple understandings and "definitions" of what is going on are likely to be in play, and that these may come from multiple sources, scholastic or everyday. It is even possible that some participants regard what is going on as "Tantric" and others do not (just as some of Pumpha Regmi Mātājī's fellow *mātājīs* were happy to see what they were doing as "Tantric" and others were not, 178). As analysts we may attempt to make sense of one or another of these understandings, but we should bear in mind that there is a wider context in which any ritual process is embedded, and from which at least some of its meanings derive. Here again the ethnographic perspective on Tantra helps to highlight the many ways in which different participants may understand what they are doing in individual cases.

The Ethics of Tantric Ethnography

In closing, I return to an issue I mentioned at the start of this chapter: the sensitivity of many of the studies in this collection to the complex postcolonial situation within which any knowledge of Tantra today is constructed. Ethnography is part of a process of knowledge generation, and ethnography, along with both anthropology and religious studies (e.g., King 1999; Nayar 2015), has been seen as arising from the colonial situation and as often complicit with it. Colonialism in its classic form may be largely in the past, but the often racialized power relationships and inequalities characteristic of colonialism are still very much present around the planet. So are the various Western and non-Western projections and misconceptions that have invested much of the field of Tantra, and which one might hope that a truly postcolonial ethnography, genuinely open to the subject position of the people with whom scholarship engaged, would help to remove. The essays here do not provide any simple solutions to this complex situation. The nature of the postcolonial situation is one in which scholars—whether members of a society or religious tradition, or outsiders—are called on to interrogate their methods, assumptions, and subject positions and develop approaches that are both honest to the reality we encounter and ethically appropriate in view of the continuing inequalities with which the field is invested. There are also limits to the degree with which any specific study, certainly a single scholarly essay, can take on all aspects of this situation, given that communication already requires a vocabulary of which much might be radically deconstructed.

We have a variety of "insider" positions in this collection: scholars who come from the society they study and scholars who come from outside; scholars who are committed practitioners of "Tantric" practices; scholars who retain a more external perspective. In any case, whether one is an insider or not is a complex matter in as ethnically varied and hierarchically structured a region as South and Southeast Asia. Being South Asian by ethnicity hardly guarantees an "insider" perspective. In addition, many researchers from outside South Asia form close and intimate friendships and relationships with their research informants over many years, and these friendships and relationships can carry with them personal and ethical obligations well beyond those involved in a brief research visit. There are questions of how open we are about those friendships and relationships. (For me, the honesty and directness of Cantú's and Hanssen's accounts of their fieldwork experience contribute much to the strength of their essays.) There are questions about how open any of us are about our own experience when, as notably in Hornbacher's chapter, it does not fit tidily into contemporary Western constructions of reality (103–4).[9] There are questions about how much any scholar tries to understand and to empathize with the experience of another, and how such an understanding can be conveyed ethnographically. Nike-Ann Schröder's essay is notable in the way she grapples with these issues.

Overall, what we read in these studies is characteristic of a lot of the best modern ethnographic work in its engagement with these difficult but vital issues. The work in this book is part of an ongoing process that bodes well for the attainment over time of a deeper understanding. I do not think there is a simple moral here beyond the need to work toward a mutually honest and respectful relationship in situations that are often marked by political and economic inequality and exploitation—but reading through these essays will give present and future scholars much food for thought regarding how they might handle these issues themselves. More generally, the wide range and perspective of these studies will provide many readers, whatever their own relationship to the topic, with a valuable opportunity to rethink and reevaluate what they think they know about "Tantra."

Notes

1. See in particular Brooks (1992) on Tantra among contemporary South Indian Brahmins, and his interview with Gorman (2017).

2. In Tibet, transference of consciousness at death (*'pho ba*) is discussed in the *Six Yogas of Nāropa,* a set of practices held to have been transmitted from the tenth-century Indian teacher Naropa. Halkias notes that "it is attested in

many Śaiva scriptures, in one Vaisṇava Saṃhitā, and a handful of Śākta Tantras" (2019, 75). The well-known *bar do thos grol* teachings are also concerned with the process of dying and include versions of *'pho ba*.

3. There are occasional exceptions, as with Goudriaan's comments on the *Vīṇāśikha Tantra* in Southeast Asia (1985, 61–62) or with some of Sanderson's more recent writings (e.g., 2004, 232–33). Note also the distinction in Kashmiri Śaiva Tantra between two types of practitioner: those "whose chosen goal was nothing but liberation (*mokṣaḥ*) from the bondage of transmigration (*saṃsāraḥ*)," and those "who elected to pursue supernatural powers and effects (*siddhiḥ*) while they lived" (Sanderson 1995, 24). Someone who intended to earn a living as a Tantric practitioner would presumably follow the second direction. As Sanderson notes, the "path of powers and rewards" was "by far the more exacting," and the religious activities involved were "much more complex, time-consuming and intense" (1995, 25).

4. Spirit mediums, including the *jhaṅkri* of Hyam's chapter or the balian of McDaniel's, and ritual dancers (such as the Keralan *teyyam* or the members of Newar ritual dance groups), oracle priests, and inspired healers might also be included as having Tantric careers with a greater or lesser spiritual component.

5. Sukanya Sarbadhikary's conch-makers are perhaps the exception. They are artisans, but they are not necessarily producing artifacts primarily for Tantric practice.

6. Wider terms here include "magic," "ritual," "sorcery," and various local equivalents.

7. Compare the use of aggressive ritual in Sax's chapter of this volume with, for example, the "dark shamans" of Amazonia (Whitehead and Wright 2004) or the sorcery of the Mekeo (Stephen 1995).

8. The overall context here was that of a weeklong practice retreat of a *tshe sgrub* ritual, a practice aimed at generating long life and health (see, e.g., Samuel 2016). Barbara Gerke, who has also carried out research on *tshe sgrub* in the same area, has written an interesting account of the differing lay understandings and uses of the related life-empowerment (*tshe dbang*) practices (Gerke 2010).

9. Here one could compare Paul Stoller's ethnographies of West African sorcery (e.g., Stoller and Olkes 1987), Edith Turner's (1994) famous encounter with a spirit, and several of the other essays in the Young and Goulet (1994) and Goulet and Miller (2007) collections.

Bibliography

Aziz, Barbara. 1976. "Reincarnation Reconsidered—Or the Reincarnate Lama as Shaman." In *Spirit Possession in the Nepal Himalayas*, edited by John Tt. Hitchcock and Rex L. Jones, 342–60. Warminster, UK: Aris and Phillips.

Bharati, Swami Agehananda. 1962. *The Ochre Robe*. Seattle: University of Washington Press.

———. 1965. *The Tantric Tradition*. London: Rider & Co.

———. 1976. *The Light at the Centre: Context and Pretext of Modern Mysticism*. Santa Barbara, CA: Ross-Erikson.

Brooks, Douglas Renfrew. 1990. *The Secret of the Three Cities: An Introduction to Hindu Śākta Tantrism*. Chicago and London: University of Chicago Press.

———. 1992. "Encountering the Hindu "Other": Tantrism and the Brahmans of South India." *Journal of American Academy of Religion* 60, no. 3: 405–36. https://doi.org/10.1093/JAAREL%2FLX.3.405.

Chawla, Janet. 2002. "*Hawa, Gola* and Mother-in-Law's Big Toe: On Understanding Dai's Imagery of the Female Body." In *The Daughters of Hāritī: Childbirth and Female Healers in South and Southeast Asia*, edited by Geoffrey Samuel and Santi Rozario, 147–62. London and New York: Routledge.

———. 2013. "The Life-Bearing Body in *Dais'* Birth Imagery." In *Religion andtheSubtle Body in Asia and the West: Between Mind and Body*, edited by Geoffrey Samuel and Jay Johnston, 48–63. London: Routledge.

Connor, Linda H. 1995. "Acquiring Invisible Strength: A Balinese Discourse of Harm and Well-Being." *Indonesia Circle* 23, no. 66: 124–53. https://doi.org/10.1080/03062849508729843.

Diemberger, Hildegard. 2021. "Did *sbas yul* Play a Part in the Development of Tibetan Book Culture?" In *Hidden Lands in Himalayan Myth and History: Transformations of sBas yul through Time*, edited by Frances Garrett, Elizabeth McDougal, and Geoffrey Samuel, 108–22. Leiden: Brill.

Dwyer, Graham. 2003. *The Divine and the Demonic: Supernatural Affliction and its Treatment in North India*. London: Routledge Curzon.

Farrow, G. W., and I. Menon. 1992. *The Concealed Essence of the Hevajra Tantra With the Commentary, Yogaratnamālā*. Delhi: Motilal Banarsidass.

Gellner, David N. 1992. *Monk, Householder, and Tantric Priest: Newar Buddhism and its Hierarchy of Ritual*. Cambridge: Cambridge University Press.

Gerke, Barbara. 2010. "The Multivocality of Ritual Experience: Long-Life Empowerments among Tibetan Communities in the Darjeeling Hills, India." In "The Varieties of Ritual Experience," edited by Jan Weinhold and Geoffrey Samuel, Section IV of *Ritual Dynamics and the Science of Ritual. Volume II—Body, Performance, Agency and Experience*, edited by Axel Michaels et al., 423–41. Wiesbaden, Germany: Harrassowitz.

Gorman, Daniel, Jr. 2017. "Studying Tantra from Within and Without." Interview with Douglas Renfrew Brooks. *Religious Studies Project*. Accessed January 20, 2022. https://www.religiousstudiesproject.com/podcast/studying-tantra-from-within-and-without/.

Goudriaan, Teun. 1985. *The Vīṇāśikha Tantra: A Śaiva Tantra of the Left Current*. Delhi: Motilal Banarsidass.

Goulet, Jean-Guy A., and Bruce Granville Miller, eds. 2007. *Extraordinary Anthropology: Transformations in the Field*. Lincoln: University of Nebraska Press.

Halkias, Georgios. 2019. "Ascending to Heaven after Death: Karma Chags med's Commentary on Mind Transference." *Revue d'Etudes Tibétaines*, no. 52: 70–89.

Harper, Katherine Anne. 2002. "The Warring Śaktis: A Paradigm for Gupta Conquests." In *The Roots of Tantra*, edited by Katherine Anne Harper and Robert L. Brown, 115–31. Albany: SUNY Press.

Headlund, Thomas, Kenneth Pike, and Marvin Harris. 1990. *Emics and Etics: The Insider-Outsider Debate*. Beverly Hills, CA: Sage.

Hofer, Theresia, ed. 2014. *Bodies in Balance: The Art of Tibetan Medicine*. Seattle: University of Washington Press.

Kapferer, Bruce. 1979. "Mind, Self and Other in Demonic Illness: The Negation and Reconstruction of Self." *American Ethnologist* 6, no. 1: 110–33. https://doi.org/10.1525/ae.1979.6.1.02a00080.

King, Richard. 1999. *Orientalism and Religion: Postcolonial Theory, India and 'The Mystic East.'* London: Routledge.

Levy, Robert I., and Kedar Rāj Rājopādhyāya. 1992. *Mesocosm: Hinduism and the Organization of a Traditional Newar City in Nepal*. Berkeley: University of California Press.

Lorea, Carola. 2016. *Folklore, Religion and the Songs of a Bengali Madman: A Journey between Performance and the Politics of Cultural Representation*. Leiden: Brill.

McCutcheon, Russell T., ed. 2005. *The Insider/Outsider Problem in the Study of Religion: A Reader*. New York: Continuum.

McDaniel, June. 2004. *Offering Flowers, Feeding Skulls: Popular Goddess Worship in West Bengal*. Oxford: Oxford University Press.

Marglin, Frédérique Apffel. 1985. *Wives of the God-King: The Devadasis of Puri*. Delhi: Oxford University Press.

Nayar, Pramod K. 2015. *The Postcolonial Studies Dictionary*. Chichester, West Sussex: Wiley Blackwell.

Needham, Rodney. 1975. "Polythetic Classification: Convergence and Consequences." *Man* 10, no. 3: 349–69. https://doi.org/10.2307/2799807.

Openshaw, Jeanne. 1998. "'Killing' the Guru: Anti-Hierarchical Tendencies of 'Bauls' of Bengal." *Contributions to Indian Sociology* 32, no. 1: 1–19. https://doi.org/10.1177/006996679803200101.

———. 2004. *Seeking Bāuls of Bengal*. Cambridge: Cambridge University Press.

Rinbochay, Lati, and Jeffrey Hopkins. 1979. *Death, Intermediate State, and Rebirth in Tibetan Buddhism*. Valois: Gabriel/Snow Lion.

Rozario, Santi, 2002. "The Healer on the Margins: The Dai in Rural Bangladesh." In *The Daughters of Hāritī: Childbirth and Female Healers in South and Southeast Asia*, edited by Santi Rozario and Geoffrey Samuel, 130–46. London: Routledge.

Samuel, Geoffrey. 2008. *The Origins of Yoga and Tantra: Indic Religions to the Thirteenth Century*. Cambridge: Cambridge University Press.

———. 2016. "Tibetan Longevity Meditation." In *Asian Traditions of Meditation*, edited by Halvor Eifring, 145–64. Honolulu: University of Hawai'i Press.

———. 2017. "The g.Yu Thog sNying thig and the Spiritual Dimension of Tibetan Medicine." In *Sharro: Festschrift for Chögyal Namkhai Norbu*, edited by Donatella Rossi and Charles Jamyang Oliphant of Rossie, 214–25. Schongau, Switzerland: Garuda Verlag.

———. 2021. "Hidden Lands of Tibet in Myth and History." In *Hidden Lands in Himalayan Myth and History: Transformations of sBas yul through Time*, edited by Frances Garrett, Elizabeth McDougal, and Geoffrey Samuel, pp.51–91. Leiden: Brill.

———. 2022. "Namkha Drimed Rinpoche and his Gesar Terchö: Gesar Ritual Practice in Western Buddhism." In *The Many Faces of King Gesar: Tibetan and Central Asian studies in Homage to Rolf A. Stein*, edited by Matthew T. Kapstein and Charles Ramble, 216–31. Leiden: Brill.

Samuel, Geoffrey, and Ann R. David. 2016. "The Multiple Meanings and Uses of Tibetan Ritual Dance: *Cham* in Context." *Journal of Ritual Studies* 30, no. 1: 7–24. http://www.jstor.org/stable/44737776.

Samuelson, Anna Katrine. 2011. "He Dances, She Shakes: The Possessed Mood of Nonduality in Buddhist Tantric Sex." Master's thesis, McGill University.

Sanderson, Alexis. 1995. "Meaning in Tantric Ritual." *Essais sur le rituel*, edited by Anne-Marie Blondeau and Kristofer Schipper, 15–95. Louvain: Peeters.

———. 2004. "Religion and the State: Śaiva Officiants in the Territory of the King's Brahmanical Chaplain." *Indo-Iranian Journal* 47: 229–300. https://doi.org/10.1007/s10783-005-2927-y.

———. 2009. "The Śaiva Age: The Rise and Domination of Śaivism during the Early Medieval Period." In *Genesis and Development of Tantrism*, vol. 23, edited by Shingo Einoo, 41–349. Tokyo: Institute of Oriental Culture.

Sardar-Afkhami, Abdol-Hamid. 2001. "The Buddha's Secret Gardens: End-Times and Hidden-Lands in Tibetan Imagination." PhD diss., Harvard University.

Sax, William S. 2009. *God of Justice: Ritual Healing and Social Justice in the Central Himalayas*. Oxford: Oxford University Press.

Smith, Frederick M. 2006. *The Self Possessed: Deity and Spirit Possession in South Asian Literature and Civilization*. New York: Columbia University Press.

Smith, Jonathan Z. 1982. "Fences and Neighbors: Some Contours of Early Judaism." Reprinted in *Imagining Religion: From Babylon to Jonestown*, by Jonathan Z. Smith, 1–18. Chicago: Chicago University Press.

Stephen. Michele. 1995. *A'aisa's Gifts: A Study of Magic and the Self.* Berkeley: University of California Press.

Stoller, Paul, and Cheryl Olkes. 1987. *In Sorcery's Shadow: A Memoir of Apprenticeship among the Songhay of Niger.* Chicago: University of Chicago Press.

Sumegi, Angela. 2010. "Being the Deity: The Inner Work of Buddhist and Shamanic Ritual." In "The Varieties of Ritual Experience," edited by Jan Weinhold and Geoffrey Samuel, Section IV of *Ritual Dynamics and the Science of Ritual. Volume II—Body, Performance, Agency and Experience,* edited by Axel Michaels et al., 443–58. Wiesbaden, Germany: Harrassowitz.

Tambiah, Stanley J. 1970. *Buddhism and the Spirit Cults in North-East Thailand.* London: Cambridge University Press.

Tannenbaum, Nicola. 1987. "Tattoos: Invulnerability and Power in Shan Religion." *American Ethnologist* 14, no. 4: 693–711. https://www.jstor.org/stable/645321.

Tannenbaum, Nicola. 1991 "Haeng and Takho: Power in Shan Cosmology." *Ethnos* 56, nos. 1–2: 67–81. https://doi.org/10.1080/00141844.1991.9981425.

Tsong-kha-pa. 2004. *The Great Treatise on the Stages of the Path to Enlightenment.* 2 vols. Ithaca, NY: Snow Lion.

Turner, Edith. 1994. "A Visible Spirit Form in Zambia." In *Being Changed: The Anthropology of Extraordinary Experience,* edited by David E. Young and Jean-Guy Goulet, 71–95. Peterborough, Ontario: Broadview Press.

White, David G. 2012. "Netra Tantra at the Crossroads of the Demonological Cosmopolis." *Journal of Hindu Studies* 5, no. 2: 145–71. https://doi.org/10.1093/jhs/his030.

Whitehead, Neil L., and Robin Wright, eds. 2004. *In Darkness and Secrecy: The Anthropology of Assault Sorcery and Witchcraft in Amazonia.* Durham: Duke University Press.

Wiener, Margaret J. 1995. *Visible and Invisible Realms: Power, Magic, and Colonial Conquest in Bali.* Chicago: University of Chicago Press.

Young, David E., and Jean-Guy Goulet, eds. 1994. *Being Changed: The Anthropology of Extraordinary Experience.* Peterborough, Ontario: Broadview.

Contributors

Sravana Borkataky-Varma is a historian, educator, and social entrepreneur. As a historian, she studies Indian religions focusing on esoteric rituals and gender, particularly in Hindu traditions (goddess Tantra). As an educator, she is the Instructional Assistant Professor at the University of Houston. At present, she is a Center for the Study of World Religions Fellow at Harvard Divinity School, Harvard University. In the past, she has taught at Harvard University, the University of North Carolina–Wilmington, the University of Montana, and Rice University. Borkataky-Varma is currently working on four book projects: *Divinized Divas: Superwomen, Wives, Hijṛās in Hindu Śākta Tantra*; *The Serpent's Tale: Kuṇḍalinī and the History of an Experience*; *Living Folk Religions*; and *Religious Responses to the Pandemic & Crises: Isolation, Survival, and #Covidchaos*. Details of her published works can be found on her website, sravana.me. As a social entrepreneur, she is the cofounder of a nonprofit, Lumen Tree Portal. Borkataky-Varma invests in building communities with individuals from various faith backgrounds who believe in kindness, compassion, and fulfillment.

Keith Edward Cantú studied in Los Angeles, Lausanne, and Seattle before obtaining his PhD at the University of California, Santa Barbara (UCSB). Following that he was an assistant professor (postdoc/eesearch associate) at the Jagiellonian University in Kraków, and he is now a visiting research fellow at FAU Erlangen-Nürnberg in the DFG-funded project "Center for Advanced Studies in the Humanities and Social Sciences, Alternative Rationalities and Esoteric Practices from a Global Perspective" (www.cas-e.de). His research focuses on intersections between yoga, esotericism, Tantra, and music in India and Bangladesh, as well as theosophy and Thelema in Europe and the United States. Some of his publications include his monograph *Like a Tree Universally Spread: Sri Sabhapati Swami and Śivarājayoga* (Oxford University Press, 2023); *City of Mirrors: Songs of Lālan Sā̃i*, a volume of songs of Lālan Fakir translated by Carol Salomon (Oxford University Press, 2017); and "Sri Sabhapati Swami: Forgotten Yogi of Western Esotericism" (2021).

Kristin Hanssen is a social anthropologist whose current research interests include caste, class, gender, and life stories. She received her PhD in 2002 from the University of Oslo, Norway. Her most recent publication is *Women, Religion, and the Body in South Asia: Living with Bengali Bauls*, published by Routledge in 2018. The ethnography is based on close participant observation for a period of more than fifteen months. Fieldwork involved living first in Burdwan town with a middle-class Brahmin family for two months before settling in a rural neighborhood with a family of heterodox Vaishnavas and singers of Baul songs, sharing their one-room hut and traveling with them to perform in different villages and towns.

Jarrod Hyam completed a doctorate in Indian subcontinental studies at The University of Sydney as a student of Geoffrey Samuel. While his research focuses on Indic Vajrayāna Buddhism and Hindu Tantra generally, his fieldwork addresses marginalized practitioners who fall outside the fold of monastic Buddhist institutions. In relation to Tantric practice, his research approaches the notion of healing as a dynamic, systemic process that occurs within oneself as well as interpersonally, sociopolitically, and ecologically. He taught for the Department of Philosophy and Religious Studies at the University of Wisconsin, Eau Claire, where he contributed to the development of a multidisciplinary medical humanities program. Dr. Jarrod Hyam passed away on May 26, 2022, while this manuscript was being finalized. He is dearly missed by all his students, friends, and colleagues.

Annette Hornbacher is a professor of cultural anthropology at the University of Heidelberg. She has conducted extensive fieldwork in Indonesia and particularly in Bali, where she worked on ritual dance drama as a kinaesthetic embodiment of cosmological knowledge. More recently, she has led several research projects on religious dynamics in Post-Suharto Indonesia (funded by German Ministry for Education and Research) and on *Local Traditions and World Religions* (funded by the German Research Council). Currently, she is also conducting a comparative research project on Tantric text practices in Bali and India. She is the author and editor of six books, including her recent *The Materiality and Efficacy of Balinese Letters* (Brill, 2016), and over twenty academic articles.

Maciej Karasinski is an associate professor in the Department of Foreign Languages at Hainan University. He has a PhD in Sanskrit literature from the University of Calicut and a master's degree in oriental philology from Jagiellonian University. He also studied at Sapienza University of Rome, participated in academic projects related to Sanskrit literature, and received an Indian Government Scholarship (2010). His current research concerns aspects of Śrīvidyā and Krama ritualism in Kerala.

Carola E. Lorea is a junior professor of Rethinking Global Religion at the University of Tübingen. She was a senior research fellow in the Religion and Globalisation Cluster of the Asia Research Institute at the National University of Singapore. She is interested in sound, oral traditions, and popular religious movements in South Asia, particularly eastern India, Bangladesh, and the Andaman Islands. Besides her monograph *Folklore, Religion, and the Songs of a Bengali Madman* (Brill, 2016), she has published numerous articles in journals such as *American Anthropologist, Asian Ethnography, Religion, Religions, History and Sociology of South Asia,* and more. She was a research fellow at the International Institute for Asian Studies (Leiden), Gonda Foundation, and the South Asia Institute at the University of Heidelberg.

June McDaniel is a professor emerita of the History of Religions in the Department of Religious Studies at the College of Charleston. Her master's degree is from Emory University, and her PhD is in the history of religions from the University of Chicago. Her research areas include mysticism and religious experience, religions of India, psychology of religion, women and religion, and ritual studies. She did field research on Tantra and mysticism in West Bengal, India, for two years, funded by the American Institute of Indian Studies and by a senior-scholar grant from Fulbright. She also did research on Tantric ritual and practitioners in Bali, Indonesia, funded by the American Academy of Religion. She has published and edited several books with Oxford University Press, SUNY Press, and Palgrave Macmillan, as well as over forty articles. Her most recent book is on the role of ecstasy in modern religion and society.

Geoffrey Samuel is an honorary associate at The University of Sydney, Australia, and Emeritus Professor at Cardiff University, Wales, UK, from which he retired in 2014 after an academic career in the UK, Australia, and New Zealand. His PhD was an anthropological study of Tibetan Buddhism in India and Nepal. His books include *Mind, Body, and Culture* (1990); *Civilized Shamans: Buddhism in Tibetan Societies* (1993); and *The Origins of Yoga and Tantra* (2008). His current research interests include Tibetan yogic health practices, Tibetan medicine, and the dialogue between Buddhism and science.

Sukanya Sarbadhikary is on the faculty at Presidency University in Kolkata. She works at the interface of the anthropology of religion, religious studies, and philosophy. In her first work she did an intensive ethnography among different kinds of Bengal-Vaishnavas, focusing on diverse experiences of religious place and discourses of sensory apprehensions of divine affect. Her book, *The Place of Devotion: Siting and Experiencing Divinity in Bengal-Vaishnavism* (University of California Press), was published in 2015. She is also passionately interested in the sociology and philosophy of aesthetics and sound, as well as their relations with sacred embodiment.

William Sax studied in Seattle, Madison, and Varanasi before beginning his PhD in anthropology at the University of Chicago, which he completed in 1987. Since then he has taught and conducted research at Harvard University; at Canterbury University in Christchurch, New Zealand; and in Heidelberg, where he has been the head of the Department of Anthropology at South Asia Institute since 2000. He has researched extensively on pilgrimage, theater, and ritual healing. He published articles and several books and volumes with Oxford University Press (1991, 1995, 2002, 2009, 2010).

Nike-Ann Schröder studied Tibetology in Berlin at the Humboldt University, learned classical and colloquial Tibetan, and graduated with a fieldwork-based Magister thesis ("Discussing Psychological Trauma with Tibetan Healing Experts: A Cultural Translation"). For her PhD, she was based at the South Asia Institute in the Department of Cultural Anthropology in Heidelberg and conducted a fieldwork- and ritual text-based research on the Tantric practice of *gcod* in Ladakh. She was a member of the Cluster of Excellence "Asia and Europe in Transcultural Contexts" and the Collaborative Research Cluster "Material Text Cultures." After completing her PhD she returned to Humboldt University and worked as a faculty member and teacher in Tibetology. Currently she is preparing her postdoc research project, which focuses on female practitioners' biographies and female agency in Tantric rituals in the Himalayas.

Rohit Singh is a Fulbright-Nehru senior scholar currently conducting fieldwork in the Indo-Himalayas. His research examines the intersections of Tantric rituals, astrology, and healing traditions among Buddhist and Muslim communities in Ladakh. He has a PhD in religious studies from the University of California, Santa Barbara. He teaches and serves as the director of Undergraduate Studies for the Religious Studies Department at the University of North Carolina–Greensboro.

Index

www.ingramcontent.com/pod-product-compliance
Lightning Source LLC
Chambersburg PA
CBHW051949270326
41929CB00015B/2583